The Testing Practitioner

The Testing Practitioner

Erik van Veenendaal

Uitgeverij
Tutein Nolthenius

UTN Publishers, Den Bosch - 2002

UTN Publishers
Willem van Oranjelaan 5
5211 CN Den Bosch
The Netherlands
www.utn.nl

ISBN 90-72194-65-9

Contents

6

Part 3   Reviews

Part 4   Test techniques

Preface

The initial idea for writing a new testing book came during a meeting in London with David Hayman and Chris Comey. We were developing the ISEB Practitioner course and needed some background papers. The idea evolved and with the support of many testing and software quality experts it turned into a full and new testing book. Using the ISEB Practitioner syllabus as a reference framework, I wanted to create a book that provides a comprehensive overview of the testing profession and in addition addresses a number of new testing challenges and topics. The book needed to be more than a set of independent papers. As a result many email discussions with leading experts in the testing field were held. To me this was probably the most interesting part of the editing and writing "The Testing Practitioner". Thank you all! It is now up to the reader to test the actual outcome.

I hope that many test professionals will be able to use the book as a basis from which to improve their testing skills by themselves. Other may need expert advice and assistance as well. The book may not contain all the answers you need, but it will set you off in the right direction. This book is intended to meet the practical needs of test engineers and test managers working in real-world businesses. Following the ISEB Practitioner syllabus this book addresses test principles, test process, test management, risk management, inspections and reviews, test techniques (both functional and non-functional), test process improvement, tools and people issues.

My thanks is due to the individuals, who have helped me by reviewing drafts and providing valuable comments. Many thanks to Jo Cowderoy, Jackie Berkery, Sarah Farrell, Julie McMullan, Fran 'o Hara, Marc Roper and Caroline Quentin. Such merits as this book displays are in large part due to them, while its defects are of course my own. Lastly, a special thank you to the testing professionals who have gone before me. Some of these are acknowledged in the bibliography, but I recall here also all those friends, and colleagues from whom I have learned everything that I know today.

Erik van Veenendaal
Dommelen, The Netherlands
September, 2002

Part 1

Test principles and process

1   Testing Fundamentals

Isabel Evans

This chapter discusses the testing basic and principles. It aims at refreshing the reader's understanding of the fundamentals of testing. The reasons for testing, the principles behind testing and the place of testing in the life cycle are described. An overview is given of the test process, the levels and types of testing, test techniques and the principal tasks in test management. This chapter also serves as a reference for standard test vocabulary and definitions.

1.1   Test principles and definitions

Testing is necessary to identify errors and faults, in order to reduce failure. Humans make mistakes, or errors and these cause faults in products. These faults may go unnoticed, or they may cause failures.

> An *error* is a mistake made by a human, a *fault* is the result of an error - it is something wrong which might occur in an interim product such as a specification, or in a final product such as code or user documentation. A *failure* is the deviation of the product from its expected delivery or service. (BS7925-1, 1998)

Many interim and final products[1] are built during a project and there will almost certainly be errors in all the activities of the build. Some of these are found and removed by the authors of the work, but it is difficult for people to find their own mistakes, while building a product. In the search for quality of product and service, testing is one of the verification and validation methods applied. Other methods include proof reading, reviewing and auditing of processes. A variety of methods may be used for checking, some of which are

---

1   In this book, "Product" is used to stand for "any deliverables of the life cycle - code, documents, diagrams, etc.". "Project" is used to stand for "any piece of work where we may need to test - project, on-going maintenance, emergency fix, etc."

done by the author of the work and some by others to get an independent view.

Definition of software quality

One definition often used for software quality is; a quality system is *delivered on time, to budget and to specification.* If this is to be achieved it requires a correct specification, a correct time scale and a correct budget. The delivered system must subsequently meet the specification. This is known as *validation* ("is this the right specification?") and *verification* ("is the system correct to specification?").

Definition of verification and validation:

Validation: Determination of the correctness of the products of software development with respect to the user needs and requirements. "Is this the right specification?" (BS7925-1, 1998)

Verification: The process of evaluating a system or component to determine whether the products of the given development phase satisfy the conditions imposed at the start of that phase. "Is the system correct to specification?" (BS7925-1, 1998)

Other definitions of quality

There are other definitions of quality, so it is important that the project and the customer have an agreed definition. Garvin showed that generally, in practice, five distinct definitions for quality could be recognised (Garvin, 1984). The definition of software quality will affect how a project defines testing and, briefly, the definitions are (Trienekens and Van Veenendaal, 1997):

The *product based definition:* Quality is based on a well-defined set of software quality attributes. These attributes must be measured in an objective and quantitative way. Differences in the quality of products of the same type can be traced back to the way the specific attributes have been implemented.

The *user based definition:* Quality is fitness for use. This definition says that software quality should be determined by the user(s) of a product in a specific business situation. Different business characteristics require different "qualities" of a software product. Quality can have many subjective aspects and cannot be determined on the basis of only quantitative and mathematical metrics.

The *manufacturing based definition:* This definition points to the manufacturing, i.e. the specification, design and construction, processes of software products. Quality depends on the extent to which requirements have been implemented in a software product in conformance with the original requirements. Quality is based on inspection, registration and (statistical) analysis of faults and failures in (intermediate) products.

The *value based definition:* This definition states that software quality should always be determined by means of a decision process on trade-off's between time, effort and cost aspects. The value based definition emphasis the need to make trade-off's, this in often done by means of communication with all parties involved, e.g. sponsors, customers, developers and producers.

The *transcendent definition:* This "esoteric" definition states that quality can in principle be recognised easily depending on the perceptions and the affective feelings of an individual or group of individuals towards a type of software product. Although the least operational one, this definition should not be neglected in practice. Often a transcendent statement about quality can be a first step towards the explicit definition and measurement of quality.

Project pressures - risk, time, budget and scope

Testers need to consider the scope of testing against the risks for the customer and the business. This is critical in understanding the test strategy, especially:

- Which of the project interim and final products must be tested? *It may be necessary to test all, or only some, depending on risk and budget.*
- What types of testing are required? *Maybe non-functional as well as functional testing is needed, depending on risk and the acceptance criteria (defined and implicit).*
- How independent must the testing must be? *Depending on the risk, we may allow people to test products they have built, or we may choose to have independent testing.*

The project pressures triangle (figure 1.1) is a reminder that changing any of project pressures (the points of the triangle) - by increasing scope for example - without adjusting the other two pressures, deforms the triangle, with a loss of quality.

Specification

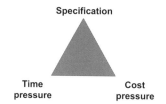

Time pressure　　**Cost pressure**

Figure 1.1: The "project pressures" triangle - balancing time, cost and specification

What needs testing?

The strategy should consider testing all intermediate and final products produced during a project. This includes:
- All levels of specification and design
- Code
- Documentation for the user group - e.g. user guides, help messages
- Operational documentation for the IT maintenance/support group
- Any service level agreements associated with the product.

Definitions of testing

The definitions of testing have changed over the last 30 years, due to a greater understanding of the psychology of testing and of the limits of testing. An initial definition is often; *"we want to know that the software works"*:

> Testing is the process of establishing confidence that a program or system does what it is supposed to. (Hetzel, 1973)

However, if the focus is on testing as a positive activity - *looking for confirmation that we were right* - it is less likely that faults will be found. Having acknowledged that people will have made mistakes, it makes sense to focus testing on finding faults:

> Testing is the process of executing a program or system with the intent of finding errors. (Myers, 1979)

This is useful, but it will now be important to define what is an error. For this it is necessary to have a specification of what the product is predicted to do and to define the precise results expected from the tests. Without knowing exactly what is expected, the tester is in danger of accepting results, which are plausible but not actually correct. Expected results are defined as part of our test cases.

A stricter definition of testing comes from IEEE:

> Testing is the process of exercising or evaluating a system by manual or automatic means to verify that it satisfies specified requirements or to identify differences between actual and expected results. (IEEE 610.12, 1990)

It is also necessary to consider the wider aspects of software quality, to look at not just the funcionaity but other capabilities or atributes of the software whether functional (for example correctness, testability) or non-functional (for example reliability, usability, maintainability) and these are measured against the requirements and risks. For example, the risks associated with an unreliable avionics program are higher than the risks with an unreliable games program, as the impact of failure is greater. There is therefore a greater emphasis on reliability testing for avionics, than for games programs. Hetzel's 1984 definition captured this and relates to the product based definition of quality:

> Testing is any activity aimed at evaluating an attribute or capability of a program or system. Testing is the measurement of software quality (note Hetzel defines quality as "meets requirements") (Hetzel, 1984)

Some people have looked for a simpler, perhaps more pragmatic definition, which emphasises that the software does not have to be perfect; *"we just expect that it will do its job"* and it does not require a greater degree of engineering than is needed for it to be *"fit for its purpose"*. This fits in neatly with consumer legislation, whereby a purchaser has a reasonable expectation that the item bought will work "as advertised" and that it will be "good enough". The definition relates to the user-based definition of quality:

> Testing is demonstrating that a system is fit for purpose. (Evans *et al.,* 1996)

A useful definition, which covers both validation and verification and also addresses non-functional testing, comes from Martin Pol and Erik van Veenendaal in TMap:

> Testing is a process of planning, preparation and execution to establish the characteristics of a software product and to determine the difference between the actual and required status. (Pol and Van Veenendaal, 1996)

Many practitioners are now seeing testing as a more inclusive activity and not just executing code. It also includes activities such as reviews and inspections:

> Testing is a process consisting of all life cycle activities concerned with checking software and software-related work products. (Gelperin and Hetzel, 1988)

Let us consider the definition from BS7925-1. This attempts to bring the other definitions together, but it misses some key questions raised by the definitions of quality and of testing, that may be important for a specific project. It is a suitable definition for component testing, but the test practitioner will also need to consider the wider definitions available. It uses a manufacturing based definition of quality:

> Testing: the process of exercising software to verify that it satisfies specified requirements and to detect errors. (BS7925-1, 1998)

In comparison, the ISEB Foundation Certificate in Software Testing Syllabus v2.0, states:

> As the objective of a test should be to detect faults, a "successful" test is one that does detect a fault. (ISEB, 1999)

This is an interesting statement for a test practitioner to debate. Notice that the definitions of testing provided do not address either the value-based or the transcendent definitions of quality, yet these are likely to be the key satisfaction triggers for both the customer of the project and the user of products. An all-inclusive definition of testing might be:

> The planning, preparation and execution of tasks to establish the characteristics of a software product and to determine the difference between the actual and required status, in order to meet the quality requirements of the customer and to mitigate risk

1.2   Test process

A test process is described in the IEEE 1008 Standard for Software Unit Testing (IEEE 1008, 1987). The test process described in this useful standard is circular; it consists of a number of steps which may need to be repeated several times (see figure 1.2). A similar process is described in the BS7925-2 Standard for Component Testing (BS7925-2, 1998).

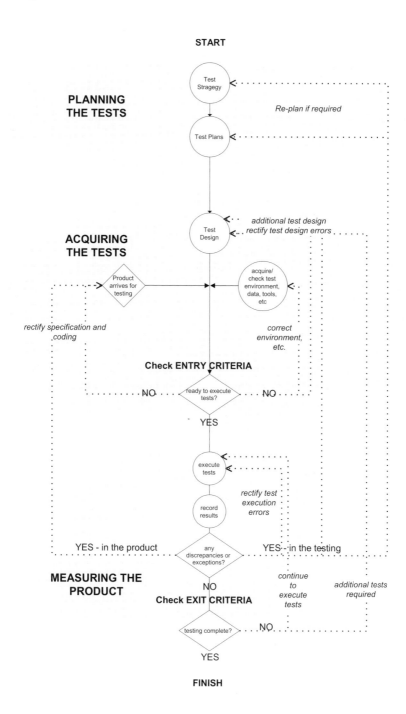

Figure 1.2: The test process - planning, acquiring and measuring

The test process may be divided into three major activities:
- Planning the testing; including test strategy and detailed test planning.
- Acquiring the tests; designing the tests, building test cases and test data, getting tools ready, getting management/reporting ready.
- Measuring the product; executing the tests, recording the results, dealing with any discrepancies and test incidents, and checking for test completion.

Planning - the test strategy

The test strategy should *at the least* give the rationale for the amount, breadth and depth of testing for the project. It should:
- Summarise the risks which the testing is addressing; this will vary from project to project and will affect how much testing is done, which non-functional tests are done, and whether there are low risk areas which the project may choose not to test.
- Summarise any constraints; time, budget, personnel, equipment, and the effect of the constraints on risk.
- Document the entry and exit criteria for each test level or phase (for example system test and acceptance test); this is to allow agreement on the minimum standard for a product entering testing, and for test completion.
- Document what types of testing will be done and decide what is out of scope; especially if results are not as the customer or the team expected.
- Document pass/fail criteria at a high level.

The test plan is a good starting place when writing a new test strategy, or reviewing an existing strategy. But, as the headings in IEEE 829 Standard for Software Test Documentation (IEEE 829, 1998), show, a full test strategy is more comprehensive. If the team is drawn from several organisations it is useful to state a glossary of terms, based on BS7925-1, in order that the project has a common vocabulary.

Note: a test policy is held in the quality management system, the quality plan or the test procedures, or the process or policy statement. Some practitioners would refer to the, so-called, test strategy, as the "High Level Test Plan" and use "Test Strategy" to mean the overall policy document.

Planning - detailed test plans

Each type of testing is planned in detail. The overall strategy may, on a large project, be broken down into several detailed strategies for different areas of the project. Each area, each level and/or each type (functional and non-functional), of testing may need detailed plans to show how the strategy is applied. Depending on the risk there may be exceptions to the strategy.

Acquiring - the tests and surrounding environment

This is also called test design or test specification. Test cases are designed for each of the functional and non-functional tests using formal techniques, error guessing or test cases from a library of previously designed tests. A number of other acquisition activities take place in parallel:

- Acquiring test data; building it or extracting it, or deciding which of a library of test databases to use.
- Acquiring the test environment in some form; being either built, booked or checked.
- Checking and making the tools ready, including: test management tools and techniques (e.g. reporting, metrics gathering, defect logging and tracking) Note: by this stage is probably too late to introduce new tools so the project needs to check the existing toolkit is ready for use.

Test readiness and entry criteria

When does the project know it is ready to start executing tests? As well as the software being ready, the tests, the test environment, the data and tools, the team and test management must all be in place. It is useful to have a test readiness process, such as a checklist or a formal meeting, to help answer the questions:

- Have we got everything we need?
- Has everything met the entry criteria, which we set in the strategy?

Testing cannot start until the product which is to be tested is ready. The entry criteria for a test phase should include checking the exits from; previous test phases, product build stages and test preparation activities. Much time is lost in projects through the test environments being ill-prepared. If there are areas that are not yet ready it may be necessary to circle back in the test process, in order to rectify problems or complete preparation. Alternatively, it may be possible to continue with a planned approach to deal with areas not yet ready.

Measuring - the product and the testing

Once the test execution has started, the product is measured against its acceptance criteria. The project must execute the test cases designed earlier, measure the coverage and log the results. It is important to manage the test configuration by recording the identity and version of the products and the tests. This must be done with the test results, for completeness and ease of audit checking.

Test incidents

Log any difference between actual and expected results, as a test incident or discrepancy. Then investigate whether the cause is:
* A test problem; it may be that the environment was wrong, the data used was wrong, the version of the test specification was wrong, or the input was mis-keyed.
* A product problem; for example, a fault in the code, an omission in the requirements, or a fault in the user documentation.
* Some other problem; for example, one where the cause is not yet clear, or where something outside the test team's control has affected the tests.

Depending on the cause of the problem, it may be necessary to repeat one or more test activities, and make changes to products, environment or test materials. Any changes can adversely affect the whole product, so retests will not only have to be carried out on the changed parts, but selective, or even complete regression tests will have to be carried out on the rest of the product. It is useful to record on the test incidents document which test cases will be run as retests and which as regression tests.

Exit criteria for test completion and test management

Use the previously defined exit criteria to check whether the tests are complete. If they are not complete, continue to execute tests, and if necessary circle back to the top of the process to plan more tests. Exit criteria include:
* Test completion criteria; based on time, budget, risk, number of requirements covered, product acceptance criteria met, black box test coverage measurements, white box test coverage measurements, number of outstanding faults and their priorities and any other coverage criteria.
* Test management criteria; including test filing in the test library, updating regression test packs and sign off for any test incidents raised.

Suspension and resumption criteria

When considering entry and exit criteria, it is also important to consider suspension and resumption criteria. Suspension criteria define when testing has to stop mid-execution because of the severity of failure and resumption criteria defines when a test execution can be restarted.

Most Important Tests firSt (MITS)

If the risks for the project have changed it may be appropriate, with agreement, to change the exit criteria. This may include deciding that the project cannot run all the tests that where planned. In order to make this possible, prioritise tests and run the most important tests first.

Document skeletons

To record the test activities use the document skeletons from IEEE 829. If the project needs to adapt these document skeletons to meet its own particular needs, use the major headings in each document as a starting point and then building document templates, which fit in with the organisation's practise. For example:
- It can be practical to combine documents.
- It can be useful on small projects to use the headings as a checklist, "have we thought about…?"
- It may be necessary to split documents or have a bigger document family for a large project.

1.3   Testing and the software life cycle

Testing throughout the life cycle

Testing throughout the life cycle is often described as the "V-model of testing". A diagram to show the major stages throughout the life cycle is in figure 1.3. It can be seen that testing activities are carried out early in the life cycle, before coding starts.

> "Test then Code" (Bill Hetzel)

Later in the life cycle, testing is executed against the code. A project with existing code (maintenance, evolutionary, prototyping) may want to apply some of the techniques described here as "late life cycle", before making any code changes. Best practice is to test throughout the life cycle for several reasons:
- Product is produced throughout the life cycle; the early products (requirements definitions and specifications) are used to build the later, final products. As errors are made in the early products, early test activities improve the development activity.
- Cost savings; the earlier we find and fix faults the cheaper it is. Some researchers quote that expenses can increase 6 to 10 times, at each stage of the life cycle.
- Time savings; the V-model allows us to get the requirements right before we build the system so less rework is needed and *prevention is better than cure!*

- Professional satisfaction, i.e. doing a good job and delivering the product that is required. The V- model encourages communication between the supplier and the customer.
- Early life cycle techniques are effective; some researchers quote static testing techniques, such as inspection, as more effective than dynamic testing.
- Late life cycle testing has a different focus; early products may be correct, but mistakes can still occur when building the late products.
- Different types of testing may be applied at different stages of the life cycle; depending on the product and the requirement to be tested.

So how does "test then code" work? At each stage in the early part of the life cycle (contract and acceptance criteria definition, requirements definition, design and detailed design) a pair of test activities are associated with a non-test activity. These two generic test activities are:

- Definition of the tests to be run later in the life cycle; this also aids the static test (review) (in figure 1.3, shown as an "operation" oval in Total Quality Management (TQM) diagramming symbols).
- Review / inspection of the products delivered at that stage; a static test activity (in figure 1.3, shown as an "operation and inspection" oval in a box, in TQM diagramming symbols).

Along with these two generic test activities, a non-test process to define the product takes place (shown in figure 1.3 as an "external process" diamond with cut corners - in TQM diagramming symbols).

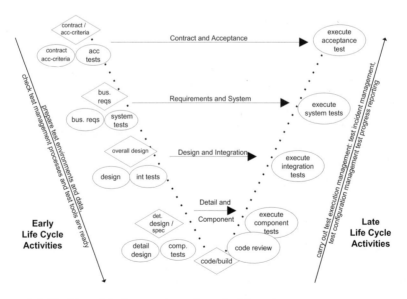

Figure 1.3: The V-model of testing throughout the life cycle

Early life cycle testing

Carry out the following testing activities before coding starts:
- Test management; strategy and test planning, risk assessment, setting of acceptance criteria for functional and non-functional requirements, auditing and reviewing of processes.
- Test design; using black box techniques (e.g. equivalence partitioning, boundary value, syntax, cause-effect, state transition) to design tests based on specifications for functional tests.
- Static testing: using review techniques (e.g. peer review, walkthrough, inspection) to test requirements, specifications and other early products
- Non-functional testing; decide which non-functional test types are required and design these non-functional tests, carry out static non-functional tests for some non-functional attributes, such as usability reviews.

Test tools may be used to support; test management, requirements management, test design and the review process.

Late life cycle testing

Carry out the following testing activities once code has been built:
- Test management; incident management, reporting, configuration management, risk assessment, audit and review of processes.
- Test design: use white box/structural techniques (e.g. statement, branch-decision, branch-condition, data flow, LCSAJ) to design tests based on code.
- Dynamic tests; run tests designed earlier, measure test coverage (white box or black box measurements), plus any additional ad-hoc testing.
- Static tests; use review techniques as before. For code use static analysis to measure code complexity.
- Non-functional testing; at suitable points run the non-functional tests designed earlier. As an example, reliability testing is run very late (after the system test), but memory management tests might be run as part of the component or integration test.

Test tools at this stage may be used to support; test management, test design, test coverage measurement, testing dynamic attributes (e.g. memory usage), static analysis, non functional testing (e.g. performance, stress, security, usability), test execution and results comparison.

1.4   Test levels

Within dynamic testing a number of different test levels can be distinguished. A test level is a group of testing activities directed and executed as one (Pol and Van Veenendaal, 1996).

Component testing:

- Is planned and designed early in the life cycle with the detailed designs, before coding starts.
- Is run late in the life cycle, but before system testing.
- Is based on the detailed design specifications.

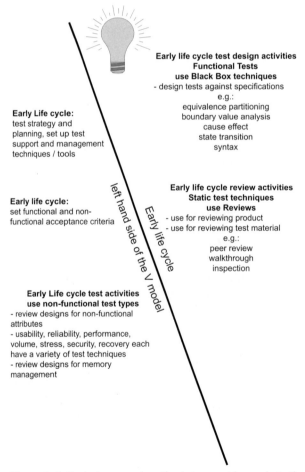

Figure 1.4: Techniques and methods to consider early in the life cycle

- Is based on the internal working of individual components, programs, objects and at extreme/failure conditions.
- May be carried out by the specialist testers or by the development team within the project.
- May require non-functional as well as functional tests.
- Will use black box (specification based) and white box (code based or structural) design techniques.
- May require tools to support the functional and / or the non-functional testing.

Integration testing "in the small":

- Is planned and designed early in the life cycle, with the system designs.
- Is run late in the life cycle, but before system testing.

Figure 1.5: Techniques and methods to consider late in the life cycle

- Is based on the design specifications.
- Is based on the parts of the system that look at links between components and subsystems and at extreme/failure conditions.
- May be carried out by the specialist testers or by the development team within the project.
- May require non-functional as well as functional tests.
- Will use black box (specification based) and white box (code based or structural) design techniques.
- Is sometimes referred to as integration "in the small", or as link testing.
- May require tools to support the functional and / or the non-functional testing.

System testing:

- Is planned and designed early in the life cycle.
- Is run late in the life cycle, but before acceptance testing.
- Is based on the acceptance criteria and requirements specifications.
- Is based on the system as a whole, looking at business processes and at extreme/failure conditions.
- May include interoperability ("integration in the large"/system to system integration).
- May be carried out by the specialist testers or by the development team within the project.
- May require non-functional as well as functional tests.
- Will generally use black box (specification based) design techniques.
- May require tools to support the functional and / or the non-functional testing.

Acceptance testing:

- Is planned and designed as early as possible.
- Is run late in the life cycle.
- Is based on acceptance criteria and a business view of the system.
- May include interoperability (integration "in the large"/system to system integration).
- May be contractual.
- Is carried out by any groups that needs to accept the system for operational usage, such as; users, IT support, IT security and database, network or operations administrators.
- May require non-functional as well as functional tests.
- Will generally use black box (specification based) design techniques.

- May require tools to support the functional and / or the non-functional testing.

1.5 Traditional versus new

The V-model method of testing may be applied, in principle, to all types of life cycles, projects, technology, and products. The essence of the process remains the same, but the risks will be different, so the project will need to apply specific techniques and types of testing.

For example:
- In each iteration of the prototyping, or evolutionary life cycle, apply the V-model in miniature and perhaps move from informal to formal application of the processes and techniques.
- In web testing there may be additional emphasis on usability, security and load testing.

References

- BS7925-1 (1998), *Software Testing – Vocabulary,* British Standards Institution

- BS7925-2 (1998), *Software Component Testing,* British Standards Institution

- Evans, I, S. Mills and R. Warden (1996), Fit for Purpose? In: *SiGiST,* February 1996

- Garvin, D. (1984), What does product quality really mean? In: *Sloan Management Review,* Vol. 26, No. 1, 1984

- Gelperin, D. and W.C. Hetzel (1988), The growth in Software Testing. In: *Communications of the ACM,* June 1988, Vol. 31, No. 6

- Hetzel, W.C. (ed.) (1973), *Program Test Methods,* Englewood Cliffs, N.J., Prentice-Hall

- Hetzel, W C (1984), *The Complete Guide to Software Testing,* QED Information Sciences Inc., ISBN 0-89435-242-3

- ISEB (Information Systems Examination Board) (1999), *Foundation Syllabus V2.0,* British Computer Society, UK

- Myers, G.J. (1979), *The Art of Software Testing,* Wiley-Interscience Publications, New York, ISBN 0-471-04328-1

- IEEE 610.12 (1990), *Standard Glossary of Software Engineering Terminology,* IEEE Standards Board

- IEEE 829 (1998), *Standard for Software Test Documentation,* IEEE Standards Board

- IEEE 1008 (1987), *Standard for Software Unit Testing,* IEEE Standards Board

- Pol, M., and E. van Veenendaal (1996), *Structured Testing of Information Systems,* Kluwer Bedrijfsinformatie, The Netherlands, ISBN 90-267-2910-3

- Trienekens, J. and E. van Veenendaal (1997), *Software Quality from a Business Perspective,* Kluwer Bedrijfsinformatie, The Netherlands, ISBN 90-267-2631-7.

2 TMap test process

Erik van Veenendaal

A test process, like a system development process, consists of numerous activities. A process model makes it possible for the various activities, their sequence and interdependence to be mapped out. The process model is divided into a number of phases, which are then subdivided into activities. The objective, input, process, output and tools of each activity are described in detail. The process model is like a tread running through the project, making it possible to retain an overview during testing. A good process model is therefore the first cornerstone supporting structured testing. This chapter provides an outline description of the Test Management approach (TMap) test process, which is applicable to both lower and higher level testing of software products. TMap provides answers to the what, when, how, where and who questions of testing. To structure the organisation and execution of the test processes, TMap is based on four cornerstones:

- *a development process-related life cycle and process model for the testing activities (L);*
- *solid organisational embedding (O);*
- *the right resources and infrastructure (I);*
- *usable techniques for various testing activities (T).*

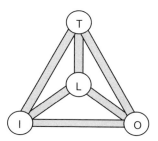

Figure 2.1: The four cornerstones for structured testing

In recent years TMap has evolved and is now recognised as the standard for software testing in The Netherlands. More than three hundred Dutch organisations, including most Dutch banks, insurance companies, pensions funds and government departments use TMap. More and more SME's are adopting TMap, and new market segments have been penetrated, such as consumer electronics, telecommunications and logistics.

2.1   Testing as a process

The main activities for all types of testing are planning, preparation and execution. A large proportion of the effort is spent during planning and preparation. As a rule of thumb, the effort distribution used is, 20% planning, 40% preparation, and "only" 40% during test execution. During the creation of the requirements specification a project (or master) test plan is established. The project test plan describes who performs which test levels, how and when. Ideally this project test plan covers all test levels, from component testing to acceptance testing, but sometimes the scope is limited to only higher level testing (system and acceptance testing) or only to development testing (component, integration and system testing). Since these types of test plans affect several disciplines, the various objectives, tasks, responsibilities, deliverables, entry and exit criteria have to be described in detail.

In larger projects the creation and subsequent co-ordination of the execution of such a test plan is usually the responsibility of an independent test team manager. On the basis of an agreed project test plan, more detailed phase test plans are made; one for lower level testing, one for system testing and one for acceptance testing. These separate test plans are the responsibility of the various parties that are involved in the testing process.

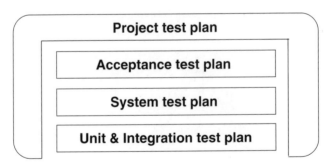

Figure 2.2: Hierarchy of test plans

After defining the phase test plans, in parallel to specification, design and coding activities, the test cases and the test infrastructure can be developed. After the delivery of the test object, the test cases are executed. In addition to system design, structured testing introduces a second design process: test design. It would appear to be an expensive activity, but with careful planning, thorough risk management, a well-founded testing strategy and an early start, costs are reduced considerably. Practice shows that the design of test cases, including the review of the requirements specification reveals a large number of defects, thus paying back the costs before the first tests have even been executed. It is known that rework effort on defects increases exponentially per development phase (Boehm, 1979).

2.2 Test process model

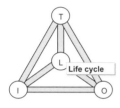

The testing activities can be organised by means of a process model that operates in parallel with the process models for system development. In the TMap® [1] process model the three main testing activities (planning, specification and execution) are divided into five phases. In addition to the planning and control, preparation, specification and test execution phase, a completion phase has been defined to finish the testing process in a structured way and to preserve the testware for the first or next maintenance release. Other standard test process models include IEEE 1008 and BS7925-2; both are directed towards component testing.

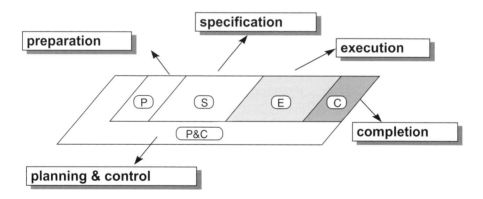

Figure 2.3: The TMap process model

The TMap process model is a generic model. It is, in principle, applicable to all test levels. However, for lower level testing it contains too many activities and

---

1   TMap is a registered trademark of Sogeti Nederland B.V.

only in highly critical circumstances will all activities be applicable. It is to up to the test manager to select the required elements from the possibilities offered by TMap. Within the hierarchy of the test plans, several tailored TMap models will be operational for different test levels. The rest of this chapter outlines the generic TMap test process model. As stated, TMap consists of four cornerstones (life cycle and process, organization, infrastructure and techniques), however, this chapter only deals with the process cornerstone.

The planning and control phase

The "planning and control" phase starts during the specification of the requirements. The test planning phase provides the basis for a manageable and high-quality testing process. It is important that all factors that make the testing process difficult to manage and control are discussed during the early stage of the system development. These factors may include, for example, the actual value of the development planning, the expected quality of the test object, the organisation of the various tasks, the availability of staff, infrastructure and time. The planning phase is the most important testing phase, however, it is often underestimated.

It is absolutely necessary to agree the test assignment, and subsequently the test team can start by studying the requirements specification, the functionality and the (project) organisation. It is impossible to test a software product completely, even if, in theory, 100% coverage is possible, no organisation has the time and money to achieve this, which is why a test strategy is determined by means of risk analysis. This will ascertain which parts of the system will get more attention during testing, depending on the risks involved. Defining the test strategy is basically a communication process, involving all parties, to establish which are the most important parts of the software product, with the aim to assign the most appropriate coverage. In addition to this, the first steps are taken towards structuring the testing organisation and defining the test infrastructure. All these activities are performed at the beginning of the testing process.

The other activities of the "planning and control" phase are carried out throughout the entire testing process, with the objective being to manage testing with regards to time and resources used. If necessary, detailed plans are drawn up for each phase of the testing process. In accordance with the test plan, reporting is done on the progress of testing and on the quality of the test object. The most important deliverable of testing is the quality report, which, also describes the accompanying risks. Right from the start of the testing process, testers are developing a view of the quality and it is important that process quality indicators are established during all phases of the testing.

Management should regularly receive, and be able to demand, a quality report on the status of the test object. This report should be continuously updated, not only at the end of the process, using test completion criteria as point of reference. It is important that the test team provides well structured management information to avoid any misunderstanding, as managers do not want to hear, unexpectedly, that they cannot go to production as the testing is not complete! A manager needs to know the risks and what actions should be taken, for example, whether to continue testing, go partly into production or to keep the old system operational in parallel to the new one (shadowing).

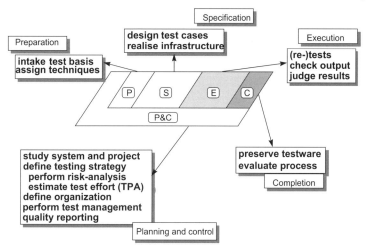

Figure 2.4: Activities within the TMap process model

The preparation phase

The preparation phase starts as soon as possible after the test plan has been drawn up and agreed upon. The first activity during this phase is the training of test staff. Once the first version of the specification is ready, and has an "adequate" level of quality, with most of the imperfections removed, the actual preparation activities can start. It most important that there is a stable version of the specification, as this is the starting point for both testers and developers. After the first version is established, the specification can only be changed by way of formal change control. In many cases, establishing the first real version takes a long time and although the aim is to have a 100% accurate specification, this, unfortunately, can not be achieved. The temptation to start test design too early is strong, but should be discouraged when a stable version of the specification does not exist. Often test design, technical design and coding activities started prematurely have to be done again. This is not only frustrating and for all parties involved, but also very expensive.

The preparation phase starts with the detailed study of the requirements specification and all other documentation that serves as a starting point for testing. Reviewing provides an insight on the testability of the specification. During the review, criteria such as the use of standard notations, understandability and recognizability are important. Using the results of the review, the quality of the test basis, namely the specification, can be improved. After the study the test basis will be divided into sub-systems that can be independently delivered and tested. Subsequently, the test techniques are allocated to each of these test units and a plan is made for the next test phase and its activities. The choice of test specification techniques will depend on the mitigating risks and should therefore be derived from the test strategy, as defined in the test plan.

The specification phase

During the specification phase the test cases are specified and the accompanying test infrastructure is realised. The creation of test cases is carried out in two phases: the logical and the physical test design. Once the test basis is available, the logical test cases are specified (test specification). A test case consists of a description of the input, the process to be executed, a prediction of the expected output (results) and any test case specific pre-requisites, such as the initial state of the software and its environment. Later, when more information is available about the technical implementation, the logical test cases are translated into physical test cases (test procedures). During this process the initial content of the test database is also defined. In parallel to the test design, the test infrastructure (the hardware- and software environment) is also being set up.

The execution phase

The execution phase starts at the moment the first testable components of the software product are available. During previous phases, agreements will have been made with the development teams about the delivery schedule and the infrastructure to be used. First the delivered parts of the software product are checked for completeness and installed in the test environment. After this a test is carried out to establish whether the application environment and technical infrastructure can run without immediate failures. To be able to start the actual tests, the initial test database has to be set up. This is a very important activity and should be done with accuracy, by using the actual software functions as much as possible. At this point, it can be considered that testing has already started.

When (parts of) the software product, the infrastructure and the test database are available, the first so called pre-tests are executed, to check whether the main functions of the object can be tested. The pre-tests provide an answer to the question, "Is the quality of the test object sufficient to be efficiently and effectively tested, using the prepared test cases?" As soon as the pre-tests have been completed successfully, test execution can start using the test procedures. The execution takes place on the basis of the agreed test strategy, giving priority to the most important parts of the system. The difference between the actual and expected test result is logged and analysed. It can indicate a software product defect, but can also indicate a defect in the specification, a defect in the test infrastructure or an invalid test case. The cause of the observed difference is investigated further during the checking and judgement activities. As soon as the rework has been completed, the tests are executed again.

During the entire test execution phase there should be an allowance for quick and reliable quality reporting. Management will expect to be informed about the risks they must consider and will want to know, for example, "What percentage of the product has been tested? What remains to be done? How many defects have been found? What are the trends? Can testing be finished?" Quality reporting should always be done against the test completion criteria. In principle, if these criteria are not met then testing is not finished and additional tests are required.

The completion phase

Even when test execution is finished, there are still some important activities to be done. Unfortunately, these activities are often carried out in a less structured way, or even forgotten. Generally, the final test execution activities take place under high pressure, which means concessions are made to the control procedures. The test scene is often chaotic at the time testing "ends" and the decision is made to go into production. An additional problem that often arises during production is that the users find new defects and these must be solved and tested without delay. As a result, the completion activities will often get low priority, and with no time and effort scheduled, the testware is not preserved in an adequate way for reuse during the first or next maintenance test.

During the completion phase, a selection is made with considering the large amount of testware available, such as test cases, test results and descriptions of the test infrastructure and the tools used. This has to be done from the perspective of required product changes, as the related maintenance tests will only need to be adjusted, and no completely new test procedures will need to be designed. During the testing process, an effort is made to keep the test cases consistent with the specification and the software product. When this is carried out successfully, it can truly be considered to be, so-called, regressive testware. Keeping the consistency between testware, specification and the actual software product is an important objective during the maintenance.

During the completion phase the testing process is also being evaluated. The data gathered and intermediate reports are combined with the results into a final report. Both the testing process and the quality of the product are being evaluated. It is recommended that an overview of costs and benefits of the testing process is drawn up, a difficult but also very engaging and necessary activity. The often large quantities of data that are available are essential to improve future planning and optimisation of the testing processes, development processes and the quality system. After the evaluation, the conservation of the testware and the presentation of the final evaluation report, management will be able to discharge the test team.

References

- Boehm, B.W. (1979), *Software engineering economics,* Prentice-Hall, Englewood Cliffs, NJ

- BS7925-2 (1998), *Software Component Testing,* British Standards Institution

- IEEE 1008 (1987), *Standard for Software Unit Testing,* IEEE Standards Board

- Pol, M,, R. Teunissen and E. van Veenendaal (1999), Testing according to TMap, 2nd edition (in Dutch), UTN Publishing, The Netherlands, ISBN 90-72194-58-6

- Pol, M., and E.P.W.M. van Veenendaal (1996), *Structured Testing of Information Systems,* Kluwer Bedrijfsinformatie, The Netherlands, ISBN 90-267-2910-3

- Pol, M., and E.P.W.M. van Veenendaal (1997), *A Test Management Approach for structured testing,* in: E. van Veenendaal and J. McMullan (eds.), *Achieving Software Product Quality,* UTN Publishing, The Netherlands, ISBN 90-72194-52-7

- Pol, M., R.A.P. Teunissen and E.P.W.M. van Veenendaal (2002), *Software Testing, A Guide to the TMap approach,* Addison-Wesley, ISBN 0-201-74571-2.

3 Testing and standards

Stuart Reid

This chapter considers how standards can be used in software testing. Two views are used to identify relevant standards. Firstly, those higher level standards that require software testing to be performed as part of a larger process are considered, and secondly, a generic software testing model is presented and standards identified that support the activities within it. The concept of integrity levels and their use in testing standards is introduced and the usefulness of application-specific standards is considered. Finally, a new framework of standards to support software testing is proposed.

3.1 Standards

What use are standards? First, we must qualify the question, as there is a consumer viewpoint and a producer viewpoint. Standards affect consumer's everyday lives and are usually considered a good thing. For instance, a standard that governs the quality of pushchairs generally meets with public approval as it is presumably safeguarding children. As such, the standard acts as a form of guarantee to the consumer that the product is of a certain quality. The vast majority of consumers have no idea what a pushchair standard might contain, but trust the authors to know. Initially, they might expect the standard to contain requirements that make a pushchair as safe as possible (so using best practice), but after a moment's reflection they will probably modify their view to expect a reasonable balance between safety and cost (good practice). After all, the manufacturer doesn't want to make the price prohibitive. So, to the consumer, standards are generally useful, their authors providing the expertise to a transaction that would otherwise be lacking.

What about the producers of pushchairs? They have a different perspective. Manufacturers benefit from complying with the standard, as it presumably means they are making 'good enough' pushchairs. They thereby avoid the dual pitfalls of bad publicity and legal liability from selling 'unsafe' pushchairs. Following the marketing theme, if the pushchair standard were not mandatory, then those manufacturers complying with it would be able to use their compliance to market their products favourably, compared with non-compliant competitors. Consider, finally, the manufacturer new to pushchairs.

The existence of a standard detailing good practice in pushchair manufacture means that they do not have to start from scratch, but can build on the experience of the standard's authors.

Unfortunately, there is no single software testing standard in the way ainlike the way single pushchair standard has been assumed here. Consumers of software testing services cannot simply look for the 'kite-mark' and testers have no single source of good practice. As will be shown, there are many standards that touch upon software testing, but many of these standards overlap and contain what appear to be contradictory requirements. Perhaps worse, there are large gaps in the coverage of software testing by standards, such as integration testing, where no useful standard exists at all. Where standards related to software testing do exist this chapter attempts to show which ones are best, for both building confidence between supplier and consumer, and providing information on good practice to the new or inexperienced tester.

A large number of standards are mentioned in this chapter, normally by reference to the originating standards body and standard number only, such as "BS7925-1". This list gives the name for each of them, along with any acronyms used.

BS	British Standard
BS7925-1	Software Testing Vocabulary
BS7925-2	Software Component Testing
CMM-SW	Capability Maturity Model for Software
CMMI-SE/SW	Capability Maturity Model Integration
Def Stan 00-55	Requirements for Safety-Related Software in Defence Equipment
DO-178B	Software Considerations in Airborne Systems and Equipment Certification
ESA	European Space Agency
IEC	The International Electrotechnical Commission
IEC 60300-3-9	Risk analysis of technological systems
IEC 61508	Functional Safety of electrical/electronic/programmable Safety-Related Systems
IEC 880	Software for computers in the safety systems of nuclear power stations
IEEE	The Institute of Electrical and Electronics Engineers
IEEE 610	Standard Computer Dictionary
IEEE 610.12	Software Engineering Terminology
IEEE 730	Standard for Software Quality Assurance Plans
IEEE 829	Standard for Software Test Documentation
IEEE 1008	Standard for Software Unit Testing
IEEE 1012	Standard for Software Verification and Validation
IEEE 1028	Standard for Software Reviews
IEEE 1044	Standard Classification for Software Anomalies
IEEE 1044.1	Guide to Classification for Software Anomalies
ISO	The International Organization for Standardization
ISO 9000	Quality management and quality assurance standards

ISO 9001	Model for quality assurance in design, development, production, installation and servicing.
ISO 9000-3	Guidelines for the application of ISO 9001 to the development, supply, installation and maintenance of computer software
ISO 9126	Software Engineering - Product quality
ISO 12207	Software life cycle processes
ISO 14598	Software Product Evaluation
ISO 15026	System and software integrity levels
ISO 15288	System Life Cycle Processes
ISO 15504	Software process assessment
MISRA	Development Guidelines for Vehicle Based Software (from the Motor Industry Software Reliability Association)
NIST	The National Institute of Standards and Technology
NIST 500-234	Reference Information for the Software Verification and Validation Process
PSS	Procedures, Specifications and Standards
PSS-05-0	ESA Software Engineering Standards
SEI	The Software Engineering Institute
TMM	Testing Maturity Model

Table 3.1: Standards list

3.2 Software testing in context

There are various definitions of software testing (see chapter 1), but BS7925-1 provides a mainstream definition, which is the "process of exercising software to verify that it satisfies specified requirements and to detect errors". Software testing is one way of performing both software verification and software validation, another being static techniques, such as reviews. Obviously, verification and validation are not performed as stand-alone processes as there has to be something to verify and validate. The verification and validation processes form part of the larger process of software engineering.

Similarly, software rarely runs as a stand-alone process - it is generally produced to run as part of a larger system. This has long been accepted by those producing embedded software, where systems engineering is already considered an acceptable and necessary encompassing discipline. Thus, from a process viewpoint, software testing, as part of verification and validation, can be included within software engineering, which, in turn, is part of systems engineering. This relationship is shown in figure 3.1.

Using the model in figure 3.1, process-oriented standards can be identified for each of the different levels identified. In fact, the systems engineering, software engineering and verification and validation processes are all covered by corresponding standards (e.g. ISO 15288, ISO 12207, and IEEE 1012 respectively). Each of these standards contains requirements relevant to the

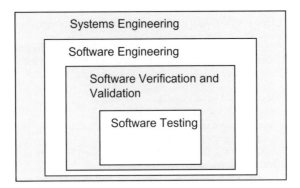

Figure 3.1: The Process Context of Software Testing

software tester. Both ISO 15288 and ISO 12207 include processes for verification and validation, and although many software developers and testers ignore the systems aspect of their work, it is impossible to deny the relevance of ISO 12207, the software life cycle processes standard. ISO 12207 is a standard that defines a framework for software throughout its life cycle and, unlike ISO 9000, has been quickly accepted in the US - it has now been accepted as the 'umbrella', or integrating standard, by the IEEE for their complete set of software engineering standards. IEEE 1012, one of this set, defines in detail the specific verification and validation processes, activities and tasks to be performed, based on integrity levels (see paragraph 3.4).

Quality provides a different perspective from which to view software testing and figure 3.2 shows how software testing fits into a quality model. From a quality perspective, testing, as part of verification and validation, can be seen as an integral part of software quality assurance. If software is part of a larger system, then software testing can also be considered as part of overall quality management and assurance. As with the process model, the higher levels are covered well by corresponding standards (e.g. ISO 9000, IEEE 730 and IEEE 1012, respectively). Most software developers will be aware of ISO 9000, but it considers testing at such a high level that non-compliance would basically mean performing no documented testing at all. IEEE 730 is similarly high level and also rather confusing as it separates testing into two parts: 'verification and validation' and 'other testing'. At a lower level, and normally considered as supporting software product evaluation, is ISO 9126, which provides a Quality Model comprised of six quality characteristics; functionality, reliability, efficiency, maintainability and portability. Each of these characteristics is broken down into sub-characteristics (see annex B) with corresponding metrics provided for their measurement. The characteristics are often used for specifying quality requirements and, with their corresponding metrics, are especially useful in supporting non-functional testing. The evaluation process that was originally part of ISO 9126 is now included in ISO 14598, and typical use of the process defined in ISO 14598 would reference the quality characteristics and metrics in ISO 9126 (*see* chapter 6 for a practical application).

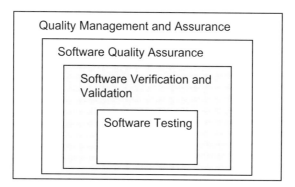

Figure 3.2: The Quality Context of Software Testing

A third model, representing a terminology perspective, can be used where software testing does have a corresponding standard is shown in figure 3.3. Natural language, as spoken in our daily lives, is at the highest level, while computing terms and software engineering terms lead eventually to software testing terms. Standards are available for each level of this model, for example starting with the Oxford English Dictionary, leading onto IEEE 610, IEEE 610.12 and finally to BS7925-1, the software testing vocabulary.

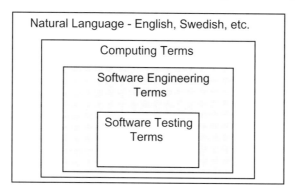

Figure 3.3: The Terminology Context of Software Testing

From the above three models a number of standards relevant to testing have been identified, albeit that many of them only consider software testing from a very high level. Some, such as ISO 9000, offer little to the software test practitioner, apart from in terms of compliance and marketing. Of the others,

ISO 12207 is expected to have a large impact, and compliance with this standard is expected to become the usual state of affairs for software developers and testers. IEEE 1012, the software verification and validation standard, is highly relevant to software testing and is covered in detail in paragraph 3.5.

So far, by only considering the context of software testing, it has been viewed as a black box, and few relevant standards concerned with the detail of the testing activity have been identified. To overcome this, paragraph 3.4 shows a white box approach where a generic software testing model is developed and then standards identified to support the different parts of the model.

3.3   A software testing model

This software test model considers software testing from all levels: from the organisation, right down to the single phase of a project. The model covers the test process, process improvement, terminology, documentation and incident management, as shown in figure 3.4. Each element of the model is considered in terms of its support by standards.

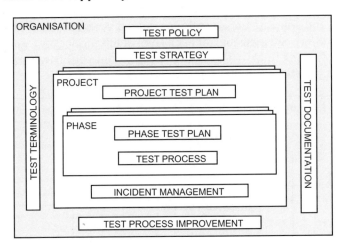

Figure 3.4: A Generic Software Testing Model

Test Terminology

A common set of terminology ensures efficient communication between all parties concerned with software testing. BS7925-1 aims to provide a specialist vocabulary for software testing, while IEEE 610.12 provides a good overall glossary of software engineering terminology. The current shortcoming of

BS7925-1 is that it is biased towards component testing. It originated as the definitions section of BS7925-2 and so initially it was purely devoted to component testing, but has since been expanded to cover software testing in general. However, further work needs to be done.

Test Policy

The test policy characterises the organisation's philosophy towards software testing. This incorporates statements to ensure compliance with standards such as ISO 9001, ISO 12207 and IEEE 730. ISO 9001 provides only a very high level requirement that suppliers perform testing as part of verification and document it. At this level ISO 12207 defines the requirement for specific verification and validation processes to support the primary processes of development, maintenance, etc. IEEE 730 requires the production of both a Software Verification and Validation Plan (and corresponding Report) and the documentation of any other tests (presumably those performed by the developers). However, it appears to be superfluous, from a testing point of view, if ISO 9001 and ISO 12207 are used.

Test Strategy

This is a high level document defining the test phases to be performed for a programme (one or more projects). ISO 9000-3 provides guidance on the application of ISO 9001 and suggests that unit, integration, system and acceptance testing be considered, basing the extent of testing on the complexity of the product and the risks. IEEE 1012 defines the verification and validation processes, activities and tasks to be performed, based on software integrity levels, and so determines which test phases are applied. ISO 15026 defines the process for determining integrity levels based on risk analysis, which is defined in IEC 60300-3-9.

Project Test Plan

This document defines the test phases to be performed and the testing within those phases for a particular project. Its content will be aligned with the test strategy, but any differences will be highlighted and explained within the document. ISO 9000-3 suggests a brief list of contents for test plans, while IEEE 829 provides a comprehensive set of requirements for test planning documentation.

Phase Test Plan

The phase test plan provides the detailed requirements for performing testing within a phase e.g. component test plan or integration test plan. IEEE 829 provides a comprehensive set of requirements for test planning. BS7925-2, which is perhaps more relevant for the unit/component testing phase, defines the detailed content of a software component test plan and provides an example set of documentation. Unfortunately, there are no standards that cover other test phases specifically.

Test Process

BS7925-2 defines a generic component test process, which is shown in figure 3.5, along with associated activities. IEEE 1008 provides similar details on the test process as BS7925-2, but labelled as unit testing. There are no standards that specifically cover other test phases.

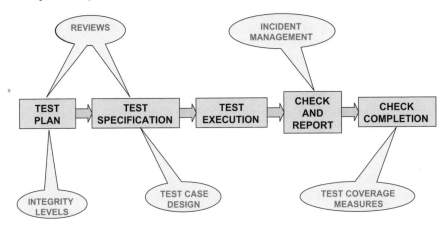

Figure 3.5: Generic Software Testing Process

The decisions made during the test phase plan activity, considered above, such as which test case design techniques to use and which test completion criteria to apply, should be dependent on the integrity levels for the software, based on some form of risk analysis. The process for determining integrity levels is defined in ISO 15026 and the risk analysis process is defined in IEC 60300-3-9. Both test plans and test specifications should be reviewed and software review techniques are defined in IEEE 1028. The techniques used to design test cases in the "test specification" activity, and the test coverage measures used in the "check completion" activity, are both defined in BS7925-2, along with examples of their use. Incident management, which forms a major part of the "check and report" activity, is covered hereafter.

Incident Management

Incident management is an essential adjunct to the testing process and is also known as problem reporting or anomaly classification. ISO 12207 includes problem resolution as a support process and IEEE 829 briefly covers incident reporting documentation. More detailed coverage is provided by IEEE 1044, which defines an anomaly classification process and classification scheme. IEEE 1044 is supported by comprehensive guidelines in IEEE 1044.1.

Test Documentation

IEEE 829 provides a comprehensive set of requirements for test planning, test specification and test reporting documentation.

Test Process Improvement

Test process improvement should be part of an organisation's test policy. If complying with ISO 12207 then an improvement process is explicitly identified, whereas process improvement is pervasive in ISO 9000. At the systems engineering and software engineering levels, SEI have produced capability maturity frameworks (CMMI-SE/W and CMM-SW) that include some testing. ISO 15504 is an international software process improvement standard that also includes some software testing. There are no process improvement standards aimed specifically at the software testing process, although proprietary schemes, such as the Testing Maturity Model (TMM), are available for software testing process improvement.

Integrity levels and risk based testing

In the field of safety-related applications, integrity levels have been around for some time. The concept of integrity levels allows a single standard to define different requirements, depending on the integrity level of the product to which the standard is being applied. The product may be a complete system, but is more often a part of a system, which means that the standard requires different parts to meet different requirements (assuming that not all parts have the same integrity level). It is sensible to partition the system; otherwise the complete system will need to meet the more rigorous requirements of the highest integrity level, which may only be a small part of the whole system. Integrity levels are normally determined on the basis of some form of risk assessment, and when used for safety-related applications this is obviously based on safety issues. Once the integrity level is determined then the corresponding requirements (methods, techniques, coverage level, etc.) are selected, based on the integrity level required.

The use of integrity levels was initially confined to application-specific standards, such as DO-178B (avionics), Def Stan 00-55 (defence) and MISRA (automotive), but this is gradually changing. The recently published IEC 61508, according to its title, is applicable to "electrical/electronic/ programmable safety-related systems". Presumably it could be used instead of the previously mentioned standards, and this has been a well-debated point. The take-up of IEC 61508 has been relatively slow in the US, as it is perceived as a European standard (despite its international title) in a similar way to ISO 9000. IEC 61508 has four integrity levels, as do most standards using this concept, and is very comprehensive, covering both hardware and software (part three of this standard covers software requirements). It currently includes some unusual software testing requirements and the relationship between the requirements for boundary value analysis and equivalence partitioning needs some work. However, part 7, when available, will provide an overview of techniques and measures, and may clarify such problems.

One thing that IEC 61508 has in common with the application-specific standards is that it is aimed at safety-related applications. IEEE 1012, published in 1998, also uses the integrity level concept, but is neither a safety-related standard, nor application-specific. This standard defines the verification and validation to be performed, again based on four software integrity levels. These integrity levels are not necessarily safety-related, but can be based on other forms of risk, such as economic or security. Also published in 1998, is ISO 15026, which defines a process for determining integrity levels based on risk analysis. This standard defines an integrity level as a range of values of a software property necessary to maintain risks within tolerable limits, where the risk can be defined under different perspectives (e.g. safety, financial, political, security). The availability of these standards (and IEC 60300-3-9 on risk analysis) supports the recent emergence and popularity of risk-based testing and provides the beginning of a framework of standards to support it.

Application-Specific Standards

There are many application-specific standards for software development and testing and nearly all of them are in the safety-related application domain. Examples of this type are DO-178B (avionics), MISRA (automotive), Def Stan 00-55 (defence), and IEC 880 (nuclear). The first three of these standards/guidelines use the concept of levels of integrity, while the last, IEC 880, does not, but this may be due to its age, as it was published in 1986.

A relevant question to be asked is why these standards are application-specific and linked to a particular application area, and not simply published as generic software development and testing standards. There are no 'special' testing techniques that are particularly appropriate for avionics systems that are not just as useful when testing automotive, or pharmaceutical, or medical, or financial software (as far as is known). As long as the perceived risks from the software failing are of a similar level, then similar amounts of effort will be appropriate for the development and testing. For instance, a safety-critical software component in a car and a financial software component, upon which an organisation's economic future is dependent, will both be rigorously tested, but there is no reason why any testing technique would work better for the automotive component than the financial, or vice versa. If both are perceived as being of similar risk by the customer, then they both deserve similar budgets and approaches for their testing, assuming all other things being equal.

Given that there appears to be no good reason for application-specific standards for software development and testing then why do they exist? Imagine that a particular industry body decides that their industry needs a software development standard and commissions a new standard from experts in software development who also work in their industrial area. On completing the work (which is a generic software development standard), the authors, who have little or no experience in other application areas, do not feel qualified to label it as a generic standard or may not want to disappoint the commissioning body by not delivering the application-specific standard they were expecting – and so another application-specific software standard is created. The developers of PSS-05-0 (the European Space Agency (ESA) software development standards) appear to have learnt this lesson. They have published the software development standards used by ESA as *generic* standards, which "provide a concise definition of how to develop quality software". PSS-05-0 is thus one step forward from application-specific standards. For testing it references IEEE 1028 for software reviews, IEEE 1012 for verification and validation, and IEEE 829 for test documentation. However, its failing is that it does not use the integrity level concept. IEC 61508 is near to fulfilling the requirement for a generic standard using integrity levels, but it states that it is specifically for safety-related applications. Why IEC 61508 could not be used for non safety-related applications, such as financially related applications, if suitable integrity levels could be determined, is not clear.

There are few application-specific standards/guidelines that solely consider software testing, although NIST 500-234 is an example of one that provides 'reference information' on software verification and validation for the US health care industry. These guidelines give good general (i.e. not especially relevant to healthcare) advice on verification and validation and also provide special sections on testing reused software and knowledge-based systems. This text of 75 pages is a good, generic introduction to software verification and validation, freely available on the Web. In general, application-specific standards for software development and testing do not appear to be worth the effort, unless some positive data confirming that application-specific requirements are valid becomes available. With no basis for making this type of standard application-specific, then the effort would be better spent on generic standards, so reducing duplicated effort. The ideal use of application area experts is to provide standards for determining integrity levels for their particular field. These can then be applied to a generic software testing standard using integrity levels, written by experts in software testing, as suggested in the next paragraph.

3.4   Software testing framework

From the previous two paragraphs, it would appear that integrity levels are the most appropriate means of defining different levels of rigour for testing different software, based on some form of risk assessment. There will always remain some application-specific knowledge that is worthy of formalisation. Therefore, application-specific standards will remain appropriate for defining how those risks that are specific to an application area are to be determined. Once integrity levels for software have been determined (ISO 15026 is available for this) then they can be applied to the verification and validation standard, which will be used to decide which testing phases and activities to apply. IEEE 1012 is suitable for this task. The integrity levels can then be used by individual test phase standards to determine which techniques and completion criteria to apply in that phase. All testing standards use a common terminology defined in a single vocabulary, an expanded version of BS7925-1. This proposed framework is shown in figure 3.6.

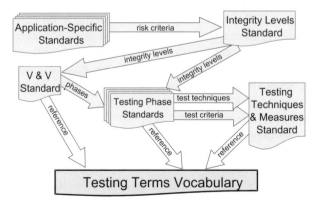

Figure 3.6: A Framework of Software Testing Standard

Currently only the component (or unit) testing phase of the life cycle is supported by standards (BS7925-2 and IEEE 1008 both cover this phase). This leaves integration, system (both functional and non-functional) and acceptance testing needing coverage by standards. A working party in the UK is currently developing a standard of techniques for non-functional testing, which should partially fill this gap (see chapter 14 on usability), but more testing standards are still required.

BS7925-2 contains both a process and definitions of techniques and measures. The techniques and measures are not only appropriate for component testing, but can also be used in other test phases. For example, boundary value analysis can be performed in all phases. Because BS7925-2 is primarily concerned with component testing, its techniques and measures are only defined from that perspective. Also, the associated guidelines that give examples of their use only cover their application to component testing. This introduces a problem when standards for the other test phases are written. It is not appropriate for the definitions in BS7925-2 to be referenced by such standards, but re-defining them is problematic, as there would be problems of consistency, but, more importantly, there would be duplication of effort. The solution is to create a single separate standard that covers the techniques and measures, which should be defined in such a way as to be applicable to whatever software testing phase is being performed. The guidelines to this standard would then need to show how the techniques could be applied at each of the test phases. A frustrating aspect of this solution is that the new techniques and measures standard would require major changes to BS7925-2, in order to remove the definitions of techniques and measures and simply leave the component test process. However, the definitions of techniques and measures from BS7925-2 would be an ideal starting place for this new standard.

3.5   Final remarks

This chapter has identified a number of high level standards that include requirements for software testing. The two most important being ISO 9000 for compliance and marketing, and ISO 12207 to define the framework of life cycle processes within which testing is performed. A generic testing model is presented and used to identify those standards that support the more detailed aspects of testing. However, the model is found to be poorly supported in one main area - that of the individual test phases. Firstly, only the unit or component test phase is adequately supported, and there are two standards available, the best of which is BS7925-2. A second shortcoming is that although information on test process improvement is available, it is proprietary, so there is a requirement for standardisation. The other parts of the generic model are generally well supported, with the areas of incident management and integrity level classification also being supported, unexpectedly, by useful standards.

The use of the integrity levels in standards is now widespread in the safety-related applications areas. This concept is gradually gaining more widespread use and IEEE 1012, a particularly good verification and validation standard published in 1998, includes integrity levels. IEEE 1012 is also generic as it applies to all software testing, but can also consider economic or other risk factors, be rather than just safety. Application-specific standards are found to be obsolete, except for those activities based on risk analysis where special application-specific knowledge is necessary. Overall, the availability of generic testing standards, using the integrity level concept, that apply to all application areas, is felt to be the way forward.

Brief subjective comments by the author on each of the standards mentioned in this chapter are provided in annex A, where each standard is also given a rating on its usefulness to a software tester. Finally, please note that standards are generally in two parts; first a normative part, which defines what the user must comply with, and then an informative part, which includes guidance on the normative part. The nature of standards is that the normative part *is* difficult to read – do not be surprised at this. Before throwing it away, try the informative part, which is generally the most useful!

References

- BS7925-1 (1998), *Software Testing – Vocabulary, British Standards Institution*

- BS7925-2 (1998), *Software Component Testing, British Standards Institution*

- Burnstein, I, T. Suwannasart and C.R. Carlson (1996), Developing a Testing Maturity Model: Part 1, in: *CrossTalk, August 1996*

- Burnstein, I, T. Suwannasart and C.R. Carlson (1996), Developing a Testing Maturity Model: Part 2, in: *CrossTalk, September 1996*

- Phillips, M. and Shrum, S., (2000), Creating an Integrated CMM for Systems and Software Engineering, in: *CrossTalk, September 2000*

- DO-178B (1992), *Software Considerations in Airborne Systems and Equipment Certification, RTCA*

- Def Stan 00-55 (1997), *Requirements for Safety-Related Software in Defence Equipment, Issue 2, UK Ministry of Defence*

- IEC 880 (1986), *Software for computers in the safety systems of nuclear power stations, Industrial Electrical Committee*

- IEC 60300-3-9 (1995), *Dependability management - Part 3: Application guide - Section 9: Risk analysis of technological systems, Industrial Electrical Committee*

- IEC 61508 (1998), *Functional safety of electrical/electronic/programmable electronic safety-related systems, Industrial Electrical Committee*

- IEEE 610 (1990), *Standard Computer Dictionary, IEEE Standards Board*

- IEEE 610.12 (1990), *Standard Glossary of Software Engineering Terminology, IEEE Standards Board*

- IEEE 730 (1998), *Software Quality Assurance Plans, IEEE Standards Board*

- IEEE 829 (1998), *Standard for Software Test Documentation, IEEE Standards Board*

- IEEE 1008 (1987), *Standard for Software Unit Testing, IEEE Standards Board*

- IEEE 1028 (1998), *Standard for Software Reviews, IEEE Standards Board*

- IEEE 1044 (1993), *Standard Classification for Software Anomalies, IEEE Standards Board*

- IEEE 1044.1 (1995), *Guide to Classification for Software Anomalies, IEEE Standards Board*

- ISO 9000-3 (1997), *Guidelines for the application of ISO 9001 to the development, supply, installation and maintenance of computer software, International Organization for Standardization*

- ISO 9001 (1994), Quality systems – *Model for quality assurance in design, development, production, installation and servicing, International Organization for Standardization*

- ISO/IEC 9126-1 (2001), *Software engineering - Software product quality - Part 1: Quality model, International Organization of Standardization*

- ISO/IEC DTR 9126-2 (2001), *Software engineering - Software product quality - Part 2: External metrics, International Organization of Standardization*

- ISO/IEC DTR 9126-3 (2000), *Software engineering - Software product quality - Part 3: Internal metrics, International Organization of Standardization*

- ISO/IEC DTR 9126-4 (2001), *Software engineering - Software product quality - Part 3: Quality in use metrics, International Organization of Standardization*

- ISO/IEC 14598 (1998), *Information technology - Software Product Evaluation, International Organization for Standardization*

- ISO/IEC 12207 (1995), *Information Technology - Software life cycle processes, International Organization for Standardization*

- ISO/IEC 15026 (1998), *Information Technology – System and software integrity levels, International Organization for Standardization*

- ISO CD 15288 (1997), *Life-Cycle Management - System Life Cycle Processes, International Organization for Standardization*

- ISO/IEC 15504 (1998), *Information technology — Software process assessment, International Organization for Standardization*

- MISRA (1994*), Development Guidelines for Vehicle Based Software,* Motor Industry Software Reliability Association

- NIST 500-234 (1996), *Reference Information for the Software Verification and Validation Process (Health Care), US Department of Commerce*

- Paulk, M.C., C.V. Weber, B. Curtis and M.B. Chrissis (1993), *The Capability Maturity Model; Guideline for Improving the Software Process, Addison-Wesley Publishing Company*

- PSS-05-0 (1991), *Software Engineering Standards, Issue 2, European Space Agency.*

Part 2

Test and risk management

4   Risk based testing

Hans Schaefer

Often the activities prior to test execution are delayed. This means testing has to be done under severe pressure. It would be unthinkable to quit the job, to delay delivery or to test badly. The real answer is a prioritization strategy in order to do the best possible job with limited resources. Which part of the systems requires most attention? There is no unique answer, and decisions about what to test have to be risk-based. There is a relationship between the resources used in testing and the cost of finding defects after testing. There are possibilities for a stepwise release. The general strategy is to test some important functions that hopefully can be released, while delaying others.

Firstly, one has to test what is most important in the application. This can be determined by looking at visibility of functions, at frequency of use and at the possible cost of failure. Secondly, one has to test where one may find most problems. This can be determined by identifying defect prone areas in the product. Project history gives some indication, and product measures give more. Using both, one finds a list of areas to test more and those to test less. After test execution has started and one has found some defects, one may analyse these in order to focus testing. The idea is that defects clump together in defect prone areas, and that defects are a symptom of particular trouble the developers had. Thus, a defect leads to the conclusion that there are more defects nearby, and that there are more defects of the same kind. Thus, during the latter part of test execution, one should focus on areas where defects have been found, and one should generate more tests aimed at the type of defect detected before[1].

---

1 The ideas in this chapter are not intended to be used with safety critical software. Some of the ideas may be useful in that area, but due consideration is necessary. The presented ideas mean that the tester is taking risks, and the risks may or may not materialize in the form of serious failures.

4.1   The bad game

The scenario is as follows: You are the test manager. You have made a plan and a budget for testing. Your plans were, as far as you knew, reasonable and well founded. When testing time approaches you might find that the product is not ready, some of your testers are not available, or the budget is just cut. You can argue against these cuts or argue for more time or whatever, but that doesn't always help. You have to do what you can with a smaller budget and time frame. You have to test the product as well as possible, and you have to make sure it works reasonably well after release. How to survive?

There are several approaches, using different techniques and attacking different aspects of the testing process. All of them aim at finding as many defects as possible, and as many serious defects as possible, before product release. Different sections of this chapter show how. At the end of the chapter, some ideas are given that should help to prevent the pressured scenario mentioned before.

In this chapter we are talking about the higher levels of testing: integration, system and acceptance test. We assume that the basic level, of testing every program, has been done by the programmers. We also assume the programs and their designs have been reviewed in some way. However, most of the ideas in this chapter are still applicable even if nothing has been done before you take over as the test manager. It is, however, easier if you know some facts from earlier quality control activities such as design and code reviews and unit testing.

You cannot win by bad testing, or by requiring more time to test. Doing bad testing will make you the scapegoat for lack of quality. Doing reasonable testing will make you the scapegoat for a late release. A good scenario illustrating the trouble is the Y2K project. Testing may be done in the last minute, and the deadline is fixed, but there are options. During this chapter Y2K examples will be used to illustrate the major points.

How to get out of the game?

You need some creative solution; namely you have to change the game. You need to inform management about the impossible task you have, in such a way that they understand. You need to present alternatives. They need a product going out of the door, but they also need to understand the risk.

One strategy is to find the right quality level. Not all products need to be free of defects. Not every function needs to work. Sometimes, you have options related to lowering product quality. This means you can cut down testing in less important areas.

Another strategy is priority: Test should find the *most important defects* first. Most important means often "in the most important functions". These functions can be found by analysing how every function supports the mission, and checking which functions are critical and which are not. You can also test more where you expect more defects. Finding the worst areas in the product soon and testing them more will give you more defects. If you find too many serious problems, management will often be motivated to give you more time and resources. Most of this chapter will be about a combination of most important and worst area priority.

A third strategy is making testing cheaper in general. One major issue here is automation of test execution. But be cautious; automation can be expensive, especially if you have never done it before or if you do it wrong! However, experienced companies are able to automate test execution with no overhead compared to manual testing.

A fourth strategy is getting someone else to pay. Typically, this someone else is the customer. You release a bad product and the customer finds the defects for you. Many companies have applied this. This is not pleasant for the customer, as he has no alternative. But it remains open to discussion as to whether this is a good strategy for long term success. So the "someone else" should be another department in your company, not the testers. You may require the product to fulfil certain entry criteria before you test. Entry criteria can include certain reviews having been done, certain test coverage in unit testing, and a certain level of reliability. The problem is: you need to have high level support to be able to enforce this. Entry criteria tend to be skipped if the project gets under pressure and organisational maturity is low.

The last strategy is prevention, but that only pays off in the next project, when you, as the test manager, are involved from the project start on.

4.2   Understanding necessary quality levels

Software is embedded in the larger, more complex business world. Quality must be considered in that context (Favaro, 1996). The relentless pursuit of quality can dramatically improve the technical characteristics of a software product. In some applications - medical instruments, air-navigation systems, and many defence-related systems - the need to provide a certain level of quality is beyond debate. But is quality really the only or most important framework for strategic decision making in the commercial marketplace? Quality thinking fails to address many of the fundamental issues that most affect a company's long-term competitive and financial performance. The real issue is which quality will produce the best financial performance. You have to be sure which qualities and functions are important. Fewer defects do not always mean more profit! You have to research how quality and financial performance interact. Examples of such approaches include the concept of Return on Quality used in corporations such as AT&T (BusinessWeek, 1994). ROQ evaluates prospective quality improvements against their ability to also improve financial performance. Also note approaches like Value Based Management. Avoid the fanatically pursuit of quality for its own sake. Thus, more testing is not always needed to ensure product success!

Example: It may be acceptable that a product fails to work on February 29, 2000. It may also be acceptable that it sorts records incorrectly if they are blended with 19xx and 20xx dates. But it may be of immense importance that the product can record orders at all in years after 1999.

4.3   Setting priorities in testing

Testing is always a sample. You can never test everything, and you can always find more to test. Thus you will always need to make decisions about what to test and what not to test, what to test more or what to test less. The general goal is to find the worst defects first, and to find as many such defects as possible. This means the defects must be important. A way to ensure this is to find the most important functional areas and product properties. Finding as many defects as possible can be improved by testing more in the bad areas of the product. This means you need to know where to expect more defects. When dealing with all the factors, the result will always be a list of functions and properties with an associated importance. In order to make the final analysis as easy as possible, we express all these factors in a scale from 0 to 5. Five points are given for "most important" or "worst", or generally for something which we want to test more, 0 points are given to areas where we feel is not necessary to include them in the testing effort at all. The details of the computation are given later.

What is important?

You need to know the most important areas of the product. In this paragraph, a way to prioritise this is described. The ideas presented here are not the only valid ones. In every product, there may be other factors playing a role, but the factors given here have been valuable in several projects. Important areas can either be functions or functional groups, or properties such as performance, capacity, security etc. The result of this analysis is a list of functions and properties or combination of both that need attention. I am concentrating here on sorting *functions* into more or less important areas. The approach, however, is flexible and can accommodate other ideas.

Major factors to look at include:

Critical areas (cost and consequences of failure)

You have to analyse the use of the software within its overall environment, analyse the ways the software may fail. Find the possible consequences of such failure modes, or at least the worst ones. Take into account redundancy, backup facilities and possible manual checks of software output by users, operators or analysts. Software that is directly coupled to a process it controls is more critical than software whose output is manually reviewed before use. If software controls a process, this process itself should be analysed. The inertia and stability of the process itself may make certain failures less interesting.

Example: The subscriber information system for a Telecom operator may uncouple subscriber lines - for instance if 31-12-99 is used as an "indefinite" value for the subscription end date. This is a critical failure. On the other hand, in a report, the year number may be displayed as blanks if it is in 2000, which is a minor nuisance.

Output that is immediately needed during working hours is more critical than an output, which could be, sent hours or days later. On the other hand, if large volumes of data sent by mail are wrong, the cost of re-mailing only may be astronomical.

A possible hierarchy is the following:
* *A failure would be catastrophic*
  The problem would cause the computer to stop, maybe even take down things in the environment (stop the whole country or business or product). Such failures may deal with large financial losses or even damage to human life. An example would be the gross uncoupling of all subscribers to the telephone network on 31 December 1999.
* *A failure would be damaging*
  The program may not stop, but data may be lost or corrupted, or functionality may be lost until the program or computer is restarted. An example is equipment that will not work just around midnight on 31 December 1999.

- *A failure would be hindering*
  The user is forced to work around, to more difficult actions to reach the
  same results.
- *A failure would be annoying*
  The problem does not affect functionality, but rather make the product less
  appealing to the user or customer.

Visible areas

The visible areas are areas where many users will experience a failure, if
something goes wrong. Users do not only include the operators sitting at a
terminal, but also final users looking at reports, invoices, or the like, or
dependent on the service delivered by the product which includes the
software. A factor to take into account under this heading is also the tolerance
of the users to such problems. It relates to the importance of different qualities,
see above. Software intended for untrained or naive users, especially software
intended for use by the general public, needs careful attention to the user
interface. Robustness will also be a major concern. Software which directly
interacts with hardware, industrial processes, networks etc. will be vulnerable
to external effects like hardware failure, noisy data, timing problems etc. This
kind of software needs thorough validation, verification and re-testing in case
of environment changes.

An example for a visible area is the functionality in a telephone switch, which
makes it possible to make a call. Less visible areas are all the value-added
services like call transfer.

Most used areas

Some functions may be used every day, other functions only a few times.
Some functions may be used by many, some by only a few users. Give priority
to the functions used often and heavily. The number of transactions per day
may be an idea in helping to find priorities.

A possibility to lower the priority of some areas is to cut out functionality which
will only be used once per quarter, half-year or year. Such functionality may
be tested after release, before its first use. A possible strategy for Y2K testing is
to test leap year functionality in January and February 2000, and then again
during December 2000 and in 2004. Sometimes this analysis is not quite
obvious. In process control systems, for example, certain functionality may be
invisible to the outside. It may be helpful to analyse the design of the complete
system.

A possible hierarchy is outlined here:
- *Unavoidable*
  An area of the product that most users will come in contact with during an average usage session (e.g. start-ups, printing, saving).
- *Frequent*
  An area of the product that most users will come in contact with eventually, but maybe not during *every* session.
- *Occasional*
  An area of the product that an average user may never visit, but that deals with functions a more serious or experienced user will need occasionally.
- *Rare*
  An area of the product which most users never will visit and which is visited only if users do very uncommon steps of action. Critical failures, however, are still of interest.

An alternative method for picking important requirements is described in (Karlsson *et al.*, 1997).

What is (presumably) worst?

The worst areas are the ones having most defects. The task is to predict where most defects are located. This is done by analysing probable defect generators. In this section, some of the most important defect generators and symptoms for defect prone areas are presented. There exist many more, and you must always include local factors in addition to the ones mentioned here.

Complex areas

Complexity is maybe the most important defect generator. More than 200 different complexity measures exist, and research into the relation between complexity and defect frequency has been going on for more than 20 years. However, no predictive measures have until now been generally validated. Still, most complexity measures may indicate problematic areas. Examples include long modules, many variables in use, complex logic, complex control structure, a large data flow, central placement of functions, and even subjective complexity as understood by the designers. This means you may do several complexity analyses, based on different aspects of complexity and find different areas of the product that might have problems.

Changed areas

Change is an important defect generator (Khoshgoftaar *et al.*, 1998). One reason is that changes are subjectively understood as easy, and thus not analysed thoroughly for their impact. Another reason is that changes are done under time pressure and analysis is not completely done. The results are side effects. Advocates for modern system design methods, like the Cleanroom process, state that debugging during unit test is more detrimental than good to quality, because the changes introduce more defects than they repair.

In general, there should exist a protocol of changes done. This is part of the configuration management system (if something like that exists). You may sort the changes by functional area or otherwise and find the areas which have had exceptional amount of changes. These may either have been badly designed from the start, or have become badly designed after the original design has been destroyed by the many changes. Many changes are also a symptom of badly done analysis (Khoshgoftaar *et al.*, 1998). Thus, heavily changed areas may not correspond to user expectations.

Impact of new technology, solutions, methods

Programmers using new tools, methods and technology experience a learning curve. In the beginning, they may generate many more faults than later. Tools include CASE tools, which may be new in the company, or new in the market and unstable. Another issue is the programming language, which may be new to the programmers, or Graphical User Interface libraries. Any new tool or technique may give trouble. A good example is the first project with a graphical user interface. The general functionality may work well, but the user interface subsystem may be full of problems.

Another factor to consider is the maturity of methods and models. Maturity means the strength of the theoretical basis or the empirical evidence. If software uses established methods, like finite state machines, grammars, relational data models, and the problem to be solved may be expressed suitably by such models, the software can be expected to be quite reliable. On the other hand, if methods or models of a new and unproven kind, or near the state of the art are used, the software may be more unreliable.

Most software cost models include factors accommodating the experience of programmers with the methods, tools and technology. This is as important in test planning, as it is in cost estimation.

Impact of the number of people involved

The idea here is the thousand monkey's syndrome. The more people that are involved in a task, the larger is the overhead for communication and the greater the chance that things will go wrong. A small group of highly skilled staff is much more productive than a large group with average qualifications. In the COCOMO (Boehm, 1981) software cost model, this is the largest factor after software size. Much of its impact can be explained from effort going into detecting and fixing defects. Areas where relatively many and less qualified people have been employed, may be identified for better testing.

Care should be taken in that analysis: Some companies (Jørgensen, 1984) employ their best people in more complex areas, and less qualified people in easy areas. Then, defect density may not reflect the number of people or their qualification. A typical case is the program developed by lots of hired-in consultants without thorough follow-up. They may work in very different ways. During Y2K testing, it may be found that everyone has used a different date format, or a different time window.

Impact of turnover

If people quit the job, new people have to learn the design constraints before they are able to continue that job. As not everything may be documented, some constraints may be hidden for the new person, and defects result. Overlap between people may also be less than desirable. In general, areas with turnover will experience more defects than areas where the same group of people has done the whole job.

Where there was time pressure

Time pressure leads to people making short-cuts. People concentrate on getting the problem solved, and they often try to skip quality control activities, thinking optimistically that everything will go fine. Only in mature organizations this optimism is controlled.

Time pressure may also lead to overtime work. It is well known, however, that people loose concentration after prolonged periods of work. Together with short-cuts in applying reviews and inspections, this may lead to extreme levels of defect density. Data about time pressure during development can best be found by studying time lists, or by interviewing management or programmers.

Areas which needed optimising

The COCOMO cost model mentions shortage of machine time and memory as one of its cost drivers. The problem is that optimisation needs extra design effort, or that it may be done by using less robust design methods. Extra design effort may take resources away from defect removal activities, and less robust design methods may generate more defects.

Areas with many defects before

Defect repair leads to changes, which lead to new defects, and therefore defect prone areas tend to persist. Experience shows that defect prone areas in a delivered system can be traced back to defect prone areas in reviews and unit and subsystem testing. Evidence in studies (Khoshgoftaar *et al.*, 1998) and (Levendel, 1991) shows that modules that had faults in the past are likely to have faults in the future. If defect statistics from design and code reviews, and unit and subsystem testing exist, then priorities can be chosen for later test phases.

Geographical spread

If people working together on a project have a certain distance between each other, communication will be worse. This is true even on a local level. Here are some ideas that haven proven to be valuable in assessing if geography may have a detrimental effect on a project:

- People having their offices in different floors of the same building will not communicate as much as people on the same floor.
- People sitting more than 25 meters apart may not communicate enough.
- A common area in the workspace, such as a common printer or coffee machine improves communication.
- People sitting in different buildings do not communicate as much as people in the same building. People sitting in different labs communicate less than people in the same lab do.
- People from different countries may have difficulties, both culturally and with the language.
- If people reside in different time zones, communication will be more difficult.

In principle, geographical spread is not dangerous. The danger arises if people with a large distance have to communicate, for example, if they work on a common part of the system. You have to check areas where the software structure requires the need for good communication between people, but where these people have geography against them.

History of prior use

If many users have used software before, an active user group can be helpful in testing new versions. Beta testing may be possible. For a completely new system, a user group may need to be defined, and prototyping may be applied. Typically, completely new functional areas are most defect prone because even the requirements are unknown.

Local factors

Examples include looking at who did the job, looking at who does not communicate well with someone else, who is new in the project, which department has recently been reorganised, which managers are in conflict with each other, the involvement of prestige and many more factors. Only fantasy sets boundaries. The message is: You have to look out for possible local factors outside the factors having been discussed here.

What to do if you do not know anything about the project, if all the defect generators can not be applied? You have to run a test. A first rough test should find defect prone areas, the next test will then concentrate on them. The first test should cover the whole system, but be very shallow. It should only cover typical business scenarios and a few important failure situations, but cover all of the system. You can then find where there was most trouble, and give priority to these areas in the next round of testing. The next round will then do deep and through testing of prioritised areas. This two-phase approach can always be applied, in addition to the planning and prioritising done before testing.

How to calculate priority of test areas

The general method is to assign weights, and to calculate a weighted sum for every area of the system. Test where the result is highest!

For every factor chosen, assign a relative weight. You can do this in very elaborate ways, but this will take a lot of time. Most often, three weights will suffice. Values may be 1, 3, and 10. (1 for "factor is not very important", 3 for "factor has normal influence", 10 for "factor has very strong influence").

For every factor chosen, you assign a number of points to every product requirement (every function, functional area, or quality characteristic. The more important the requirement is, or the more alarming a defect generator seems to be for the area, the more points. A scale from 0 to 3 or 5 is normally good enough.

The number of points for a factor is then multiplied by its weight. This gives a weighted number of points between 0 and 50. These weighted numbers are then summed up. Testing can then be planned by assigning the greatest number of tests to the areas with the highest number of points.

An example:

Area to test	Business criticality	Visibility	Complexity	Change frequency	SUM
Weight	3	10	3	3	
Order registration	2	4	5	1	64
Invoicing	4	5	4	2	78
Order statistics	2	1	3	3	34
Management reporting	2	1	2	4	35
Performance of order registration	5	4	0	1	58
Performance of statistics	1	1	0	0	13
Performance of invoicing	4	1	0	0	22

Table 4.1: Risk score table

The table suggests that function "invoicing" is the most important to test, "order registration" and "performance of order registration" are next. The factor that has been chosen as the most important is visibility. Computation is easy, as it can be programmed using a spreadsheet. A more detailed case study is published in (Amland, 1997).

A word of caution: This calculation is not mathematically correct. Actually you are multiplying apples with oranges and summing up fruit salad. Thus, the number of points can only be a rough guideline. It should be good enough to distinguish the high-risk areas from the medium and low risk areas. That is its main task. This also means you don't need to be more precise than needed for just this purpose.

4.4   More effective testing

More effective testing aims to find more and more important defects in the same amount of time. The strategy to achieve this is to learn from experience.

First, the whole test should be broken into four phases:
* test preparation
* pre-test
* main test
* after-test.

Test preparation sets up areas to test, the test cases, testy programs, databases and the whole test environment. In particular setting up the test environment can give a lot of trouble and delay. It is generally easy to install the program itself and the correct operating system and database system. Problems often occur with the middleware, i.e. the connection between software running on a client, and software running on a server. Care should be taken to thoroughly specify all aspects of the test environment, and dry runs should be held, in order to ensure that the test can be run when it is time to do it. In a Y2K project, care should be taken to ensure that licenses are in place for machine dates after 1999, and the licenses allow resetting of the machine date. Another area to focus on is that the included software is Y2K compliant.

The pre-test is run after the software under test is installed in the test lab. This test contains just a few test cases running typical day to day usage scenarios. The goal is to test if the software is ready for testing at all, or totally unreliable or incompletely installed. Another goal may be to find some initial quality data, i.e. find some defect prone areas to focus the further tests on.

The main test consists of all the pre-planned test cases. They are run, failures are recorded, defects found and repaired, and new installations of the software made in the test lab. Every new installation may include a new pre-test. The main test takes most of the time during a test execution project.

The after-test starts with every new release of the software. This is the phase where optimisation should occur. Part of the after-test is regression testing, in order to find possible side effects of defect repair. But the main part is a shift of focus.

The type of defects may be analysed. A possible classification is described in (Bach, 1999). In principle, every defect is a symptom of a weakness of some design, and it should be used to actively search for more defects of the same kind.

Example: In a Y2K project, it was found that sometimes programs would display blank instead of zeroes in the year field in year 2000. A scan for the corresponding wrong code through many other programs produced many more instances of the same problem.

Another approach is to concentrate more tests on the more common kinds of defects, as these might be more common in the code. The problem is; however, that such defects might already have been found because the test was designed to find more of this kind of defects. Careful analysis is needed. Generally, apply the abstractions of every defect found as a checklist to more testing or analysis. The location of defects may also be used to focus testing. If a particular area of code has many failures, that area should be a candidate for even more testing (Levendel, 1991), (Khoshgoftaar *et al.*, 1998). But during the analysis, care should be taken to ensure that a high level of defects in an area is not caused by especially high test coverage in that area.

4.5   Making testing cheaper

A viable strategy for cutting budgets and time usage is to do the work in a more productive and efficient way. This normally involves applying technology. In software, not only technology, but also personnel qualification, seem to be ways to improve efficiency and cut costs. This also applies in testing.

Automation

There exist many test automation tools. Tool catalogues list more tools for every new edition, and the existing tools are more and more powerful while not costing more. Automation can probably do most in the area of test running and regression testing. Experience has shown that more test cases can be run for much less money, often less than a third of the resources spent for manual testing. In addition, automated tests often find more defects. This is fine for software quality, but may hit the testers, as the defect repair will delay the project. Still, such tools are not very popular, because they require an investment in training and learning at start. Sometimes a lot of money is spent in fighting with the tool. For the productivity improvement, nothing general can be said, as the application of such tools is too dependent on platforms, people and organizations. Anecdotal evidence prevails, and for some projects automation has had a great effect.

An area where test is nearly impossible without automation is stress, volume and performance testing. Here, the question is either to do it automatically or not to do it at all.

Test management can also be improved considerably using tools for tracking test cases, functions, defects and their repairs. Such tools are now more and more often coupled to test running automation tools.

In general, automation is interesting for cutting testing budgets. You should, however, make sure you are organised, and you should keep the cost for start-up and tool evaluation outside your project. Tools help only if you have a group of people who already know how to use them effectively and efficiently. To bring in tools in the last moment has a low potential to pay off, and can do more harm than good.

The people factor - Few but good people against many who don't know

The largest obstacle to an adequate testing staff is ignorance on the part of management. Some of them believe that "development requires brilliance, but anybody can do testing." Testing requires skill and knowledge. Without application knowledge your testers do not know what to look after. You get shallow test cases, which do not find defects. Without knowledge about common errors the testers do not know how to make good test cases[2]. Again, they do not find defects. Without experience in applying test methods people will use a lot of unnecessary time to work out all the details in a test plan.

If testing has to be cheap, the best is to get a few highly experienced specialists to collect the test candidates, and have highly skilled testers to improvise the test instead of working it out on chapter. Skilled people will be able to work from a checklist, and pick equivalence classes, boundary values, and destructive combinations by improvisation. Non-skilled people will produce a lot of chapter before having an even less destructive test.

The test people must be at least equally smart, equally good designers and have equal understanding of the functionality of the system. One could let the Function Design Team Leader become the System Test Team Leader as soon as functional design is complete. Pre-sales, Documentation, Training, Product Marketing and/or Customer Support personnel should also be included in the test team. This provides early knowledge transfer (a win-win for both development and the other organization) and more resource than exist full-time. Test execution requires lots of bodies that don't need to be there all of the time, but who do need to have a critical and informed eye on the software. You probably also need full-time testers, but not as many as you would use in the peak testing period. Full-time test team members are good for test design

---

2   Good test cases, i.e. test cases that have a high probability of finding errors, if there are errors, are also called "destructive test cases".

and execution, but also for building or implementing testing tools and infrastructure during less busy times.

If an improvised test has to be re-done, a problem will occur. But modern test automation tools can be run in a capture mode, and the captured test may later be edited for documentation and rerunning purposes. The message is: Get highly qualified people for your test team!

4.6   Cutting testing work

Another way of cutting costs is to get rid of part of the task. Get someone else to pay for it or cut it out completely!

Who pays for unit testing?

Often, unit testing is done by the programmers and never turns up in any official testing budget. The problem is that unit testing is often not really done. Test coverage tool vendors often report that without their tools, 40 - 50% of the code are never unit tested. Many defects then survive until the later test phases. This means later test phases have to test better, and they are delayed by finding all the defects that could have been found earlier. As a test manager, you should require higher standards for unit testing!

What about test entry criteria?

The idea is the same as in contracts with external customers: If the supplier does not meet the contract, the supplier gets no acceptance and no money. Problems occur when there is only one supplier and when there is no tradition in requiring quality. Both conditions are true in software. But entry criteria can be applied if the test group is strong enough. Criteria include many, from the most trivial to advanced. Here is a small collection of what makes the life in testing easier:
- The system delivered to integration or system test is complete.
- It has been run through static analysis and defects are fixed.
- A code review has been done and defects have been corrected.
- Unit testing has been done to the accepted standards (near 100% statement coverage, for example).
- Any required documentation is delivered and is of a certain quality.
- The units compile and can be installed without trouble.
- The units may even have been run through some functional test cases by the designers.

- Really bad units are sorted out and have been undergone special treatment like extra reviews, reprogramming etc.

You will not be allowed to require all these criteria. You will maybe not be allowed to enforce them. But you may turn projects into a better state over time by applying entry criteria. If every unit is reviewed, statically analysed and unit tested, you will have a lot less problems to fight with later.

Less documentation

If a test is designed by the book, it will take a lot of chapter to document. Not this entire chapter is needed. A test log made by a test automation tool may do the job. Qualified people may be able to make a good test from checklists, and even repeat it. Check out exactly which documentation you will need, and prepare no more. Most important is a test plan with a description of what is critical to test, and a test summary report describing what has been done and the risk of installation.

Cutting installation cost - strategies for defect repair

Every defect delays testing and requires an extra cost. You have to rerun the actual test case, try to reproduce the defect, document as much as you can, probably help the designers debugging, and at the end install a new version and retest it. This extra cost is impossible to control for a test manager, as it is completely dependent on system quality. The cost is normally not budgeted for either. Still, this cost will occur. Here some advice about how to keep it low.

When to correct a defect, when not?

Every installation of a defect fix means disruption: Installing a new version, initialising it, retesting the fix, and retesting the whole. The tasks can be minimised by installing many fixes at once. This means you have to wait for defect fixes. On the other hand, if defect fixes themselves are wrong, then this strategy leads to more work after finding new defects. There will be an optimum, dependent on system size, the chance to introduce new defects, and the cost of installation. For a good description of practical test exit criteria, see (Bach, 1997). Here are some rules for optimising the defect repair work:

- Rule 1: Repair only important defects!
- Rule 2: Change requests and small defects should be assigned to next release!
- Rule 3: Correct defects in groups! Normally only after blocking failures are found.

4.7   Strategies for prevention

The starting scenario for this chapter is the situation where everything is late and where no professional budgeting has been done. In most organizations, there exist no experience data and there exists no serious attempt to really estimate costs for development, testing, and error cost in maintenance. Without experience data there is no way to argue about the costs of reducing a test.

The imperatives are:
- You need a cost accounting scheme.
- You need to apply cost estimation based on experience and models.
- You need to know how test quality and maintenance trouble interact.

Measure:
- Size of project in lines of code, function points etc.
- Percentage of work used in management, development, reviews, test preparation, test execution, and rework.
- Amount of rework during first three or six months after release.
- Fault distribution, especially causes of user detected problems.
- Argue for testing resources by weighting possible reductions in rework before and after delivery against added testing cost.

A different way to prevent trouble is incremental delivery. The general idea is to break up the system into many small releases. The first delivery to the customer is the least commercially acceptable system, namely, a system that does exactly what the old one did, only with new technology. From the test of this first version you can learn about costs, error contents, bad areas etc. and then you have an opportunity to plan better.

4.8   Priority rules

Testing in a situation where management cuts both budget and time is a difficult game. You have to endure and survive this game and turn it into a success. The general methodology for this situation is not to test everything a little, but to concentrate on high-risk areas and the worst areas.

> Priority 1: Return the product as fast as possible to the developers, with a list of as serious deficiencies as possible.
>
> Priority 2: Make sure that, whenever you stop testing, you have done the best testing in the time available!

References

- Amland, S. (1997), Risk Based Testing of a Large Financial Application, in: *Proceedings of the 14th International Conference and Exposition on Testing Computer Software,* June 16-19, 1997, Washington, D.C., USA

- Bach, J. (1997), Good Enough Quality: Beyond the Buzzword, in: *IEEE Computer,* August 1997, pp. 96-98

- Bach, J. (1998), A framework for good enough testing, in: *IEEE Computer Magazine,* October 1998

- Bach, J. (1999), Heuristic Risk-Based Testing, in: *Software Testing Quality Engineering,* Vol. 1, Issue 6, November/December 1999

- Boehm, B.W. (1979), *Software engineering economics,* Prentice-Hall, Englewood Cliffs, NJ

- Business Week (1994), Quality: How to Make It Pay, in: *Business Week,* August 8, 1994

- Favaro, J. (1996), When the pursuit of quality destroys value, in: *Testing Techniques Newsletter,* May-June 1996

- IEEE 1044 (1993), *Standard Classification for Software Anomalies,* IEEE Standards Board

- Jørgensen, M. (1994), *Empirical studies of software maintenance,* Thesis for the Dr. Sceintific degree, Research Report 188, University of Oslo

- Karlsson, J. and K. Ryan (1997), A Cost-Value Approach for Prioritizing Requirements, in: *IEEE Software,* September 1997

- Khoshgoftaar, T.M., E.B. Allan, R. Halstead, G.P. Trio and R. M. Flass (1998), Using Process History to Predict Software Quality, in: *IEEE Computer,* April 1998

- Levendel, Y. (1991), Improving Quality with a Manufacturing Process, in: *IEEE Software,* March 1991.

5 Good enough testing

Paul Gerard

Are you ever asked as a tester, "is the system good enough to ship?" Given our normal experience, testers are never given enough time to do the testing and the system cannot be as good as it should be. When the time comes to make the release decision, how can one answer that question? James Bach introduced the idea called "Good Enough" in 1997 (Bach, 1997). It is helpful to understanding the risk-based test approach, as it seems to be a framework for release decision-making, at least in projects where risks are being taken. So, what is "Good Enough?" and how does it help with the release decision?

Many consultants advocate 'best practices' in books and conferences. Usually, they preach perfection and they ask leading questions like, "would you like to improve your processes?" "Do you want zero defects?" Could anyone possibly say "no" to these questions? Of course not. Many consultants promote their services using this method of preaching perfection and pushing mantras that sound good. It's almost impossible to reject them.

'Good enough' is a reaction to this compulsive formalism, as it is called. It's not reasonable to aim at zero-defects in software and your users and customers never expect perfection, so why do you pretend that you're aiming at perfection? The zero-defect attitude just doesn't help. Compromise is inevitable. The challenge ahead is to make a release decision for an imperfect system based on imperfect information.

The definition of "Good Enough" in the context of a system to be released is:
1. X has sufficient benefits.
2. X has no critical problems.
3. The benefits of X sufficiently outweigh the problems.
4. In the present situation, and all things considered, improving X would cause more harm than good.
5. All the above must apply.

To expand on this rather terse definition, X (whatever X is) has sufficient benefits means that there is deemed enough of this system working for us to take it into production, use it, get value, and get the benefit. It has no critical problems i.e. there are no severe faults that make it unusable or unacceptable.

At this moment in time, with all things considered, if we spend time trying to perfect X, that time is probably going to cost us more than shipping early with the known problems. This framework allows us to release an imperfect system early because the benefits may be worth it. How does testing fit into this good enough idea?

Firstly, have sufficient benefits been delivered? The tests that we execute must at least demonstrate that the features providing the benefits are delivered completely, so that we have evidence of this. Secondly, are there any critical problems? Our incident reports give us the evidence of the critical problems and many others too. There should be no critical problems for it to be good enough. Thirdly, is our testing good enough to support this decision? Have we provided sufficient evidence to say these risks are addressed and those benefits are available for release?

It is not for a tester to decide whether the system is good enough. An analogy that might help here is to view the tester as an expert witness in a court of law. The main players in this courtroom scene are:
• The accused (the system under test)
• The judge (project manager)
• The jury (the stakeholders)
• Expert witness (the tester).

In our simple analogy, we will disregard the lawyers' role. (In principle, they act only to extract evidence from witnesses). Expert witnesses are brought into a court of law to find evidence and present that evidence in a form for laymen (the jury) to understand. When asked to present evidence, the expert is objective and detached. If asked whether the evidence points to guilt or innocence, the expert explains what inferences could be made based on the evidence, but refuses to judge innocence or guilt. In the same way, the software tester might simply state that based on evidence "these features work, these features do not work, these risks have been addressed, these risks remain". It is for others to judge whether this makes a system acceptable.

The tester simply provides information for the stakeholders to make a decision. Adopting this position in a project seems to be a reasonable one to take. After all, testers do not create software or software faults; testers do not take the risks of accepting a system into production. Testers should advocate to their management and peers this independent point of view. When asked to judge whether a system is good enough, the tester might say that on the evidence we have obtained, these benefits are available; these risks still exist. The release decision is someone else's decision to make.

However, you know that the big question is coming your way so when you are asked, "Is it ready?" What should you do? You must help the stakeholders make the decision, but not make it for them. The risks, those problems that we thought could occur some months ago, which, in your opinion would make the system unacceptable, might still exist. Based on the stakeholders' own criteria, the system cannot now be acceptable, unless they relax their perceptions of the risk.

The judgement on outstanding risks must be as follows:
- There is enough test evidence now to judge that certain risks have been addressed.
- There is evidence that some features do not work (the feared risk has materialised).
- Some risks remain (tests have not been run, or no tests are planned).

This might seem like an ideal independent position that testers could take but you might think that it is unrealistic to think one can behave this way. However, this stance is unassailable since the alternative, effectively, is for the tester to take over the decision making in a project. Testing may still be forced to give an opinion on the readiness of a system, but taking this principled position (at least at first) might raise the profile of testing and credibility with management. They might also recognise the role of testing in projects in future - as an honest broker.

References

- Bach, J. (1997), Good Enough Quality: Beyond the Buzzword, in: *IEEE Computer*, August 1997, pp. 96-98

- Bach, J. (1999), Heuristic Risk-Based Testing, in: *Software Testing Quality Engineering*, Vol. 1, Issue 6, November/December 1999.

6 Measuring Software Quality

Rob Hendriks, Erik van Veenendaal and Robert van Vonderen

Quality requirements of software products are often described in vague and general terms. As a consequence it is difficult for test engineers to evaluate the quality of the software product as no unambiguous and quantitative reference, of what quality in that context means, exists. This chapter describes a method to identify the most important quality characteristics by means of a risk assessment, to define completion criteria and to subsequently measure software quality characteristics using the ISO 9126 standard. The authors have applied this method, amongst others, during testing of copier/printer controller software at Océ Technologies, a Dutch developer and manufacturer of copying and printing equipment.

6.1 Project context

In 1997 Océ Technologies started the development of a new line of copier/printer controllers, to be used in a new family of monochrome high-volume hybrid copier/printers. In April 1999 this development entered the engineering phase. The engineering of the software for this controller line took place on three sites, of which two were in the Netherlands and one was in France. Approximately 60 software engineers were involved in development of this software product, hereafter referred to as the "controller software". The controller software was developed in an incremental way, with each development cycle conforming to the V-model. Each increment taking between 3 and 5 months.

At the start of the engineering phase a test team was formed with the assignment to verify correct functional behaviour and to determine product quality of the controller software. One of the main problems that occurred for the test team was the fact that the required quality level of the controller software was not specified. The only quality requirements available referred to the copier/printer product as a whole and not in particular to its software components. However, those requirements were easily measurable and easy to understand. E.g. the mean number of copies between failures (MCBF, which pertains to all system errors) and the average copies per repair (ACPR, which is the average number of copies made between visits of a service engineer).

6.2   Quality model: ISO 9126

The objective of the test team was to get a clear baseline of the quality requirements before the testing phase would actually start. Therefore a quality model had to be found that could help in defining and measuring software product quality. In 1977 McCall *et al.*, (McCall, 1977) proposed the idea of breaking down the concept of quality into a number of quality factors. The idea has been followed by many other authors who have tried to capture software product quality in a collection of characteristics and their depending sub-characteristics, which in turn are connected to indicators and metrics. By doing so, every author imposes his or her own hierarchically layered model of software product quality. In these varying models some elementary characteristics keep on reappearing, although their place in the hierarchy can differ. In recent years the International Organization for Standardisation (ISO) and the International Electrotechnical Commission (IEC) have defined a standard set of quality characteristics. This set reflects a big step towards consensus in the software industry and thereby addresses the general notion of software quality. This ISO 9126 standard (ISO 9126-1, 2000) defines six quality characteristics and the subdivision of each quality characteristic in a number of sub-characteristics (see figure 6.1). The six quality characteristics defined in ISO 9126 are functionality, reliability, usability, efficiency, maintainability and portability. A full definition of the ISO 9126 quality characteristics and subcharacteristics is provided in annex B.

Figure 6.1: ISO 9126 quality characteristics overview

6.3   Selection of quality characteristics

Terminology

Not all quality characteristics are of equal importance to a software product. Portability may be unimportant when the development aims at a dedicated platform and maintainability may not be an issue when it's a product with a short life cycle. The (most) important quality (sub-) characteristics need therefore to be identified and selected by means of a risk assessment. This can be done by interviewing stakeholders in- and outside the project. Inside the project one can think of the product manager, the project manager and the software architect. Outside the project the various types of users are important. Copier users are not only limited to the persons operating the copier, often forgotten are stakeholders such as the service engineer and the system administrator.

The quality characteristics as defined by the ISO 9126 standard are not always easy to interpret. What does maintainability, or even worse co-existence mean? It's difficult to communicate regarding these quality characteristics in an unambiguous way. As it will be hard to understand for IT professionals, it will be even harder for users of the copier, who, in general, have no or limited IT knowledge. Most of the users don't even perceive that the product contains software. The quality characteristics are usually not part of the stakeholders' terminology. It will therefore be difficult to determine those quality characteristics that are important for the software component of the product just by asking, "Do you think resource-behaviour is important?" The persons interviewed have their own definition of the characteristics and their own view of what the system should do and therefore what is important.

Structured questionnaire

To overcome the problems mentioned above, a questionnaire risk-based method has been developed and empirically validated in the European ESPRIT project SPACE-UFO (Trienekens and Van Veenendaal, 1997). This method has been further elaborated by Improve Quality Services in numerous real-life projects (Hendriks *et al.*, 2001). The method relates the wishes and needs of stakeholders regarding the software product to software quality characteristics. The stakeholders' needs and requirements are explored and identified by using a structured questionnaire. The questionnaire consists of a number of questions regarding so-called generic product characteristics. These product characteristics are intended to be stated in the stakeholders' language. Instead of asking whether usability is important one asks questions about the characteristics of the users that influence the usability requirements, e.g. the number of different users, their experience with the product (or a similar one) and their educational level. Similar questions are asked for the other quality characteristics. The answers given are used to deduct the most relevant quality (sub-) characteristics by means of two-dimensional matrices. A part of the structured questionnaire is shown in table 6.1. For each question the related quality (sub-) characteristics are indicated.

Question	Quality Characteristic
What kind of market type is the product oriented towards? 1. Business market 2. Consumer market	Suitability Interoperability Learnability Resource utilisation Time behaviour
What is the number of products to be sold in a certain market area? 1. 1 - 1000 2. 1000 – 10000 3. more than 10000	Suitability Maturity
Does the product belong to a product family? 1. No 2. Yes	Analysability Changeability
Can software product failures cause damage? 1. Some economic loss 2. Serious economic loss 3. Safety damage or environmental disaster	Maturity Operability
What is the average experience of the recognised user groups with regard to the product? 1. More than one year experience 2. Less than one year experience 3. No experience	Understandability
How many users can be identified per product? 1. 1 – 10 2. 10 – 100 3. more than 100	Maintainability Reliability Usability
Are there any alternatives to carry on with the activities when the software fails? 1. Yes 2. No	Reliability
Are certain parts of the software available on more than one platform? 1. No 2. Yes	Portability

Table 6.1: Sample questions Structured Questionnaire

Quality Profile

Within the copier/printer project 4 key-persons were selected. In addition 3 representatives of the different types of users were selected. Thus 7 persons were interviewed, each having their typical view on the copier/printer product. From the answers given by the participants, a list of important quality characteristics can be deducted. Furthermore, importance levels can be identified (from level D to level A). This whole process results in a so-called quality profile (ISO/IEC 14598-5, 1996). A quality profile reflects the notion of quality for a certain software product and makes quality more tangible for all stakeholders (including testing). Once the initial quality profile has been defined, a consensus meeting is organised with all stakeholders to discuss the quality profile, the results of the interviews and the observed differences. Table 6.2 shows the resulting quality profile (on a quality characteristic level) for the controller software.

	Quality Level				
	-	D	C	B	A
Functionality				X	
Reliability				X	
Usability			X		
Efficiency		X			
Maintainability			X		
Portability	X				

Table 6.2: Quality Profile

As can be observed in the quality profile, the quality characteristics functionality, reliability, usability and maintainability were considered to be most important for the controller software. This can be explained for the type of copier the project is developing: it is expected to run in a highly professional document production environment, where the uptime (highly related to "reliability" and "maintainability") is of utmost importance. Also, the copier/printer will be the successor product of an analogue high-volume copier model, where a clear functionality demand (being compatible with existing products as well as providing an extension) is expressed. Usability scores high but was not taken further into account for testing the controller software. The reason for this is that usability is a property of the user interface, which was not part of the controller software development project as it is developed in a separate project.

As a result, the test team decided to focus on three quality characteristics primarily (functionality, reliability and maintainability), and to develop a set of completion criteria (metrics) for these quality characteristics.

6.4   Identification of quality metrics

Once the quality profile has been determined, it is time to start focusing on how to evaluate and measure the relevant quality (sub-) characteristics. The ISO 9126 standard defines in part two ("External metrics") and three ("Internal metrics") a large number of possible metrics per characteristic, including measurement scales and application guidelines. A selection needs to be made of the metrics provided and, if necessary, extended with self-defined metrics. Within the project for each quality characteristic, a selection of metrics was made either based on ISO 9126 or based on the product requirements (e.g. Mean Copies Between Failures). The selection of metrics to be used was mainly based on the fact whether it was possible and easy to measure them, since this was considered to be a pilot project within Océ for measuring software product quality.

Most of the metrics were used directly from the ISO standard, but some of them had to be fine-tuned to the project's definitions. An example is the ISO 9126 metric Mean Time Between Failures (MTBF). This metric is often used to give an indication of the maturity of the system. For copier/printers the maturity is often indicated by means of the metric Mean Copies Between Failures (MCBF) as the number of copies made is leading instead of the up-time. Therefore a slight change for some metrics was desirable. Furthermore, the product requirements often include quality statements applicable to the product as a whole. As only the controller software was taken into account, these quality statements needed to be translated to the controller software. E.g. the MCBF is higher for the controller software than for the product, because only failures caused by the controller software are taken into account. For example paper jams are not important when evaluating the maturity of the software.

In total sixteen metrics were defined, of which one was defined additional to the internal and external metrics provided in the ISO 9126 standard. The availability of design documentation was considered to be a good indication of the maintainability. Therefore a metric was added to verify the amount of design documentation that was available versus the amount of design documentation planned. An overview of some of the metrics defined can be found in table 6.3.

Quality characteristic	Sub-characteristic	Metric	Explanation
Functionality	Suitability	*Functional implementation completeness:* Number of missing functions detected during system testing / Number of functions described in requirement specifications.	How many functions have been implemented in relation to the number of functions specified in the requirement specifications?
		Functional implementation correctness: Number of correctly implemented functions confirmed during system testing / Number of functions described in requirement specifications.	What is the amount of functions that have been implemented according to the requirement specifications?
Reliability	Maturity	*Mean Copies Between Failures:* Total number of copies during system testing / Number of defects, caused by controller software, detected during operation time.	How frequent are the defects of the controller software in operation?
		Defect detection: Absolute number of defects detected during all test phases / Number of estimated defects to be detected. Measured for each release.	What's the proportion of the defects found?
		Test completeness: Number of actually executed test cases / Number of test cases to be executed.	How reliable is the test process for product quality statements?
Maintainability	Analysability	*Availability of design documentation:* Available design documentation (i.e. SW architecture, top-level design, analysis views, design views and interface specifications) / Identified design documentation.	What's the proportion of design documentation available?
		Inspected design documentation: Inspected design documentation / Available design documentation	How reliable and correct is the content of design documentation?

Table 6.3: Examples of product quality metrics

6.5   Defining completion criteria

It was decided that completion criteria, as a hypothetical baseline, had to be defined before starting actual measurement. The goal was not to measure relative improvement with each test-cycle, but to compare the measured quality against the completion criteria, which has to be reached before the product could be released. Defining completion criteria in advance forces people to start discussion when quality targets are not met. If no baseline is defined one is tempted to accept the quality as is, because no tangible reference exists. The product is easily considered to be "good enough".

These completion criteria were defined by individually asking a number of experienced engineers within the project and of comparable software projects for an estimate on each metric. These estimates were then compared and discussed in a team meeting. Each estimate needed to state the "minimum but sufficient quality level' for release. E.g., the metric Mean Copies Between Failures was defined to be 100,000. This means that only one failure, caused by the controller software, may occur every 100,000 copies. It was decided to measure all criteria (when applicable) during the system test phase of each incremental development cycle. The result of each development cycle could thus be scored against the defined baseline. In this way, both the improvements per development cycle, as well as the discrepancy with the "minimum but sufficient quality level" could be depicted and reacted upon.

Collection of the measurement data during the system test phases implied that thorough administration was necessary during test execution. In addition to defects found, it was important to record the number of copies made, the total down time of the copier/printer, the number of failures successfully restored by the system itself, etc. It was important to clearly instruct the test engineers on what data should be recorded, otherwise important information necessary to calculate the metrics could be missing. The test engineers were given instructions on how to collect the metrics and a set of supporting forms was established.

After each system test phase the measured values were evaluated to see whether the product was approaching its completion criteria. If necessary the completion criteria can be modified, but not after a thorough discussion within the steering committee regarding the desired quality levels. Management should always formally approve the changing of completion criteria.

6.6   Real-life measurements

Until the first commercial release of the controller software, 5 development increments were evaluated and measured. For one increment, an additional system test phase was added, leading to a sixth measurement (C2 patch). Some measurement results of the increments are presented in the table below.

Quality-charac-teristic	Sub-charac-teristic	Metric	Completion Criteria	Value C1	Value C2	Value C2 patch	Value C3	Value C4	Value C5
Functio-nality	Suit-ability	Functional implementation completeness	0.90	0.91	1.0	1.0	0.82	0.90	0.91
		Functional implementation correctness	0.80	0.45	0.80	0.84	0.61	0.70	0.64
Reli-ability	Maturity	Defect detection	0.75	0.46	0.63	0.63	1.08	1.19	1.43
		Mean copies between failures	100000	not avai-lable	93	175	4880	11204	6560
		Test completeness	0.90	0.75	0.78	0.33	0.92	0.97	0.95
Maintain-ability	Analys-ability	Available design documentation	not defined	0.70	0.62	0.62	0.66	0.73	0.70
		Inspected design documentation	0.75	0.71	0.67	0.67	0.59	0.49	0.49

Table 6.4: Measurements results

From the table it can be observed that the Mean Copies Between Failures (MCBF) was far below the completion criteria defined. Still the completion criterion was not adjusted. The low number for MCBF for increments C1, C2 and C2 patch was mainly caused by the fact that the controller software was not yet robust for failures in the scanner or printer. E.g. a paper jam also resulted in a failure in the controller software. From increment C3 onwards the software was robust for paper jams and one can see that the MCBF increased tremendously. Still the value was far below what the initially defined quality target. It appeared that during the initial estimation it was not taken into account that the tests were aiming at finding functional defects in the software and not were not defined, as usually, with the objective of finding defects by producing large amounts of copies.

It is interesting to compare the measurements from increment C2 patch to those from increment C2. The software test on increment C2 was hindered by major instability and performance problems. These problems were resolved, after which measurement C2 patch took place. Although the difference between the metrics of increment C2 and increment C2 patch is only relatively small (only 9 major defects were solved, approx. 5% of the total number of defects solved), the users perceived increment 2 patch as a much "better" system. This example shows that the metrics and values indicated in the previous table should be interpreted with great care. For instance, when a system only shows a few critical defects in the most important part of that system, it will be of an unacceptable quality level, however the metrics may show otherwise. The severity of a defect and its location in the system are not taken into account. This means in addition to the metrics also an experienced based quantitative evaluation is needed.

From increment C3 onwards one can see that the defect detection rate is higher than 1, which shows that more defects have been found than initially expected. The estimation for the defects expected to be found may be incorrect, this needs further investigation. Literature and historical metrics of the Océ organisation were used to estimate the number of defects expected to be found. The main assumption was that on average 6 defects could be found per thousand lines of code (KLOC). For re-used code this value was adapted to 2 defects per KLOC. Furthermore automatically generated code was seen as newly developed code and therefore also 6 defects per KLOC were expected.

The number of defects found versus the number expected should be approximately 1 for each increment. Note that this is a cumulative value. However, in the project it was experienced that defects were found rather late over the increments. At increment C3 the integration test process was strengthened, which may be an explanation for the rise of defect detection from that moment onwards.

After increment C3 a major shift of responsibilities between the test team of the controller software and the system test team of the copier/printer took place. From that point on the functional tests were the responsibility of the copier/printer test team, while integration testing remained the responsibility of the controller software test team. Due to this shift a different test strategy was applied to system testing. The printer/copier test team did not only focus on functionality, but also on performance and duration. Therefore more copies were made with a minimum number of user interactions, which affected the total number of copies made during a system test phase. This affected the metric Mean Copies Between Failures. The types of tests that have been executed are important to take into account when evaluating the metrics.

6.7   The release decision

The software quality metrics have been measured within the project for over 2 years. During that period a lot of experience was gained on the metrics themselves, how to interpret them and how they could be used e.g. for setting project priorities. The metrics were initially only applied to provide visibility on software product quality. The next step was to submit changes in the development process to improve the quality of the software itself and the process. E.g. if the defect detection rate is lower than expected, as can be seen for releases C1 to C2 patch, but the test completeness is quite high (75% - 78%) it is be necessary to evaluate the effectiveness of the test process. It's of course also possible that the engineering team makes fewer errors as expected.

Of course, if the completion criteria are not met, normally additional tests are required. However, the tension between time-to-market and product quality will always remain. The metrics as provided by using this method are a major input for management to support the release decision process. They allow a thorough discussion with all stakeholders on product quality and the identification of outstanding risks. As a result, the test plan may be revised to permit the relaxation (or strengthening) of the test completion criteria.

The reporting on product quality has been received well within the project, both by people involved in the quality profile definition and those (only) receiving the test results. The discussions on product quality are now based on more than "just" the number of defects and the subjective perception of stakeholders.

References

- Hendriks, R., E. van Veenendaal and R. van Vonderen (2001), *Measuring Software Product Quality during Testing,* in: *Professional Tester*, Volume Two, Issue No. 1, March 2001

- ISO/IEC 9126-1:2000, *Information technology - Software product quality - Part 1: Quality model,* International Organization for Standardization

- ISO/IEC 9126-2:1999, *Information technology - Software product quality - Part 2: External metrics,* International Organization for Standardization

- ISO/IEC 9126-3:2000, *Information technology - Software product quality - Part 3: Internal metrics,* International Organization for Standardization

- ISO/IEC CD 14598-5 (1996), *Information technology - Software product evaluation - Part 5: Process for evaluators,* International Organization for Standardization

- McCall, J.A., P.K. Richards and G.F. Walters (1977), *Factors in software quality,* RADC-TR-77-363 Rome Air Development Center, Griffis Air Force, Rome, New York

- Solingen R. van and E. Berghout (1999), *The Goal Question Metric method, a practical method for quality improvement of software development,* McGraw-Hill, UK, ISBN 007-709553-7

- Trienekens J.J.M. and E.P.W.M. van Veenendaal (1997), *Software Quality from a business perspective,* Kluwer Bedrijfsinformatie, Deventer, The Netherlands, ISBN 90-267-2631-7

- Veenendaal, E.P.W.M. van and J. McMullan (eds.) (1997), *Achieving Software Product Quality*, UTN Publishing, 's-Hertogenbosch, The Netherlands, ISBN 90-72194-52-7.

7 Test Point Analysis: a method for test estimation

Erik van Veenendaal and Ton Dekkers

This chapter describes the test estimation technique known as test point analysis (TPA). TPA can be used to objectively prepare an estimate for a system test or an acceptance test. TPA covers only high level testing. Estimates for the test activities, which precede high-level testing (i.e. activities during low-level testing), have already been included in the estimate produced by function point analysis (FPA). So, while the function point analysis productivity factor covers the low-level testing, it does not cover system testing or acceptance testing.

TPA can also be used in cases where the test hour budget has been predetermined. By performing a TPA, any risks involved can be clearly identified by comparing the objective TPA estimate with the predetermined number of test hours. With TPA, it is also possible to determine the relative importance of the various functions, with a view to using the available testing time as efficiently as possible.

7.1   Philosophy

When establishing an estimate for a high-level test, three elements are relevant: the size of the software product to be tested, the test strategy (selection of system units and quality characteristics to be tested and the coverage of testing) and the level of productivity. The first two elements together determine the volume of testing work to be carried out (expressed in test points). If the number of test points is multiplied by the productivity (the amount of time needed to perform a given volume of testing work), then the result is a test estimate in hours. The three elements, (size, test strategy and productivity) are considered in more detail below.

Size

The first element to be considered is the size of the software product. For TPA[1] purposes, the size of a software product is determined mainly by the number of function points (Albrecht, 1984) assigned to it. FPA is a technique that measures the functional size of a software product and expresses the size in function points (FPs). The International Function Point User Group (IFPUG, 1999) has developed a well known and internationally accepted function point standard. Although sometimes a FPA also includes an estimate for high-level tests, this estimate is generally too rough. The huge difference between the estimates from TPA and FPA is that in TPA the risk-based test strategy is taken into account. In an FPA, high-level tests are included by increasing the productivity factor. This is like saying that testing takes x% of the development effort, regardless of the risks involved. To summarize, while the FPA productivity factor covers the component and integration test levels; it lacks sufficient coverage of system and acceptance testing.

In the context of size a number of additions or adjustments need to be made on the FPA, because certain factors, which have little or no influence on the number of function points, are pertinent to testing.

The factors in question are the following:
- *Complexity:* complexity relates to the number of conditions in a function. More conditions almost always means more test cases and therefore a greater volume of testing work;
- *Interfacing:* the degree of interfacing of a function is determined by the number of data sets maintained by a function and the number of other functions, which make use of those data sets. Interfacing is relevant because these "other" functions will require testing if the modifying function is changed;
- *Uniformity:* it is important to consider the extent to which the structure of a function allows it to be tested using existing or slightly modified specifications, i.e. the extent to which the software product contains similarly structured functions.

Test strategy

During development or maintenance, quality requirements will have been specified for the software product. The test activities are focused on

---

determining the extent to which these requirements have been satisfied. In co-operation with all stakeholders, the system and/or subsystem quality characteristics to be tested are identified and their relative importance determined. The importance of each characteristic influences the thoroughness of the related test activities. The more important a quality characteristic, the more accurate and thorough the tests have to be, and the larger the volume of work. The importance of the various characteristics should be determined in consultation with the stakeholders when the test strategy is being formulated; the information can then be used as TPA input. In the course of the TPA process, the volume of testing work is calculated on the basis of the test strategy.

While certain general quality requirements apply to the software product as a whole, there are also differences between the various functions in terms of the requirements to be met. From the user's point of view, a data entry function, which is utilized throughout the day, may be much more important than a batch processing function that creates a weekly report for management. For each function, therefore, there are two (subjective) factors that influences the thoroughness of testing:
- *User-importance of the function*
- *Usage-intensity.*

The user-importance and usage-intensity factors should, of course, be derived from the test strategy.

As previously indicated, the importance attached to the various quality characteristics for testing purposes and the importance of the various subsystems and/or functions determine the test strategy. The test strategy specifies which quality characteristics are to be tested for each subsystem or function, and the relevant degree of coverage. Thus, TPA and strategy determination are closely related and in practice are often performed in parallel.

Productivity

Productivity is not a new concept to anyone who has produced estimates on the basis of function points. In function point analysis, productivity is an expression of the relationship between the number of hours necessary for a task and the measured number of function points. In TPA, productivity relates to the time necessary to realize one test point, as determined by the size of the software product and the test strategy. Productivity has two components:

- *Productivity number*: the productivity number is based on the knowledge and skill of the test team, and is therefore specific to the individual organization or project.
- *Environmental factor*: the environmental factor indicates the degree to which the environment influences the test activities to which the productivity is related. Influential environmental considerations include the availability of test tools, the level of experience the team has with the test environment, the quality of the test basis and the availability of testware.

7.2   Basic procedure

The TPA procedure is illustrated below.

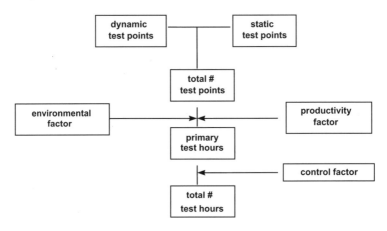

Figure 7.1: Overview of the test point analysis procedure

The number of test points necessary for dynamic testing is calculated for each function on the basis of the number of function points assigned to the function, the function-dependent factors (complexity, interfacing, uniformity, user-importance and usage-intensity) and the quality requirements that will be tested dynamically. The sum of the test points assigned to the individual functions is the number of "dynamic test points". The number of test points necessary for static testing is calculated on the basis of the total number of function points for the software products and the quality requirements that will be tested statically. This gives the number of static test points.

The total number of test points is the sum of the dynamic and static test points. The number of primary test hours can then be calculated by multiplying the total number of test points by the calculated environmental factor and the applicable productivity factor. The primary test hours represents the volume of work involved in the primary testing activities, i.e. the time required for completion of the test phases preparation, specification, execution and completion (see chapter 2 for the TMap life cycle).

Finally, the total number of test hours is obtained by adding an allowance for secondary test activities (test management, test planning and control) to the primary number of test hours. The size of this allowance, which represents the volume of work involved in the management activities, depends on the size of the test team and the availability of management tools. The total number of test hours is an estimate of the time required for all test activities, excluding the establishment of the test plan.

7.3   Principles

Regarding TPA, the following principles apply:
- TPA is concerned only with the measurable quality characteristics (according to ISO 9126, 2001), which fall within the scope of system testing and/or acceptance testing. A characteristic is considered "measurable" if an appropriate test technique is available. Sufficient practical experience should already have been acquired using the test technique for the quality characteristic in question, to allow the volume of work to be predicted with reasonable accuracy.
- The consequence of the first principle is that, using the TPA technique in its present form, it is not possible to allow for all the quality characteristics that might be addressed by acceptance testing and/or system testing. The characteristics for which allowance cannot be made are those for which no pre-defined test technique (yet) exists and those in relation to which insufficient practical experience has been acquired. It is likely that any subsequent version of the TPA system would cover more quality characteristics.
- TPA is in principle analyst-independent. In other words, if two different people performed a TPA of the same software product, they should obtain the same result. This is because clear rating definitions are provided for all factors, which can be rated on an objective basis, while the stakeholders determine all other factors.
- TPA depends on the availability of a function point count produced using IFPUG (IFPUG, 1999). For TPA, the gross function point count is used as the basis for analysis.
- For TPA purposes, the test team's domain knowledge is not treated as a variable, which affects the amount of work involved in the tests. Naturally, it is assumed that the team does have a certain amount of domain knowledge.

Sufficient domain knowledge is thus a precondition, satisfaction of which has to be assured at the test planning stage.
- TPA estimates are made on the assumption that, on average, one complete re-test will be conducted. This is a weighted average based on the size of the functions, expressed in test points. This implies that if one of the functions in a system needs more than one retest, this will be compensated for internally by other functions requiring no retest.

7.4   The technique in detail

Input and starting conditions

To conduct a TPA, one needs to have a functional design available, consisting of detailed process descriptions and a logical data model, preferably including a Create, Read, Update, Delete (CRUD) table. In addition, a function point count made using the IFPUG technique is necessary. A count made using one of a different function point "dialect" can also be used as input for the TPA. However, when determining a productivity factor from the historical data, it is important that only one function point counting method is used; different methods should not be combined. The choice of function point counting technique does not affect test point calculation, but it can influence the productivity factor.

For TPA purposes, the function point count is amended as follows:
- The function points for the various (logical) data sets, defined within the function point count, are assigned to the function(s) which provide(s) the input for those (logical) data sets.
- The function points for the various external data sets, defined within the function point count, are assigned to the function(s) which use(s) those external data sets.
- The number of function points for a clone-class FPA function is the same as the number of points assigned to the relevant original FPA function. A clone is an FPA function, which has already been specified and/or realized within the same or another user function in the same project.
- The number of function points for a dummy-class FPA function is, if possible, calculated; otherwise, such functions are treated as being of average complexity and the corresponding number of function points are assigned. A dummy is an FPA function whose functionality does not need to be specified and/or realized, but which is nevertheless available because specification and/or realization has been undertaken outside the project.

If no function point count is available, but one is desirable (for TPA purposes), the time needed to carry out the count can be determined as follows:
The number of logical data sets is counted and multiplied by
- 28 in the case of a system with low data complexity (less than 10 LDSs)
- 35 in the case of a system with average data complexity (between 10 and 25 LDSs)
- 42 in the case of a system with high data complexity (more than 25 LDSs).

This provides a very rough approximation of the function point count. This approximation is divided by four hundred to obtain the number of days necessary for the count. (Note: it is generally possible to count four hundred to five hundred function points a day depending and the quality of the system documentation.)

Dynamic test points

The number of dynamic test points is the sum of the test points assigned to the individual functions. To calculate the test points for the individual functions, the influential variables and factors are divided into two categories:
- Function-dependent (D_f)
- Quality requirements relating to the quality characteristics to be tested dynamically (Q_d).

The FPA function is used as the unit of function. The calculation of user-importance and usage-intensity is based largely on the user function as communication medium. The importance which users assign to a user function applies to all subsidiary FPA functions as well.

Function-dependent factor (D_f)
The various function dependent factors and the associated ratings are described below. One of the ratings given must be selected; intermediate ratings are not allowed. If insufficient information is available to enable rating of a given factor, the nominal rating (that in bold) should be assigned.

User-importance
The user-significance is an expression of the importance that the user attaches to a given function relative to the other system functions. A useful rule of thumb is that about 25 percent of functions should be placed in the "high" category, 50 percent in the "normal" category and 25 percent in the "low" category. User-importance is assigned to the functionality identified by the user. This means assigning user-importance to the user function. The user-importance of a function should, of course, be determined in cooperation with all stakeholders.

Rating:
3   Low: the importance of the function relative to the other functions is low
6   Normal: the importance of the function relative to the other functions is normal
12 High: the importance of the function relative to the other functions is high.

Usage-intensity
The usage-intensity has been defined as the frequency with which a certain function is processed by the users and the size of the user group that uses the function. As with user-importance the usage-intensity is being determined at a user-function level.

Rating:
2   Low: the function is only used a few times per day or per week.
4   Normal: the function is being used a great many times per day
12 High: the function is used continuously throughout the day.

Interfacing
Interfacing is an expression of the extent to which a modification in a given function affects other parts of the system. The degree of interfacing is determined by ascertaining first the logical data sets (LDSs), which the function in question can modify, then the other functions that access these LDSs.

An interface rating is assigned to the function by reference to table 7.1, in which the numbers of LDSs affected by the function are ranged vertically and the numbers of other functions accessing the LDSs are ranged horizontally. When determining the number of "other functions" affected, a given function may be counted several times if it accesses several LDSs, all of which are maintained by the function for which the calculation is being made.

LDS \ functions	1	2 - 5	> 5
1	L	L	A
2 - 5	L	A	H
> 5	A	H	H

Table 7.1: Complexity table interface factor

Explanation: L : Low interfacing
                 A : Average interfacing
                 H : High interfacing

If a function does not modify any LDSs, it is given a low interface rating. A CRUD table is very useful for determining the degree of interfacing.

Rating:
2   The degree of interfacing associated with the function is low.
4   The degree of interfacing associated with the function is normal.
8   The degree of interfacing associated with the function is high.

Complexity
The complexity of a function is determined on the basis of its (logical) algorithm. The general structure of the algorithm may be described using pseudo code, Nassi-Shneiderman or ordinary text. The complexity rating of the function depends on the number of conditions in the function's algorithm. When counting the conditions, only the processing algorithm should be considered. Conditions, which are the result of syntax checks, such as domain validations, should not be counted, since these are implicitly included in the function point count.

Compound conditions such as "IF A AND B, THEN" count twice, since, without the "AND" statement, two "IF" statements would be needed. Similarly, a "CASE" statement with n cases counts as n-1 conditions, since replacement of the "CASE" statement with a series of "IF" statements would result in n-1 conditions. To summarize: count the (single) conditions, not the operators.

Rating:
3   The function contains no more than five conditions.
6   The function contains between six and eleven conditions.
12 The function contains more than eleven conditions.

Uniformity
Under the following circumstances, only 60% of the test points assigned to the function under analysis are actually counted:
• In the case of a second occurrence of an almost similar function: the test specifications can be largely reused.
• In the case of a clone function: the test specifications can be reused for clone functions.
• In the case of a dummy function (provided that reusable test specifications have already been drawn up for the dummy).

A uniformity factor of 0.6 is assigned in the circumstances described above; otherwise a uniformity factor of 1 is assigned. A software product may therefore contain functions that possess a degree of uniformity for test

purposes, even though they are regarded as unique in the context of a function point analysis. In function point analysis, the term "unique" is applied to the following:
- A function which uses a combination of data sets which is not used by any other FPA function
- A function which, although it does not use a unique combination of data sets, does use a unique processing technique (e.g. a unique method of updating a data set).

Conversely, a software product may contain functions which, although they are regarded as completely uniform in the context of a function point analysis and therefore are not warranted any function points, do count in TPA, since they do need to be tested. Clones and dummies come under this heading.

Method of calculation
The D_f factor is calculated by adding together the ratings for the first four function-dependent variables (user-importance, usage-intensity, interfacing and complexity) and dividing the sum by twenty (the nominal rating). The result should then be multiplied by the uniformity factor. The D_f factor is calculated for each function.

$$D_f = ((Ue + Uy + I + C) / 20) * U$$

Where D_f = weighting factor for the function-dependent factors, Ue = user-importance, Uy = usage-intensity, I = interfacing, C = complexity and U = uniformity.

Standard functions
If, as is often the case, the function point count includes the error message function, help-screen function and/or menu structure function, standard numbers of test points can be assigned, as indicated in the table below.

Function	FP's	Ue	Uy	I	C	U	D_f
Error message	4	6	8	4	3	1	1,05
Help screens	4	6	8	4	3	1	1,05
Menu structure	4	6	8	4	3	1	1,05

Table 7.2: Test points standard functions

Dynamic quality characteristics (Q_d)

The paragraphs below describe how the requirements relating to quality characteristics (ISO 9126-1, 2001) that will be tested dynamically, are taken into account in the TPA process.

In this context, distinction is made between quality characteristics that will be tested by means of executing dedicated test cases. This so-called dynamic explicit testing is the most common way of testing. During the course of explicit testing, data from the test process may be collected simultaneously with the execution of the test cases. Information about the good and bad characteristics of the system may be derived from these data. An evaluation of the system's reliability may be based on its behaviour during the test period: noting the frequency of failures and specifically looking for trends will allow the tester to estimate the number failure that are likely to occur during operation. This is called implicit testing.

In TPA, four quality characteristics are distinguished, that can be tested explicitly and dynamically:
- Suitability
- Security
- Usability (regarding usability no distinction has (yet) been made in sub characteristics, since there are no usability testing techniques available that have this level of accuracy.)
- Efficiency (for the same reason as mentioned for usability, efficiency is not split up into time-behaviour and resource-utilization).

The importance of the requirements relating to each quality characteristic is rated; if necessary, this is done separately for each subsystem.

Rating:
0   Quality requirements are not important and are therefore disregarded for test purposes.
3   Quality requirements are relatively unimportant but do need to be taken into consideration for test purposes.
4   Quality requirements are of normal importance. (This rating is generally appropriate where the software product relates to a support process.)
5   Quality requirements are very important. (This rating is generally appropriate where the software products relate to a primary process.)
6   Quality requirements are extremely important.

Dynamic, explicitly measurable quality characteristics:
Characteristic / Rating: 0   3   **4**   5   6
Functionality   (weighting 0.75)
Security   (weighting 0.05)
Usability   (weighting 0.10)
Efficiency   (weighting 0.10)

Where black-box test techniques are concerned, the elementary comparative test (ECT), data combination test (DCT), semantic test and syntactic test are available for testing suitability; the semantic test (SEM) is available for testing security; the process cycle test (PCT), use cases and SUMI (see chapter 14 on Usability) are available for testing usability and the real-life test (RLT) is available for testing efficiency (time-behaviour and resource-utilization) For more information on the various testing techniques see TMap (Pol *et al*, 2002).

The table below illustrates how the choice of test specification techniques is related to the rating given to the dynamic quality characteristics.

Rating	3	4	5	6
Suitability - Processing : - Screen checks:	DCT and Error Guessing Error Guessing	DCT Sample SEM and Error Guessing	EVT and DCT Sample SEM and SYN	EVT* SEM and Sample SYN
Security	Error Guessing	SEM sample user profiles	SEM user profiles	SEM user profiles and overall system **
Usablility	No test-spec's and SUMI	Use Case or PCT and SUMI	Use Case or PCT and SUMI	Usability laboratory test
Efficiency	The thoroughness of the RLT is variable and will thus be determined by the rating and the amount of hours that comes available as a consequence.			

Table 7.3: Test techniques versus quality characteristics

*   ECT is a more thorough technique than DCT, so testing all functions with ECT is more thorough that testing some functions with ECT and others with DCT, as is done for rating 5.

**   If the security characteristic is given a rating of six, the semantic test should be used to examine the user profiles and associated access privileges, both for the software product to be tested and for the infrastructure or information network as a whole.

The test manager has to determine which quality characteristics will be tested dynamic implicitly. A statement regarding these quality characteristics can be done by gathering data during test execution. ISO 9126 part 2 "External Metrics" can be used as a source of information or inspiration for this (ISO 9126-2, 2001). For instance Efficiency (time-behaviour) can be explicitly tested applying the Real-life test or implicitly by gathering data and establishing metrics. The quality characteristics to be tested implicitly and dynamically need to be specified. Subsequently the number of quality characteristics can be determined to which metrics will be applied. Per characteristic a rating of 0.02 is applicable in the context of Q_d.

Method of calculation (Q_d)
The rating for each dynamic, explicitly tested quality characteristic is divided by four (the nominal rating), then multiplied by the weighting factor. Subsequently, the ratings thus calculated for the five quality characteristics, to be tested dynamically and explicitly, are added together.

If certain implicitly to be tested quality characteristics are to be included in the test; the appropriate weighting (0.02 for each characteristic) should be added to the result obtained for the dynamic quality characteristics so far. The figure thus calculated is the Q_d factor. Normally, a single Q_d factor can be calculated for the system as a whole. However, if different test strategies are to be used for the various subsystems, a separate Q_d factor calculation should be made for each subsystem.

Dynamic test point formula
The number of dynamic test points is the sum of the test points assigned to the individual functions. The number of test points assigned to each function can be calculated by entering the data obtained so far into the following formula:

$$TP_f = FP_f * D_f * Q_d$$

TP_f = number of test points assigned to the function
FP_f = number of function points assigned to the function
D_f = weighting factor for the function-dependent factors
Q_d = weighting factor for the dynamic quality characteristics

Static test points

The number of static test points depends mainly on the function point count for the system as a whole. The static test points are also influenced by the requirements regarding the quality characteristics to be tested statically (the Q_s factor).

In the context of TPA, a static test is carried out using a checklist. In principle all ISO 9126 quality characteristics can be tested using a checklist. These checklists provide possible measures with a positive influence for a quality characteristic that can be taken throughout development. By scoring the product and its process against such a checklist, an experienced tester can formulate an indication of the expected quality level (Pol *et al.*, 2002). E.g. Security can therefore be tested dynamically, using a semantic test, and/or statically, by evaluating the security measures with the support of a checklist.

Method of calculation (Q_s)
If a quality characteristic is tested by means of a checklist (static test), the factor Qs is given the value sixteen. For each subsequent quality characteristic to be included in the static test, another sixteen is added to the Q_s factor rating.

Total number of test points

The total number of test points assigned to the system as a whole is calculated by entering the data obtained so far, into the following formula:

$$TP = \Sigma TP_f + (FP * Q_s) / 500$$

Where TP = total number of test points assigned to the system as a whole, ΣTP_f = sum of the test points assigned to the individual functions (dynamic test points), FP = total number of function points assigned to the system as a whole (minimum value 500), and Q_s = weighting factor for the quality characteristics to be tested statically

Primary test hours

The formula presented in previous the paragraph gives the total number of test points assigned to the system as a whole. This total number of test points is a measure of the volume of the primary test activities. The primary number of test points is multiplied by the productivity factor and the environmental factor to obtain the primary test hour count. The primary test hour count is the number of hours required for carrying out the test activities involved in the test life cycle phases' preparation, specification, execution and completion.

Productivity factor
The productivity factor indicates the number of test hours required per test point. The higher the productivity factor, the greater the number of test hours required. The productivity factor is a measure of the experience, knowledge and skill of the test team. The productivity factor can vary from one organization to the next, or from one organizational unit to the next.

Productivity factors can be calculated by analysing completed test projects; thus, historical data on such projects is necessary for productivity factor determination.

In practice the productivity factor has shown to have a value between 0.7 and 2.0.

Environmental factor

The number of test hours required for each test point is influenced not only by the productivity factor, but also by the environmental factor. A number of environmental factors are defined for calculating the environmental factor. The various environmental factors and the associated ratings are described below. Again, one of the ratings given must be selected; intermediate ratings are not allowed. If insufficient information is available to enable rating of a given variable, the nominal rating (in bold type) should be assigned. Note that even if TPA is not applied, the productivity factor may still be applied as part of another test estimation technique.

Test tools

The test tools variable reflects the extent to which the testing activities are automated. For the purpose of calculating this factor, the term "test tools" covers tools that are used for the primary test activities. The availability of test tools means that some of these activities can be performed automatically and therefore more efficient.

Rating:
1   During testing, supporting tools are used for test specification and test execution.
2   During testing, supporting tools are used for test specification or test execution.
4   No test tools are available.

Development testing

The development testing factors reflects the quality of preceding tests. If the test estimate is for an acceptance test, the preceding test will be the system test. If the estimate is for a system test, the preceding test will be the component and integration test. The quality of these preceding tests influences the amount of functionality (features/functions?) that may require less thorough testing, with less coverage, as well as the duration of the test activities. For, the better the preceding tests, the less likely one is to encounter time-consuming problems during the test under consideration.

Rating:
2   A plan for the preceding tests is available and the test team is familiar with
    the actual test cases and test results
4   A plan for the preceding tests is available.
8   No plan for the preceding tests is available.

Test basis
The test basis factor reflects the quality of the (system) documentation upon
which the test under consideration is to be based. The quality of the test basis
influences the amount of time required for the test preparation and test
specification phases.

Rating:
3   During the system development documentation standards and templates
    are being used. In addition the inspections are organized
6   During the system development documentation standards and templates
    are being used.
12 The system documentation was not developed using a specific standard
    or template.

Development environment
The development environment factor reflects the nature of the environment
within which the software product will be developed. In this context, the
degree to which the development environment will have prevented errors and
inappropriate working methods is of particular importance. If errors of a given
type cannot be made, it is of course not necessary to test for them.

Rating:
2   The system was developed using a 4 GL programming language with an
    integrated DBMS containing numerous constraints.
4   The system was developed using a 4 GL programming language, possibly
    in combination with a 3 GL programming language.
8   The system was developed using only a 3 GL programming language
    (such as C, COBOL, PASCAL or RPG).

Test environment
The test environment factor reflects the extent to which the test environment,
in which the testing is to take place, has previously been tried out. In a well-
tried test environment, fewer problems and delays are likely during the
execution phase.

Rating:

1 The environment has been used for testing several times in the past.

2 The test is to be conducted in a newly equipped environment similar to other well-used environments within the organization.

4 The test is to be conducted in a newly equipped environment, which may be considered experimental within the organization.

Testware

The testware factor reflects the extent to which the tests can be conducted using existing testware. The availability of usable testware mainly influences the time required for the test specification phase.

Rating:

1 A usable, generic initial data set (tables, etc.) and specified test cases are available for the test.

2 A usable, generic initial data set (tables, etc.) is available for the test.

4 No usable testware is available.

Method of calculation (E)

The environmental factor (E) is calculated by adding together the ratings for the various environmental factors (test tools, development testing, test basis, development environment, test environment and testware), then dividing the sum by twenty-one (the sum of the nominal ratings). Normally, one environmental factor is worked out for the system as a whole, but separate factors can be calculated for the individual subsystems if appropriate.

Primary test hours formula

The number of primary test hours is obtained by multiplying the number of test points by the productivity factor and the environmental factor:

$$PT = TP * P * E$$

Where PT = the total number of primary test hours, TP = the total number of test points assigned to the system as a whole, P = the productivity factor, and E = the environmental factor.

Total number of test hours

Since every test process involves tasks which may be placed under the heading 'test management" or "planning and control", allowance needs to be made for such activities. The number of primary test hour and the planning and control allowance together give the total number of test hours.

The standard (nominal) allowance is 10 per cent. However, the allowance may be increased or decreased, in line with the following two factors:
- Team size
- Management tools.

Team size
The team size factor reflects the size of the team (including the test manager). Note: count part time testers also as one person.

Rating:
3   The team consists of no more than four people.
6   The team consists of between five and ten people.
12 The team consists of more than ten people.

Management tools
The management tools factor reflects the extent to which automated tools are to be used for planning and control.

Rating:
2   Both a time tracking tool and a defect management tool are available and used.
4   Either a time tracking tool or a defect management tool is available.
8   No supporting management tools are available.

Method of calculation
The planning and control percentage is obtained by adding together the ratings for the two influential factors (team size and planning and control tools). The allowance in hours is calculated by multiplying the primary test hours count by this percentage. Addition of the planning and control allowance to the number of primary test hours gives the total number of test hours.

Breakdown over phases

The result of a TPA is an estimate for the complete test process, excluding the test planning phase. If a structured testing approach is used, the test process is divided into a number of life cycle phases; many stakeholders will need to see estimates for the individual phases, as well as for the complete test process. The estimate for the test management will normally be the same as the planning and control allowance, i.e. the primary test hour count multiplied by the planning and control percentage. The primary test hours are then divided between the preparation, specification, execution and completion phases (see chapter 2 on Test life cycle). The breakdown between the phases can of course vary from one organization to another, or even from one project to another. Suitable phase percentages can be calculated by analysing completed test projects; thus, historical data on such projects is necessary for breaking down the total estimate.

Experience with the TPA technique suggests that the following percentages are generally appropriate:
- Preparation: 10 percent
- Specification   40 percent
- Execution   45 percent
- Completion   5 percent

7.5   Test Point Analysis at an early stage

A test project estimate is often needed at an early stage. Until detailed functional specifications are obtained, however, it is not possible to determine factors such as complexity, interfacing and the like. Nevertheless, a rough function point analysis can often be performed on the basis of very general specifications. If an indicative function point count is available, a rough TPA can be performed as well.

For a rough TPA, a single function is defined whose size is determined by the total (gross) function point count. All function-dependent factors (user-importance, user-intensity, complexity, interfacing and uniformity) are usually assigned the neutral value, so that D_f has a value of 1. A TPA can then be carried out as described in paragraph 7.4. The environmental factor will often have to be based on assumptions; any such assumptions should be clearly documented and stated on the test estimate when it is presented to the customer.

7.6   An example calculation

This paragraph provides a small TPA example; a more elaborate example can be found in TMap (Pol *et al.*, 2002).
An information system has two user functions and one internal logical dataset:

Registration (11 function points) broken down in the following FPA-functions:
- Create   3 function points
- Update   4 function points
- Delete   4 function points.

Processing (12 function points) broken down in the following FPA-functions:
- Output 1 5 function points
- Output 2 7 function points

7 function points are assigned to the internal logical data set; for the TPA these are added to the input function.

Calculation of dynamic test points

Calculation of the function dependent factors (D_f)

	Registration	Processing
User importance	6	12
User intensity	8	2
Interfacing	2	2
Complexity	3	6
Uniformity	1	1

$D_f =$ 19/20 x 1 = 0,95   22/20 x 1 = 1,10

(In this example, it as assumed that the interface and complexity ratings are the same for the FPA functions within a given create function.)

Calculation of quality characteristics to be tested dynamically (Q_d)

Suitability	5	5/4 x 0,75 = 0,94
Security	4	4/4 x 0,05 = 0,05
Usability	0	
Efficiency	0	

Dynamic implicit testing (gathering metrics) is carried out for:

Time-behaviour	= 0,02
Resource-utilization	= 0,02
Maintainability	= 0,02

$Q_d = 0,94 + 0,05 + (3 * 0,02) = 1,05$

Calculating the number of dynamic test points

	FP_f	D_f	Q_d		TP_f
Registration	18	0,95	1,05	=	18
Processing	12	1,10	1,05	=	14
Total number of dynamic test points					32

(Note the number of function points for the registration function is based on the 11 function points from the individual FPA functions and the 7 function points from the internal logical data set.)

Calculation of static test points
Static testing (by means of a checklist) is carried out for:

Reliability $\quad$ = 16
Q_s $\qquad$ = 16

Calculation of the total number of test points

$TP = \Sigma TP_f + (FP * Q_s) / 500$
$TP = 32 + (500 \times 16) / 500 = 48$

Calculation of the number of primary test hours

Productivity factor
For this organization (project) a productivity factor of 1.2 applies.

Environmental factor
The ratings given to the various environmental factors are as follows:

Test tools $\qquad$ 4 (no test tools)
Development testing $\qquad$ 4 (a development test plan is available)
Test basis $\qquad$ 3 (documentation standards, templates and
$\qquad$ inspections)
Development environment $\qquad$ 4 (4 GL (Oracle) in combination with
$\qquad$ COBOL)
Test environment $\qquad$ 1 (proven environment)
Testware $\qquad$ 4 (no usable testware available)

$$E = 20/21 = 0,95$$

$PT = TP * P * E$
Primary test hours (PT) = 48 x 1,2 x 0,95 = 54,72 (55 hours)

Calculation of planning and control allowance

Team size $\qquad$ 3 (the team consists of two people)
Planning & control tools $\qquad$ 4 (time registration tool available)

Planning and control allowance 7%

Calculation of the total number of test hours

Primary test hours   55

P & C allowance   55 * 0,07 = 3,85 (rounded to 4)
Total number of test hours   55 + 4 = <u>59</u>

References

- Albrecht, A.J. (1984), *AD/M productivity measurement and estimate validation,* IBM Guideline

- IFPUG (International Function Point User Group) (1999), *Function Point Counting Practices, release 4.1,* IFPUG, January 1999

- ISO/IEC 9126-1 (2001), *Software engineering - Software product quality - Part 1: Quality model, International Organization of Standardization*

- ISO/IEC DTR 9126-2 (2001), *Software engineering - Software product quality - Part 2: External metrics,* International Organization of Standardization

- Pol, M., R.A.P. Teunissen and E.P.W.M. van Veenendaal (2002), *Software Testing, A Guide to the TMap approach,* Addison-Wesley, ISBN 0-201-74571-2

- Veenendaal, E.P.W.M. van (1995), Test Point Analysis: a method for estimating the testing effort (in Dutch), in: *Computable,* May 1995

- Veenendaal, E.P.W.M. van and J.E. Dekkers (1999), Test point analysis: a method for test estimation, in: R. Kusters, A. Cowderoy, F. Heemstra and E. van Veenendaal (eds.), *Project Control for Software Quality,* Shaker Publishing BV, The Netherlands, ISBN 90-423-0075-2.

Part 3

Reviews

8 Formal review types

Erik van Veenendaal and Mark van der Zwan

A number of formal review types are applied in the software community and inspection is perhaps the one most engineers are familiar with. However, within an inspection there is little or no room for discussion or to ask detailed questions. Other review types, such as technical reviews and walkthroughs, are more suitable for these purposes. Using the three formal review types presented in this paper at the right life cycle phase and for the right purposes improves the efficiency and effectiveness of the review process and improves the quality of the (work) product.

In this chapter three types of formal review are described: inspection, technical (peer) review and walkthrough. The goals, participants and procedures are described. In addition some practical tips are given for each type of review.

8.1 Document reviews

Formal reviews

There are a number of ways to improve a document. Studies have shown that as a result of formal reviews, a significant increase in productivity and product quality can be achieved (Gilb and Graham, 1993), (van Veenendaal, 1999). Reducing the number of defects in the final product means that less time has to be spent on testing and maintenance. Although inspection is perhaps the most documented (and notorious) formal review technique, it is certainly not the only one (Bisant and Lyle, 1989), (Freedman and Weinberg, 1990). The IEEE 1028 standard on software reviews distinguishes three types of formal reviews (IEEE 1028, 1998):

- *Inspection*
  Inspection is a formally defined and rigorously followed review process. The process includes individual and group checking, using sources and standards, according to detailed and specific rules or checklists, in order to support the author by finding as many defects as possible in the available amount of time.

- *Technical review*
  The objective of a technical review process is to reach consensus on technical, content related issues. Domain or technical experts check the document-under-review, prior to the meeting, based on specific questions of the author. In this meeting, the approach to be taken is discussed by the experts, under guidance of a moderator or technical leader.
- *Walkthrough*
  In a walkthrough, the author guides a group of people through a document and his or her thought processes, in order to gather information and to reach consensus. No formal preparation is required and defects are found during the meeting. People from outside the software discipline can participate in these meetings. In walkthroughs, dry runs and task scenarios are often applied.

The different review types have a different focus and are applicable at a different life cycle phase. All three types, however, aim to explain and evaluate the contents of the document in order to improve its quality. In other words, the goal of the reviews is to find defects. The types of defects that are found differ for the three review types. Using the right type of review at the right place in the software life cycle ensures a more effective and efficient review process.

In addition to formal document reviews, the IEEE 1028 standard mentions two other types of formal reviews:
- *Management review*
  A systematic evaluation of a project performed by, or on behalf of, management in which the project status is evaluated against the plan (resources, costs, progress, quality) and appropriate actions are defined.
- *Audit*
  An audit is the independent examination of a product or process against an agreed reference base. The examination is based on a problem definition and/or set of questions and carried out from a certain viewpoint (e.g. engineering, management or customer).

The focus of these two review types is clearly very different from the formal document review types already mentioned. The focus of this chapter is on effective and efficient improvement of document quality through the use of (formal) document reviews. Therefore, 'management review' and 'audit' will not be elaborated further.

Informal reviews

The informal review is perhaps the most common type of review. In practice, these reviews are applied at various times during the early stages in the life cycle of a document. A two-person team can conduct an informal review, as the author can ask a colleague to review a document. In later stages these reviews often involve more people and a meeting. This normally involves peers of the author, who try to find defects in the document-under-review and discuss these defects in a review meeting. The goal is to help the author and to improve the quality of a document. Informal reviews come in various shapes and forms, but all have one characteristic in common - they are not documented.

Although these reviews do not follow a documented procedure, they do have added value and organisations have reported a returns-on-investment of up to four. Besides the difference in formality, informal reviews have a number of other differences compared to formal reviews:

- In general there is no guidance or help on what and how to check the document-under-review. The reviewers are simply asked to review it, and so the effectiveness of the review depends largely on the availability, review experience and actual effort of experts
- Reviewers do not use different viewpoints to prepare the document-under-review. Therefore the same defects are found by multiple reviewers, which has a negative effect on the efficiency
- No limitations are set on the number of pages to be reviewed, so typically this means that reviewers have to prepare dozens of pages. As a result, not all of these pages will be reviewed thoroughly enough
- Some informal reviews do not have meetings, the comments are simply sent to the author
- When a meeting is held, it typically lasts for over two hours, with a lot of discussion about technical approaches, but also about trivia, which influences both the efficiency and effectiveness of the process
- No process data (effort, throughput time, results) is collected to improve the review process. Since data is not stored, the possible benefits cannot be shown, which puts future reviews in a difficult spot when the project is under pressure.

Reviews are a prescribed part of the development process in most organisations. Using both formal and informal reviews, based on a documented strategy, will improve the efficiency and effectiveness of the review and development process. The challenge within each project is to define a strategy that is best for the project, applying the appropriate type of review at the appropriate moment in time.

8.2   Participants, roles and responsibilities

The participants in any type of formal review should have adequate knowledge of the review process. The best, and most efficient, review situation occurs when the participants can gain some kind of advantage for their own work during the process. In the case of an inspection or technical review participants should have been properly trained as both types of reviews have proven to be far less successful without trained participants.

The best formal reviews come from properly organised teams, guided by trained moderators (or review leaders). Within a review team five types of participants can be distinguished: moderator, author, scribe, reviewer and trainee.

- *The moderator*
  The moderator leads the review process. He or she determines, in co-operation with the author, the review strategy and the composition of the review team. The moderator performs the entry check and the follow-up on the rework, in order to control the quality of the input and output of the review process. They also schedule the meeting, disseminate materials before the meeting, coaches other team members, paces the meeting, leads possible discussions, and stores the data that is collected on the process form (see annex B for examples of review forms).

- *The author*
  As the writer of the document-under-review, the author's basic goal should be to learn as much as possible with regards to improving the quality of the document, in order to improve his or her ability to write future documents. The author's task is to illuminate unclear areas and to understand the defects found.

- *The scribe*
  During the logging meeting the scribe has to record each defect mentioned and any suggestions for improvement, on the logging form (see annex B). This is usually the author's task, ensuring that logging form is readable and understandable. If the author records their *own defects*, in their own words, it helps them to understand these better during rework.

- *The reviewers*
  The task of the reviewers is to check any material for defects, prior to the meeting. The level of thoroughness required depends on the type of review. The level of domain knowledge or technical expertise needed by the reviewers also depends on the type of review. In addition to the document-under-review, the material will include source documents, standards, checklists, etc. In general, the less source and reference documents provided, the more domain expertise regarding the content of the document-under-review is needed.

- *The trainee*
  An additional and optional role is that of a trainee. It is difficult to educate and train new employees to become 'good' engineers. One technique is to include new engineers in the review process (only one or two per team). The trainee(s) then gets a detailed look inside the organisations development process, to develop an understanding of how it works. E.g. a trainee could check whether the document-under-review complies with the standards.

8.3   Inspections

Background, definition, goal and timing

Inspections are the most formal type of review (see also chapter 10). The document-under-inspection is prepared and checked thoroughly by the inspectors. In the inspection meeting the defects found are logged, but any discussion is postponed until the discussion phase. This makes the inspection meeting a very efficient meeting. A well-disciplined team, with an experienced moderator, will be able to log between one and two defects per minute at the meeting.

The reason for carrying out inspections can be explained by using Wienberg's concept of egoless engineering (Weinberg, 1971). Weinberg refers to the human tendency to self-justify actions. Since we tend not to see evidence that conflicts with our strong beliefs, our ability to find errors in our own work is impaired. Because of this tendency, many engineering organisations have established independent test groups that specialise in finding defects. Similar principles have led to the introduction of inspections.

> *Inspection definition:*
> *Inspection is a structured review of an engineers' work product against sources and other documents, carried out by his colleagues to find defects and to enable the engineer to improve the quality of his product (Fagan, 1986).*

Depending on the organisation and the objectives of a project, inspections can serve a number of goals. For example, if the time-to-market is extremely important, the emphasis in inspections will be on efficiency. In a safety critical market the focus will be on effectiveness.

The generally accepted goals of an inspection are to:
- Help the author to improve the quality of the document-under-inspection.
- Remove defects efficiently, as early as possible.

- Improve product quality, by producing documents with a higher level of quality.
- Create a common understanding by exchanging information among the inspection participants.
- Training new employees on the organisations development process.
- Learn from defects found and improve processes in order to prevent reoccurrence of defects.

The authors of this chapter carried out a survey in which engineers, practising inspections, were asked to indicate the benefits of the inspection process. Almost 100 engineers were asked to rate the benefits on a scale of 1 to 10. In table 8.1 some of the results of this survey, on the engineers' opinions, are reported.

Results of inspections	Average	Median
Improved product quality	8.0	8.0
Software process improvement	7.7	8.0
Better controlled project	7.3	8.0
Improved efficiency of development process	7.2	7.0
Motivated to do good work	7.0	8.0
Training of new engineers	6.7	7.0

Table 8.1: The engineers' opinion

When should an inspection be held?

In general, an inspection should be held before a document transfers from one phase to another. Subsequently, the inspected and reworked document can be subject to formal approval.

An inspection can be organised in all phases of the development process, from requirements up to coding. It should be organised when the author thinks that their document is ready, i.e. when they feel confident with the document's quality and are prepared to join the inspection team.

The inspection procedure consists of seven steps:

1. Initiation & planning
The inspection process begins with a "request for inspection" by the author to the moderator. For each document to be inspected, a moderator should be

assigned to take care of the scheduling (dates, time, place and invitation) of the inspection.

The moderator always performs an entry-check; to be sure that the document submitted is 'inspection-ready'. This check is done against entry criteria to ensure that the reviewers' time is not wasted on a document that is not ready for inspection. A document containing too many obvious mistakes is clearly not ready to enter an inspection process and it would be very harmful to the inspection process. It would de-motivate both reviewers and the author, since too many obvious and minor defects are found. Also, the inspection cannot be effective because the numerous obvious and minor defects will conceal the major defects.

Although more entry criteria can be applied, the following can be regarded as the minimum for performing an entry-check:
• A short check of a product sample by the moderator (or expert) does not reveal a large number of major defects. E.g.: After 30 minutes of checking, no more than 3 major defects are found on a single page, or less than 10 major defects in total in a set of 5 pages
• The document to be inspected is printed with line numbers
• The document has been cleaned up by a spelling-checker or other computer "diagnosis"
• References needed for the inspection are stable and available
• The document author is prepared to join the inspection team and feels confident with the quality of the document.

If the document passes the entry-check, the moderator and author decide which part of the document to inspect. Because the human mind can 'only' comprehend a limited set of pages, the number should not be too high. The right size of a document-under-inspection depends, amongst other things, on the type of document and should be derived from practical experiences within the organisation. Usually the maximum size is between 10 and 20 pages.

After the document size has been set and the pages to be checked have been selected, the moderator determines the composition of the inspection team in co-operation with the author. The team normally consists of 4 to 6 participants, including moderator and author. To improve the effectiveness of inspections, different roles are assigned to each of the reviewers. These roles help the reviewers focus on particular types of defects during checking. This reduces the chance of different reviewers finding the same defects. The moderator assigns the roles to the reviewers.

The following figure shows the different roles within an inspection. The roles represent views on the document-under-inspection.

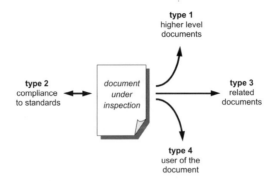

Figure 8.1: Four basic review roles for a document-under-inspection

Within inspections the following review roles can be identified:
- Focus on higher level documents, e.g. does the design comply to the requirements.
- Focus on standards, e.g. internal consistency, clarity, naming conventions, templates.
- Focus on related documents at the same level, e.g. interfaces between software functions.
- Focus on use, e.g. for feasibility, maintainability and/or testability.

The author may raise additional specific roles that have to be addressed. The moderator has the option to also fulfil a role, alongside the task as inspection leader. Checking the document improves the moderator's ability to lead the meeting, because it ensures better understanding. Furthermore, it improves the inspection efficiency because the moderator replaces an engineer that would otherwise have to check the document and attend the meeting. It is recommended for the moderator to take the type two role (compliance to standards), since this is a more objective role, which leads to less discussion on the defects found.

2. Kick-off
An optional step in an inspection procedure is a kick-off meeting. The goal of this meeting is to get everybody on the same wavelength regarding the document-under-inspection and to commit to the time that will be spent on checking. This step is highly recommended since there is a strong positive effect of a kick-off meeting on the effectiveness of the inspection.

During such a meeting the reviewers receive a short introduction on the objectives of the inspection and the document(s). The relationships between the different documents are explained, especially if the number of related documents is high.

Role assignments, checking rate, the pages to be checked, process changes and possible other questions are also discussed during this meeting. Of course the distribution of the document-under-inspection, sources and other related documentation, can also be done during the kick-off.

The next table shows the results of a study carried out by the authors. The effect of a kick-off on the number of major defects found is measured.

Inspection process	Without Kick-off	Including Kick-off
Number of inspections	165	145
Major defects per page (per participant)	0.32	0.52 (+63%)

Table 8.2: Kick-off effect

In the case of inspection with a kick-off, engineers were able to find over 60% more major defects per page. This supports the notion that a kick-off helps make reviewers focus on the right issues and, as a result, they are motivated and able to do thorough checking.

3. Preparation

The participants work individually on the document-under-inspection using the related documents, procedures, rules and checklists provided. The individual participants identify the defects, according to their understanding and viewpoint or role (see chapter 9 for specific reading techniques). All defects are recorded on a logging form. Spelling mistakes are recorded on the document-under-inspection but not mentioned during the meeting. The annotated document will be given to the author at the end of the logging meeting.

A critical success factor for a thorough preparation is the number of pages checked per hour. This is called the checking rate. The optimum checking rate is the result of a mix of factors, including the type of document, its complexity, the number of related documents and the experience of the reviewers. Usually the checking rate is in the range of 5 to 10 pages per hour. During preparation, participants should not exceed this criterion.

The size of the document is another critical success factor in the initiation and planning step. Reasonable criteria should be used as a starting point, for both the checking rate and the document size. By measuring the inspection process (collecting metrics), company specific criteria for checking rate and document size can be set, preferably document type specific.

4. Inspection meeting

The meeting is divided in three sequential parts:
1. Logging phase
2. Discussion phase
3. Decision phase.

Ad 1. Logging
During the logging phase the individual defects that have been identified during the preparation are mentioned page-by-page, reviewer-by-reviewer and are logged by the author. To ensure progress and efficiency no real discussions are allowed during the logging phase. If a defect needs discussion, the item is logged and then handled in the discussion phase. Discussion on whether or not it is a defect is not allowed, as it is much more efficient to simply log it and proceed to the next one. Furthermore, in spite of the opinion of the team, a discussed defect might turn out to be a "real" one during rework.

Every defect and its severity should be logged. The participant who identifies the defect proposes the severity. Severity classes are:
*   *Critical* defects will cause, so-called, downstream damage; the scope and impact of the defect is beyond the document-under-inspection.
*   *Major* defects could cause a downstream effect (e.g. an fault in a design can result in an error in the implementation).
*   *Minor* defects are not likely to cause downstream damage (e.g. non-compliance with the standards and templates).

Spelling related remarks are not part of the defect classification. As stated in the paragraph on preparation, these defects are noted, by the participants, in the document-under-inspection and given to the author at the end of the meeting.

During the logging phase the focus is on logging as many defects as possible within a certain timeframe. To ensure this, the moderator tries to keep a good logging rate i.e. the number of defects logged per minute. In a well led and disciplined meeting the logging rate will be between 1 and 2 defects logged per minute.

In the survey mentioned earlier, engineers were asked to rate the benefits of the logging meeting, in addition to the logging of defects and the explanation of the defects found to the author. In table 8.3 the results of this part of the survey are reported.

Results of inspection meetings	Average	Median
Learn how to check	7.4	8.0
Motivated to do good work	7.1	8.0
Learn how to specify	7.0	7.0
Common understanding is reached	7.0	7.0
Find new defects	6.6	7.0

Table 8.3: The engineers' opinion on meetings

Ad 2. Discussion
The items classified as discussion items will be handled during this phase of an inspection meeting. Participants can take part in the discussion by bringing forward their arguments. As chairman of the discussion meeting, the moderator takes care of people issues. For example, the moderator prevents discussions getting too personal, rephrases remarks if necessary and calls for a break to cool-down 'heated' discussions and/or participants.

Reviewers who do not need to be in the discussion may leave, or stay as a learning exercise. The moderator also paces this part of the meeting and ensures that all discussed items either have an outcome by the end of the meeting, or are defined as an action point if a discussion cannot be solved during the meeting. The outcome of discussions must be written down for future reference.

Ad 3. Decision
At the end of the inspection meeting a decision on the document-under-inspection has to be made by the participants, based on the exit criteria. The most important exit criteria are the average number of critical and major defects found per page (e.g. no more than 3 criticals/majors per page). If the number of defects found per page exceeds a certain level, the document must be inspected again, after it has been reworked. If the document complies with the exit criteria, the document will, after rework, be checked by only the moderator or one or more participants. Subsequently, the document can leave the inspection process.

If a project is under pressure, the moderator sometimes will be forced to skip re-inspections and exit a defect prone document. Setting, and agreeing, quantified exit level criteria, helps the moderator to make firm decisions at all times.

In addition to the number of defects per page, other exit criteria measure the thoroughness of the inspection process. Such as seeing if all pages have been checked at the right rate? The average number of defects per page is only a valid quality indicator if these process criteria are met.

The possible options for decision are:
a) The document fails the exit criteria which means:
    - A new inspection of the updated document must be scheduled.
b) The document passes the exit criteria and the follow-up will be carried by either the:
    - Moderator, only the moderator checks the updated document
      or
    - Participants; all or some participants check the updated document to determine whether their comments are addressed.

5. Causal analysis

A causal analysis meeting is used to immediately analyze defects, in order to find common causes and to define possible actions for improvement. Causal analysis leads to bottom-up, and practical, process improvement. Provided the process owners are in place, the software development processes and the inspection process itself can continuously be improved.

The objective of a causal analysis is to initiate examination and action on the organizational and process causes of the defects found. This will be done using Pareto analysis (Juran, 1970) of reoccurring defects over a number of inspections. A causal analysis meeting will focus on 3-5 critical defects. It will follow inspection meetings on a regular basis (e.g. every sixth, every tenth), and is conducted according to the following procedure:
1. Select 3-5 critical defects.
2. Categorise each defect to focus the analysis. Possible categories are: organisation, people, architectural, technology and process.
3. Every participant provides a number of possible causes in a brainstorm manner. One or two possible causes are selected.
4. Every participant provides a number of possible cures, again in a brainstorm manner. The moderator, who leads the process, encourages everybody to think of cures that "they could and would do themselves" within a certain timeframe (e.g. 3 months). The cures are prioritised.
5. Improvement actions are defined by the end of the meeting, based on the cures mentioned.
6. The improvement actions are communicated to the QA-department or a similar group within the organisation.

A causal analysis enables immediate improvements, based on the inspection cycle. Through causal analysis the focus of inspections shifts from detection and removal of defects towards prevention.

6. Rework

Based on the defects logged, the author will improve the document-under-inspection step by step. The author may also make other improvements or corrections to the document, not based on the inspection's defect log. Not every defect that is found leads to rework. It is the author's responsibility to judge if a defect has to be fixed. If nothing is done about a defect for a certain reason, it should be reported on the logging form to indicate that the author is addressing the defect.

Changes that are made to the document should be easy to identify during follow-up. Therefore the author has to indicate where changes are made (e.g. using "Track changes" in Microsoft Word).

7. Follow up and exit

The moderator is responsible for ensuring that satisfactory actions have been taken on all logged defects, improvement suggestions and change requests. Although the moderator checks to make sure that the author has taken action on all known defects, he does not necessarily have to check the corrections in detail himself. If it is decided that all participants check the updated document, the moderator takes care of the distribution and collects the feedback.

In order to control and optimise the inspection process, a number of measurements are collected at each step of the process, on the review process form. It is the responsibility of the moderator to ensure that the information is correct and stored for future analysis.

8.4   Technical reviews

Background, definition, goal and timing

A technical review is a discussion meeting that focuses on achieving consensus on the technical content of a document. Compared to inspections, technical reviews are less formal and there is little or no focus on defect identification on the basis of referenced documents, intended readership and rules. Defects are found by experts, who focus only on the content of the document. The experts that are needed for a technical review are, for example, architects, chief designers and key-users. Technical reviews are also known as peer reviews.

> *Technical review definition:*
> *A technical review is typically a peer group discussion activity that focuses on achieving consensus on the technical approach to be taken. A technical review is also known as a peer review. (Gilb and Graham, 1993)*

The goals of a technical review are to:
* Assess the value of technical concepts and alternatives in the product and project environment.
* Establish consistency in the use and representation of technical concepts
* Ensure, at an early stage, that technical concepts are used correctly.
* Inform participants of the technical content of the document.

When should a technical review be held?

In general, technical reviews are held during the early stages in the life cycle of a document. The review focuses on discussing the approach taken, technical feasibility and such like. A technical review should be held whenever issues arise during specification, design or coding that need to be discussed and solved. Unlike inspections, this can be done as early as possible since there is no need to finish the document first.

Inspections and technical reviews are complementary and a document may undergo both formal review types. An inspection, having the objective to identify defects, needs a "complete" document to be efficient and effective. A technical review will precede an inspection and can be done on, for example, a 70% complete document. After the technical review, the discussed technical concepts can be reworked in the document or software code. In other words, the document can be made "ready" in order to enter the inspection process.

The technical review procedure consists of five steps, described hereafter.

1. Initiation & planning
As with inspections, a moderator should be assigned for each document to be reviewed. The moderator will take care of the organisation and scheduling of the review. The technical review process begins with a 'request for technical review' by the author to the moderator. The moderator, in co-operation with the author, will formulate the specific questions that need to be answered during the technical review. A formal entry-check is not possible, since the document is often only 70% complete.

The moderator and author will select the participants for the technical review based on their domain and/or technical knowledge. In contradiction to inspections, only experts are selected, to ensure a thorough content related discussion on the technical concepts and possible alternatives. The recommended team size for a technical review is five or six, including moderator and author.

A project leader may participate as a reviewer, especially if resource or issues such as planning need to be addressed and project decisions need to be taken. Of course they can also participate based on their expert knowledge.

It is recommended that technical leaders act as the moderator for a technical review. They should have sufficient knowledge to chair the technical meeting effectively. Alternatively, moderators who also normally fulfil this task during inspections can be chosen. Authors should not take this task, as they have to be fully focussed on the discussion.

In technical reviews there are no strict criteria for the checking rate and document size, and these can both be higher compared to an inspection. However, appropriate upper limits should be determined, by means of measuring the technical review process (collecting metrics).

2. Kick-off
An optional, but highly recommended, step in a technical review is the kick-off meeting. As with inspection, the goal of this meeting is to get everybody on the same wavelength regarding the document-under-review and to commit to the time that will be spent on preparation. During the kick-off the participants receive a short introduction on the objectives of the technical review and the document-under-review. The strong positive effect of a kick-off meeting on the effectiveness of an inspection, as shown in the previous section, is even stronger for technical reviews. Because the document is not yet complete, the author must point out where to look for defects and which sections to skip, because they are not yet ready. The different viewpoints of the reviewers are determined by the specific questions of the author. At the end of the meeting all participants must be absolutely clear on what contribution, for example focus or pages, is expected from them.

3. Preparation
The participants work individually on the document-under-review using their technical skills and their domain knowledge. During the preparation they should focus on the specific questions that were raised by the author and try to find as many major defects as possible. In a technical review, defects often 'act' as issues, because in most cases the mistakes have not yet been made. In this chapter the generic term defect is used for issues found during inspections, technical reviews or walkthroughs.

Defects, not directly related to the specific questions, can be identified according to the understanding of the individual participants. The focus should be on critical and major defects. Minor defects and spelling mistakes are not even noted during checking nor mentioned in the review meeting.

In the inspection process preparation means checking the document against sources, standards and rules. However, the focus in a technical review is on the document itself and the defects found relate to the content and approach presented in the document.

Technical review meeting

The meeting is divided in two sequential parts:
1. Discussion and logging phase.
2. Decision phase.

Ad 1. Discussion and logging

In a technical review there is no distinction between logging and discussion, since discussion requires most of the time needed and is thus allowed. Questions raised by the author need to be answered in this phase. Additional defects identified during the individual preparation are discussed either defect by defect or, if preferred, page by page.

Due to the nature of the meeting, only the more severe defects (critical or major) are discussed and logged. There is no sense in logging, nor mentioning minor defects because the document is not yet ready for inspection. As with inspections, the participants propose a classification when mentioning the defect.

Participants can take part in the discussion by bringing forward their arguments. It is the moderator task to keep the meeting focussed on providing answers to the questions raised and find as many as possible additional defects. The moderator, authors and reviewers, will decide if a defect needs further discussion, in or outside the meeting.

At the end of this phase of the meeting the moderator does a final check. The moderator finds out from the author whether the technical review has been successful, by asking if, "All initial questions raised by the author, have been answered with the expected level of detail?"

Ad 2. Decision

At the end of the review meeting a decision on the document-under-review has to be made by the participants. This decision focuses on the question how to improve the document. The logged defects form a list of action items. This list indicates what improvements are to be made. Based on the action items, the knowledge of the reviewers and the experience of the author, a decision regarding the outcome must be made. No strict exit criteria apply to technical reviews. The decision itself is less formal and more expert based than the decision in an inspection process.

Three possible outcomes are:
a) The updated document will re-enter a new technical review, which needs to be scheduled;
b) The updated document will be checked by the moderator (technical leader);
c) The updated document will be inspected.

5. Rework, follow-up and exit
Based on the action items, the author will improve the document-under-review step by step. The author may also make other improvements or corrections to the document, which are not based on logged defects.

Although the follow-up is not as formal as with inspections, the moderator checks whether all action items have been addressed. If it is decided at the end of the technical review meeting that a new review is needed, the procedure is started all over again.

In general, there will be no change requests on other documents, since the focus during a technical review is entirely on the document-under-review. Possible improvement suggestions could be made regarding template issues, etc, but generally no action is needed from the moderator at this point.

8.5 Walkthroughs

Definition, goal and timing

A walkthrough is characterised by the author of the document-under-review guiding the participants through the document and his or her thought processes, so they achieve a common understanding. This is especially useful if people from outside the software discipline are present, who are not used to, or able to read, software documents. The content of the document is explained step-by-step by the author, to reach consensus on changes to make, or information to gather.

> *Walkthrough definition:*
> *A step-by-step presentation by the author of a document in order to gather information and to establish a common understanding of its content. (Freedman and Weinberg, 1990)*

Within a walkthrough the author does most of the preparation. The participants, who are selected from different departments and backgrounds, are not required to do a detailed study of the documents in advance. Because of the way the meeting is structured, a large number of people can participate and this larger audience can bring a great number of diverse viewpoints regarding the contents of the document being reviewed as well as serving an educational purpose. If the audience represents a broad cross-section of skills and disciplines, it can give assurance that no major defects are "missed" in the walkthrough. A walkthrough is especially useful for higher-level documents, such as a software requirement specification and architectural documents.

The specific goals of a walkthrough depend on its role in the creation of the document. In general the following goals can be applicable:
- To present the document to stakeholders both within and outside the software discipline, in order to gather information regarding the topic under documentation.
- To explain and evaluate the contents of the document (knowledge transfer).
- To establish a common understanding of the document content.
- To examine and discuss the validity of proposed solutions and the viability of alternatives: establishing consensus.

When should a walkthrough be held?

A walkthrough is considered to be most useful during two particular stages of a document. It can be held during an early stage of its development (a 'working document'), or just before the document is to be released (a 'draft document'). A walkthrough meeting can take anywhere from four hours or even a full day, since the entire document must be explained and evaluated.

Working document
An example of a higher-level document in an early development phase is a Software Requirements Specifications (SRS). A number of information sources are needed as input for a SRS, such as a customer requirement specification, software prototypes, customer visit reports and any other form of information and documentation. The goal of the walkthrough on a working document is to get feedback and discussion on the documented interpretation of these inputs. The walkthrough of a working document is part of the validation process. Information is gathered in order to establish if the right product is being developed.

Draft document
A walkthrough on a document that is almost ready for release will focus on the common understanding of the presented document, which contains the

solution to the earlier defined opportunity or problem. This walkthrough will be more like a presentation and will focus on achieving consensus, sometimes with the objective to prepare for a sign-off.

A group of 2 to 7 project members, that are directly involved and including members from outside the software discipline, may be invited for a walkthrough meeting. To be able to be effective in the walkthrough, participants do not have to study the documents in detail. Reading through the document without trying to comprehend every detail, is enough to enable them to fully participate in the meeting.

The walkthrough procedure consists of four steps. Each of these steps is described hereafter. Participants need no special training to contribute to a walkthrough. The general procedure can be explained in a kick-off meeting.

1. Initiation & planning
The walkthrough process begins with a 'request for walkthrough' by the author to the moderator. A specific entry check, such as during an inspection, does not take place for a walkthrough. In co-operation with the moderator, the author can identify specific topics that need clarification during the walkthrough. Furthermore, the moderator and author will select the participants for the walkthrough, based on their domain knowledge and background. The moderator distributes all necessary input materials to the participants, allowing for enough time for reading.

Since the author is busy throughout the meeting guiding the participants through the document and the moderator is involved in chairing the meeting, a separate scribe is needed. During the meeting the scribe has to record each defect discussed, any suggestions for improvement made and/or alternative approaches proposed.

2. Preparation
The preparation for a walkthrough is not extensive. Participants need to familiarise themselves with the document-under-review. The reviewers will be asked to read the document before the meeting and prepare a list of questions and defects for discussion. In a walkthrough defects often act as action items or recommendations on how to improve the document. The word defect is used as a generic term in this chapter, although no strict definition of defects can be given in a walkthrough.

3. Walkthrough meeting
The meeting is divided into two sequential steps:
1. The kick-off
2. The walkthrough.

Ad 1. The kick-off
The moderator states the objectives of the walkthrough and the author presents an overview of the document. The participants can make general remarks and ask questions. The agenda for the meeting is determined and agreed upon, based on the lists of questions and defects that are prepared by the reviewers.

Ad 2. The walkthrough
The author walks through the document page-by-page (or feature-by-feature) so that the team members may ask questions, raise issues, recommend improvements etc. The author presents the document step-by-step, possibly focussing only on the most important parts. Task scenarios and dry runs can be applied to illustrate and explain the document. The moderator paces the meeting.

The output of the meeting is a list of recommendations and action items with respect to the document-under-review.

4. Rework, follow-up and exit
Based on the action items, recommendations and defects logged, the author will improve the document-under-review, step-by-step. The author may also make other improvements or corrections to the work product, not based on the defects logged.

The moderator checks whether the action items are closed, using the updated document. In the case of a working document is most likely to be reviewed in a technical review or inspection at a later stage. It is the author's responsibility to improve the document based on the defects logged. The defect log may even be used as an input document during an inspection. In the case of a more final document, which is already put under configuration management, the defects logged lead to change requests on the document. It is the moderator's tasks to check whether these change requests are recorded.

If the document is updated, action items are closed and change requests are documented, the document may exit the walkthrough process.

8.6   Combining the review types

This section elaborates on the role of the different review types during the establishment of a document. In the previous paragraphs, the goals and characteristics of various review types are described. It is apparent that none of these types is the "winner", but the different types serve different purposes at different stages in the life cycle of a document.

Reviews are a time consuming activity that must be applied with care. Not every type of document should be subject to both an inspection and a technical review. The testing principle of Myers (Myers, 1979) also applies to reviews: "Testing is setting priorities". Therefore, a strategy is needed to ensure the most feasible and applicable document coverage. A review strategy should aim at optimising the total amount of undetected defects. The review effort needed for finding a next defect should be less than the cost of it occurring during testing or in operation. However, finding the next defect is not merely a matter of review costs. If the testing phase or even the starting of operation is delayed, large sums are often involved. Also the likelihood of a specific defect occurring during testing or operation should be considered. A defect that never evolves into a failure during testing or in operation is not an important defect. Like a test strategy, a review strategy is based on a risk assessment and the probability and impact of defects, both detected and undetected during review, needs to be assessed.

An important distinction should be made between product and project documents, for example, project plan, test plan, software quality assurance plan. A thorough discussion on the content of project documents, is often much more effective than checking whether a plan is written in accordance to rules and standards. A technical review focussing on the content and feasibility is more applicable in this case. Inspection of a product document, such as a SRS, is always worthwhile because this document forms the basis for all subsequent development. Therefore, the review should focus on higher-level documents. To ensure that no content related discussions arise during an inspection, a walkthrough or technical review should be held beforehand.

The goal of a formal review should match with the type of document and its life cycle stage. Figure 8.2 shows a possible positioning of the various review types in the life cycle of a document.

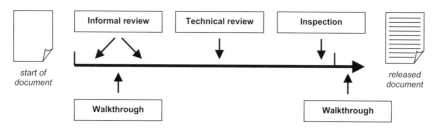

Figure 8.2: Document review types and the life cycle of a document

The review types, shown in the figure above, are complementary to each other. They serve different objectives and deliver different defects.

Comparing the review types

Formal reviews are an effective and efficient means of improving the quality of the software product. The three formal review types described in this chapter are used based on their specific objectives. In table 8.4 the three formal review types are compared with regards to their objectives, phases, participants, sizes and materials needed.

	Walkthrough	**Technical Review**	**Inspection**
Objectives	Gather information, evaluate content, establish consensus, forum for learning	Discuss technical (alternative) concepts, establish consistency, inform others	Find defects, verify product quality, exchange information
Phase	Start of - and released document	"70%" document	Almost finished document
Participants	Peers, technical leaders and participants from ouside the software discipline	Experts (technical leaders), peers and sometimes project leaders	Peers
Preparation	Not extensive. Defects are found during the meeting. Roles are not needed	Roles based on specific question of the author. Not to many pages	Formal preparation using roles, based on rules, at a slow checking rate
Meeting	Presentation like, discussion. Author is the leader	Discussion. The technical leader (or alternatively the moderator) is the meeting leader	Formal, focus on logging, no discussion. Moderator is the leader
Logging	Separate scribe	Author	Author
Follow-up	Moderator checks if action items are closed	Expert-based decision regarding the follow-up	Formal check by the moderator and/or the participants
Materials needed	Document-under-review	Document-under-review	Document-under-review, source documents, standards, rules & checklists
Process leader	Moderator	Technical leader will act as a moderator	Moderator
Team size	5 - 8	4 - 6	2 - 6

Table 8.4: Three formal review types

Different responsibilities

The approval of a document is not part of figure 8.2. This is because the primary objective of the reviews is to improve the quality of documents. The reviews described are applied to help the author. The moderator is responsible for ensuring that these goals are met. However, approval of a document is a different objective, for which the review leader is not responsible. The leader co-ordinates and controls the review process to achieve efficient and effective document quality. Management decides whether or not to approve a document and allow it to be used as a basis for the next development step. It is highly recommended to use the results of the formal review as a basis for the approval decision, since the risks of approving the document are made visible by the review process.

8.7 Success factors of implementation

Implementing formal reviews is not easy as there is no 'one way' to success and there are a numerous ways to fail. The next list contains a number of critical success factors that improve the reviews chances of success. It aims to answer the question, "How do you start formal reviews?"

- *Find a "champion"*
  A champion is needed, who will lead the process on a project or organisational level. They need expertise, enthusiasm and a practical mindset in order to guide moderators and participants. The authority of this "champion" should be clear to the entire organisation.
- *Pick thing that "really count"*
  Select the documents for formal review that are the most important in a project. Reviewing highly critical, upstream documents like requirements and specifications will most certainly show the benefits of the review process to the project. These invested reviews hours will have a clear and high Return-on-Investment.
- *Explicitly plan and track formal review activities*
  To ensure that reviews become part of the day-to-day activities, the hours to be spent should be made visible within each project plan. The engineers involved are prompted to schedule time for preparation and, very importantly, rework. Tracking these hours will improve the next review planning.
- *Follow the rules but keep it simple*
  Follow all the formal rules until you know why and how to modify them, but start simple and make the process as formal as the project culture or maturity levels allows. However, do not be too theoretical.

- *Respect optimum checking rates*
  The checking rate is a very important success factor. If this rate is too high, no real defects will be found and the number of minor defects that are found will frustrate the whole process. Only by applying the optimum checking rate, will the truth of the document be found.
- *Collect data and provide feedback*
  If no data is collected the process cannot properly be managed nor improved and will vanish within a few months. Provide feedback to everyone involved so they can interpret the data correctly. Both data and feedback are essential for understanding and improving the review processes.
- *Continuously improve process and tools*
  Continuous improvement of process and supporting tools (e.g. checklists), based upon the ideas of participants, ensures the motivation of the engineers involved. Motivation is the key to a successful change process.
- *Use a thorough entry check*
  Only documents that are ready for inspection should enter an inspection process, otherwise valuable time is lost finding obvious defects. "Garbage in" will lead to "garbage out", so documents should be cleaned up and free of obvious defects and too many annoying minors or even spelling mistakes.
- *Report results*
  Report quantified results and benefits to all those involved as soon as possible, and discuss the consequences of defects if they had not been found this early.
- *Just do it!*
  The process is simple but not easy. Every step of the process is clear, but experience is needed to execute them correctly. So, try to get experienced people to observe and help were possible. But most importantly, start doing reviews and start learning from every review.

References

- Bisant D.B. and J.R. Lyle (1989), A two-person inspection method to improve programming productivity, in: *IEEE Transactions on software engineering*, October 1989

- IEEE 1028 (1998), *Standard for Software Reviews,* IEEE Standards Board

- Fagan, M. (1986), Advances in software inspections, in: *IEEE Transactions on Software Engineering*, Vol. 12, no 7, July 1986

- Freedman, D.P. and G.M. Weinberg (1990) *Handbook of Walkthroughs, Inspections, and Technical Reviews*, Dorset House Third edition, New York, ISBN 0-932633-19-6

- Gilb, T. and D. Graham (1993), *Software Inspection*, Adison-Wesley, London, ISBN 0-201-63181-4

- Juran, J.M. and F.M. Gryna (1970), *Quality Planning and Analysis*, McGraw-Hill, New York

- Myers, G.J. (1979), *The Art of Software Testing*, Wiley-Interscience, New York, ISBN 0-471-04328-1

- Veenendaal, E.P.W.M. van (1999), Practical Quality Assurance for Embedded Software, in: *Software Quality Professional*, Vol. 1, no. 3, American Society for Quality, June 1999

- Weinberg, G.M. (1971), *The psychology of Computer Programming*, Van Nostrand Reinhold, New York.

9 Reading Techniques

Forrest Shull and Victor Basili

Too little attention has been paid to the development of effective procedures for the individual defect detection phase of an inspection. Often, reviewers are left to their own implicit procedures and experience for detecting defects, which can be effective for more experienced reviewers but provides little guidance for the less experienced and inhibits learning about effective approaches. "Reading techniques" are a procedural approach to defect detection that addresses these issues. By focusing reviewers on the perspective of a downstream user of the document being reviewed, reading techniques represent an improvement over ad hoc approaches. This chapter presents a description of reading techniques and guidelines for creating and tailoring them.

9.1 Current practices

In the current state of the practice, software developers often rely on ad hoc techniques for their individual review of a software document, to read the document and detect defects. An ad hoc approach is one that is nonsystematic, nonspecific, and nondistinct.

Nonsystematic means that inspectors have no set procedure or rules to follow; they use whatever processes or tools seem useful to them at any given time. While this may seem like an appealing approach (it asks inspectors to rely on their own practical experience to decide how to inspect the document), there are some drawbacks. First, because there is no set procedure, it is difficult to provide training to inexperienced inspectors. New inspectors are required to build up their own experience over time; it is difficult for them to learn what other inspectors are already doing in order to build on their experience. Secondly, it is difficult to improve a process that is not even informally defined. If an inspector learns, for example, that a particular type of defect is consistently not being detected in the inspections, it is difficult for him or her to know how to alter the inspection process in order to detect defects of that type more effectively.

Nonspecific detection techniques mean that inspectors are required to find defects of all types. Again, at first this may seem like a benefit since all types of defects have to be removed from the document. But from the viewpoint of an individual inspector, a lack of a specific goal can make the defect detection process harder. When an inspector is equally responsible for finding typos as well as all kinds of omitted functionality, it becomes harder to do the search because the inspector is looking for many different things. Limiting the search makes the inspector responsible for only a subset of the defects, but allows that inspector to spend more energy and concentration looking for fewer types.

Nondistinct techniques mean that all inspectors have the same goals and responsibilities. In short, there is some duplication of work since all inspectors are reading the document looking for the same things. This approach does have its advantages; some defects are more likely to be found since there are more inspectors examining the same material looking for the same things. On the other hand, inspectors are motivated to do a better job when they know that they are the only people responsible for a particular part of the inspection, and can't rely on other inspectors to find the defects they missed. Giving different inspectors distinct responsibilities also allows different inspectors to become "experts" in different aspects of a document, rather than requiring all inspectors to have the same, overview level of knowledge.

Inspections using rules and checklists represent an improvement over ad hoc approaches, largely by making the review process more specific and systematic. By providing focus for the inspectors, they can also support distinct roles or responsibilities. However, they still leave crucial information to be discovered in an ad hoc way. For example, a checklist may say what issues to check for but not *how* an inspector gets the information to do so.

In contrast to other approaches, the use of a defined, systematic process for individual defect detection (known as a reading technique, since it helps reviewers to inspect, or read, a document more effectively) allows reviewers to focus better on the important aspects of the document being reviewed. More importantly, by making the review process explicit, reading techniques allow inspections to be adapted over time to better meet the needs of the organization. For example, if a particular type of defect is consistently missed by inspections, then a procedure for how that type of defect could be found should be developed and applied by at least one of the inspectors in the future. On the other hand, if a particular part of the procedure is felt by the inspectors to never lead to any defects being detected, then it might be dropped from the procedure, rather than continue to use inspectors' time for little gain.

This chapter provides an overview of reading techniques for software inspections. It provides a description of reading techniques and the underlying models, of the document being inspected and the types of defects sought, which are necessary for their use. A set of dimensions is presented along which any reading technique must be tailored to the specific organization doing the inspections, and examples are presented to illustrate the discussion. Finally, a summary of experiences with these techniques is discussed.

9.2   A reading procedure template

When reading techniques are used to perform an inspection, a family of related reading techniques is used in which each technique captures an important aspect of the information contained in the document under review. Each reading technique captures a different perspective on the information and all together the family of techniques should cover all the perspectives of interest. Since each inspector on the inspection team applies a particular reading technique, from a particular perspective, team members have unique (rather than redundant) responsibilities.

The use of perspectives reflects a belief that the correctness of software artifacts must be evaluated, not according to some global and static definition of quality, but according to how such documents will be used during the software lifecycle. That is, software artifacts are created not for any intrinsic value, but in order to be used by some stakeholder at some later stage of software development. If these stakeholders can be identified and the artifact reviewed from their perspectives, then greater confidence can be had that the artifact will be able to meet all the downstream expectations for it. On the other hand, if any of these stakeholders' needs are not met, this represents a deficiency in the quality of the requirements that has the potential to negatively impact software development. This is what is referred to as a requirements defect.

Perspectives should be chosen so as to minimize the overlapping responsibilities among inspectors, while achieving a high level of coverage of the defects. This goal is illustrated by Figure 9.1, in which each of the tables represents the set of defects in a document. An "X" in the column for that defect means it is targeted by one of the three review perspectives (Rev1, Rev2, or Rev3). The table on the left illustrates the situation in which an ad hoc approach is used for individual defect detection. In ad hoc reviews, each reviewer is asked to inspect the entire document but typically focuses on some subset of the possible defects, perhaps because the reviewer has more experience with a particular defect type, considers certain types of defects to be more important to find, or finds certain types of defects more easily.

However, because this focusing is not made explicit, often during the review certain defects happen to be covered more thoroughly, by multiple reviewers (such as D2, D3, D4, D5), and other defects not at all (D7). The idea behind reading techniques is that each technique provides the reviewer with a process for reviewing the document from a certain perspective, and thus focuses the reviewer on a certain subset of defects. Perspectives are chosen with the goal that all possible defects of interest are the target of at least one technique, with minimal overlap between them. This ideal situation is illustrated in the table on the right.

Ad hoc coverage:

	D1	D2	D3	D4	D5	D6	D7
Rev1	X	X	X				
Rev2		X	X	X	X		
Rev3				X	X	X	

Reading technique coverage:

	D1	D2	D3	D4	D5	D6	D7
Rev1	X	X					
Rev2			X	X			
Rev3					X	X	X

Figure 9.1: Simulated defect coverage of different inspection approaches, for three review perspectives (Rev1…Rev3) over a set of defects (D1…D7)

For example, for an inspection of requirements in a particular environment the following perspectives were found to be useful:
• The perspective of a designer, who uses the requirements as the basis for the system design;
• The perspective of a tester, who uses the requirements to determine whether the system exhibits proper behavior for each test case;
• The perspective of the customer, who has certain needs for the system functionality, which are described in the requirements.

Each reviewer is assigned only one perspective from which to inspect the document (i.e. the reviewers have distinct responsibilities) and focus on the particular defects relevant to that perspective (i.e. have a specific focus). If the perspectives have been chosen wisely then the union of these inspectors covers all of the relevant defects in this document with a minimum of overlap. More information on identifying perspectives is given in paragraph 9.5.

Inspectors receive guidance for staying within their perspective by means of an operational procedure, a set of process steps, or guidelines that keep them focused on just the information in the artifact that is important for their perspective (allowing a systematic inspection preparation). For each perspective, the operational procedure is created by first identifying an abstraction of the document, i.e. a way of modeling only the information in the document that is important for the perspective. Choosing the right abstraction requires answering the question of *what* information should be important to the inspector. Next, a model of *how* that information can be used to detect defects is necessary. This requires deciding which quality aspects are of interest in the document and understanding how the abstraction addresses those aspects.

These two models (the "what" and the "how") must be used to create procedures for the reviewers to follow. As shown in Figure 9.2, the reading technique for reviewing the document is a combination of these specific procedures. The procedure that says what to look for is called the "abstraction procedure"; the procedure that says how to use the abstraction to look for defects is the "use procedure."

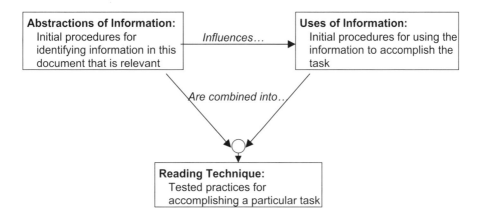

Figure 9.2: Building focused, tailored software reading techniques

An abstraction procedure is necessary to describe how the abstraction should be built. This procedure can be thought of as a "traversal" algorithm that instructs the reviewer in how to read through the document and find the information necessary for building the abstraction. Creating the abstraction procedure usually involves determining what are the relevant organizing structures for the given document from the reviewer's perspective. This information helps the reviewer concentrate on just the relevant pieces of the document rather than the document as a whole. For example, if a requirements document is reviewed from the perspective of a tester, the reviewer needs to worry about how to make each requirement testable. The organizing structure is thus the requirements themselves. The abstraction procedure could step through each requirement at a time and help the reviewer to identify the relevant aspects, such as the expected inputs, the different classes of input values, and the expected outputs. However, from the perspective of a user, thinking about individual requirements might not be very useful, so instead the abstraction procedure could help the reviewer to think about the larger functionalities involved and to abstract modes of behavior from the requirements. For a user, these modes of behavior can be easier to analyze for defects than lists of individual requirements.

Next, for each of the steps of the abstraction procedure generated above, a use procedure must be provided that contains guidance as to how the information seen so far can be checked for defects. The abstraction procedure gives the inspector the right information; the use procedure should provide a step-by-step way to check that information for defects. Once these procedures have been identified, the reading technique can be created by interleaving them in such a way that every step of the abstraction procedure is followed by a step of the use procedure, that uses the information just identified in the abstraction to look for defects.

9.3   Example 1: The requirements customer perspective

This paragraph contains the full text from a reading technique created for the perspective of the customer in a requirements review. It represents the set of instructions given to a reviewer and corresponds to the outline for reading techniques described in paragraph 9.2, in which abstraction steps (here, the set of instructions that guide the reviewer through the process of building use cases) are followed by use steps (here, the sets of questions) that help the reviewer find defects in that information. It should be noted that this is only one possible instantiation for this perspective and that others could be created by tailoring along the dimensions identified in paragraph 9.5, for example, the level of detail, the abstraction chosen, or the defect taxonomy that yields the sets of questions. Another example of a reading technique is described in paragraph 9.4.

The goal for this procedure is to provide a comprehensive review of the quality aspects that would be relevant for the customer (i.e. to review whether the requirements correctly describe all of the necessary functionality for the system), regardless of quality aspects for other stakeholders of the requirements (e.g. whether the requirements are easily translatable into a design). This procedure includes a set of steps for developing use cases that describe the system functionality (the abstraction procedure), each of which is followed by associated questions (the use procedure). For example, Step 1 includes guidelines for identifying system "participants," a necessary first step toward developing the system abstraction, the use cases. The series of questions immediately following aim to uncover any defects in the information about the participants in the requirements.

The procedure:
Create use cases to document the functionality that users of the system should be able to perform. This will require listing the functionality that the new system will provide and the external interfaces that are involved. Identify actors (sets of users) who will use the system for specific types of functionality. Remember to include all of the functionality in the system, including special/contingency conditions. Follow the procedure below to generate the use cases, using the questions provided to identify faults in the requirements:

1) *(abstraction step)* **Read through the requirements once, finding participants involved.**
   a) Identify and list the participants in the new requirements. Participants are the other systems and the users that interact with the system described in the requirements – that is, they participate in the system functionality by sending messages to the system and/or receiving information and instructions from it. You may use the following questions to help you identify participants:
      - Which user groups use the system to perform a task?
      - Which user groups are needed by the system in order to perform its functions? These functions could be its major functions, or secondary functions such as system maintenance and administration.
      - Which are the external systems that use the system in order to perform a task?
      - Which are the external systems that are managed or otherwise used by the system in order to perform a task?
      - Which are the external systems or user groups that send information to the system?
      - Which are the external systems or user groups that receive information from the system?

   (use step)
   Q1.1 Are multiple terms used to describe the same participant in the requirements?
   Q1.2 Is the description of how the system interacts with a participant inconsistent with the description of the participant? Are the requirements unclear or inconsistent about this interaction?
   Q1.3 Have necessary participants been omitted? That is, does the system need to interact with another system, a piece of hardware, or a type of user that is not described?

Q1.4 Is an external system or a class of "users" described in the requirements, which does not actually interact with the system?

2) *(abstraction step)* **Read through the requirements a second time, identifying the product functions.**
   a) Identify and record the set of functionality that the system must be able to perform. That is, what activities do the requirements say the system must do? (E.g. display a database record, print a report, create and display a graph.)
   b) Now consider how a user of the system will view it. The user is probably not concerned with the individual activities that the system can perform, but instead thinks about using the system to achieve some goal (e.g. adding information to an existing database, computing a payment, viewing the current status of an account). These user goals will be the set of use cases for the system.
   c) For each use case, decide which of the system activities you previously recorded are involved, and note them. Sketch out, from the user's point of view, what steps are required to achieve the goal and use arrows to identify the flow of system control ("First this functionality happens, then this…"). Use branching arrows to signify places where the flow of control could split. Remember to include exception functionality in the use case. Check the appropriate functional requirements to ensure that you have the details of the processing and flow of control correct.
   d) For each use case you create, remember to signify what class(es) of users would use the functionality (the user classes should be already recorded in the list of participants), as well as the action that starts the functionality (e.g. "selecting option 2 from the main menu" might start a use case for deleting records from a database). Record both of these pieces of information with the use case. Finally, give the use case a descriptive name that conveys the functionality it represents and assign it a number for future reference.

(use step)
Q2.1 Are the start conditions for each use case specified at an appropriate level of detail?
Q2.2 Are the class(es) of users who use the functionality described, and are these classes correct and appropriate?
Q2.3 Is there any system functionality that should be included in a use case but is described in insufficient detail or omitted from the requirements?
Q2.4 Has the system been described sufficiently so that you understand what activities are required for the user to achieve the goal of a use

case? Does this combination of activities make sense, based on the general description and your domain knowledge? Does the description allow more than one interpretation as to how the system achieves this goal?

Q2.5 Do the requirements omit use cases that you feel are necessary, according to your domain knowledge or the general description?

3) *(abstraction step)* **Match the participants to all of the use cases in which they are involved.**
Remember that if two participants are involved in all of the same use cases, they might represent a single unique actor and should be combined.

(use step)

Q3.1 Is it clear from the requirements which participants are involved in which use cases?

Q3.2 Based on the general requirements and your knowledge of the domain, has each participant been connected to all of the relevant use cases?

Q3.3 Are participants involved in use cases that are incompatible with the participant's description?

Q3.4 Have necessary participants been omitted (e.g. are there use cases which require information that cannot be obtained from any source described in the requirements)?"

9.4   Example 2: The requirements test perspective

As a further example, this paragraph provides an instantiation of a reading technique for requirements review representing the perspective of a tester. It represents the set of instructions given to a reviewer and corresponds to the outline for reading techniques described in paragraph 9.2. The goal of this perspective is to evaluate whether the functionality contained in the requirements is well specified (i.e. that test cases can be constructed to demonstrate the adherence of the system to the requirements) regardless of quality aspects for other stakeholders (e.g. whether the complete set of functionality has been described).

As with the customer perspective given in 9.3, it should be noted that this example is only one possible instantiation for this perspective and that others could be created by tailoring along the dimensions identified in paragraph 9.5.

The procedure:

For each requirement, generate a test or set of test cases that allow you to ensure that an implementation of the system satisfies the requirement. Follow the procedure below to generate the test cases, using the questions provided to identify faults in the requirements:

1) *(abstraction step)* **For each requirement, read it through once and record the number and page on the form provided, along with the inputs to the requirement.**

   (use step)
   Q1.1   Does the requirement make sense from what you know about the application or from what is specified in the general description?
   Q1.2   Do you have all the information necessary to identify the inputs to the requirement? Based on the general requirements and your domain knowledge, are these inputs correct for this requirement?
   Q1.3   Have any of the necessary inputs been omitted?
   Q1.4   Are any inputs specified which are not needed for this requirement?
   Q1.5   Is this requirement in the appropriate section of the document?

2) *(abstraction step)* **For each input, divide the input domain into sets of data (called equivalence classes), where all of the values in each set will cause the system to behave similarly.**

   Determine the equivalence classes for a particular input by understanding the sets of conditions that affect the behavior of the requirement. You may find it helpful to keep the following guidelines in mind when creating equivalence classes:
   - If an input condition specifies a range, at least one valid (the set of values in the range) and two invalid equivalence sets (the set of values less than the lowest extreme of the range, and the set of values greater than the largest extreme) are defined.
   - If an input condition specifies a member of a set, then at least one valid (the set itself) and one invalid equivalence class (the complement of the valid set) are defined.
   - If an input condition requires a specific value, then one valid (the class containing the value itself) and two invalid equivalence classes (the class of values less than, and the class greater than, the value) are defined.

   Note: Each equivalence class should be recorded with the appropriate input.

(use step)

Q2.1 Do you have enough information to construct the equivalence classes for each input? Can you specify the boundaries of the classes at an appropriate level of detail?

Q2.2 According to the information in the requirements, are the classes constructed so that no value appears in more than one set?

Q2.3 Do the requirements state that a particular value should appear in more than one equivalence class (that is, do they specify more than one type of response for the same value)?

Q2.4 Do the requirements specify the result for an invalid equivalence classes?

3) *(abstraction step)* **For each equivalence class write test cases, and record them beneath the associated equivalence set on the form.** Select typical test cases as well as values at and near the edges of the sets. For example, if the requirement expects input values in the range 0 to 100, then the test cases selected might be: 0, 1, 56, 99, 100. Finally, for each equivalence class record the behavior, which is expected to result (that is, how do you expect the system to respond to the test cases you just made up?).

(use step)

Q3.1 Do you have enough information to create test cases for each equivalence class?

Q3.2 Are there other interpretations of this requirement that the implementer might make based upon the description given? Will this affect the tests you generate?

Q3.3 Is there another requirement for which you would generate a similar test case but would get a contradictory result?

Q3.4 Can you be sure that the tests generated will yield the correct values in the correct units? Is the resulting behavior specified appropriately?

9.5 Customizing reading techniques

Paragraph 9.2 provided a generic outline for how reading techniques are constructed. To be effective in practice, however, reading techniques must be tailored to the needs of the project and the organization. In the following subsections, several dimensions are identified along which the customization that should be performed. In performing the customization, it is helpful to reuse prior knowledge whenever possible. That is, the reading technique should borrow from other methods, or incorporate tools, that have already been proven successful in the environment. In some cases, ethnographic studies may be necessary to understand exactly what techniques and tools developers have already found to be useful. For example to uncover particular types of defects that reviewers have determined are important, or a particular order for doing the analysis of the document that avoids repetition, or an existing tool that automates some portion of the checking. This attention to tested tools can result in a more effective technique for the environment and aid in overcoming developer resistance at being asked to use a "new" technique.

Tailoring Perspectives

To detect defects in a document that would hinder its downstream use in software development, it is necessary to identify properly all of the stakeholders in later development phases. This selection of stakeholders has to be done according to organization or project needs. To do so, answering the following questions can be helpful:
- In what other phases of the software lifecycle is this document needed?
- In each phase, what other specific software tasks does the document support?

For example, for a requirements inspection the following simple waterfall model of the software lifecycle could be sketched (figure 9.3).

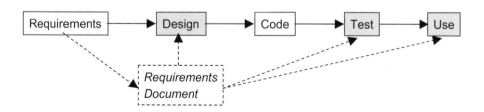

Figure 9.3: Simple model of requirements' use in the lifecycle

Thinking about how the requirements document is used in each of these phases could yield the following:
- As a description of the needs of the customer: The requirements describe the set of functionality and performance constraints that must be met by the final system.
- As a basis for the design of the system: The system designer has to create a design that can achieve the functionality described by the requirements, within the allowed constraints.

- As a point of comparison for system test: The system's test plan has to ensure that the functionality and performance requirements have been correctly implemented.

These uses suggest perspectives from which the requirements document should be reviewed. The designer needs a set of requirements that are correct and described in sufficient detail for the major system components to be identified and correctly designed. As the tester is concerned about whether the requirements are testable and described in sufficient detail, a test plan, or set of test cases for the entire system can be created. The customer (or user) of the system requires that the functionality he or she needs the system to have be completely and correctly captured by the requirements.

However, these are by no means the only perspectives that can be appropriate for a requirements review. The simple lifecycle model should be used as a tool to help identify the right perspectives for a given environment. For example, it may be that the needs of the stakeholders already identified (designer, tester, and customer perspectives) are not entirely applicable to another environment, and should be modified or dropped. Or, there might be a stakeholder identified in the coding phase (e.g. someone who has to integrate the functionality described for the new system with existing components). It is also possible that other phases need to be added to the lifecycle model for a given environment. For example, if the system was being developed incrementally, such that multiple future versions of the system are planned, a maintainer perspective could be added that is responsible for reviewing the requirements for their extensibility (i.e. for evaluating how easy the next extension to such a system would be). The right mix of perspectives depends on the expected uses of the document being reviewed in the organizational environment.

Tailoring Abstraction Models

Using the right abstractions for a set of reading techniques is especially crucial because the abstractions created, when a reviewer applies the techniques during a review, will be used in two ways. First, they have to support defect detection as they are created. Therefore the abstractions chosen should be as simple as possible, so that the effort required for their construction does not distract from their use as a tool for finding defects. But, secondly, they must also be abstractions that are useful in some later lifecycle phase for the development of the system. That is, the effort expended to analyze the system and create the abstraction should also directly support system construction.

For example, in the previous paragraph designer, tester, and customer perspectives were discussed as examples for a requirements review. During the inspection, reviewers in each perspective could be asked to translate the information in the requirements into a high-level design sketch, a high-level test plan, and a set of use cases, respectively. Each of these abstractions was chosen because it gives the reviewer a new perspective on the information contained in the requirements relevant to that stakeholder (e.g. translating the requirements into use cases helps the "customer" reviewer think about how the functionalities specified will be implemented). The abstractions were also chosen for their usefulness in constructing the system. As shown in figure 9.4, use cases and design notes can be used in the design phase as a basis for system design, use cases can also be useful as the basis for a user manual, and the high-level test cases can be used as a starting point for the test phase.

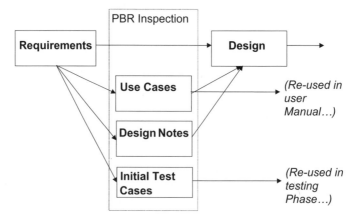

Figure 9.4: Use of abstractions created during a review elsewhere in the lifecycle.

Perhaps most importantly, abstractions should be chosen with which the likely reviewers have some expertise. Often, in organizations just introducing inspections, there are likely to be more personnel with expertise in creating the system abstractions (e.g. test plans) than in looking for requirements defects. Using the test case as an abstraction for a reading technique helps reviewers leverage their existing experience for a new goal.

The following questions will be helpful for identifying the right abstractions:
- What information must the document contain to support each perspective identified?
- What is a good way of organizing that information, so that attributes of interest are readily apparent to the inspector?
- What artifacts are being created in other lifecycle phases to support downstream development?

Tailoring the Defect Taxonomy

The questions that the inspector is asked about the abstraction correspond directly to the types of defects being sought. In order to target questions effectively, it is useful to create a taxonomy of the important issues. This requires an analysis of exactly what types of issues are of most concern to the project and organization. What constitutes a defect is largely situation-dependent. For example, if there are strong performance requirements on a system, then any description of the system that might lead to those performance requirements being unfulfilled contains a defect; however, for other systems with fewer performance constraints the same artifacts could be considered perfectly correct. Similarly, the types of defects in a textual requirements document could be very different from what would be used for a graphical design representation.

As a starting point, however, a generic defect taxonomy can be identified which can then be instantiated for specific circumstances. One such taxonomy that has proven useful is based on the idea of the software development lifecycle as a series of transformations of a system description to increasingly formal notations, and adding increasing levels of detail. For example, a set of natural-language requirements can be thought of as a loose description of a system that is transformed into high- and low-level designs, more formal descriptions of the same basic set of functionality. Eventually these designs are translated into code, which is more formal still, but describes the same set of functionality (hopefully) as set in the original requirements.

So what can go wrong during such transformations? Figure 9.5 presents a simplified view of the problem, in which all of the relevant information has to be carried forward from the previous phase into a new form, and has to be

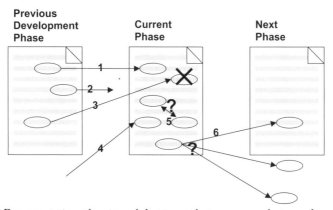

Figure 9.5: Representation of various defect types that can occur during software development

specified in such a way that it can be further refined in the next phase. The ideal case is shown by arrow 1, in which a piece of information from the artifact created in the previous phase of development is correctly translated into its new form in the artifact in the current phase. There is, however, the possibility that necessary information is somehow left out of the new artifact (omitted information, arrow 2) or translated into the new artifact but in an incorrect form (incorrect fact, arrow 3). In the current phase artifact, there is always the possibility that extraneous information has been entered (arrow 4), which could lead to confusion in the further development of the system, or that information has been specified in such a way as to make the document inconsistent with itself (inconsistent information, arrow 5). A related possibility is that information has been specified ambiguously, leading to multiple interpretations in the next phase (ambiguous information, arrow 6), not all of which may be correct or appropriate[1].

It is important to note that the classes are not orthogonal (i.e. a particular defect could possibly fit into more than one category) but are intended to give an idea of the set of possible defects that can occur. These broad categories need to be tailored to the document being inspected. For a requirements inspection, for example, the categories can be defined more exactly as:
• Omitted Information: some significant requirement related to functionality, performance, design constraints, attributes or external interface is not included, or the response of the software to all realizable classes of input data in all realizable classes of situations is not defined.
• Incorrect Fact: a requirement asserts a fact that cannot be true under the conditions specified for the system.
• Extraneous Information: information is provided that is not needed or used.
• Inconsistent Information: two or more requirements are in conflict with one another.
• Ambiguous Information: a requirement has multiple interpretations due to multiple terms for the same characteristic, or multiple meanings of a term in a particular context.

---

1   Of course, figure 9.5 is a simplified view. In reality, many of the implied 1-to-1 mappings do not hold. There may be multiple artifacts created in each stage of the lifecycle, and the information in a particular phase can influence many aspects of the artifact created in the next phase. For example, one requirement from a requirements specification can impact many components of the system design. When notational differences are taken into account (e.g. textual requirements are translated into a graphical design description) it becomes apparent why performing effective inspections can be such a challenging task.

The important point is not the defect taxonomy itself, which is probably similar to the information given to reviewers during "traditional" inspections, which is expected to be tailored to the needs of a particular environment anyway. In a reading technique, the taxonomy is not given directly to the reviewer (except as supplemental material), but used instead to create a set of questions aimed at eliciting defects, for each step of the abstraction procedure. Taken as a whole, the reading technique provides the reviewer with a tested process to follow in order to answer the questions and find defects, rather than leaving it up to the reviewer how to look for defects of each type.

To illustrate, consider step 1 of the reading technique shown in paragraph 9.3. Following an abstraction step for eliciting information about participants comes a set of questions that check that information for ambiguous information (Q1.1), inconsistent information (Q1.2), omitted information (Q1.3), and extraneous information (Q1.4). The question list does not include defects of incorrect facts because that type of defect was not felt to be relevant for the information about participants, but other questions in this procedure (e.g. Q2.4) do search for that defect type in other information.

It is worth repeating that this is not a definitive taxonomy of defects, but a tool that can be used to start reasoning about the types of issues of relevance to a particular organization. Clearly, the taxonomy can be augmented (e.g. with performance issues) or shortened (e.g. if the organization does not find extraneous information to be important to consider in an inspection) or replaced altogether.

Tailoring the Level of Detail

The level of detail used in the procedure must also be seen as a dimension along which reading techniques can be customized to a particular organization, in order to yield higher effectiveness. Most importantly, the level of detail needs to vary with the expertise of the inspectors who will be applying the techniques: experienced reviewers should be free to make use of their own hard-won experience, while inexperienced reviewers may be more comfortable with more step-by-step guidelines.

Recall from paragraph 9.2 that the steps of a reading technique interleave abstraction steps (that help the reviewer identify information and build a model) and use steps (that give the reviewer a set of questions to answer about that information). Typically, varying the level of detail means varying the number of abstraction steps (and adjusting the associated use steps accordingly). For example, for experienced reviewers in the customer perspective there might be a single abstraction step ("Use whatever technique you normally do to reason about functionality") and a single associated use step ("Keep the following questions in mind while you do so..."). For less experienced reviewers a very specific abstraction may be chosen (e.g. use cases) so that multiple abstraction steps can be identified each with an associated set of questions.

Although more detailed procedures can be very useful for less experienced reviewers, there are tradeoffs to keep in mind. First, no procedure no matter how detailed will be effective if the reviewers don't have enough training to make effective use of the abstraction. Thus, the technique demonstrated in paragraph 9.3 will not be effective if the reviewers that use it have not received at least minimal training with use cases. Secondly, choosing a very detailed abstraction means reducing flexibility. Suppose, for the requirement review tester perspective, that "equivalence partitioning test cases" (BS7925-2, 1998) are selected as the abstraction. The resulting procedure may be useful for novice reviewers but some flexibility has been lost; not every requirement is well suited to the equivalence partitioning approach. The lack of applicability of the more detailed procedure to some requirements has to be balanced against how well the inexperienced reviewers could do if allowed to select their own test approach on a requirement-by-requirement basis.

It is important, for both the software engineers tailoring the reading techniques and the inspectors applying them, to keep in mind the purpose of the model-building: the models are not important in themselves but as tools to find defects. It is sometimes tempting for software engineers to make the techniques too detailed, or for reviewers to spend too much time on model creation during a review, adding more detail than is necessary for finding defects in the document being inspected. Unfortunately there are no hard-and-fast guidelines that can be given; developers must use their own judgment as to when additional detail will not help find additional defects.

Tailoring Team Composition

A more advanced level of tailoring involves changing the composition of the inspection team. Typically, teams are composed of one member for each perspective, so that all-important aspects of the document are covered by at least one member of the team. As data is collected concerning the effectiveness of a particular set of reading techniques for an organization, it becomes possible to tailor team composition better to larger organizational goals. For example, suppose the customer perspective for requirements review is found to be especially effective for finding defects in which important functionality has been omitted (reviewing from the customers' perspective helps focus on whether all the functionality they expect will be there). Then, organizations which have a history of problems with omitted functionality, or projects for which omitted functionality would be especially problematic, could add extra· reviewers from this perspective to improve the chances that these important issues would be found.

Such tailoring cannot be done without enough measurement having been performed to be able to draw connections between the individual perspectives and their effectiveness for types of defects. For this reason, measurement and a well thought-out defect taxonomy are especially important for improving inspection practices.

9.6   Experiences

This chapter has concentrated on the family of reading techniques for requirements inspections (known as Perspective-Based Reading, or PBR). PBR focuses requirements inspection on catching inconsistent or incorrect requirements before they form the basis for design or implementation, necessitating rework, and on verifying that information is complete and correct enough to support all stakeholders in downstream phases of development.

A number of studies have been run to assess the effectiveness of PBR in comparison to less procedural review techniques. Researchers in the U.S. (Shull, 1998), Norway (Sørumgård, 1997), and Germany (Ciolkowski et al., 1997) have run studies in university classes using over 150 software engineering students to evaluate and evolve the techniques. These students have run the gamut from undergraduates, with little previous review experience, to professionals with over 20 years of experience in industry who were returning for advanced degrees. In 1995 and 1996, studies were run using 25 professional developers from the NASA Goddard Space Flight Center (Basili et al., 1996). These developers were asked first to apply the requirements review technique they used at NASA, then were trained in PBR and asked to apply the new technique to a similar requirements document. In this way, researchers could assess how well these professionals performed using PBR compared with how they performed using their usual review technique.

These studies support the notion that PBR leads to improved rates of defect detection for both individual reviewers and review teams, for unfamiliar application domains. For example, in the 1995 NASA study, teams using PBR to review one document did on average 30% better than teams using their usual approach (finding 62% versus 48% of all defects in the document). For this document, individual reviewers also did significantly better when using

PBR, with a 30% improvement over the non-PBR detection rate. On a second document, on which PBR and non-PBR individual reviewers performed about the same, PBR teams still had a higher effectiveness (finding 8% more of the total defects), perhaps because the use of perspectives reduced overlap between the reviewers. The NASA study also demonstrated that, for a familiar application domain, one danger is that experienced reviewers ignore the PBR procedure and go back to using the heuristics they had previously acquired. For this type of reviewer, training and reinforcement are needed to overcome this tendency.

Another benefit from these studies is that, by observing the use of PBR in a large number of environments and by large numbers of reviewers, researchers better understand the effects of PBR in different contexts and for different types of users. For example, PBR seems best suited to reviewers with a certain range of experience. Reviewers who have previously inspected requirements documents on multiple industrial projects have, over time, typically developed their own approaches, and do not benefit significantly from the introduction of PBR. Reviewers with very low experience (i.e. who have never been trained, or have been trained but never applied their training on a real project) with the relevant work products (e.g. designs or test plans) need to receive sufficient training before they can effectively apply PBR (Shull, 1998). This training seems to be necessary so that the difficulties of creating the representation of the system do not distract from the process of checking for defects.

Reading techniques are procedural guidelines that can be used by reviewers to improve the effectiveness of the individual defect detection phase of software inspections. Typically, reading techniques ask each reviewer of a document to take on the viewpoint of a downstream user of that document, looking for issues that would hinder its use from their perspective. To help keep reviewers focused on their perspective, reading techniques guide the reviewer through a relevant abstraction of the information in the document (e.g. through a set of use cases, for a customer perspective) and provides questions aimed at eliciting defects in that information.

The reading technique approach has been used to develop and refine multiple sets of reading techniques. This text has concentrated on the family of reading techniques for requirements inspections (known as Perspective-Based Reading, or PBR) but the idea has been tailored to other document types as well (Shull, 2002), most recently for high-level Object-Oriented designs (using Object-Oriented Reading Techniques or OORTs).

References

- Basili, V., S. Green, S., O. Laitenberger, F. Lanubile, F. Shull, S. Sørumgård, and M. Zelkowitz (1996), The Empirical Investigation of Perspective-Based Reading, in: *Empirical Software Engineering*, 1996, pp. 133-164.

- BS7925-2 (1998), *Software Component Testing*, British Standards Institution

- Ciolkowski, C., C. Differding, O. Laitenberger, and J. Muench (1997), *Empirical Investigation of Perspective-based Reading: A Replicated Experiment*, Technical Report ISERN-97-13, International Software Engineering Research Network.

- Shull, F. (1998), *Developing Techniques for Using Software Documents: A Series of Empirical Studies*, Diss. Computer Science Department, University of Maryland

- Shull, F. (2002), Software Reading Techniques, in *Encyclopedia of Software Engineering*, ed. John J. Marciniak, John Wiley & Sons.

- Sørumgård, S. (1997), *Verification of Process Conformance in Empirical Studies of Software Development*, Diss. Norwegian University of Science and Technology.

10 Making inspections work

Tom Gilb

Inspection, a proven technique for achieving quality and identifying process improvements, should be applied to documents throughout software development. The greatest value from inspection can be gained through a proper understanding of its purposes and benefits. Newer practices, such as sampling, should be incorporated into the more traditional application of this technique. The full benefit of inspection can be found as it contributes to measurement, exit control, and defect injection prevention. This chapter aims to provide direction on getting the most value from inspections. It will also update readers on new practices, such as sampling.

10.1 Basic definitions

Inspection is a proven technique for achieving quality control of specifications and identifying associated process improvements. In fact, inspection can be applied to any discipline that produces documents. It has been applied with excellent results to hardware engineering, management planning, and sales contract documentation. Software inspections are widely known within the software industry, but most organizations do not make the most of them. This is because many people misunderstand and misinterpret inspection. Often, they assume there is only one inspection method – the 1976 IBM version (Fagan, 1976).

The author's process of inspection consists of two main processes: the defect detection process and the defect prevention process. The *defect detection process* is concerned with document quality, especially identifying and measuring defects in the documentation submitted for inspection and using this information to decide how best to proceed with the main (product) document under inspection.

The *defect prevention process* is concerned with learning from the defects found and suggesting ways of improving processes to prevent them from reoccurring. Note, the causal analysis component of the defect prevention process is not a costly, in-depth examination of all defects; for each inspection, it simply involves brainstorming the reasons and preventive cures for several selected defects. The major part of the defect prevention process involves in-depth process analysis, and it is actually carried out off-line from the normal day-to-day inspection of specific documents.

A *major defect* is a defect that, if not dealt with at the requirements or design stage, will probably have an order-of-magnitude or larger cost to find and fix when it reaches the testing or operational stages. On average, the find-and-fix cost for major defects is one work hour upstream but nine work hours downstream (Gilb and Graham, 1993).

A *page* is a logical page. It is defined as a unit of work on which inspection is performed. A page must be defined as a quantity of noncommentary words (for example, 300 words).

10.2 Benefits and current best practice

Given adequate management support, inspection can quickly be turned from the initial chaos phase (20 or more major defects per page) to relative cleanliness (two or fewer major defects per page at exit) within a year (Mays *et al.*, 1990). A good example is the experience of the British Aerospace Eurofighter Project. In software documentation, more than 20 defects per page were reduced to 1 to 1.5 defects per page within 18 months.

On one pass, the defect detection process can find up to 88 percent of existing major defects in a document (Gilb and Graham, 1993). This is important, but there is actually greater benefit achieved by the teaching effect of inspection feedback. By attending inspections, software engineers go through a rapid learning process, which typically reduces the number of defects they make in their subsequent work by two orders of magnitude within about five inspection experiences, and within a few weeks.

The defect detection process can and should be extended to support continuous process improvement by including the associated defect prevention process. The defect prevention process is capable of at least 50 percent (first year of project) to 70 percent (second or third year) defect cause reduction, and more than 90 percent in the longer term. It has also shown at least 13-to-1 return on investment (ROI) for the ratio of the downstream cost savings of engineering time (rework cost saved by using inspection) compared to the operational cost of carrying out the inspections (Haley *et al.*, 1995), (Kaplan, *et al.*, 1994).

The defect prevention process is the model for the Software Engineering Institute's Capability Maturity Model (SEI CMM) level 5. Robert Mays worked with Ron Radice, who developed the CMM[1] model at IBM. This model was the basis for the SEI model (Radice *et al.*, 1999), (Radice and Phillips, 1988). Radice himself co developed inspection with Michael Fagan (Kohli and Radice, 1976).

Raytheon provides a good case study. In six years, from 1988 to 1994, using the defect detection process combined with the defect prevention process, Raytheon reduced rework costs from about 43 percent to between 5 percent and 10 percent, and, for process improvement, achieved ROI of 7.7-to-1. It improved software code generation productivity by a factor of 2.7-to-1, reduced negative deviation from budget and deadlines from 40 percent to near zero, and reduced defect density by about a factor of three (Haley *et al.*, 1995).

Smaller software producers (30 to 60 programmers) have also experienced major business improvements as a result of using inspection (Holland, 1999).

10.3 Improving inspections

The following sections contain tips for improving the inspection process and achieving the kinds of results cited previously. The tips are grouped under the part of the inspection process they chiefly apply to. Readers should keep in mind that some tips do cover a broader section of the process.

Inspection Strategy

- *Don't misuse Inspection as a clean-up process. Use it to motivate, teach, measure, control quality, and improve processes.*
  Many people think inspection is for cleaning up bad work, embedded faults, and other defects. the greatest payback, however, comes from the improved quality of future work. ensure that the inspection process fully supports the aspects of teaching and continuous process improvement.
  For continuous process improvement, integrate the defect prevention process into conventional inspections. The defect prevention process must be practiced early and should be fully integrated into inspection. CMM level 5 is too important to be put off until later – it needs to be done from the start.

---

1   CMM is a registered trademark of Carnegie Mellon University

- *Use inspection on any technical documentation.*

  Most people think Inspection is about source code inspection. Once one realizes that Inspection is not a clean-up process, it makes sense to use it to measure and validate any technical documentation – even technical diagrams. Requirements and design documentation contribute 40 percent to 60 percent of code defects anyway (Pence and Hon, 1993).

- *Inspect upstream first.*

  By the end of the 1970s, IBM and inspection-method founder, Michael Fagan, recognized that defects, and thus the profitable use of Inspection, actually lie upstream in the requirements and design areas. Bellcore found that 44 percent of all defects were due to defects in requirements and design reaching the programmers (Pence and Hon, 1993). Because systems development starts with contracts and management and marketing plans, the Inspection activity must start there, where the problems originate.

  One of the most misunderstood dictums from early inspections is "No managers present." This is wrong. Managers should only be excluded from Inspection that they would corrupt by their presence. They should not be excluded from Inspection of management-level documents, such as requirements or contracts. Nor should they be excluded if they are trying to experience the method with a view to supporting it. Having managers take part in Inspections is a great way to get their understanding and support. "No managers present" is a rule from the past when IBM was doing source code inspections.

- *Make sure there are excellent standards to identify defective practices.*

  Inspection requires that good work standards (Juran, 1995) be in place. Standards provide the rules for the author when writing technical documents and for the Inspection process to subsequently check against. An example of a simple, powerful generic rule is "specifications must be unambiguous to the intended readership and testably clear." Violation of this rule is a defect.

  Standards must be built by hard experience; they must be brief and to the point, monitored for usefulness, and respected by the troops. They must not be built by outside consultants or dictated by management. They must be seen as the tool to enforce the necessary lessons of professional practice on the unwary or unwilling.

- *Give inspection team leaders (moderators) proper training, coaching after initial training, certification, statistical follow-up, and, if necessary, remove their "license" to inspect.*

  Proper training of team leaders takes about a week (half lectures and half practice). Experience shows that less than this is not adequate. Inspection team leader certification (an entry condition to an inspection) should be similar in concept to that for pilots, drivers, and doctors – based on demonstrated competence after training. Note, at present there is no industry-recognized license or certification standard for inspection.

Team leaders, who will not professionally carry out the job, even if it is because their supervisor wants them to cut corners, should have their "licenses" revoked. Professional inspection team leadership must be taken seriously so that checkers will take inspection seriously. Ensure that there are enough trained inspection team leaders to support Inspections within an organization – at least 20 percent of all professionals. Some clients train all their engineers on a one-week team leader course.

Entry Conditions

- *Use serious entry conditions, such as minimum level of numeric quality of source documents.*

  Lack of discipline and lack of respect for entry conditions wastes time. One of the most important entry conditions is mandating the use of upstream source documents to help inspect a product document. It is a mistake to try to use the experts' memory abilities (instead of updated, inspection-exited source documents). It is also a mistake to use source documents with the usual uncontrolled, uninspected, unexited, 20-or-more major defects per page to check a product document (The figure "20 or more" comes from the author's experience over several years. In fact, from 20 up to 150 major defects per page is not uncommon in environments where Inspection is new).

  It is not a good idea for the author to generate a product document using a poor quality source document. It is easy to check the state of a source document by using inexpensive sampling. A half-day or less on a few pages is a small price to pay to ensure the quality of a document. Another serious entry condition is carrying out a cursory check on the product document and returning it to the author if it has too many remaining defects. For example, if while planning the Inspection, the team leader performs a 15-minute cursory check that reveals a few major defects on a single page, it is time for a word with the author in private. If necessary, pretend the document was never seriously submitted. Do not waste the Inspection team's time to try to approve shoddy work.

  In short, learn which entry conditions have to be set and take them seriously. Management needs to take a lead on this. It is often managers who are actually responsible for overriding the entry criteria. For example, carrying out an inspection is often mistakenly seen as fulfilling a quality process (regardless of the Inspection results). Managers have been known to demand that Inspections proceed even when a team leader has determined that the entry condition concerning majors per page is violated.

Planning

- *Plan inspections well using a formal review process form.*
  Use the one-page review process form with all relevant information rather than the conventional invitation. Document the many supporting documents needed, assign checkers special defect-searching roles, and carefully manage the rates of checking and the total checking time needed. Establish the formal purpose(s) of each specific inspection – they do vary. Ensure a team numeric stretch goal is established and that there is a specific strategy to help attain it. A well-used process form avoids senseless bureaucracy and lays the groundwork for intelligent inspections.
- *Plan inspection to address the inspection purposes.*
  There are more than 20 distinct purposes for using inspection, including document quality, removing defects, job training, motivation, helping a document author, improving productivity, and reducing maintenance costs. Each inspection will address several of these purposes to varying degrees. Be aware which purposes are valid for a specific inspection and formally plan to address them (that is, by choosing checkers with relevant skills and giving them appropriate checking roles).

1. Reducing time to delivery	11. Training the team leader
2. Measuring document quality	12. Certifying the team leader
3. Measuring the quality of the process producing the document	13. Peer motivation
	14. Motivating the managers
4. Enabling estimation of the number of remaining defects	15. Helping the author
	16. Reinforcing conformance to standards
5. Identifying defects	
6. Removing defects	17. Capturing and reusing expert knowledge (by use of rules and checklists)
7. Preventing additional downstream defects being generated by removing existing defects	
	18. Reducing costs
8. Improving the document production process	19. Team building
	20. Fun – a social occasion
9. Improving the inspection process	
10. On-the-job training for the checkers	Note: This list is not necessarily complete.

Figure 10.1: Purposes for inspection

- *Inspect early and often while documents are still being written.*
  Leaving inspection until after a large technical document is finished is a bad idea. If the process that generates the document is faulty, discover it early and fix it. This saves time and corrects bad processes before they cause too much damage. This is one form of sampling.
- *Use sampling to understand the quality level of a document.*
  It is neither necessary nor desirable to check all pages of long documents.

Representative samples should provide enough information to decide whether a document is clean enough for exit, for example, "0.2 major defects per page maximum remaining".

The main purpose of inspection is economic – to reduce lead time and people costs caused by downstream defects. As in Harlan Mills' IBM "clean room" method (Mills and Linger, 1987), defects should be cleaned up or avoided using disciplines such as Watts Humphrey's Personal Software Process (PSP) (Humphrey, 1995), structured programming (Mills, 1972), (Mills and Linger, 1987), defect prevention/continuous improvement (Gilb and Graham, 1993), inspection, and verification. If all this works as it should, cleaning is unnecessary and sampling provides the information to decide if it is economically safe to release the document. Perfection is not required; it costs infinite resources and is dangerous as a guiding concept.

- *Use an optimum number of people on a team to serve the current purpose of inspection, for example, effectiveness, efficiency, and training.*
  For 13 years, one large U. S. telecommunications company had 12 to 15 people on each inspection team because each person "had" to be sent there to protect territorial interests. There seemed to be no motivation to cut these costs.

  The number of people needed on an inspection team is a function of the inspection purposes. By measuring inspection experiences, it has been established that best effectiveness at finding major defects uses four to six people; best efficiency (effect over cost) needs two to four people; and only 'teaching as a purpose' justifies larger numbers (Kelly, 1990), (Weller, 1993). The results of varying team sizes should be monitored within an organization to discover the optimum for a given document type.

- *Allocate special defect-searching roles to people on the team.*
  Each person on an inspection team should be finding different defects. Much like a coach on a ball team, the inspection team leader should assign specialist roles to team members (for example, identify time and money risks, check against corporate standards for engineering documentation, and check security loopholes) when planning the inspection. Special role checklists help people know exactly what to look for.

Individual preparation

- *Check against source and kin documents; check them for defects, too.*
  Because of potentially poor quality control practices and craftsmanship, and because inspection is imperfect on first pass (30 percent to 88 percent effective) (Gilb and Graham, 1993), one must focus on the major defects that still persist in source and kin documents. Source documents are input documents used as upstream engineering process inputs to produce the product document being evaluated for possible exit. Kin documents are

documents derived from the same source documents as the product document. For example, a requirements document can be a source document and used to produce a design specification (a product document) that requires inspection. Associated kin documentation to consider, including in the inspection, would be the testing specification.

Most people over focus on the product document. In fact, the aim should be to find roughly 25 percent of the total defects external to the product document, mainly in source documents, even when they have exited with no more than one major defect per page.

- *Check the significant portions of the material – avoid checking commentary.*
  Most organizations waste time checking nonsignificant document areas. It is a waste of checker energy to check at optimum rates to uncover minor defects with no downstream savings. It is necessary to go at optimum rates to find the major defects but ensure that time is not wasted at those rates (one logical page of 300 noncommentary words checked per hour plus or minus 0.9 logical pages is the expected optimum checking rate range). The result of indiscriminate checking of trivia at an optimum rate could be 90 percent minor defects and 90 percent waste of time. It is equivalent to checking comments for 90 percent of the time instead of real code.

  From practical experience, it pays to have a general specification rule that technical authors must distinguish between noncommentary and commentary text (or diagrams). Noncommentary (or "meat") text is text where any defects might translate into serious downstream costs (that is, major defects could be found). Commentary (or "fat") text can only contain minor defects and so is less important.

  The distinction between "meat" and "fat" can be achieved, for example, by using italics for the fat. Some clients have even created Microsoft Word macros to count the volume of noncommentary text (nonitalics) and print the logical page count on the first page (Holland, 1999). Of course, the checker is allowed to scan and reference the commentary words but is not obliged to check them against all sources, rules, and checklists; it is not worth it.

- *Define a major defect as "possible larger costs downstream".*
  It does not matter if a defect is not precisely a nonconformance or if it is visible to a customer. If it could lead to significant costs if it escapes downstream, classify it as a major defect, and treat it with due respect.

  Note major and minor defects after the checklist questions or rule statement. It is often useful to indicate criticals. These are defects where the downstream effect could be an order of magnitude bigger than an average major, which is about nine hours downstream loss average. Criticals are also called super majors or showstoppers and can be highlighted for management attention.

  Concentrate on the major defects. This helps avoid the "90 percent minor syndrome" that often hampers inspection. As mentioned previously, employees will waste time identifying 90 percent minor defects, unless strongly redirected. There are at least 18 different tactics that shift the focus from minor to major defects (see figure 10.2). For example, using checklists

1. Plan special roles with special role checklists that only ask questions directed at major defects.

2. Teach at kick-off meeting that the search for majors is primary.

3. Hand out checker procedures that define the fact that majors are the primary concern.

4. Use rule sets that for approximately 19 out of 20 rules are identifying major defects.

5. Limit rule sets and checklists to a maximum of one page. This has the effect of squeezing trivial ideas "off the page," as soon as higher priority major defect identification rules, task activities, and checklist questions are gradually identified.

6. Identify the probable classification of an issue identified in a checklist question next to the question itself as major or minor.

7. Ask checkers to do their own personal classification of major/minor during the checking activity.

8. Ask checkers to report (at the bottom of the inspection-plan form) how many issues they found during checking in the various severity categories. This is done orally with the team. Those who report numerous issues categorized as minors and few as majors will feel motivated to do better next time.

9. Have checkers always state orally "major" or "minor" when they report an issue to be logged at the "public" logging meeting. It's embarrassing to constantly cite "minor" when others are stating "major."

10. Calculate inspection "return on time invested" based on major defects found, never on minors.

11. State numeric inspection team process improvement objectives in terms of major defects per page and per hour. Never have it a team objective to get better at finding minor defects.

12. Never discuss the root causes of minor defects at the causal analysis meeting. Only majors are worth discussing.

13. When time for logging is particularly short, report only major defects. If time permits, allow the reporting of minors and formally log them.

14. Report only a symbolic sample of minors, for example, on a single page. The rest, if checkers have notes of them, can be handed informally to the editor. They are simply not worth more formal treatment or priority.

15. If editing time is under pressure, only major defects might actually be fixed.

16. If edit audit has an overwhelming number of things to check, then the leader would take majors seriously and skim over the minors, perhaps looking at a sample only.

17. Report inspection statistics to management based only on major defects.

18. Determine optimum rates of checking that ignore minors and use only majors found per hour per page as the basis for calculation of rates.

Note: This list is not necessarily complete.

Figure 10.2: List of tactics to encourage checkers to focus on critical and major defects

can help people identify majors rather than minors. The checklist contents should aim to detect majors and not minors. (Note: checklists are only allowed to help interpret the rules, which are an organization's official standards for writing a given document, and which define what constitute defects).

Another useful tactic is to log only majors at a meeting and calculate the ROI for inspections only on the basis of the majors. This sends a clear message not to waste time on minor defects.

- *Check at an organization's optimum (coverage) checking rates to find major defects.*

This is the big one. Most people, including many teachers of inspection, manage to miss this point. Or worse, they recommend checking rates that are 10 times optimum speed (Kelly, 1990), (Haley *et al.*, 1995). Optimum checking rate is not a reading rate. Checking in real inspections involves checking a page against all related documents. This can involve up to 10 or 20 individual documents; these are source documents of large size, checklists, and standards. The requirement is to check a single product document line against many sources, and it takes time.

Adequate inspection statistics can prove that an organization's employees have a clear, dramatic, and consistent optimum checking rate on specific document types. The expected optimum checking rate range is between 0.2 and 1.8 pages of 300 noncommentary words per checking hour. For example, at Raytheon it was about 20 plus or minus 10 lines per hour (0.3 pages) (Haley *et al.*, 1995). Unfortunately, in spite of its own data, Raytheon suggested rates of about 100 to 250 lines per hour. This was probably because it had finite deadlines and did not understand sampling. Figure 10.2 is a diagram from the Raytheon Report (Haley, 1995). It shows that their optimum checking rate is probably about 10 to 20 statements per hour for an individual checker.

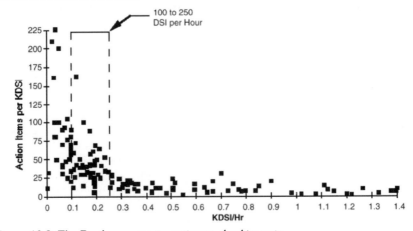

Figure 10.3: The Raytheon report - optimum checking rate

As the checking speed moves toward an optimum speed for effectiveness of finding major defects, the curve for optimum checking rate moves dramatically upward in terms of major defects identified per logical page. The optimum may seem slow, but considering the amount of checking that has to be done, it is fast. The point is that there is a best speed at which to check, and an organization could easily be operating at only 1 percent of defect identification effectiveness if it fails to heed it.

Note that the optimum checking rate applies both to the checking carried out during the individual checking phase (also known as preparation) and to the optional checking carried out during the logging meeting. This second logging-meeting check will produce roughly an additional 15 percent defects (Arksey, 1989). In fact, there is no need to carry out this extra checking if the document is found to be clean enough to exit as a result of initial checking sampling, or if it is so polluted that a major rewrite is required anyway. It is only useful in clean-up mode.

- *Use the individual checkers' personal notes instead of proper meeting defect logs when the major-issue density is (non-exit level) high, or when there are many minor defects.*

Checkers should not be required to use any particular method to make notes during the checking process. In practice, most checkers choose to mark the defective words on a paper document, using underlines, circles, or highlights. Some use electronic notes. It is important that they note, against the defective words, exactly which rule was broken (the issue). A note classifying subjective decisions as to severity (major or minor) of the issue is also required.

Whenever there are more issues than would allowable for exit level, it is suggested that, with author agreement, the notes made during individual checking (sometimes known as 'scratchings') be simply handed over to the author. This is better than pedantically logging all the issues. In such situations, authors must rewrite and resubmit their documents, and they might as well use the rough checking information to correct their work. The usual problem leading to a high defect density is that the author fails to take sources and rules sufficiently seriously.

Logging meeting

- *Decide whether it is worth holding a logging meeting, based on checking phase data.*

Use checking phase data that are collected at the beginning of a logging meeting or beforehand (such as pages checked, majors found, time used, and checking rate) from individual checkers to decide whether it is worth holding a logging meeting. Less mature inspections plunge into the logging meeting without forethought and consequently waste time. A process of logging meeting entry evaluation must be carried out before holding a logging meeting. To do this, collect the data from the checkers about their checking rates and major issue density (Note, to avoid personal conflict, issues – not defects – are logged during the logging meeting. An issue may or may not become a defect, as judged by the responsible product document editor later). Based on this checking-phase data, make a series of decisions about the logging meeting and the rest of inspection. The most critical decision is whether a meeting is necessary. Other decisions include whether to log minors and whether to continue checking. Shutting down the rest of the inspection entirely is also a possibility.

- *At logging meetings, avoid discussions and suggesting fixes.*
  Inspection is not for talkers and quibblers – it is for professionals committed to making maximum, meaningful progress on the project. It is important to have a good time but not by detailed technical discussion, idle gossip, or insults.

Causal analysis

- *Use the defect prevention process on inspection itself for continuous improvement.*
  Recognize that systematic continuous improvement of the inspection process is necessary. Initially, this is required not only to improve the inspection process but also to learn to implement the correct inspection process and tailor it to the organization.

Exit criteria

- *Use serious exit criteria.*
  Exit criteria, if correctly formulated and taken seriously, can be crucial. An example of an exit is "the maximum probable remaining major defects per page is 0.2 for exit". It is wrong to have the customary vote to accept a document once the logged defects are fixed, because this ignores the known factor of the number of remaining unfound defects (a value that is computable and verifiable from past data and experience).
  Remember that inspection processes, like other testing processes, have a maximum effectiveness for a single pass in the range of 30 percent to 88 percent of existing defects. If the maximum probable remaining defect density is a high-quality low count, such as 0.2 majors per page, then it does not matter much if the detected defects are removed at this stage; the document is clean enough (economically speaking) to exit without fixing them. It is probably better to catch them later.
  If defect density is high, for example, 20 or more majors per page (quite common), the undetected defects, at say 50 percent effectiveness, are more

than enough to make exit uneconomical. If there are 10 majors remaining per page in a 100-page document, there are an expected 9 x 10 x 100 hours of additional project work to clean them up by testing and discovery in the field. It costs an order of magnitude less to find them now. Admittedly, this situation is only the lesser of two evils. Ideally they should have been prevented in the first place using the defect prevention process rather than being cleaned up, even if at an earlier stage than test, using the defect detection process. Management must understand the large-scale economics of this and take action to make clear policy about the levels of major defects per page that will be allowed to escape.

Inspection metrics

- *Build or buy an automated software tool to process inspection basic data.*
  Use automated software to capture data-summary data and to present trends and reports. Inspection generates a lot of useful data. It is vital that good computer support be given early, so the process owners and management take the data seriously and the early champions are not overwhelmed.
  The key distinction between inspections and other review processes is the use of data to manage inspections. For example, the optimum checking rates must be established early and updated as they change, through continuous improvement. It also is vital to statistically see the consequences of inadequate exit levels (too many major defects floating downstream), which then must be caught with expensive testing processes.
- *Put inspection artifacts on a company web site.*
  If an organization has an intranet, all relevant inspection artifacts, standards, experiences, statistics, and problems should be added as soon as possible.
- *Measure the benefit from using inspections.*
  Inspection should always be highly profitable, for example, 10-to-1 ROI. If not, then it is time to adjust the inspection process or to stop it. Benefits to be measured include rework costs, predictability, productivity, document quality, and ROI (Haley *et al.*, 1995). Inspection profitability must be evaluated for each type of specification individually. In general, the upstream inspections (requirements, contracts, bids) will be the most profitable.

The art of inspection has progressed considerably since it was first publicly documented by IBM. It has shifted focus from clean up to sampling, measurement, exit control, and defect injection prevention. By taking the technical points that made inspection strong at IBM and elsewhere and combining them with the recent process improvements, inspection will continue to be a powerful software process tool. Ignoring the process improvements makes it likely that one will end up with a costly failure of a process.

References

- Arksey, C. (1989), *Fagan method pilot*, final report, Internal Technical Report, Boeing, Seattle

- Fagan, M. (1976), Design and code inspections to reduce errors in program development, in: *IBM Systems Journal*, Vol. 15, no. 3: 182-211 (Reprinted in IBM Systems Journal 38, no. 2: 259-287).

- Gilb, T. and D. Graham (1993), *Software Inspection*, Adison-Wesley, London, ISBN 0-201-63181-4

- Haley, T., B. Ireland, E. Wojtaszek, D. Nash, and R. Dion. (1995), *Raytheon electronic systems experience in software process improvement*, (CMU/SEI-95-TR-017), Software Engineering Institute, Carnegie Mellon University, Pittsburgh, USA

- Holland, D. (1999), Document inspection as an agent of change, in: *Software Quality Professional*, pp. 22-33, December 1999

- Humphrey, W.S. (1995), *A discipline for software engineering*, Addison-Wesley, New York, ISBN 0-201-54610-8

- Juran, J.M. (1995), *Managerial breakthrough: the classic book on improving management performance*, McGraw-Hill, London, ISBN 0-07-034037-4

- Kaplan, C., R. Clark, and V. Tang (1994), *Secrets of software quality: 40 innovations from IBM*, McGraw Hill, New York

- Kelly, J.C. (1990), An analysis of Jet Propulsion Laboratory's two year experience with software inspections, in: *Proceedings of the Minnowbrook Workshop on Software Engineering*, Blue Lake, NY, USA

- Kelly, J. (1990), An analysis of defect density found during software inspection, in: *Proceedings of 15th Annual Software Engineering Workshop*, (NASA SEL-90-006), Jet Propulsion Labs, Pasadena, California, USA

- Kohli, O.R., and R.A. Radice (1976), *Low-level design inspection specification*, IBM Technical Report (TR 21.629), Armonk, IBM, NY, USA

- Mays, R.G., C.L. Jones, G.J. Holloway and D.P. Studinski, (1990), Experiences with Defect Prevention in: *IBM Systems Journal*, 29 (1), 4-32, 1990

- Mills, D., and Linger (1987), Cleanroom software engineering, in: *IEEE Software*, pp. 19-25, September 1987

- Mills, H.D. (1972), *Mathematical foundations for structured programming*, (FSC 71-6012), IBM Corporation Federal Systems Division, Bethesda, Md

- Paulk, M.C., C.V. Weber, B. Curtis and M.B. Chrissis (1993), *The Capability Maturity Model; Guideline for Improving the Software Process*, Addison-Wesley Publishing Company

- Pence, J.L.P., and S.E. Hon III. (1993), Building software quality into telecommunications network systems, in: *Quality Progress*, pp. 95-97, October, 1993

- Radice, R.A., J.T. Harding, P.E. Munnis, and R.W. Philips (1999), A programming process study, in: *IBM System Journals* 2 and 3.

- Radice, R.A. and R.W. Phillips (1988), *Software engineering, an industrial approach*, vol. 1, Englewood Cliffs, Prentice Hall

- Weller, E.F. (1993), Lessons from three years of inspection data, in: *IEEE Software*, pp. 38-45, September, 1993.

Part 4

Test techniques

11 Static Analysis[1]

Les Hatton

There is much to be done examining system artifacts without actually running the system. For example, we saw in the previous chapters that we can carefully review requirements, designs, code, test plans and more, to find faults and fix them before we deliver a product to a customer. In this chapter, we focus on a different kind of review, where we carefully examine designs and code, usually with some automated assistance, to ferret out additional problems before the code is actually run. Thus, what we call static analysis is just another form of testing. Static analysis is an examination of design and code that differs from more traditional testing in a number of important ways:

- *Static analysis is performed on a design or code without execution.*
- *Static analysis is performed before the kinds of peer reviews discussed in chapter 8.*
- *Static analysis is unrelated to dynamic properties of the design and code, such as test coverage.*
- *The goal of static analysis is to find faults, whether or not they may cause failures.*

Let us look more closely at the nature of static analysis, to see why it is essential for building solid software.

11.1 Static fault versus dynamic failure

Static analysis is called "static" because there is no actual run-time behavior involved. That is, examining the code, either by eye or with a tool, with two goals in mind. First, as with reviews, the nature of the design or code is studied to see if there is something clearly amiss, such as a reference to a non-existent item. In this sense, reviews are a form of static code analysis. Second, tools and

---

1   This chapter by Les Hatton is based on chapter 8 from the book "Solid Software", by Pfleeger, Hatton and Howel © 2001 reprinted by permission of Pearson Education, Inc.

techniques are used to examine characteristics of the design or code, to see if some of these characteristics warn us that the design or code may be faulty. For example, looking at the levels of nesting; a large number may warn us that the code is difficult to understand or maintain.

In addressing both goals, the design or code are intellectually interpreted and it is decided that the predicted behavior is inconsistent with our understanding of what the program will actually do at run-time. As we noted in chapter 1, this mismatch in behavior is a software fault. Because no verifcation (by running the program or enacting the design) that the behavior is incorrect is taking place, it is assumed that the observations are correct. Of course, there is always a possibility that they are wrong, based on incorrect understanding of what the system is supposed to do or an incorrect assessment of what the code should be doing. For this reason, and especially for solid software, static analysis is used in concert with other techniques. By contrast, in dynamic analysis the program is actually run and an observation is made on what happens. If the program exhibits behavior different from that which was expected, this is called a software failure. Failures are often easier to identify, in that it is generally obvious when the system has breached a fundamental requirement for its behavior.

11.2 When faults cause failures

It is very important to distinguish faults from failures and to understand the relationship between the two. The ultimate goal in building solid software is to make it reliable and dependable—that is, at best to try to keep the software from failing, and at least to make sure that if the software fails, it does so in a way that does no physical, environmentalor financial harm. So it is essential to remember that every failure is the result of one or more faults. But in practice, it can be exceptionally difficult to figure out which faults are responsible when a system fails. This diagnostic problem is generally getting worse as systems become more complex (Hatton, 1999). It would seem that the easiest solution to this problem is to eliminate all faults. But of course not all faults cause failures during the life-cycle of the code. In fact, the number of failure-causing faults is actually significantly smaller than the number of all faults in a typical piece of code; this relationship is depicted in figure 11.1.

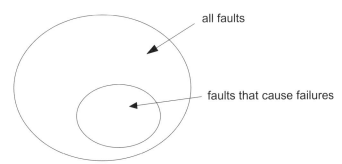

Figure 11.1: The relationship between fault and failure

To see why, consider a few lines of a program that are unreachable. One may think this a silly example, but experience shows that unreachable code occurs far more often than we would like to admit. This piece of code could be full of faults, but it would be impossible for any to lead to a system failure because the lines are never executed. For a less trivial example, consider the inertial reference system of the Ariane-4 rocket. It never failed in Ariane-4, but when re-used in the Ariane-5 rocket, it led to the rocket's destruction, (Lions, 1996), As this example shows, sometimes faults are latent, causing failures only when certain conditions are met - conditions that occurred for Ariane-5 but not for Ariane-4. The notion of latency was explored in some depth by Adams (1984) at IBM. He examined data for nine operating systems software products, each with many thousands of years of logged use world-wide. His data, shown in table 11.1, related detected faults to their manifestation as observed failures. For example, the table shows that for product 4, 11.9% of all known faults led to failures that occur on average every 160 to 499 years of use. That is, for this class of faults, one would have to use the product for at least 160 years before the faults would cause the product to fail.

Product	1.6 years	5 years	16 years	50 years	160 years	500 years	1600 years	5000 years
1	0.7	1.2	2.1	5.0	10.3	17.8	28.8	34.2
2	0.7	1.5	3.2	4.5	9.7	18.2	28.0	34.3
3	0.4	1.4	2.8	6.5	8.7	18.0	28.5	33.7
4	0.1	0.3	2.0	4.4.	11.9	18.7	28.5	34.2
5	0.7	1.4	2.9	4.4	9.4	18.4	28.5	34.2
6	0.3	0.8	2.1	5.0	11.5	20.1	28.2	32.0
7	0.6	1.4	2.7	4.5	9.9	18.5	28.5	34.0
8	1.1	1.4	2.7	6.5	11.1	18.4	27.1	31.9
9	0.0	0.5	1.9	5.6	12.8	20.4	27.6	31.2

Table 11.1: Adams data: Fitted percentage defects - mean time to problem occurrence in years

In fact, Adams discovered that about a third of all detected faults led to the "least frequent" types of failures, namely those that required on average at least 5000 years of run-time to fail. Conversely, a small number of faults (less than 2%) caused the most common failures, namely those occurring at least once every 5 years of use. In other words, a very small proportion of the faults in a system can lead to most of the observed failures in a given period of time. Conversely, most faults in a system are benign, in the sense that in the same given period of time they will not lead to failures. A summary of the data is shown in figure 11.2, which classifies faults by their mean time to failure.

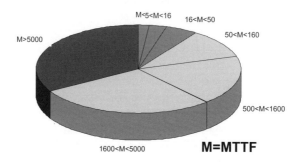

Figure 11.2: Adams' data, with faults classified by mean time to failure

The Adams data show that some products with a very large number of faults can in fact fail very rarely, if at all. This relationship is easy to see in figure 11.3, an alternative depiction of the Adams data. Ordinarily, such products would be called "high quality", since they are reliable - they rarely fail. That is, our notion of quality is not based on fault counts or fault density but instead on lack of failure. So the usual approach to quality, finding faults and fixing them, may not actually lead to improved reliability. And using fault rate or fault density as a predictor may be misleading; the code may be better than we think!

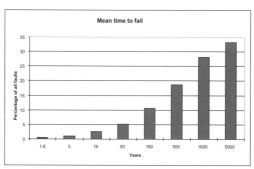

Figure 11.3: Adams' data, showing length of time for fault to be manifested as failure

11.3 Early versus late detection

Even if we think that failure data is a better indicator of quality than fault data, we cannot wait until the product is finished to see if it is any good. So both both static and dynamic analysis are used to get a snapshot of quality at different times. Static analysis is applied at a much earlier stage of development than dynamic analysis. By definition, dynamic analysis can be carried out only when enough of the product has appeared to allow it to be compiled, linked and executed in various test scenarios. A great advantage of static analysis is that it can start very early and applied with varying degrees of tool support, from requirements capture all the way to their implementation as source code.

Why do static analysis as early as possible? Simply because it is much cheaper to detect faults early than late. The dramatic difference in cost can take people by surprise. Figure 11.4 illustrates the relative cost to fix a fault during the development process compared with the cost of fixing it in the requirements stage of the life cycle. The chart, from Boehm (1981), contains two curves, one with a smaller slope for systems where failures have low cost of failure, and one with a steeper slope where failures have high cost of failure. Note that systems requiring solid software, such as embedded control systems, tend to follow the high curve.

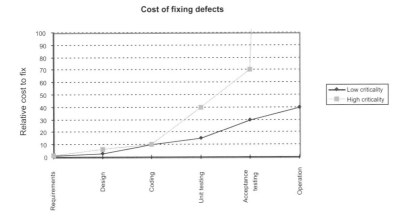

Figure 11.4: Cost escalation of fixing a fault as a function of development stage at which it is discovered (Boehm, 1981)

Thus, there is a strong financial incentive for finding faults and fixing them early in the process. Even if several faults are found and fixed that might not have become failures, we are still ahead of the game by finding one early and avoid a substantial increase in cost. In other words, "an ounce of prevention is worth a pound of cure."

11.4 Measurement for static analysis

When performing static code analysis, usually information is calculated about structural attributes of the code, such as depth of nesting, number of spanning paths, cyclomatic number, number of lines of code, and unreachable statements. This information can be computed not only as the design and code are being created but also as changes are made changes to a system, to see if the design or code is becoming bigger, more complex and more difficult to understand and maintain. The measurements also help us to decide among several design alternatives, especially when redesigning portions of existing code.

There are many different kinds of structural measures, each of which tells us something about the effort required to write the code in the first place, to understand the code when making a change, or to test the code using particular tools or techniques. It is often assume that a large module takes longer to specify, design, code and test than a smaller one. But in fact the code's structure plays a big part.

There are several aspects of code structure to consider:
• control flow structure
• data flow structure
• data structure.

The control flow addresses the sequence in which the instructions are executed. This aspect of structure reflects the iterations and loops in a program's design. If only the size of a program is measured, no information is provided on how often an instruction is executed as it is run.

Data flow follows the trail of a data item as it is accessed and modified by the code. Many times, the transactions applied to data are more complex than the instructions that implement them. Thus, using data flow measures it is shown how the data act as they are transformed by the program.

Data structure refers to the organization of the data themselves, independent of the program. When data are arranged as lists, queues, stacks or other well-defined structures, the algorithms for creating, modifying or deleting them are more likely to be well-defined, too. Thus, the data structure provide much information about the difficulty in writing programs to handle the data, and in designing test cases to show program correctness. That is, sometimes a program is complex because it has a complex data structure, rather than because of complex control or data flow.

Fenton and Pfleeger (1997) discuss static code measures in great detail. The important thing for you as a tester is to be aware that you can ask for many of these measures as early warning signals of how good the code is likely to be when it is finished. A tester can ask to see measures of:

- *problem complexity* to understand the complexity of the underlying problem that is being solved
- *algorithmic complexity* to understand the efficiency of the solution implemented by the software.
- *structural complexity*, as noted above, to see how the code structure affects overall quality
- *cognitive complexity*, to understand the effort that is likely to be required to understand and maintain the software.

Table 11.2 lists examples of these kinds of measures.

Type of measure	Examples
Problem complxity	Number of requirements, lines of code, function points
Algorithmic complexity	$O(n)$, $O(n^2)$, $O(\log n)$, number of comparisons
Structural complexity	
- Control flow	Depth of nesting, cyclomatic number
- Data flow	Mumber of transformations
- Data structure	Number of data items, number of links
Cognitive complexity	Gunning' fog index (applied to written text)

Table 11.2: Example static measures

11.5 Coverage: how much is enough?

How do we know how much static analysis to do? Coverage of static analysis means how much of the system has been analyzed. Because static analysis is independent of execution issues, this notion of coverage has nothing to do with concepts like test coverage, a dynamic issue. However, test coverage is a good model for the thinking about the thoroughness of static analysis. Test coverage is, because testing needs to be able to say things like, "We have tested ten percent of this program," or "We have exercised fifty percent of all paths." So testing measures at a very crude level to determine how many of the functions present in a system are exercised. At a finer level of granularity, discussion takes place refering to statement coverage or various kinds of decision coverage. However, Myers (1979) notes that many noble coverage goals, such as loop and path coverage, to all intents and purposes are unachievable in any reasonable time. That is, there are serious trade-offs between test coverage and business needs: getting the product out the door.

This tension means in essence that a program can never be exhaustively tested dynamically. Unfortunately, some significant amount of the program is delivered to the customer without having been tested as thoroughly as we would like.

Static analysis suffers from the same problem but in a rather different way. In this case, coverage relates to how much of the source code and design have been analyzed, and to what depth. These issues are very different from those in dynamic analysis. In static analysis, failure to cover part of the system adequately is essentially a management or an educational issue. In dynamic analysis, failure to cover parts of the system is an architectural issue strongly related to the ability of the test engineers to design suitable test cases. Static and dynamic testing must be designed and organised to deliver a system that has been evaluated enough to meet the contractual and ethical needs (remember, this may be software whose failure could kill or maim a person or a business), but not so much as to exceed the business needs (and put the company or jobs in jeopardy).

11.6 Approaches to static analysis

Many techniques classify as static analysis, since they share the property that the code is not actually executed. In addition to design or code review, walkthrough or inspection, also the extraction of any static property of the code is considered, such as its component calling tree, to be a form of static analysis.

Static analysis of designs

Much as we would like to use sophisticated design techniques and uniform notations (much as music is written in the same notation worldwide), in fact design techniques and notations vary dramatically, even within a single project. The design process itself is very creative, much more art than engineering in many ways. So usually designers are allowed to create and document their designs in whatever way suits them; we do not want to sacrifice creativity and originality to formalism and rigidity.

However, this lack of uniformity and formality means that it is no easy to do static design analysis. Even when projects use a formal approach to design, it is subject to the dozens of design methodologies and related measurements. It is very difficult to calibrate design measures across design techniques; automation is variable, and often the nomenclature of static design analysis is particular to a project. It seems that the only thing static analysis has in common for designs is an intrinsic belief in the view that "all bugs are shallow to enough eyeballs". Fortunately, this statement seems to be true (Hatton, 1997), and the previous chapters showed that there is ample evidence that reviews can be very effective.

Source code is much more standardized than design, and it is easier to define relationships between code expressed one way and code expressed in another. Witness, for example, tools that translate code from one language to another. Thus, for the remainder of this chapter, the concentration is on static code analysis. Static code analysis is examined from two perspectives: using automated tools, and manual inspection.

Using automation to find code faults

There are many tools to support static code analysis, including those that calculate many of the static code measures mentioned earlier. The tools can show not only numbers, such as depth of nesting or cyclomatic number, but also graphic depictions of control flow, data relationships, and number of distinct paths from one line of code to another. Even the compiler can be considered a static analysis tool, since it builds a symbol table and points out some incorrect and inconsistent usage.

In fact, engineers often rely on the compiler, and on programming standards in general, to find many faults. Indeed, for many programs, they rush to compile the code so that the nastiest or most obvious faults are eliminated automatically. So it may be a surprise to learn that compilers are not really reliable in this way. Programming languages, even those standardized by hard-working standardization committees, are a rich source of statically detectable faults. Here is why:
- programming languages contain well-known fault modes
- these faults are often missed during testing and so appear in released products
- then the products fail.

These concerns will be addressed in order.

Programming languages contain well-known fault modes
There are two reasons why programming languages contain well-known fault modes: politics and mistakes. As a tester, you know how politics can be a formidable force in any organization. Consider then the politics involved in a standards committee. With 40 or 50 people on such a committee, it is very, very difficult to get their necessary agreement to standardize an aspect of a language. Indeed, complete agreement is almost never reached, so ISO

committees resolve an issue or aspect in a standard if as few as 75 percent are in favor of it. As a result, all programming languages contain holes resulting from one of the following:
- the standard is so badly written as to be confusing
- the standard doesn't say anything at all
- the standard is inconsistent.

Some languages are worse than others, but all have problems. In addition, the language standardization process itself is inherently flawed. The essence of incremental improvement in engineering is the recognition of failure modes and their subsequent elimination. Unfortunately, standardization does not usually lead to fewer failure modes, because standards committees are always very willing to add new features. In fact, most modern programming languages grow substantially when they are re-standardized. For example, compare Fortran 77 with Fortran 90 and its later incarnation, Fortran 95; each one is significantly bigger than its predecessor. This enthusiastic experimentation with a language is not necessarily a bad thing; sometimes the committees add capabilities that lead to ease of use (of the language) or more protection from known problems. However, the new features leave the language open for new problems. Moreover, another feature that characterizes standards committees is their requirement for preserving "backwards compatibility": the notion that programs that worked for previous versions of the standard must still work in the new version. The combination of these two goals, capability expansion and backwards compatibility, creates a lethal cocktail. Backwards compatibility sanctions the idea that breaking existing code is an unforgivable sin. Hence, the new standard gives us a mechanism for injecting experimental features into a programming language but no comparably efficient mechanism for removing the significant number that are found to be inappropriate or simply wrong. (One could consider using obsolescence as a mechanism, but in practice it proves to be almost useless.)

To see that this is not an exaggerating regarding the vulnerability of upgraded languages, consider the programming language C as an example. C is the result of the classic formula for success in software engineering: the efforts of a small number of very able people. Originally created in the 1970s, C is a programming language of enduring appeal; today it is the dominant force in embedded programmable control systems. The genesis of the C standard (first ISO C90 9899:1990 and recently ISO C99 9899:1999) is typical of the way modern programming languages are standardized and specified; it is by no means a bad example of the genre.

When first released in 1990, the C standard contained 201 items on which the committee could not agree sufficiently to standardize completely. These items were split into four severity categories, varying from completely benign to potentially catastrophic (like division by zero). The 1999 standard contains nearly twice as many such items, 366 in all. The nature of many of these items is such that if a program depends on any of these features, *its behavior is not defined*. Not only is this a horrific situation, but also there is no provision or requirement to detect these problems. Other programming language standards are in the same predicament to a greater or lesser degree.

One may think that the language is still safe to use, because at least the standards committee knows where the problems are. But this would be wrong. Adding to the holes left by the standardization process, programmers continue to report features of the language, which though well-defined, lead to recognizable fault modes. By the end of the 1990s, approximately 700 of these additional problems had been identified in standard C90 (Hatton, 1995).

These faults are often missed during testing and so appear in released products
It is now clear that such fault modes exist. Now we can demonstrate that they frequently escape the scrutiny of conventional testing, ending up in commercial products. These problems can be found by producing compiler-like tools to detect them. In fact, many of the 700 fault modes reported in C can be detected in this way. Figure 11.5 depicts the results of a scan of a number of a large number of commercial products around the world over several years (Hatton, 1997). One can see that the fault rates are not only non-trivial, they are completely unacceptable in solid software.

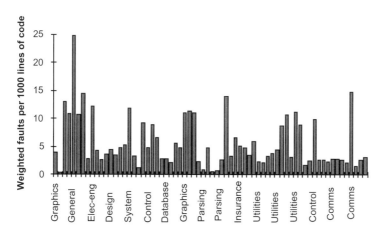

Figure 11.5: The occurrence rate of a class of statically detectable faults known to cause problems in C, as reported in Hatton (1995)

In other words, in a typical C program, there is an average of approximately 8 such faults per 1000 lines of source code; they are embedded in the code, just waiting to cause the code to fail. Conventional testing simply did not detect them. C is not the culprit here; this exercise can be carried out for other languages with broadly the same results (Hatton, 1995 and 1997). All programming languages have problems, and programmers cannot assume that they are protected against them. And nothing in the current international process of standardizing languages will prevent this from happening in future.

For readers who are still skeptical, consider the following example from the author's (Hatton's) recent products.

```
case ET_FLOATING_CONST:
/*              :ISOC90:SEMANTICS:6.4:18:p56:                    */
if (    ev_flags->syntax_check                 &&
            ev_flags->must_be_integral )          <---- A
            {
                    p_val->cv_is_computable = FALSE;
                    ok = FALSE;
            }
            /*      Lots more code here  */
            break;

case ET_CAST:
/*              :ISOC90:SEMANTICS:6.4:20:p56:         */
            if (    ev_flags->syntax_check                 &&
            myc_is_integral                )          <---- B
            {
            if( !myc_is_integral(expr->ex_type->ty_code))
                    {
                            /* Lots more code here */
                    ...
```

Line B should be the same as line A. The code turns out to be legal in the language (C in this example), but it is completely wrong. The confusion arose because of the similarity of the line following B.

When a system fails, a root-cause analysis can be performed to determine not only the cause of the problem but why the fault was missed. Forensic techniques can be used to discover exactly when the fault was injected into the system. For the example above, this fault was created after design and during coding. It could have been found by static analysis during a compile, but in fact it is (unfortunately) a legal (although odd) statement in the language. In principle, tools could be written to detect this kind of fault, but tools in use at the time did not reveal the problem.

In actuality, the fault was injected not during the first incarnation of the system, but several months after the product was released. In this case, regression testing would be expected to find the fault before it causes any damage. The pre-delivery testing alone involved regression tests against 2500 test files, including the entire official validation suite for the C language. None of the regression tests revealed this problem either. Thus, it is essential that we rely on more than just the compiler to find faults.

The systems fail

Although there is no model to show whether and when a particular fault contributes or not to a failure, in fact steps can be taken to resolve this question. A begin can be made by measuring the detection rates of each class of faults over a period of usage time. If the faults in a class fail, their detection rate should gradually decline as the faults fail - because then they are detected and corrected the hard way. Figure 11.6 shows that that is precisely what happens. The system represented by the bar on the left is quite young and has been subjected only to an average amount of dynamic testing. The bar on the right represents the system after it has matured; it has been subjected to very thorough dynamic testing. The difference in statically detectable faults rates for the same faults is very marked, showing that this class of fault does in fact fail (and is subsequently corrected) during the life cycle.

Data derived from CAA CDIS

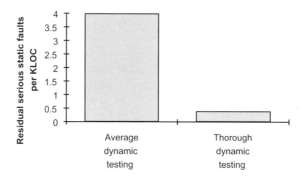

Figure 11.6: The fault rates of a class of statically detectable faults measured in faults per 1000 lines of source code in two different populations.

Thus far, it has been shown that a percentage of the faults do in fact fail in the life cycle of the code. However, which ones? Sadly, no prediction method can answer this question. It has been demonstrated that flaws inherent in the programming language can creep all the way through the development process and into the final products, whereupon some percentage of them fails. The course of action to eliminate this form of repetitive failure is simply to remove all of the language-standard faults by using only those parts of the language not subject to these problems. This subset of the language is called a *safer subset*, and it is known how to create and use it for a number of years. Sadly, most organizations do not bother. Instead, they move on rapidly to new and frequently more complex languages. They have no data about the faults in the new standard, but use it nevertheless and call it progress. Fun it may be, but progress it decidedly is not.

Code faults that cannot be found by automation

Many kinds of faults are detectable using automation. However, there will always be code faults that cannot be detected automatically, even though refinement of the tools can be done systematically as experience is gained with faults creation and discovery. For example, logic errors in requirements cannot generally be detected automatically; they will remain in the province of the human reviews discussed in Chapter 8.

Static noise

Because overdoing static analysis is still much cheaper than waiting until testing to find faults, static analysis emerges as strongly preferable and in some cases a replacement for the traditionally much more expensive dynamic testing (Gilb and Graham, 1993). So what is the downside to using static analysis?

The downside is quite simple. As has already been noted, static analysis finds faults whilst dynamic analysis finds failure. A closer look at figure 11.3 suggests that most of the things an inspection would find are unlikely to fail in the lifetime of the product, whereas everything found during dynamic analysis failed by definition. So static analysis may be inherently more inefficient than dynamic analysis in that it finds many false positives.

To understand this problem in a different light, the discovery of faults can be considered that are never likely to fail; they are called inherent "noise" in the static analysis process. It would be desirable to assign a likelihood of failure to each fault discovered during static analysis, but such a model has so far evaded software engineering. The essentially chaotic nature of software failure, whereby a small change in the source code can lead unpredictably to benign or catastrophic failure, may mean that software engineering can never predict such things.

The noise analogy is apt, and it shows us that static analysis has something in common with signal processing, where one are trying to infer the nature of a signal in the presence of noise. If the noise is overwhelming or is insidiously similar to the signal, this identification can be exceedingly difficult if not impossible. But the success of most static analysis, in spite of the noise, is compelling. Inspection data alone still overwhelmingly favor static analysis techniques, as has been observed by many authors, including Humphrey (1990 and 1995), Gilb and Graham (1993), and Liedtke (1995). Careful control of the noise problem is still necessary, though, and, as will be shown, it can be addressed with some kinds of static analysis tool.

To deal with static noise, one must understand its nature. It manifests itself in at least two important ways:
1.   Static noise greatly complicates manual code reviews.
2.   In the output of static analysis tools, static noise frequently hides faults more likely to fail from faults less likely to fail.

Let us examine each problem in turn. There is a great deal of discussion in the literature about what happens at a review or inspection meeting, where different inspectors discuss what they have found individually. Many of the items revealed to the group turn out to be false positives and are dismissed as noise. For static analysis tools, such noise has long been a problem. If the use of tools were to follow traditional inspection techniques, the output of the tool would be discussed at an inspection meeting and the noise eliminated. Unfortunately, such tools are usually applied by the programmer rather than the inspector. As a result, hard-pressed by deadlines and the pressures of getting the product to market, developers often suppress tool output completely, so that even in organizations that claim to use such tools, released products are still rife with statically-detectable faults.

Controlling static noise in tools and with tools requires considerable language and system expertise. The best way to achieve control is probably to apply the rules and tools in the form of checklists. That is, small subsets of items are formed to watch for, such as data-flow problems, or interface inconsistency. Lutz (1993) demonstrated the effectiveness of such checklists in finding faults early at the Jet Propulsion Laboratory. Thus the practice of applying a safer subset becomes simply the practice of iteratively applying very targeted checklists and tools in digestible quantities. When static analysis tools look in an unconstrained way for statically detectable faults, they sometimes annotate every line of code with so many messages that the analysis is virtually ineffective; we cannot really tell what is going on. With techniques and tools targeted at narrow subsets of problems, we know right away what is happening in the code and can fix it quickly.

In this discussion is has been assumed that, as engineers find and fix a fault, they have not introduced new faults into the product Unfortunately, this assumption is not valid. Configuration management is essential for making sure that what worked in a system before a change was made is still working after the change.

References

- Adams, E. (1984), Optimizing preventive service of software products, in: *IBM Journal of Research and Development*, 28(1): 2–14

- Boehm, B.W. (1981), *Software Engineering Economics*, Englewood Cliffs, NJ: Prentice Hall

- Fenton, N. and S. L. Pfleeger (1997), *Software Metrics: A Rigorous and Practical Approach*, 2nd edition, London: PWS Publishing

- Gilb, T., and D. Graham (1993), *Software Inspection*, Addison-Wesley, London, ISBN 0-201-63181-4

- Hatton, L. (1995). *Safer C: Developing Software for High-integrity and Safety-critical Systems*. New York: McGraw-Hill

- Hatton, L. (1997), *Reexamining the fault density-component size connection*, in: *IEEE Software*, Vol. 14 Issue 2, March 1997: pp. 89–97

- Hatton, L. (1999), Repetitive failure, feedback and the lost art of diagnosis, in: *Journal of Systems and Software*, October 1999

- Humphrey, W. S. (1990), *Managing the Software Process*, Addison-Wesley, ISBN 0-201-18095-2

- Humphrey, W. S. (1995). *A Discipline for Software Engineering*. Addison-Wesley, New York, ISBN 0-201-54610-8

- Koenig, A. (1988), *C traps and pitfalls*, Addison-Wesley, ISBN 0-201-17928-8

- Liedtke, T. and H. Ebert (1995), On the benefits of reinforcing code inspection activities, in: *Proceedings EuroStar conference*, London 1995

- Lions, J.L. (1996), *Ariane 5 Flight 501 Failure: Report by the Inquiry Board*, European Space Agency

- Lutz, R. R. (1993), Targeting safety-related errors during requirements analysis, in: *ACM Software Engineering Notes*, Vol. 18, Issue 5, pp. 99–105

- Myers, G. J. (1979), *The Art of Software Testing*, Wiley-Interscience Publications, New York, ISBN 0-471-04328-1.

12 Testing Techniques; why bother?

David Hayman

Formal and informal test case design techniques have been around for many years. Their use has, to say the least, been spasmodic in medium to low risk systems. However, the recent focus on risk based testing has brought many techniques to the forefront of the testing activity. There are many sources of information with respect to test techniques, their methods and coverage measures. It is not the intention of this chapter to repeat or re-iterate such information. References are included at the end of this chapter. This chapter looks at a number of reasons why we should consider the use of test case design techniques as a part of our everyday testing activities and who should be looking to use them.

12.1 What are techniques?

According to the Oxford English Dictionary (OED) a technique is:
• Mode of artistic execution in music, painting, etc.;
• Mechanical skill in art;
• Means of achieving one's purpose, esp. skilfully.

What do these definitions mean and what is the relationship to the software testing activity?

Mode of artistic execution in music, painting, etc.: Testers would be stretching a point to call test cases 'artistic'. Testers are expected to use artistic license with some of the tests created, especially those using ad-hoc or error guessing 'techniques'. Perhaps the artistic element surrounding test cases is that testers use their own imagination and experiences to produce executable tests.

Mechanical skill in art: A method of using a medium e.g. water colour or oils to produce a desired effect - the same could be said to apply to test case design techniques. The techniques used must be best suited to the application, environment or test phase in which the testers are working. Mechanical indicates that the activity being undertaken is repeatable amongst other things. Repeatable, in turn, provides testers with measures that are objective and as a result they have control over their tests.

Means of achieving one's purpose, esp. skilfully: The use of 'purpose' in this context can translate directly to the objective of the test phase or level – what are the objectives? Scope, coverage, risk whatever you wish to call it, it is in effect the end result. Techniques, therefore, provide a means to an end. The testers job in part, is to ensure that the 'end' is objective and measurable.

The art of testing

Software testing has been referred to as an "art", amongst other things, for many years. Perhaps parts two and three of the OED definition should be combined. Yes; testing techniques make a part of the exercise mechanical in that the production of the test cases becomes formalised. However, the overriding need for test techniques, is the need to achieve our purpose. The purpose being; to provide objective and measurable tests and results to allow users to make an objective decision about the likely impact of taking the system into live operation.

What subset of all possible test cases has the highest probability of detecting most errors? (Myers, 1979). Well that is a loaded question if ever there was one! Although published in 1979 many others probably asked that question well before that time and certainly many thousands have asked it since. The testing fraternity are still trying to answer it. However, it may well be that there is no definitive objective answer! The question has an implicit measure within it; in that 'subset' implies that testers cannot/will not/should not even try to run every possible test case, even if they have been able to identify them. That being the case, the very simple question requires a very complicated answer, within which there will be caveats, compound decisions and 'what if?' statements abounding.

This chapter has been produced to discuss some of the issues surrounding the need for, and the use of, testing techniques. Testing techniques come in many shapes and sizes, some formal some not, some dynamic and some static. It is not the intention of this chapter to detail or explain the functions, coverage or methods of any of these techniques. These are very well covered in BS7925-2 (BS7925-1, 1998) and many textbooks (see references at the end of this chapter). However, aspects of some techniques may be used to clarify a point or to highlight a specific issue. The overall objective is to discuss the issues surrounding the use, selection, advantages and disadvantages of testing techniques as a set of tools.

Inevitably, the focus will be drawn to the dynamic test case design techniques and activities. Coverage measures are more easily defined and the definition of a single test case or test script is as easily identifiable from the testers point of view. However, static testing techniques must always be borne in mind; prevention will always be better than cure. The bottom line is that there may not actually be one complete answer to suit every situation, type of application or degree of quality required.

12.2 An overview

Dynamic vs. Static

The key difference is the point in the lifecycle that the test activities are carried out. Based on the early lifecycle V-model systems development approach, dynamic test case design activities are carried out at the same time as the static 'review' activities. The dynamic test cases are executed once the system has been built and delivered into the test environment. It could be argued that the act of producing test cases for dynamic execution is in itself a static test.

Static testing (reviews and static analysis) are primarily techniques aimed at preventing faults being propagated into the next phase or into the test environment. Dynamic techniques (either black or white box) are intended to find faults in the translation of the specifications into the actual system.

Systematic vs. Non-systematic techniques

As the heading suggests, the distinction is in the formality. Systematic techniques are based around a set of rules that make the activity mechanistic, repeatable and measurable. Non-systematic techniques are based on the experience of the tester, either at product level or within the testing function. Identifying test cases using non-systematic techniques has gathered some credibility using techniques such as exploratory testing (see chapter 13) and the testing aspects of extreme programming (XP). These techniques seek to put some process rigor around testing using experienced testers or developers carrying out the testing. The biggest draw back with these and other techniques is the lack of documentary evidence and therefore repeatability of the test scenarios. Although these techniques have a number of value added attributes they are not a panacea (cure all) for all testing functions.

Functional vs. Non-functional techniques

The majority of the dynamic techniques discussed in this chapter relate to establishing what the system does, i.e. Do the functions work (regardless of granularity)? Non-functional techniques focus on establishing how the system does what it does, i.e. is it secure? How quickly does it respond? Is it reliable?

Etc. There is little information available relating to non-functional techniques other than details of what they are. Creating non-functional test cases tends to be more of a strategic activity based on a series of inter-related requirements. For example, performance tests are based around the application operational profile, the number of concurrent users, the application mix and background system activities, rather than a condition within a function or a business scenario. As a general point, non-functional techniques often use tools to execute the tasks with supporting tools analyzing the dynamic system activity, e.g. memory use, concurrent threads etc.

12.3 Are techniques for testers only?

> *The development of technology will leave only one problem: The infirmity of human nature.*
>
> *Karl Kraus*

Absolutely not! Everyone who is involved in the system definition, development, implementation, support or use has a vested interest in establishing the quality of the system to be delivered. As identified earlier in this chapter, specific techniques should be used to look for specific types of fault. The tester should be taught techniques that will reflect the phase of system development in which that tester is involved. It could be argued that techniques for reviewing system documentation, at whatever level of formality, should be a natural and normal part of the fundamental tool set. Basic review methods should be an integral part of the process at every stage. Reviews are often considered to be "tester" driven, i.e. the only reason reviews are carried out is because the testers want them. The concept of what you don't see can't be there and certainly won't hurt is naive in the extreme. The human condition appears to override every other requirement when considering the delivery of systems. The implication is that deliverables shouldn't be challenged for content because if a problem is found the author may be upset - perhaps implying they are careless, stupid or worse incompetent.

This approach to IT systems delivery means that many faults are found very late and many not found until the system has gone live. Those with a vested interest only find the faults. This approach does not tackle the root of the problem. Everyone should be made aware of the type of tests they could carry out and the value they would add. If everyone in the IT systems environment was aware of and took the time to apply the basic aspects of test case design techniques then many, many, many faults would either not happen in the first place or be found before they could have an impact.

This may sound like a spleen venting exercise, however, allowing the current situation to remain will lead to no improvement in the quality of the systems delivered despite being aware of the problems. The 'head in the sand' approach is no defense for an ostrich and it is certainly no defense for a supposedly professional body of systems deliverers.

12.4 Why use techniques at all?

> *The most perfect technique is that which is not noticed at all.*
> *Pablo Casals*

By using testing techniques all the time they will become an integral part of the fabric of the testing and systems development process. Why use test case design techniques at all? Maybe the following will convince you of their value:
* Objectivity; guarantees a certain level of coverage linked to an identifiable process of achieving it.
* Increase in the defect finding capability.
* The ability to reproduce tests.
* Long term system maintainability and change control.

Much is espoused in the testing fraternity about the need to ensure the activities are measurable, controllable and repeatable (objective in word). Many techniques and supporting tools have been developed to allow testers to meet those objectives, it would seem churlish to avoid them even though they require some effort to implement and manage. The benefits usually far outweigh the costs. Testers have to document the tests whichever approach is taken, why not take advantage of what is already in place? Re-inventing the wheel is a tedious and time wasting exercise.

Test techniques provide an understanding of the complexities imposed by most systems. The use of techniques forces testers into thinking about what they test and why they are testing it. In many cases, techniques identify a level of coverage that would otherwise be a mystery. Remember techniques will not provide a mechanism to exercise 100% test coverage. However, if information regarding the level of coverage to be achieved is available, then objective decisions can be made, based on the risk of the system under test and on which tests to leave out.

The decision on which test case design techniques are to be used and when is entirely dependent on the understanding of the risk and in which component parts of the system it lies. Risk identification, assessment, management and mitigation are a fundamental part of the testing function. The identification and assessment of risk provides a focus to the testing, the management of risk is included as a part of the test process controls and mitigation is achieved when the correct coverage of tests is performed.

The use of test techniques is methodical and mechanical for the core tests but used properly they are flexible. Used together formal and informal techniques create an entire re-usable test package. Consider a situation where there is a need to test a new function in a system and a few bug fixes in the same package. It is likely that there will be a basic set of reference tests executed to ensure the build has some integrity before moving into the detailed aspects of re-testing, regression tests and the new tests. The outcome is that the package of change has just been given a 'quick check', often referred to as a 'shakedown'.

Question: Have techniques been used?
Answer: Yes.

The testers will have identified which functions are critical to the functionality of the system. They will have used some existing scripts or the error guessing technique to create values for input. Almost certainly they will have applied the rules for equivalence partitioning, boundary value analysis and state transition (Beizer, 1990), (BS7925-2, 1998), without formally documenting them. There will be expected results, albeit implicit, in that the system does not crash, users can log on, the passwords are valid, the menus are in place etc. The principles of test techniques are used all the time, however, they are not always documented or formally applied. Therefore the question should not be "why use techniques?" but "which techniques should be used?"

12.5 When should techniques be used?

> *Is it time to make time?*
>
>   *Henry Dumas*

It is often easy to say or be lead by those who say; "we don't have time to use techniques, we just need to get on with the testing." The pressure to start "playing" with the system as soon as it arrives is tremendous. This is the worst form of false economics in the system delivery process that can be propagated. If testers are fortunate enough to work in an environment where early life cycle principles are practiced then the "when" is not an issue. From discussion with many testers it is apparent that those working within a formal framework are in the minority. So how do testers know when to use test techniques if there is no structure to the testing?

To attempt to answer that it must first be understood and appreciated that using techniques has an initial cost and time overhead. The long-term benefits must also be factored into the tester's planning and cost benefit analysis. Finding the time to utilise test techniques is a major problem in the real world. In many cases as soon the system is delivered it is expected that the dynamic testing activities will start. Almost certainly the proposed system will be seen at the last moment and, as such, have no time to prepare any test cases. Although the discussion in this chapter has been in respect of dynamic test design techniques, their early use can also act as a great static testing technique as they will find a lot of defects in the specification.

Regardless of the situation testers find themselves in, it is suggested that they must always consider the tests they are going to run. Test cases do not just appear as if by magic! Time always has to be spent establishing and creating test cases and associated scripts. So whenever testers are presented with a new system it is up to the test team to ensure that test case design techniques are applied. Obviously the amount of time available and the test stages required will dictate which techniques and how much detailed documentation can be completed.

The simplest techniques to apply, equivalence partitioning and boundary value analysis, will provide a start point for the test scoping activity. These are probably the easiest to understand, and are perhaps the most directly relevant to most users. Error guessing (informal technique) can be utilised to provide a wider range of tests quickly.

Testers should use test case techniques at all times. This fundamental principle ensures that techniques will be used at every stage. The only question remaining is; "which techniques are the most appropriate?" Many of the test case design techniques have been developed to find defects of a certain type. Defects and testing go hand-in hand, however, the view that the only reason for testing is to find bugs is more fundamental and conceptual than the need to find them. Different types of test cases are executed for many reasons; a side effect of executing those tests will be to find defects. The test case design techniques chosen should be focused on the type of bugs that the testers are expecting to find, or that should be looked for at any given stage of the system delivery cycle. For more detailed information on the types of bugs and when they will most likely be found see, "The Taxonomy of Bugs" (Beizer, 1990).

12.6 Software and system modeling

Every picture tells a story.

Proverb

It is readily agreed that by painting a picture or drawing a diagram thought processes can be explained to others, and perhaps ourselves, more clearly. How often has a meeting finished with the users or technical architects, with the tester wandering back to their desk clutching a ragged piece of chapter (system specification) upon which the whole testing scope is going to be based?

This method of "documenting" systems has been prevalent for many years and is still in existence today. In fact, the need for rapid delivery and change to new technologies has exacerbated the situation and unfortunately this approach (documentation is produced as the system is built - if you are lucky) is being given credibility as a "formal design method" by the introduction of Extreme Programming methodology! That is one view of the usefulness or otherwise of producing diagrams. However, from the testing perspective, modelling techniques should be used to their full capacity. Across the spectrum of computing, models are used in the form of flowcharts, data flow diagrams, control flow graphs, Bachman diagrams, network/comms diagrams, etc. to represent some part of the physical or logical system. Modelling software or interfaces within systems will provide a 'picture' to some degree of how that part of the system is intended to operate.

The vast majority of formal dynamic test techniques identified in BS7925-2 utilise one method or other to model the system component under test. This is not a coincidence. Modelling software is often considered the most complete method of establishing paths, decisions, branches and statements. The objective of formal test techniques is not just to provide an objective coverage measure but also to document the decision making process, whilst making the component clear to both technical and non-technical staff.

Documentation of test coverage is critical in a function where objectivity is the be all and end all. Testers must ensure they know what they are going to test from the possibilities and perhaps more importantly they must be able to identify which situations are not going to be executed. The level and detail of the modelling is dictated by the technique chosen and often these models are not feasible without the use of automated tools. Not every tool used in testing is a pure "test" tool, for example a path analyser can be used for much more than identifying possible test cases. Some techniques use more than one method for example cause effect analysis. This uses condition and action tables to document results of flows established through the cause effect graphing method. Some models are relatively simple e.g. state transition, some very complex e.g. LCSAJ's. The commonality is that they all use some form of modelling without which carrying out test coverage analysis (regardless of whether the tests are focussed on requirements or code paths), identifying highly complex components and providing an objective measure would be impossible. Testers must ensure they use these models to the best advantage to provide this objectivity hand in hand with a deeper understanding of how the system works.

12.7 New technology and techniques

Don't stand in the doorway,
Don't block the hall,
For he that gets hurt,
Will be he who has stalled...
For the times they are a-changin'

Bob Dylan, 1963

Just because the technology is changing it does not mean that the techniques used to test it must change as well! There may well be many new tools flooding the market to cover a gap and to compliment what is already in place. However, they are still looking for the same type of bug it just may be with a different focus or having used new technology to create the component in the first place. Lets take a quick look at the Internet. (Maybe not quite so new now, nonetheless a good enough example.) The basic language has been changed from code to HTML, interfaces are dynamic and the risks have been refocused.

Firstly lets look at HTML; it is a language to ensure the data required can be used by any version of a web browser and be displayed onto a desktop. What techniques are required to test HTML? A basic static test tool called a complier is used to check the syntax. The HTML compiler can be configured to adhere to a specific HTML standard but this is fundamentally no different to the syntax checks carried out by code compilers.

Secondly, interfaces are now created to other web pages or sites using URL hyperlinks or bookmarks. A tool would almost certainly be used to check these interfaces. Why? No other reason than shear volume. Hyperlinks are easy to create and easy to use – great. Therefore they are used more. The interfaces or links are tested using a tool for expediency. Testing the validity of internal bookmarks and external URL links could take many days; a tool can usually check 2-3000 links in less than an hour. This, and the HTML testing, will almost certainly move away from the tester to become a development based set of techniques

Thirdly, the risks surrounding web sites are now considered to be issues such as Usability, Performance, Reliability, Availability, and Security etc. These non-functional techniques have been in existence for many years. All that new technology has done is to bring seldom used and therefore slightly dated methods to the fore and up to date.

New development techniques such as Extreme Programming are methods of delivering a system to live. Different people, using different tools may carry out the test techniques used at different times, but nonetheless the techniques remain the same. Regardless if it is the technology or the delivery methodology that changes, the techniques remain the same. This situation enforces even more the argument made in paragraph 12.3 that everyone should be aware of and trained in at least the most common test techniques.

12.8 Advantages / disadvantages

So should testers use formal and informal test case design techniques? The decision to use or not use test case design techniques is directly related to the risk of the products being tested. Initially a basic view of both the advantages and disadvantages must be taken.

Advantages	Disadvantages
Objectivity	Require training to some degree
Formal coverage measures	Time to implement - culture change
Early defect finding	Everyone must be 'bought in'
Traceability	Not seen as useful for all applications
Covergae independent of the tester	Take more time than less formal design
Way to differentiate test depth based on risks using different techniques	Do not cover all situations (error guessing still useful)
High level of re-use (re-usabale testware)	Little use of domain and product knowledge of tester
Repeatability and Reproduceability	
Audit trails	
Higher defect finding capability	

Table 12.1: Advantages / Disadvantages Testing Techniques

Whether testers like it or not, test case design techniques, whether formal or not, are an integral part of everyday testing life. If testing is to keep up in these ever changing times the testing discipline must ensure the validity of its function by continuing to be objective. In order to remain objective the level of testing must be measurable. The only measure available is coverage and only formal test case techniques and static testing methods provide this framework. If testing is to be taken seriously, the testing function must take itself seriously and ensure its objective is to make any testing objective. So should formal and informal test case design techniques be used? In a word YES.

References

- Beizer, B. (1990), *Software Testing Techniques*, 2nd edition, Van Nostrand Reinhold, ISBN 1-850-32880-3

- BS7925-2 (1998), *Software Component Testing*, British Standards Institution

- Kit, E. (1995), *Software Testing in the Real World*, Addison-Wesley, London

- Myers, G.J. (1979), *The Art of Software Testing*, Wiley-Interscience, New York, ISBN 0-471-04328-1

- Roper, M. (1994), *Software Testing*, McGraw-Hill, New-York

- Pol, M., R. Teunissen and E. van Veenendaal (2002), *Software Testing; A Guide to the TMap approach*, Addison-Wesley, ISBN 0-201-74571-2.

13 Exploratory testing

James Bach

Exploratory software testing is a powerful approach, yet widely misunderstood. In some situations, it can be orders of magnitude more productive than scripted testing. All testers practice some form of exploratory testing, unless they simply do not create tests at all. Yet few of us study this approach and it does not get much respect in our field. This attitude is beginning to change as companies seek ever more agile and cost effective methods of developing software.

13.1 Introduction

Among the hardest things to explain is something that everyone already knows. We all know how to listen, how to read, how to think, and how to tell anecdotes about the events in our lives. As adults, we do these things everyday. Yet the *level* of any of these skills, possessed by the average person, may not be adequate for certain special situations. Psychotherapists must be *expert* listeners and lawyers *expert* readers; research scientists must scour their thinking for errors and journalists report stories that transcend parlour anecdote.

So it is with exploratory testing (ET): the simultaneous design and execution of tests. This is a simple concept. But the fact that it can be described in a sentence can make it seem like something not worth describing. Its highly situational structure can make it seem, to the casual observer, that it has no structure at all. That is why textbooks on software testing, with few exceptions, either do not discuss exploratory testing, or do so only to dismiss it as an unworthy practice.

Exploratory testing is also known as ad hoc testing, but unfortunately, *ad hoc* is too often synonymous with sloppy and careless work. So, in the early 1990s a group of American test methodologists (now called the Context-Driven School) began using the term "exploratory" instead. With this new terminology, first published by Cem Kaner in his book Testing Computer Software (Kaner *et al.*, 1993), they sought to emphasise the dominant thought process involved in unscripted testing, and to begin to develop the practice into a teachable discipline. Indeed, exploratory testing can be as disciplined as any other intellectual activity. Microsoft practices a formalised process of exploratory testing for the purposes of certifying third-party applications for Windows compatibility[1], and session-based test management is a method specifically designed to make exploratory testing auditable and measurable on a large scale (http://www.satisfice.com). Our use of the word "exploratory" echoes its usage in geography, as the explorers of the Royal Geographic Society, in the eighteenth and nineteenth centuries, struggled with similar issues of methodology:

> *"So, to qualify as exploration a journey had to be credible, had to involve hardship and risk, and had to include the novelty of discovery. Thereafter, like cricket it was somewhat hard to explain to the uninitiated. But one element was absolutely vital; indeed it was precisely that which distinguished the age of exploration from previous ages of discovery and which necessitated the adoption of the word 'exploration.' It was, quite simply, a reverence for science."*
>
> John Keay, The Permanent Book of Exploration

Just as a star may seem dim in the spectrum of visible light, yet burn brightly in the infrared, the simple idea of exploratory testing becomes interesting and complex when viewed in the spectrum of *skill*. Consider chess: the procedures of playing chess are far less interesting than the skills. No one talks about how Emanuel Lasker followed the rules of chess when he defeated Steinitz in 1894 to become world champion. The procedures of chess remain constant, it's only the choices that change, and the skill of the players who choose the next move. What makes exploratory testing interesting, and in my view profoundly important, is that it when a tester has the skills to *listen, read, think* and *report,* rigorously and effectively, without the use of pre-scripted tests, the exploratory approach to testing can be many times as productive as the scripted variety (predefined test procedures, whether manual or automated). And when properly supervised and chartered, even testers without special skills can produce useful results that would not have been anticipated by a script. Drawing a historical analogy, the Lewis and Clark expedition is an excellent example of the role of skill in exploration:

---

1   For an example of a fully defined process of exploratory testing, see the General Functionality and Stability Test Procedure for MicroSoft's Windows 2000 Compatibility Certification Program at http://msdn.microsoft.com/certification/downloads/GenFSTest.doc.

> *"Lewis was the diplomatic and commercial thinker, Clark the negotiator. Lewis, who went especially to Philadelphia for training in botany, zoology, and celestial navigation, was the scientific specialist, Clark the engineer and geographer as well as master of frontier crafts...Both men were of great intelligence, of distinguished intelligence. The entire previous history of North American exploration contains no one who could be called their intellectual equal."*
>
> *Bernard De Voto, The Journals of Lewis and Clark*

Now, let me come back from the frontier, for a moment. Of course, tests may be worth reducing to a repeatable scripted form for a variety of good reasons. You may have special accountability requirements, perhaps, or maybe there are certain tests that must be executed in just the same way, every time, in order to serve as a kind of benchmark. Exploratory testing is not against the idea of scripting. In some contexts, you will achieve your testing mission better through a more scripted approach; in other contexts, your mission will benefit more from the ability to create and improve tests as you execute them. Most situations benefit from a mix of scripted and exploratory approaches.

Two Definitions

There are two prevailing uses of the term exploratory testing, a broad view and a narrow view. First, the broad view:

> *Exploratory testing* is any testing to the extent that the tester actively controls the design of the tests as those tests are performed and uses information gained while testing to design new and better tests.

In the broad view of ET, virtually all testing performed by human testers is exploratory to some degree. The broad view treats ET as a thought process that infuses much of what all good testers do. Often the broad view is preferred, but many people, including Cem Kaner, prefer a narrower definition of ET:

> *Exploratory testing* is any testing to the extent that the tester actively controls the design of the tests as those tests are performed and uses information gained while testing to design new and better tests, and where the following conditions apply:
> * The tester is not required to use or follow any particular test materials or procedures.
> * The tester is not required to produce materials or procedures that enable test re-use by another tester or management review of the details of the work done (Kaner *et al.*, 1993).

This narrow view, which we will call "pure" exploratory testing for the purposes of this chapter, is what most test managers think of when they consider using ET on a project. In this view, ET is a *tactic* to employ at particular times on a project, rather than a thought process that is more or less always present.

These two views are compatible and simply represent different styles of test management. Test managers who work in organizations that accept the value of exploratory testing can choose to take the narrow view, in which case ET becomes another task that is placed on the official test plan. Test managers who work in an environment that believes everything should be pre-scripted can still apply the broad view of ET, however, by allowing the testers to improvise on those scripted tests; thus discretely bringing the value of exploration into the test process.

Exploratory testing is an interactive test process. It is a free-form process in some ways and has much in common with informal approaches to testing that go by names like ad-hoc testing, error guessing, or intuitive testing. However, unlike traditional informal testing, this procedure consists of specific tasks, objectives, and deliverables that make it a systematic process.

Exploratory Testing is a Profoundly Situational Practice
Have you ever solved a jigsaw puzzle? If so, you have practised exploratory testing. Consider what happens in the process. You pick up a piece and scan the jumble of unconnected pieces for one that goes with it. Each glance at a new piece is a test case ("Does this piece connect to that piece? No? How about if it is turned around? Well, it almost fits but now the picture doesn't match…"). You may choose to perform your jigsaw testing process more rigorously, perhaps by concentrating on border pieces first, or on certain shapes, or on some attribute of the picture on the cover of the box. Still, can you imagine what it would be like to design and document all your jigsaw "test cases" before you began to assemble the puzzle, or before you knew anything about the kind of picture formed by the puzzle?

When we solve a jigsaw puzzle, we change how we work as we learn about the puzzle and see the picture form. If we notice a big blotch of colour, we might decide to collect all the pieces of that approximate colour into one pile. If we notice some pieces with a particularly distinctive shape, we might collect those together. If we work on one kind of testing for a while, we might switch to another kind just to keep the mind fresh. If we find we've got a big enough block of pieces assembled, we might move it into the frame of the puzzle to find where it connects with everything else. Sometimes we feel too disorganised, and when that happens, we can step back, analyse the situation, and adopt a more specific plan of attack. Notice how the process *flows* and how it remains continuously, *each moment*, under the control of the practitioner. Isn't this very much like the way one would assemble a jigsaw, too? If so, then perhaps we would agree that it would be absurd for us to carefully document these thought processes in advance. Reducing this activity to one of the following explicit instructions would only slow down our work.

This is a general lesson about puzzles: *the puzzle changes the puzzling.* The specifics of the puzzle, as they emerge through the process of solving that puzzle, affect our tactics for solving it. This truth is at the heart of any exploratory investigation, be it for testing, development, or even scientific research or detective work.

What kinds of specifics affect ET? Here are some of them:

• The mission of the test project
• The mission of this particular test session
• The role of the tester
• The tester (skills, talents and preferences)
• Available tools and facilities
• Available time
• Available test data and materials
• Available help from other people
• Accountability requirements
• What the tester's clients care about
• The current testing strategy
• The status of other testing efforts on the same product
• The product, itself
  • its user interface
  • its behaviour
  • its present state of execution
  • its defects
  • its testability
	• What the tester knows about the product
	  • what just happened in the previous test
	  • known problems with it
	  • past problems with it
	  • risk areas and magnitude of perceived risk
	  • recent changes to it
	  • direct observations of it
	  • rumours about it
	  • the nature of its users and user behaviour
	  • how it's supposed to work
	  • how it's put together
	  • how it's similar to or different from other products
	• What the tester would like to know about the product

Figure 10.1: Specifics that affect ET

Exploratory testers ask, *"What's the most powerful test I can perform, right now?"* The power of a test is how much useful information it reveals about the product. Each of the considerations in the list above contributes to designing a powerful test. These factors change continuously throughout the course of the test project, or even from moment to moment during a test session. The power of exploratory tests can be optimised throughout the test process, whereas scripts, because they don't change, tend to become less powerful over time. They fade for many reasons, but the major reason is that once you've executed a scripted test one time and not found a problem, the chance that you will find a problem on the second execution of the script is, in most circumstances, substantially lower than if you ran a new test instead.

13.2 Practicing exploratory testing

The external structure is easy enough to describe. Over a period of *time*, a *tester* interacts with a *product* to fulfil a testing *mission*, and *reporting* results. There you have the basic external elements of ET: time, tester, product, mission, and reporting. The mission is fulfilled through a continuous cycle of aligning ourselves to the mission, conceiving questions about the product that if answered would also allow us to satisfy our mission, designing tests to answer those questions, and executing tests to get the answers. Often our tests don't fully answer the questions, so we adjust the tests and keep trying (in other words, we explore). We must be ready to report our status and results at any time.

A pure exploratory test session often begins with a charter, which states the mission and perhaps some of the tactics to be used. The charter may be chosen by the tester himself, or assigned by the test lead or test manager. Sometimes charters are written down. In some organizations, test cases and procedures are documented so vaguely that they essentially serve as charters for exploratory testing.

Here are some example testing charters for DecideRight, a decision analysis product:
- Explore and analyse the product elements of DecideRight. Produce a test coverage outline.
- Identify and test all claims in the DecideRight manual, (either use checkmark/X/? notation on the printed manual, or list each tested claim in your notes).
- Define workflows through DecideRight and try each one. The flows should represent realistic scenarios of use, and they should collectively encompass each primary function of the product
- We need to understand the performance and reliability characteristics of DecideRight as decision complexity increased. Start with a nominal scenario and scale it up in terms of number of options and factors until the application appears to hang, crash, or gracefully prevent the user from enlarging any further.

- Test all fields that allow data entry (you know the drill: function, stress, and limits, please)
- Analyse the file format of a DecideRight scenario and determine the behaviour of the application when its elements are programmatically manipulated. Test for error handling and performance when coping with pathological scenario files.
- Check UI against Windows interface standards.
- Is there any way to corrupt a scenario file? How would we know it's corrupted? Investigate the feasibility of writing an automatic file checker. Find out if the developers have already done so.
- Test integration with external applications, especially Microsoft Word.
- Determine the decision analysis algorithm by experimentation and reproduce it in Excel. Then, use that spreadsheet to test DecideRight with complex decision scenarios.
- Run DecideRight under AppVerifier and report any errors.

If you find any of these charters ambiguous, I'm not surprised. They are intended to communicate the mission of a test session clearly and succinctly to testers who have already been trained in the expectations, vocabulary, techniques and tools used by the organization. Remember, in ET we make maximum use of skill, rather than attempting to represent every action in written form.

In pure exploratory testing, the only official result that comes from a session of ET is a set of bug reports. In session-based test management, each session of ET also results in a set of written notes that are reviewed by the test lead. It may also result in updated test materials or new test data. If you think about it, most formal written test procedures were probably created through a process of some sort of exploratory testing.

The outer trappings, inputs and outputs to exploratory testing are worth looking at, but it is the inner structure of ET that matters most - the part that occurs inside the mind of the tester. That's where ET succeeds or fails; where the excellent explorer is distinguished from the amateur. This is a complex subject, but here are some of the basics:

- *Test Design:* An exploratory tester is first and foremost a test designer. Anyone can design a test accidentally; the excellent exploratory tester is able to craft tests that systematically explore the product. That requires skills such as the ability to analyse a product, evaluate risk, use tools, and think critically, among others.
- *Careful Observation:* Excellent exploratory testers are more careful observers than novices, or for that matter, experienced scripted testers. The scripted tester need only observe what the script tells him to observe. The

exploratory tester must watch for *anything* unusual or mysterious. Exploratory testers must also be careful to distinguish observation from inference, even under pressure, lest they allow preconceived assumptions to blind them to important tests or product behaviour.

- *Critical Thinking:* Excellent exploratory testers are able to review and explain their logic, looking for errors in their own thinking. This is especially important when reporting the status of a session of exploratory tests, or investigating a defect.
- *Diverse Ideas:* Excellent exploratory testers produce more and better ideas than novices. They may make use of heuristics to accomplish this. Heuristics are mental devices such as guidelines, generic checklists, mnemonics, or rules of thumb. The Satisfice Heuristic Test Strategy Model (http://www.satisfice.com) is an example of a set of heuristics for rapid generation of diverse ideas. James Whittaker and Alan Jorgensen's "17 attacks" is another (Whittaker and Jorgensen, 2000). The diversity of tester temperaments and backgrounds on a team can also be harnessed by savvy exploratory testers through the process of group brainstorming to produce better test ideas.
- *Rich Resources:* Excellent exploratory testers build a deep inventory of tools, information sources, test data, and friends to draw upon. While testing, they remain alert for opportunities to apply those resources to the testing at hand.

Managing Exploratory Testing

In many organizations, it's important to distinguish between a test manager and a test lead. The test manager usually has hiring and firing authority and other administrative responsibilities, whereas the test lead is focused only on the test strategy and tactics. For the purposes of discussing ET test management, the term test lead will be used, even though a test manager may be fulfilling that role.

Pure exploratory testing can be managed in two ways: delegation or participation. With delegation, the test lead specifies the charters. Then the testers go off on their own, design and execute the tests to fulfil the charters, and report back. In practice, a particular tester is often permanently assigned to one set of components, so that the project benefits from an uninterrupted learning curve. The test reports that come back may be written or oral. Cem Kaner suggests regular meetings with testers to discuss test progress, at least once per week. He finds it useful to open the meeting with a standard question, "What is the most interesting bug you've found recently? Show it to me." In the session-based approach, test reports are written, and testers are interviewed at least once per day.

Managing by delegation essentially treats each tester as an executive who manages the value of his own time. Just as with executives, a tester who hasn't earned credibility as a productive and responsible tester is not given big assignments, but rather is restricted to shorter exploratory sessions and subjected to more scrutiny. Being a leader of exploratory testers means being a coach of semi-independent creative agents.

Managing by participation means that the lead tests right alongside the rest of the testers. In practice, this is best for leads that have otherwise delegated their administrative and meeting attendance responsibilities to other people. Participation allows the lead to direct the test strategy in real time and continuously demonstrate the behaviours he expects from the team. Since the test manager is ultimately responsible for the performance of the team, participation puts him in an excellent position to fulfil that responsibility. Many concerns about the potential for confusion or inefficient testing during ET tend to disappear when a test lead is intimately involved with the testing.

Most test leads will use a test coverage guide of some kind to help them organise the test effort. This guide may take the form of a test coverage outline or matrix, a list of risks, or even an old fashioned To Do list.

Team exploratory testing can be extremely powerful. In the experience of many test leads who have tried it, the social energy of people working together, hunting for bugs on the same equipment at the same time, often leads to more and better ideas than would otherwise come out if the same people worked independently. One way to organise team ET is to put testers into pairs and have them share one computer as they test. Another way I've done it is to have one tester "drive" at the keyboard while several others watch and comment. If the driving tester discovers a problem or has a question that needs to be researched, one of the watchers can break away to attempt to investigate that issue using another test platform. That frees the driving tester to continue the main thread of testing with less distraction. This method is especially useful as a blockbusting tool to get the test effort out of a rut or to help train testers in the technology of the product or about methods of test design.

13.3 Where exploratory testing fits

In general, ET is called for in any situation where it is not obvious what the next test should be, or when you want to go beyond the obvious tests. More specifically, pure exploratory testing fits in any of the following situations:
* You need to provide rapid feedback on a new product or feature

- You need to learn the product quickly
- You have already tested using scripts and seek to diversify the testing
- You want to find the single most important bug in the shortest time
- You want to check the work of another tester by doing a brief independent investigation
- You want to investigate and isolate a particular defect
- You want to investigate the status of a particular risk, in order to evaluate the need for scripted tests in that area.

According to the broad definition of exploratory testing, ET fits anywhere that testing is not completely dictated in advance. This includes all of the above situations, plus at least these additional ones:
- Improvising on scripted tests
- Interpreting vague test instructions
- Product analysis and test planning
- Improving existing tests
- Writing new test scripts
- Regression testing based on old bug reports
- Testing based on reading the user manual and checking each assertion.

ET is powerful because of how the information flows backward from executing testing to re-designing them. Whenever that feedback loop is weak, or when the loop is particularly long, slow, or expensive, ET loses that power. Then, we must fall back on carefully pre-scripted tests. Another place to use scripted tests is in any part of our testing that will be subjected to extreme retrospective scrutiny. But don't settle for weak tests just because they please the auditors. Consider using a combined exploratory and scripted strategy, and get the best of both worlds.

13.4 Exploratory testing in action

I once had the mission of testing a popular photo-editing program in four hours. My mission was to assess it against the specific standards of the Microsoft Windows Compatibility Certification Program. The procedure for performing such a test is laid out as a formalised exploratory testing process. My goal was to find any violations of the compatibility requirements, all of which were clearly documented for me.

With this rather clear charter in mind, I set myself to test. Applying one of the simplest heuristics of exploring, I chose to begin by walking through the menus of the application, trying each one. While doing so, I began creating an outline of the primary functions of the product. This would become the basis for reporting what I did and did not test later.

I noticed that the Save As… function led to a very sophisticated set of controls that allow the user to set various attributes of image quality. Since I knew nothing about the technical aspects of image quality, I felt unprepared to test those functions. Instead, I started an issues list and made a note to ask if my client was willing to extend the time allowed for testing so that I could study documentation about image quality and form a strategy for testing it. Having made my note, I proceeded walking through menus.

A basic strategy of ET is to have a general plan of attack, but allow yourself to deviate from it for short periods of time. Cem Kaner calls this the "tour bus" principle. Even people on a tour bus get to step off it occasionally and wander around. The key is not to miss the tour entirely, nor to fall asleep on the bus. My first urge to leave the tour of the menus happened when I found a dialog box in the program that allowed me to control the amount of memory used by the application. This immediately gave me an idea (sudden ideas are encouraged in exploratory testing). Since one of the requirements of the Windows Compatibility program is stability, I thought it would be useful to set the product to use the minimum amount of memory, and then ask it to perform memory intensive functions. So I set the slider bar to use 5% of system memory, then visited the image properties settings and set the image size to 100 inches square. That's a big canvas. I then filled the canvas with purple dots and went over to the effects menu to try activating some of the special graphical effects.

Okay, here comes an important part: I chose a "ripple" effect from the menu and *bam*, the product immediately displayed an error message informing me that there was not enough memory for that operation. This is very interesting behaviour, because it establishes a standard. I have a new expectation from this point forward: a function should be able to prevent itself from executing if there is not enough memory to perform the operation. This is a perfect example of how, in exploratory testing, the result of one test influences the next, because I then proceeded to try other effects to see if the rest of them behaved in the same way. Verdict? None of the others I tried behaved that way. Instead, they would crank away for five minutes, doing nothing I could see other than drive the hard disk into fits. Eventually an error popped up, "Error -32: Sorry this Error is Fatal," and the application crashed.

This is a nice result, but I felt that the test would not be complete (exploratory testers strive to anticipate questions that their clients will ask later on) unless I set that memory usage lever all the way up, to use the most memory possible.

To my surprise, instead of getting the Error -32, the entire operating system froze. Windows 2000 is not supposed to do that. This was a far more serious problem than a mere crash.

At this point in the process, I had spent about 30 minutes of a 4-hour process, and already found a problem that disqualified the application from compatibility certification. That was the good news. The bad news is that I lost my test notes when the system froze. After rebooting, I decided I had learned enough from stress testing and returned to the menu tour.

I submit that this test story is an example of disciplined, purposeful testing. I can report what I covered and what I found. I can relate the testing to the mission I was given. It was also quite repeatable, or at least as repeatable as most scripted tests, because at all times I followed a coherent idea of what I was trying to test and how I was trying to test it. The fact that those ideas occurred to me on the fly, rather than being fed to me from a document, is immaterial. I hope you see that this is a far cry from unsystematic testing. It *would* be unsystematic "ad hoc" testing if I couldn't tell the story of my tests, couldn't remember what I tested or what my test strategy was, and couldn't relate my testing to my mission.

13.5 Productivity

There are no reasonable numbers; no valid studies of testing productivity that compares ET with scripted testing. All we have are anecdotes. Here are a couple anecdotes of mine.

I taught testing classes where exploratory testers, testing on a system that automatically logged their work, have designed and executed almost a hundred tests each. Then, when challenged to write a repeatable test procedure in the same amount of time, each person managed to create only one. One can argue that the repeatable test procedure was better, in some ways than the exploratory tests. Maybe it was or maybe it wasn't. Personally, I felt that the test scripts produced were far less powerful than were the exploratory tests. None of the scripted tests found bugs that were not first found while performing the exploratory testing needed to create the scripted tests.

I led teams in the testing of applications that had already been tested by scripted means and found dramatic problems in them. In one case, without any preparation or test materials, it took my team only ten minutes to crash a network appliance so badly that its internal hard drive had to be reformatted.

True, it took longer than ten minutes to investigate and isolate the problem, but that would also have been true for a scripted test procedure, assuming it found the problem in the first place.

These vignettes do not prove anything. I include them simply to pique your interest. The truth is, productivity depends upon a lot of factors. So, work with it, and gather your own experiences.

Exploratory testing can be described as a martial art of the mind. It's how you deal with a product that jumps out from the bushes and challenges you to a duel of testing. Well, you don't become a black belt by reading books! You have to work at it. Happy practising.

References

- Bach, J. (1999), Heuristic Risk-Based Testing, in: *Software Testing Quality Engineering*, Vol. 1, Issue 6, November/December 1999

- Bach, J. (2001), Where does Exploratory Testing fit? in: *StickyMinds*, Issue July 2001

- Bach, J. (2001), What is Exploratory Testing? in: *StickyMinds*, Issue January 2001

- Kaner, C., J. Falk and H.Q. Nguyen (1993), *Testing Computer Software*, Van Nostrand Reinhold, ISBN 1-85032-847-1

- Whittaker, J.A. and A.A. Jorgensen (2000), How to Break Software, in: *Proceedings EuroStar conference*, Kopenhagen 2000.

14 Usability testing

Isabel Evans

This chapter aims to increase the reader's understanding of usability and usability testing. Discussed here are the importance of usability, including contexts of use and accessibility, and how to set usability acceptance criteria that are measurable. Usability design and test activities are positioned within the project life cycle. A thorough introduction is given to BCS usability test techniques standard[1], and how this standard may be applied in projects.

14.1 What is usability?

Usability is the quality of a product (software or other) which addresses its suitability for the people who will use it. Consideration of usability affects the definition of the requirements, the design and the build of the product and the testing of the product. Usability and usability testing have aspects in common with other types of testing, but there are specific differences which affect how usability testing is set up, executed and reported on. Good usability is as vital as good functionality and reliability to delivering products which can be used successfully, are appealing and encourage people to use and re-use the product.

The usability requirements include consideration of the context within which the product is used, the people who will use it and the environment within which it will be used. Usability is defined by different authors under either a narrow or a broad focus. The usability of a product can be tested from both perspectives. Quite often the scope is limited to the narrow focus, also called the "ease-of-use" perspective. The ease or comfort during usage is mainly determined by characteristics of the software product itself, such as the user-

---

1   A number of references in this chapter are made to the usability testing section of the non-functional testing standard being drawn up by the BCS Special Interest Group in Software Testing (SIGiST). At the time of publication this standard is in draft. Further information, copies and status of the draft may be obtained from the BCS SIGiST. The draft standard is referenced in the chapter as (Usability SIGiST, 2000)

interface. Within this type of scope usability is part of product quality characteristics. The usability definition of ISO 9126-1 (see hereafter) is an example of this type of perspective.

In a broader scope, usability is determined by using the product in its (operational) environment. The type of users, the tasks to be carried out, physical and social aspects that can be related to the usage of the software products are taken into account. Usability is being defined as "quality-in-use". The usability definition of ISO 9241-1 (see hereafter) is an example of this type of perspective. Clearly these two perspectives of usability are not independent. Achieving "quality-in-use" is dependent on meeting criteria for product quality. The interrelationship is shown in the figure below:

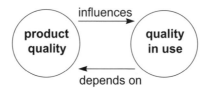

Figure 14.1 : Relationship between different types of usability

Narrow focus definition of usability

The narrow focus definition of usability describes usability as a set of attributes that can be measured, but it does not take account of the context of use or tasks. These attributes directly affect how people perceive the product. They impact on the effort needed for use, as well as the attitude to, or assessment of the product by the people using it. In summary the narrow band attributes give a measure of the usability of the software by looking at:

> *"The capability of the software to be understood, learned, used and liked by the user when used under specified conditions" (ISO 9126-1, 2001).*

These attributes are qualities of the software including understandability, learnability, operability, and attractiveness. They are defined as:
- *Understandability:* attributes of the software that bear on the users' effort for recognising the logical concept and its applicability;
- *Learnability:* attributes of software that bear on the users' effort in learning the application;
- *Operability:* attributes of the software that bear on the users' effort for operations and operation control;
- *Attractiveness:* the capability of the software to be liked by the user (ISO 9126-1, 2001).

Although this is described as a "narrow focus" it is important to assess a broad range of aspects of the product, and indeed with a software product we may consider surrounding manual processes. In this context Nielsen defines usability as "not just the property of the user-interface but a multiple component issue associated with the attributes of learnability, efficiency, memorability, errors and satisfaction" (Nielsen, 1993).

Broad focus definition of usability

The broad focus definition of usability is:

> *"The effectiveness, efficiency and satisfaction with which specified users can achieve specified goals in particular environments" (ISO 9241-1, 1998).*

Effectiveness, efficiency and satisfaction are defined as:
* *Effectiveness:* the capability of the software product to enable the people who use it to achieve specified goals with accuracy and completeness in a specified context of use.
* *Efficiency:* the capability of the software product to enable the people who use it to expend appropriate amounts of resources in relation to the effectiveness achieved in a specified context of use.
* *Satisfaction:* the capability of the software product to satisfy users in a specified context of use (ISO 9241-1, 1998).

Various methods are suggested for measuring effectiveness, efficiency and satisfaction, but it should be noted that research and debate continues, for example both in considering how a "fair test" of satisfaction can be carried out, and in defining what attributes make up satisfaction. It may be that some of these attributes can only be measured qualitatively. Projects, including their customers, designers and testers need to have a clear understanding of what is required for usability and what can be measured for the project. More information on setting criteria for effectiveness, efficiency and satisfaction can be found in ISO 9241-11 (1998): Guidance on usability, and ISO/IEC 9126-4 (2000): Quality in use metrics. Quality in use is defined is a similar way to "usability" in ISO 9241-11.

Good usability is vital to delivering products that can be used successfully and which are appealing, encouraging people to use and re-use the product. Consider an ATM (Automatic Teller Machine), an everyday example of a product used by a wide variety of people. The factors affecting how we think about usability for the ATM include:

- Tasks: include withdrawing money, checking bank account balance, paying bills
- People who will use the ATM: Anyone with a bank card
- Environment: Typically the machines may be placed outside or inside banks, and are set in the wall at a fixed height. If the ATM is outside, then it may be used in bright sunshine or at night.
- Human Computer Interface: Typically, information is displayed on screen and buttons are pushed or the screen is touched in order to carry out the tasks.

Figure 14.2 : Usability factors for an ATM

Decisions taken during the design of the ATM, including the software, the interface, the machine itself, and the placing of the machine in its environment, will affect the usability of the ATM for some or even all of the people who want to use it.

Examples of an ATM's design and installation that will affect its usability:
- The colours used on the ATM screen
- The font size and font shape on the ATM screen
- The complexity of language used on the screen and use of jargon
- Wording and provision of information and help messages
- Suitable help versus speedy navigation
- The height of the screen and controls above the ground
- Ambient light on the screen
- Privacy and safety for the person using the ATM

Figure 14.3 : Example design decisions for an ATM that affect usability

Some of these considerations affect the design of the ATM software and interface. Others (such as consideration of the privacy and safety of the person using the ATM) will also affect where it is placed - the design of the environment in which it is used. Understanding usability is vital for building acceptable systems. If people find the system difficult, irritating, unsatisfactory or inefficient to use, they will avoid using the system. Usability has always been a factor in the success of software provision, whether for in-house or third party, bespoke or package systems. With the increase in e-commerce and the use of Intranets and Extranets to deliver information, usability is critical to the success of the organisation. If potential customers cannot use the web-site or on-line transaction effectively, or if the experience is unsatisfactory, they will "vote with their finger/mouse" and click elsewhere or ignore the information. A message is not delivered and a sale is lost.

14.2 Contexts of use

The context of use for a product is particularly used in broad focus usability testing, where the product is tested and used in its operational environment.

Considering many viewpoints

It is important to understand the people who will be using the product. They may be a relatively uniform group or a very disparate group. The more public the product, the broader the potential group of people who will attempt to use it. A site on the World Wide Web may be accessed by anyone with the means worldwide. Similarly a product sold for home or office use could be purchased by a very wide range of people, with widely differing requirements and expertise. The designers and testers working with the product need to identify and empathise with those people; indeed it is valuable to include them or their representatives in the design and test teams. In order to do this the *contexts of use* must be identified.

Understanding the contexts of use

In order to confine the definition of usability requirements to a manageable level, the project will need to define the contexts of use for the product. This includes understanding who will be using the product, how they will be using it and where they will be using it. The characteristics of these aspects must be must be identified. Contexts of use include the people who will use the product, the tasks and the environment, and some example considerations under those headings are:

- The people
    - type of people who will use the product, their interests and attributes, including access for people with special needs (accessibility is a legal, a business and a moral consideration (DDA, 1995))
    - type of people who will use the product, their skills and knowledge, including levels of technical ability with IT and in the application area
    - changing levels of ability as people become accustomed to the product
    - side effects of using the product
    - physical and mental demands.
- The tasks
    - goals for the system
    - tasks to be performed, including steps, frequency, task goal, outcome, duration
    - flexibility of the product to different approaches for carrying out tasks.

- The environmental context
    - environment of use - home, office, outside or indoors
    - computer environment - control of, knowledge of, private, public, extremes of environment
    - dependencies on other products.

The example context checklist in the figure below shows how for an ATM, the designers and testers have started to list characteristics that make up the contexts of use. It is only partially completed. Other types of checklist are available, for example from the MUSiC (Measuring Usability in Context) project (Kelly, 1994).

Example: ATM - Context Checklist			
Goals for this system: encourage the majority of cash withdrawals to take place at the ATMs not the counters			
Users			
Skills and knowledge	No / low / good IT knowledge No / low/high previous experience of ATMs		
Attributes (people)	With sight / hearing / language / mobility difficulties With other special needs / without special needs		
List of tasks	Withdrawing cash Withdrawing cash with receipt Checking balance, etc.		
Task checklist			
	Withdrawing cash	Receipts	Balances
Goal for user	Cash withdrawn	Receipt with cash	Balance received
Goal for XYZ bank	Fast delivery minimise enqs	Fast delivery minimise enqs	Fast delivery minimise enqs
Output	Cash deliver	Receipt delivered with cash	Balance delivered
Frequency	5000 hits per day per machine	5000 hits per day per machine	500 per month per machine
Duration	Less than 1 minute Less than 4 actions to complete	Less than 1 minute Less than 4 actions to complete	Less than 1 minute Less than 4 actions to complete
Environment in which ATM is to be used	Inside bank branch Outside bank branch (main street - well lit at night) Outside bank branch (side street - query make unavailable at night?)		

Figure 14.4 : Example context checklist for ATM

The goals of the ATM include enabling people to withdraw money, check their bank accounts, and pay bills. The attributes to consider include consideration of special needs. The system may be used by experienced or by inexperienced people - there will always be someone for whom this is their first use of an ATM, or of this type of ATM. In the list of "people" attributes above, accessibility for people with special needs was mentioned. Access for everyone who wants to use the software product should be considered as part of the context of use: "Usability and accessibility work hand in hand. You can't claim that your Web site is usable without ensuring it's accessible to everyone." (Splaine, 2001). In the ATM design, the context of use includes people with special needs. Ambient light, colours, font size and font shape used on the display all affect the ability of customers, and especially visually impaired customers, to use the screen successfully. Usability considerations also include setting an acceptable maximum number of selections of commands to achieve a task. If the people find they cannot use the ATM easily then they will not use the ATM, and if this means they cannot draw money then they may change bank.

A context of use checklist helps in setting usability acceptance criteria. Having agreed a checklist, the project has a better understanding of tasks and contexts, a better understanding of the user profile and has started to set and agree measurable acceptance criteria.

14.3 Designing for usability

As with all requirements for a product development, the most cost-effective time to validate usability requirements is during the requirements definition and design phase. Information gathering and design techniques are available which specifically address usability. The techniques are drawn from social sciences, industrial product design and software design. These are a selection of methods that gather information as a system is in use, either by observation of the user, or by asking the user to comment. They are not explained in detail here, but the following are examples.

* *Contextual design-* a structured field interviewing method based on a discovery process rather than an evaluative process; more like learning than testing. Contextual enquiry is carried out to understand the context in which a product is used, with the person will use the product as a partner in the design process. The usability design process, including assessment methods like contextual inquiry and usability testing, must have a clear focus, and contextual enquiry has the establishment of this focus as one of its goals (Bawa *et al.,* 2001).

- *Ethnographic study / field observation* - a sociology/anthropology method, used to see how people actually behave in their work environment. Rather than studying the user and interface in laboratory or test conditions this method uses an observer watching the actual work and the actual reaction to the product (Bawa *et al., 2001*).

- *Interviews and focus groups* - formal, structured events where the designers and testers directly interact with the people who will use the product, asking them to voice their opinions and experiences (Nielsen 1993).

- *Prototyping models* - including low fidelity (e.g. paper mock-ups of screen layouts) is useful to help people understand the proposed product and suggest improvements (Bawa *et al., 2001*).

- *Affinity Diagrams* - can be useful to help people categorise their views about a system / interface / problem / requirement. This method is used by a team to organise a large amount of data according to the natural relationships between the items. Often this is done using Post-It notes to gather and group the ideas. Team members move the notes to groups based on how they feel the concept belongs with other concepts (Bawa *et al., 2001*).

Designing for usability includes good information design, for example minimising what is often called "chart junk" - the spurious addition of complexity to a display's or graph's shading or colour scheme with the effect of reducing the information impact.

14.4 Planning and managing usability testing

What is usability testing?

Usability testing is one part of the process of evaluating the usability of software. It is described in the Usability SIGiST Draft standard as follows:

> *"Usability testing measures the suitability of the software for its users, and is directed at measuring the effectiveness, efficiency and satisfaction with which specified users can achieve specified goals in particular environments or contexts of use" (Usability SIGiST, 2000)*

Other definitions have been offered in the literature, for example:

> "A process of planning, preparation and measurement regarding a software product and related (work) products with the objective to determine the effectiveness, efficiency and user satisfaction" (Van Veenendaal, 1998)

In the requirements and design process, the usability attributes are defined for the broad and narrow focus, which are important for this system. The specific requirements for each attribute are listed, together with acceptance criteria. An assessment of the risks associated with each attribute is required:
- how likely is it that this will cause a problem?
- how large is the impact if it goes wrong?

During usability testing, each usability requirement is checked against the specification, including, as appropriate, both broad and narrow focus tests. Usability and usability testing have aspects in common with other types of testing, but there are specific differences which affect how usability testing is set up, executed and reported on.

Usability requirements may need evaluation as well as testing

It is easy to make non-measurable usability requirements that cannot be tested. It is also easy to tie down the usability requirements so that the requirements are easy to measure as opposed to addressing people's usability needs. The project will need to agree a balance for usability requirements. Usability testing requires the tester to carry measurement against defined requirements and measurable acceptance criteria.

> "Usability evaluation has two purposes: the first is to remove usability defects (sometimes referred to as formative evaluation) and the second is to test against usability requirements (sometimes referred to as summative evaluation). It is important to have high level goals for effectiveness, efficiency and satisfaction, but not all means to achieving these goals can be precisely specified or measured. It is important that usability evaluation has the objective of "getting inside the user's head" and understanding why they have a difficulty using the proposed design, using methods that help understand the problems." (Usability SIGiST, 2000).

Both static and dynamic testing have a part to play; static testing using some of the specialised inspection techniques developed for usability, such as Heuristic Evaluation (Nielsen and Mack, 1994), and dynamic testing using some of the observation techniques developed for usability.

Building a strategy for usability testing

The recommended three-step approach in the Usability SIGiST Draft Standard is derived from (Van Veenendaal, 1998). This is a four-step approach overlaid on the V-model:
• Establish and validate usability requirements
• Inspect or review the specification and designs from a usability perspective
• Verify the implementation against the requirements (narrow focus usability testing)
• Validate the implementation (broad focus usability testing)

The figure below shows the V-model from chapter 1, Testing Fundamentals, with the four steps described in (Van Veenendaal, 1998) overlaid on it.

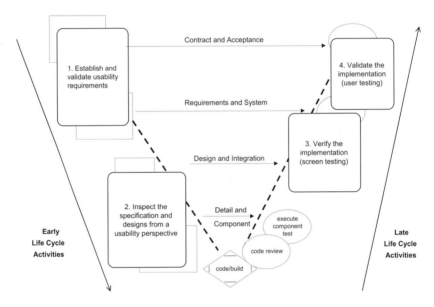

Figure 14.5: V-model with usability steps overlaid

Thus, as with other types of testing, usability testing starts as early as possible in the product life cycle. It may continue after the product launch, with on-going usability assessment during live use. Once the product is in use, usability evaluations can be drawn from survey techniques, as well as from information gathering techniques used during requirements gathering such as focus groups and ethnographical studies.

14.5 Why is usability testing different?

Usability testing is planned and managed in the same way as other types of testing. A test strategy, high level and detailed plans will be required. However, there are significant differences or issues to consider in some areas:

- Usability testers have a special role in observing the test rather than executing the test
- Sampling and sample sizes, as well as choice of participants to meet the contexts of use requires considerable planning
- Designing a fair test requires additional thought compared with other tests
- Usability metrics are not necessarily easy to define quantitatively
- The test environment must closely match the environment in which the product is to be used (this is not just the computer environment but also the surroundings)
- There is a specific industry standard for documenting usability testing
- Usability issues may have a wider scope than testers normally deal with.

Role of the usability tester

The usability tester may not be the person who executes the test; instead the tester's role may be to set up and control the test, and to observe/measure the effect of the product on people chosen to meet the context checklist.

Sampling and sample sizes

There is some argument amongst usability experts about what size sample is required in order to make a meaningful assessment of usability. If only a small number of people use the product it may be possible to include all of them in the usability evaluation. If a large number of people will use the system, a sample will be needed, based on the context of use analysis. In practice the number required would depend on the variance in the data, which will determine whether the results are statistically significant. Some research appears to show that if users are selected who are representative of each user group, then a sample size of as small as three to five users is sufficient to identify problems, while a sample size of eight or more users of each type is required for reliable measures (Macleod *et al.*, 1997).

Once the sample has been selected, its characteristics should be logged, in order that the actual coverage of the identified contexts of use is captured as part of the test results. An example is shown below:

Participant number	Time in job (years)	Windows experience (years)	Internet / web site experience (years)	Attitude to computers / web (1-7) *	Gender	Age group
1	5.5	3.5	0	6	F	20-35
2	0.8	2.1	0.8	1	F	20-35
3	2.1	2.5	2.1	3	M	20-35
4	4.9	3.5	1.5	2	F	36-50
5	0.7	0.7	0.7	2	M	20-35
6	1.6	2.1	0	3	F	36-50
7	4.3	1.4	0	4	M	36-50
8	2.7	4.6	2.7	4	M	20-35

* 1 = prefer to use a computer as much as possible, 7 = prefer to use as little as possible

Figure 14.6 : Example user group characteristics from the Usability SIGiST Draft Standard

Designing a fair test

In functional testing, and in some other non-functional testing, the performance of the test and the observation of results would not significantly affect the outcome of the test. However, in usability testing there is a significant problem in that the way the usability tester introduces and observes the test will affect how the people using the product react to it. Therefore, the usability tester must set up the test to produce a fair result and the test scenarios must include

- instructions for the participants
- allowance of time for pre-test interviews for giving instructions
- allowance of time for post test interviews for receiving feedback
- logging the session
- observer training
- an agreed protocol for running the sessions.

The protocol includes a description of how the test will be carried out (welcome, confirmation that this is the correct user, timings, note taking and session logging, interview and survey methods used). The test must be run with an agreed level of help or intervention provided for the participants, perhaps none or perhaps the help desk provision normally available.

The way in which the instructions are given to the participants affects the test. Consider a usability test where ten participants are to use the product one after another:

- The tester should give the same instructions to all the participants; the way the instructions are given will affect the attitude of the participants.

- The participants all need the instructions immediately before they participate in the test.
- Only one participant will be using the project at a time.
- Examples of factors that may affect the outcome include the usability tester's body language, tone of voice, degree of enthusiasm, the wording which is used.

The example participant instructions in the figure below are to be used. What is the affect if the tester gives instructions verbally and ad hoc to each person, reads the same words to each participant, or gives out the instructions for people to read?

> Thank you for helping us in this evaluation. The purpose of this exercise is to find out how easily people like you can use this ATM. To achieve this, we will ask you to perform some tasks, and your performance will be observed. Then, to help us understand the results, we will ask you to complete a standard questionnaire, and to answer a few questions about yourself. The aim of this evaluation is to help assess the product, and the results may be used to help in the design of new versions. Please remember that we are testing the software, not you.
>
> For this exercise, you will use a Debit Card and a Bank Account set up to help us test the equipment. You own bank account is not known to us and will not be affected. The "money" which you withdraw from the ATM will be "dummy money" and not real money! When you have finished each task, or got as far as you can, please phone us by dialling 1234. I am afraid that we cannot give you any assistance with the tasks.
>
> You have just been shown the XYZ ATM. You now need to find out whether it would be helpful to you to have an ATM like this one at your bank. You will perform the following tasks:
>
> - Withdraw £50 and request a receipt
> - Check your balance
>
> We are interested to know how you go about these tasks and whether you find the instructions helpful or not. LET US KNOW WHEN YOU ARE READY TO BEGIN
>
> - Task 1 – withdraw £20 with receipt (you have about 2 minutes for this task).
>
> Let us know when you have finished.
>
> - Task 2 - check your balance (you have about 2 minutes for this task).
>
> Let us know when you have finished.

Figure 14.7: Example participant instructions

Deciding what it is reasonable to measure

There is not one set of "off the shelf" measurements which may be used for every project. Instead for a particular project, the usability measurements must be agreed. Some examples are shown in the figure below, and there are others in ISO 9126 part 2 and 4.

Effectiveness:

- completion rate: percentage of participants who completed each task correctly;
- mean goal achievement: mean extent to which each task was completely and correctly achieved, scored as a percentage.

Efficiency:

- task time: mean time taken to complete each task (for correctly completed tasks);
- completion rate efficiency: mean completion rate/mean task time;
- goal achievement efficiency: mean goal achievement/mean task time.

Satisfaction:

- measure using a questionnaire, at the end of the session, giving scores for each participant's perception of overall satisfaction, efficiency, affect, controllability and learnability (*see SUMI method, explained hereafter and in annex D*)

Figure 14.8 : Example measurements for effectiveness, efficiency and satisfaction

Environments for usability testing

Testing should be done under conditions as close as possible to those under which the system will be used "in real life". It may be necessary to build a specific test environment, but many of the usability tests may be part of other tests, for example during functional system test. The test environment is part of the context, so thought should be given to different contexts, including environment, and to the selection of specified users. Consideration should be given to how the environment supports the execution, observation and recording of the tests, for example by use of a usability lab (see hereafter).

Reporting on and documenting usability testing

Usability test documentation is covered in the Usability SIGiST Draft standard. A Common Industry Format (CIF) is being developed by the Industry USability Reporting project (IUSR) (Bevan, 1999). If the project is required to meet the CIF standard then the documentation of the usability testing will need to include the test's purpose, product types, the quality model, contexts of use for the product and for the test (including users, goals and environment), metrics (normally at least one for each of effectiveness, efficiency, satisfaction and, where relevant, safety), assessment criteria, and an interpretation of the usability measures of the usability.

Usability problems and issues

Usability problems should be logged and tracked in the normal way. All aspects of the product and environment are open to comment, and usability problems may be raised by anybody, regardless of the documented requirements. This includes documentation, installation, misleading messages, return codes. These can often be perceived as low priority if the functionality is correct even if the system is awkward to use. For instance a spelling mistake or obvious GUI problem in a screen that is frequently in use will be more serious than one in an obscure screen that is only occasionally seen.

It is important to decide how test participants' comments will be considered. If only one person from the sample raises a particular usability problem, that should still be regarded as a problem which needs a solution. Agreement will be needed within the project of how to treat usability problems which are outside the documented usability requirements; these need to be dealt with, but the decision about whether they are treated as "faults to be fixed" or "changes to be negotiated" may have contractual implications.

14.6 Designing usability tests

Many techniques for designing usability tests are available, and a selection is described in the next paragraphs. Whatever techniques are used, there must be a clear definition of the goals for the test. Appropriate narrow and broad focus measures must be agreed. Each project or business would make its own decision about selection of techniques, depending on cost and risk. The use of specialist organisations, in other words outsourcing the usability activities, may be considered. This allows the use of specialist knowledge in designing and running the tests, as well as use of specialist equipment in a usability laboratory. Specialists would also be able to help with usability requirements gathering and in the design process, particularly with their knowledge of use of special usability design and early testing techniques.

In order to save costs, the usability review process may be carried out by the development and testing team. This incurs lower preparation and meeting costs but does not involve the users, so it only addresses in theory how a user might react to the system to be built. A review with users costs more to prepare and run, but the user involvement will be cost effective in finding problems early. The level of complexity of the recording equipment also affects cost. A usability lab costs a great deal to set up (video cameras, mock up office, review panel, users, etc) but enables the development staff to observe the effect of the actual system on real people. This option may be attractive where usability is high priority. It is also possible to set-up a simpler, cheaper environment; for example, Perlman's use of a mirror on the monitor with an over-the-shoulder video camera, so that one can record the screen and the user's expression (Perlman, 1995).

14.7 Early life cycle techniques

Some techniques can be used early in the lifecycle and so influence and test the design and build of the system. Many of these are variations on review, walkthrough and inspection. Examples found in the literature (Nielsen and Mack, 1994) and by an Internet search include:

Heuristic evaluation

Heuristic evaluation is a systematic inspection of a user interface design for usability (Nielsen, 1993). This technique takes the software inspection methodology and adapts it to usability evaluation. The goal of a heuristic evaluation is to find the usability problems in the design so that they can be attended to as part of an iterative design process. Heuristic evaluation involves having a small set of evaluators examine the interface and judge its compliance with recognised usability principles (the "heuristics"). The heuristics defined by Nielsen are:

- visibility of system status
- match between system and the real world
- user control and freedom
- consistency and standards
- error prevention

- recognition rather than recall
- flexibility and efficiency of use
- aesthetic and minimalist design
- help users recognise, diagnose, and recover from errors
- help and documentation

Cognitive walkthrough

Cognitive walkthrough is a review technique where expert evaluators construct task scenarios from a specification or early prototype (Nielsen and Mack, 1994). They then role play the part of a user working with that interface, by "walking through" the interface, working through typical tasks. They act as if the interface was actually built. Each step the user would take is examined. Where the evaluator is blocked by the interface and cannot complete the task, this indicates that the interface is missing something. If the path through the task is convoluted and circuitous this indicates that the interface and the software need simplifying.

Pluralistic walkthroughs

Pluralistic walkthroughs are meetings where users, developers, and usability professionals step through a task scenario, discussing and evaluating each element of interaction (Nielsen and Mack, 1994). Group walkthroughs have the advantage of providing a diverse range of skills and perspectives to bear on usability problems.

Standards inspections

Inspections may be used to ensure consistency across multiple products from the same development effort (Nielsen and Mack, 1994). Standards inspections may be used to ensure compliance with industry standards. In such inspections, a usability professional with extensive knowledge of the standard checks for compliance to industry standards. Consistency inspections begin with a usability professional analysing the interfaces to all of the products and noting the various ways that each product implements a particular user interaction or function. An evaluation team then meets, and using the usability analysis as a basis, negotiates and decides on the implementation for the usability attributes of each product. Guidelines and checklists may help to ensure that consistency is checked and that usability principles will be considered in a design. Usually, checklists are used in conjunction with a usability inspection method. The checklist gives the inspectors a basis by which to compare the product.

Feature inspections

Feature inspections analyse only the feature set of a product, usually given end user scenarios for the end result to be obtained from the use of the product (Nielsen and Mack, 1994). For example, a common user scenario for the use of a word processor is to produce a letter. The features that would be used include entering text, formatting text, spell-checking, saving the text to a file, and printing the letter. Each set of features used to produce the required output (a letter) is analysed for its availability, understandability, and general usefulness.

14.8 Late life cycle techniques

Some techniques are used post software build, for example the use of survey and questionnaire techniques where the system is in use and observations of behaviour with the system in a usability test lab. These techniques are typically used in test levels such as system and/or acceptance test.

Thinking aloud protocol

An example of an observation technique is the "Thinking Aloud Protocol" (Nielsen, 1993). In this method the participants talk while using the product, to describe what they are doing, why they are doing it, and their reaction to the system - they "think aloud". This monologue is recorded, either on a video recorder, an audiotape or by an observer sitting with the participant. The usability laboratory setting may mimic the normal office set up. Before the test, the purpose of the test is explained to the participants - that it is a test of the system's usability not a test of the participants. They are given instructions as to how to run the test, and also the observation and reporting rules. This type of test is explorative, using test scenarios which would be done first by the usability tester to ensure that the tests can be run, and then brought into the usability lab for a "thinking aloud" session with the participant. It is important to consider the effect on the participant of being observed; the tests must take place in an atmosphere of trust and honesty. Additionally it should be noted that the fact of being observed, and the fact of articulating one's thoughts affect one's reaction; thus the test in itself effects the outcome of the test.

Co-discovery

Variations on "thinking aloud" include "Co-discovery" where two participants attempt to perform tasks together while being observed, allowing interaction and mutual help during exploration of the product; and the "Question asking protocol" where instead of waiting for users to vocalise their thoughts, the tester prompts them by asking direct questions about the product. Their ability (or lack of it) to answer questions can help show what parts of the product interface were obvious, and which are not. Note that the approach must be consistent for all the usability tests, because the protocol used will affect the way the participant uses the product and their reaction to it. The observation /

recording may be of sound (verbal comments), video (body language and facial expression) or even of detail such as tracking of eye movements. The recording may be of just the participants, or in some usability laboratories, the observers include the product designers to record their reactions to the participants' reaction to the product.

SUMI

In addition to, or instead of observation techniques, it is possible to use survey techniques and attitude questionnaires both during testing and once the product is used live. These surveys may be "home grown". However, it is also possible, and recommended, to measure against a benchmark, by using standardised questionnaires such as SUMI (Software Usability Measurement Inventory) and WAMMI (Website Analysis and MeasureMent Inventory). (Kirakowski and Corbett, 1994).

SUMI is a brief questionnaire that is marked against a benchmark of responses to surveys of systems. SUMI has been rigorously tested and is regarded as a proven method of measuring software quality from the end user' point of view. WAMMI gives ongoing feedback to continue monitoring how a web site is used. WAMMI is a short questionnaire, which is placed on a website, with a request for visitors to complete comments about the web site. These are marked against a database of previous usability measurements to give a measure of the product against the industry mean score. Both SUMI and WAMMI are brief questionnaires. An example of a SUMI case study can be found in annex D (see also Van Veenendaal, 2000).

Functional testing techniques

The techniques for drawing up specific test cases may be drawn from BS7925-2, The Standard for Component Testing (BS7925-2, 1998), or the tester may wish to use use-cases or scenarios to describe the tests (for a good example see Collard, 1999). In order to observe the person using the system, it is possible to re-use some of the functional tests in the sense of the same inputs and system outcomes being exercised, but the focus of the outcomes are now re-defined to describe the affect of the system on the user. The tests may appear to be the same as the functional tests but the expected results will not be defined in terms of functional correctness. They will be defined in terms of the users' responses to the system - not just that it does what it is supposed to do but that it does it in a way that supports the users.

The system must be understandable, easy to learn, attractive, efficient, and so on. So the expected results are defined to reflect usability requirements rather than functional requirements, and the test set up will be different because we are collecting different types of information. For usability testing we may be interested in the skill sets of the people who will input the customer details, how the system supports that skill set, how efficiently people can process their work, that the system supports them by preventing errors in input, or that the system supports ergonomic keyboard and screen use. It happens that our tests still output letters - but we are interested not so much in the content of the letters but in the human activities and attitudes around the system:

- Can the person using the system get the level of help they require?
- How efficiently can they work?
- How attractive is the system?
- Are they going to use it again by choice?
- Did it help or hinder?

Possible test scenario:

User profile: expert user - 15 of the expert users asked to perform this task and rate it on the usability questionnaire

- Input 1: age = 18
- Input 2: value of goods: £20,000
- System outcome: refuse insurance

Usability outcome:

- User able to work with help prompts switched off.
- Input and letter produced from one screen with two input fields, and confirmation (OK) button.
- 80% of the expert users rate the system as efficient.
- 80% of the expert users rate the system as attractive.

Figure 14.9 : Example functional test with added usability expected results

Tests may be developed to test the syntax (structure or grammar) of the interface, for example what can be entered to a field as well as the semantics (meaning) for example that each input required, system message and output is reasonable and meaningful to the user. These tests may be derived using black box or white box methods (for example those described in (BS7925-2, 1998) or (Pol *et al.*, 2002)). The context of use checklist may be used to develop tests using equivalence partitioning and boundary value analysis. These techniques make it easier to define tests across the range of contexts without repetition or missing contexts. The partitions and boundaries are those between the contexts of use, rather than partitions and boundaries between inputs and outputs. Use risk analysis for the effect of usability problems to weight the partitions and therefore include the most important tests.

An example is the ATM discussed earlier in the chapter. It must be available to everyone. Some of the partitions to consider are shown in the example below, with notes made by the design team to show further areas for consideration and research.

Partition number	Partition description	Notes
Partition 1	User over 2.4 tall	Very tall people sometimes have back problems - bending may be a problem - check what height is suitable
Partition 2	User 2.4 to 1.2 tall	Check if this is the average range
Partition 3	User is less than 1.2 tall or has restricted length	Someone in a wheelchair, for example, must be able to reach. Check what height is suitable
Partition 4	User without visual impairment	What proportion of the population have no visual impairment? What environmental factors will affect them?
Partition 5	User with colour deficit	Which colour combinations?
Partition 6	User with other visual impairment - e.g. central visual defect	Check what visual impairments need to be catered for and how. Check best methods e.g. could there be Braille options, could we use sound (only if private booth available)

Figure 14.10: Example of Partitioning and Boundary Value Analysis for an ATM

Consideration of these partitions and boundaries leads us to question where to place the ATM, or indeed if more than one is required at different heights, as well as the colour and fonts to be used on the display and print out. Example test cases are shown below.

ACTION/TASK: Use the ATM				
Test case	Parti-tions tested	User type / skill / Attribute (people)	Actions	Expected outcome
1	1, 4	A person of over 2.4m with no visual impairment	Withdraw £50 and get receipt	An ATM is available that can be used without excessive bending or stretching. The on-screen instructions can be clearly read and understood. The person can withdraw the money and get a receipt in less than 1 minute. The receipt is readable. Positive feedback in survey.
2	2, 5	A person of between 2.4m and 1.2m tall with red-greencolour deficit	Withdraw £50 and get receipt	An ATM is available that can be used without excessive bending or stretching. The on-screen instructions can be clearly read and understood. The person can withdraw the money and get a receipt in less than 1 minute. The receipt is readable. Positive feedback in survey.
3	3, 6	Person in wheelchair with central visual defect	Withdraw £50 and get receipt	An ATM is available that can be used easily from a wheelchair, without excessive bending or stretching. The on-screen instructions can be clearly read and understood. The person can withdraw the money and get a receipt in less than 1 minute. The receipt is readable. Positive feedback in survey.

Figure 14.11 : Action/task list – example test cases for an ATM

Techniques outside BS7925-2, for example use cases, may also be used (Collard, 1999). An example of a simple use case for an ATM is shown below. Note that in this format, the alternative flow is not a continuation of the main flow but a separate test. Once the tests have been designed they can be run in a usability lab, as described earlier, or using one of the other observation techniques.

Scenario name:	Use of ATM		
System:	XYZ Bank ATM	V0.9	12-7-2001
Goal of test	The goal of this use case is to test the withdrawal of cash from the ATM		
Description	**Context:** This is core functionality, so this is an important test of a frequent usage function		
	Actors: Any user may use this function	Chec-ked	Com-ments
Preconditions	The ATM is on and functional The user has a current debit card		
Description of main flow	ATM start screen is showing 1. the user inserts card 2. the user types in PIN 3. the user selects "cash with receipt" 4. the user selects £50 5. the user selects "no further service"		
Expected results	The ATM returns the card, delivers £50 and a receipt, clears the screen and displays the start screen		
Alternative flows	The user wants to have a balance printed not displayed. ATM start screen is showing 1. the user inserts card 2. the user types in PIN 3. the user selects "print balance" 4. the user selects "no further service"		
Expected results	The ATM returns the card and balance slip, clears the screen and returns to start screen		
Failure conditions	On screen instructions not clearly displayed On screen instructions not simple to follow Card not returned (see functional tests)		
Additional attention points	Note response times		

Figure 14.12 : Example use case for usability test scenario

14.9 Additional sources of information

Many organisations and individuals have an interest in usability and accessibility, either in setting standards or in providing services. Many publications and web sites offer additional information about requirements, usability techniques and tools, usability services or case studies. These include campaigning organisations, government organisations, standards organisations, and interest groups. Campaigning organisations are worth looking at both for examples of well thought out accessible information design and for their own accessibility/usability checklists. IT Organisations such as

IBM, Microsoft and the World Wide Web Consortium Web Accessibility Initiative have usability and accessibility guidelines. Special interest groups and specialist help can be found on many web sites. However, as web sites change or are removed, web site addresses are not referenced here. A search in the literature or on the Internet with keywords will quickly uncover a wealth of information.

References

- Bawa, J, P. Dorazio and L. Trenner L (2001), *The Usability Business - making the web work*, Springer

- Bevan, N, (1999),   *Industry Standard Usability Test Reports*, Industry USability Reporting project (IUSR) CIF IEEE

- BS7925-2 (1998), *Software Component Testing*, British Standards Institution

- Collard, R (1999), Developing test cases from use cases, in: *Software Testing Quality Engineering*, Vol. 1, Issue 4, July 1999

- DDA (1995), *Disability Discrimination Act 1995* (c. 50), Stationery Office Ltd, ISBN 0-10-545095-2

- ISO/IEC 9126-1 (2001), *Software engineering - Software product quality - Part 1: Quality model,* International Organization of Standardization

- ISO/IEC DTR 9126-2 (2001), *Software engineering - Software product quality - Part 2: External metrics,* International Organization of Standardization

- ISO/IEC DTR 9126-4 (2001), *Software engineering - Software product quality - Part 4: Quality in use metrics,* International Organization of Standardization

- ISO 9241-1 (1997), *Ergonomic requirements for office work with visual display terminals (VDT's), part 1: General introduction,* International Organization of Standardization

- ISO 9241-11 (1998), *Ergonomic requirements for office work with visual display terminals (VDT's), part 11: Guidance on usability,* International Organization of Standardization

- Kelly, M. (ed.), (1994), *MUSiC Final Report Part 1 and 2: the MuSiC project*, BRAMEUR ltd, Hampshire, UK

- Kirakowski, J. and M. Corbett (1994), SUMI: the Software Usability Measurement Inventory, in: *British Journal of Educational Technology*, Vol. 24 No. 3 1994

- Macleod M, R. Bowden, N. Bevan and I. Curson (1997*)*, *The MUSiC Performance Measurement method*, in: Behaviour and Information Technology, Vol.16, pp. 279-293.

- Nielsen J., (1993) *Usability Engineering*, Academic Press, ISBN 0-12-518406-9

- Nielsen, J. and R.L. Mack (eds.) (1994), *Usability Inspection Methods,* John Wiley & Sons, Inc.

- Perlman, P, (1995), Practical Usability Evaluation, in*: Conference Proceedings of ACM CHI'95*, v2, no.13, pp.369-370

- Pol, M., R.A.P. Teunissen and E.P.W.M. van Veenendaal (2002), *Software Testing, A Guide to the TMap approach,* Addison-Wesley, ISBN 0-201-74571-2

- Splaine, S and S.P. Jaskiel (2001) *The Web Testing Handbook,* ISBN 0-9704363-0-0

- Usability SIGiST (2000), *Usability testing standard* (draft), BCS Special Interest Group in Software Testing (SIGiST)

- Veenendaal, E. van (1998), Usability Testing, in: *Proceedings EuroStar conference,* Barcelona 1999

- Veenendaal, E. van (2000), Questionnaire-based usability testing, in: *Professional Tester* Vol. 1 Issue 4, September 2000.

15 Performance Testing

Dirk Meyerhoff

This chapter discusses guidelines and recommendations for planning, designing and carrying out a performance test for commercial software applications. These guidelines have been successfully applied in classical monolithic mainframe applications as well as today's client-server and web-based architectures. The recommendations are based on experience gained in numerous performance testing projects. Finally, the performance problems of an actual Internet application and the performance testing measures taken to identify the causes of those problems are described.

15.1 Performance testing

In practice, performance testing often has the goal to measure the load-dependent characteristics of time-critical transactions. Performance testing can be used to benchmark the performance of an application or to understand the scalability of an IT infrastructure. Performance testing of client-server and web-based applications is becoming more and more important due to their increasing role in today's commercial application market. Many companies however have yet to gather experience in performance testing client-server and e-business systems. Long system response times or low transaction rates can reduce the productivity of end-users significantly and subsequently lead to drastically increased monitoring and system-support efforts in production. This can be disastrous for the end-user's acceptance and for a software project's success. This is especially true for web-based systems where the low user tolerance to poor performance and the availability of competitor sites means that customers are easily lost.

Various definitions for performance can be found in testing literature standards. In ISO 9126-1 the software quality characteristic efficiency is defined as having three dimensions, namely time behaviour, resource utilisation and efficiency compliance.

Efficiency: The capability of the software to provide appropriate performance, relative to the amount of resources used, under stated conditions.

Time behaviour: The capability of the software product to provide appropriate response and processing times and throughput rates when performing its function, under stated conditions.

Resource utilisation: The capability of the software product to use appropriate amounts and types of resource when the software performs its function under stated conditions.

Efficiency compliance: The capability of the software product to adhere to standards or conventions relating to efficiency. (ISO 9126-1, 2001)

Currently a detailed performance testing section of the non-functional testing standard is being developed by the BCS Special Interest Group in Software Testing (SIGiST) working party (Performance SIGiST, 2002).

Performance issues often arise in software development projects, which assign too low a priority to performance in the early project phases. This is where performance-engineering methods should be implemented. It is recommended to begin quality assurance with respect to performance issues during requirements analysis.

1. One should start with a realistic estimate of the data volumes and user behaviour to be managed.
2. In addition, a specification of acceptable response times from the end-user's point of view is needed. It is recommend to define a set of measurable performance quality requirements that can be used as acceptance criteria at a later stage, e.g. using the metrics from ISO 9126 part 2 (ISO 9126-2, 2001).
3. During the conceptual phases, lean throw-away prototypes can accompany key decisions in the functional model of an application. At this point, the testability of the application using standard load-generation tools will be decided, too. Selecting a non-standard client-server communication protocol usually significantly increases the effort for introducing a load-generation tool or makes it even impossible.
4. Once the functional specification is available, performance testing activities can start.

15.2 Motivation

Why conduct a performance test?

Past commercial-software projects often placed a higher priority on functional aspects than on performance aspects. Performance testing became relevant only when performance issues disturbed or even blocked production. In many of today's projects, the system's architectural components are very new and there is little or no experience in integrating these components into larger systems. It becomes very difficult to anticipate or plan a system's transaction processing power because of the complexity and the number of components involved. There is usually a multitude of potential bottlenecks for system performance. Therefore performance becomes one of the key risk factors and performance testing helps to avoid such risks.

Additional important reasons for conducting a performance test are to answer the following types of questions:
- What are the major technical and functional performance characteristics of the application? Examples: How does the system react to additional concurrent users? Would it be better to invest more in network bandwidth or in faster I/O components?
- How can the application's performance behaviour in production be estimated?
  Example: Will call centre agents be able to access needed information within a second?
- Is the current hardware-software configuration capable of managing future data volumes and what must be done to keep the application productive until another solution becomes available?
  Example: Should performance be improved by using hardware that is more powerful or by splitting a large database into several smaller ones?
- What, if any, are the differences in performance between this version and the previous one?
  Example: Have software changes improved the performance?

The specific project-related questions that are to be answered during performance testing should be compiled beforehand and be included in the project or phase test plan as major goals of performance testing. This allows an assessment of the performance test's success upon completion.

When should performance testing be conducted and by whom?

When performance issues appear they are usually causing problems for production. Therefore performance testing is often pushed or demanded by production departments, especially when performance engineering methods have not been applied properly. Performance testing in production is definitely the latest possible test. It is also the most expensive (and the least useful) test because only minor environment tuning is possible and the end-user's acceptance of the software has already been jeopardised. It is therefore a good idea to begin performance testing as early as functional system testing or - even better - a couple of weeks before. This is particularly important when additional hardware must be ordered and when results from performance testing are to be addressed by tuning the software before roll-out. It is even more cost effective to conduct a performance analysis and create a performance-test design based on the first architecture descriptions available, since the architecture decisions are among the most important regarding system performance. Here also reviews of architecture and design documents are very important to find and address bottleneck candidates early in the development process.

Performance tests are similar to scientific experiments (Basili *et al.*, 1986). Consequently, performance testing requires highly skilled staff with thorough technical expertise and experience in testing and tools. In most companies, personnel with such a profile are very scarce. External consulting companies offering services in this area can help here. In many cases, performance testing is well suited to be conducted as a small stand-alone project by external resources or even for complete outsourcing to external test laboratories at a fixed price. This is because the knowledge of the functionality required for performance testing is relatively low and any necessary information needed can be acquired in interviews and review meetings with key persons from the business departments. The limiting factors are then whether
- the company wants to distribute core know-how to an outside party,
- the test environment can be set up with a reasonable effort,
- support from in-house experts can be guaranteed, for example via a hotline.

15.3 Conducting a performance test

Prerequisites

Before performance testing can begin, all parties involved should clearly agree upon the major objectives of the test. It is better to reduce the test focus than to overwhelm all participants with the technical and functional complexity of a commercial client-server or web-based application. A few questions must be answered before the performance testers can begin test design. Among these are

- What are the business departments' requirements in detail (e.g. business transactions, test load)?
  Example: How many users log on to the server every Monday morning between 9:00am and 10:00am?
  Example: What is the maximum time in seconds that is acceptable for a transaction?
- How can the performance test expertise that currently exists in the company be expanded?
  Example: Is the performance test team joined by at least two employees from other departments?
- What sort of test data is needed in order to run the test?
  Example: What are the names and passwords of the customers used during testing? What are their account numbers?
- Which tools can be used for performance testing and how can a test environment be set up to automate regression tests?
  Example: Which capture-playback tool should be used and can tools also be used for load generation and performance measurement?

A detailed functional and technical specification is necessary to begin preparation for performance testing. Minimal requirements for response times, maximum data volumes and test data must be defined by the business departments. Performance test tools and at least one production-like test environment should be available; otherwise, activities for test tool evaluation and test environment set-up must be added to the test plan. In cases in which applications are already running in production, sometimes mass data from production can be made available as an initial data load. In such situations security aspects and restrictions, for example the legal aspects concerning the access of performance testers to production data, need to be clarified ahead of time.

In order to begin with test execution and performance analysis, the core functionality of the application should have reached a minimal maturity with respect to stability and correctness. Otherwise, it will be difficult to actually use the test results. The performance requirements regarding the loads and the transaction times should be defined in measurable terms.

Tool evaluation and selection guidelines

The use of testing tools in performance testing is essential for an efficient test execution. At least a capture-playback tool for the automated recording and replaying of user activities is strongly recommended. Such tools allow for the simulation of many users in parallel by running them on different machines or in different environments at the same time. A load-generation tool can simulate many users while only running on one machine. Load-generation tools can significantly reduce the effort needed for multi-user tests, which are often the most interesting scenarios. Monitoring tools for test transaction measurement on the client and on the server are also required. A test management tool for the remote execution of processes, archiving and test script organisation is also strongly recommended, because otherwise too much time is spent on manually preparing the environment for test execution (start each computer, user login, start of client application, start of client, start measurement tools on each server and start execution).

For evaluating and selecting tools, it is useful to apply a standard process, which involves:
• analysis of business requirements and needs,
• documentation checks (basic usefulness of tool for required purpose is checked using available tool documentation),
• on-site evaluation (most tool providers offer evaluation licenses) and
• decision after first successful tests using the tool.

Often the tool provider offers support as part of the evaluation license. The trial use of tools is recommended because the hardware and software in the target environment often conflict with the hardware and software requirements of the test tools or the tool documentation raises expectations, which sometimes simply are not met.

Important questions for the evaluation and selection of capture-playback tools in the context of performance testing are:
• Does the capture-playback tool recognise the GUI controls (GUI objects) of the application under test?
• Can the recorded scripts be easily parameterised and how reliable is the replaying of scripts?
• What are the hardware requirements of the tool and what is their impact on the performance behaviour of the application under test?
• What initial effort is required for learning how to use the tool?
• Can the tool access system resource information (CPU time, memory usage, etc.)?

Important questions for the evaluation and selection of load-generation tools are:
• Does the load-generation tool support the client-server protocol of the application?
• How does the tool support script parameters?
• Can scripts from a capture-playback tool be imported into the load-generation tool?

- How many virtual users can the tool simulate?
- What are the hardware requirements of the tool and what is their impact on the performance behaviour of the application under test?
- Can the virtual-user scripts run directly on the server?
- Is the communication between client and server encrypted? If yes, can the tool handle this?

Important questions for the evaluation and selection of monitoring tools are:
- Is it possible to measure key parameters such as network traffic, client-server CPU and memory usage?
- Can the results be stored as protocols in the test archive?
- Can the results be visualised as graphs?
- What is the accuracy and resolution of the measurement?
- What is the measurement error caused by the tool itself?

Test items and test cases in performance testing

In order to ensure that the entire test process remains goal-oriented, the performance-critical functional transactions should be identified together with key representatives from the business units. These transactions are the test items in performance test. An example of a performance test item could be the login step of an application. Performance test results based on critical transactions are easily understood because end-users can compare the test results with their intuitive expectations. This also facilitates the final assessment of the test results, because recommendations on performance improvements can be expressed in terms of the possible performance gains for those critical user transactions.

In practice, test results show that only between 50% and 70% of the transactions that are initially identified as not performing adequately are actually problematic. The other transactions are affected by bottlenecks lying elsewhere – so they appear to be performing poorly themselves – or they are identified as problematic based on the personal (biased) judgement of users.

During system analysis, the performance-relevant parameters, like database configurations, number of simultaneous session's etc., are identified for each test item. Test cases are then derived through systematic variation of those parameters.

Each test item – for example the user login, a buy transaction, or a user function to display all transactions of the user – should be covered by at least one business workflow executed during the performance test. These workflows are also called test scenarios. The so-called production mix, a model of the expected production load, is obtained by mixing all test scenarios according to the expected operational load profile. The underlying idea of such an operational profile is that all relevant transactions and functions are actually executed in the frequency that are to be expected in or known from production. (for more information see TMap "Real-life" testing technique, (Pol *et al.*, 2002))

When developing performance test designs and procedures one should keep in mind that performance testing does not replace functional testing as only a few business processes are considered. Accordingly, performance test scenarios should be kept as simple as possible and should not contain functionally different test cases for a transaction unless additional insights regarding the performance are expected. The content of the test cases is not the focus of performance test, rather the number and type.

Test execution

The activities of test execution as well as test validation and documentation in performance testing are just as important as they are in functional system testing. However, the high number of test cases run in performance testing can produce measurement result data that is distributed over several protocol files instead of a simple yes-or-no test result. Immediate test result validation is therefore mandatory. For test execution, the test environment has to be prepared. The background test data must be prepared in such a way that they are compatible with the performance tests, i.e. with the transactions and functions to be executed by the performance tests. When the background data and the system is ready the manual or – more likely – the automated load can be placed on the system. This means that the performance tester either enters the performance test scenarios manually or starts a load generator, which will then simulate the defined load using the test scenarios. Often these load generators also take an important role in test monitoring and evaluation.

Every aspect of test execution should be documented carefully. Automated logging of (screen) output is strongly recommended for some representative test cases, while logging of output for all test cases may lead to invalid performance test results due to the extensive use of system resources by the logging processes.

Test evaluation

A large amount of runtime data is collected during test execution. Therefore, an overview of test results that directly addresses the questions described in paragraph 15.2 should be created for all functional and technical key parameters. Using statistical methods dependencies between technical key parameters and measured runtime data can be proved. In order to answer questions concerning stability it is highly recommended to observe the distribution of the measured runtime data.

It is also important to check not only the time needed for transactions but also, at least to some extent, the accurateness of the results produced by the system. This is due to the experience that applications under high load do not always produce the same results (functionally) as they do with a low load. If for example a certain number of stock orders were created during the performance test, it is recommended to verify a few orders in the database in detail and check the total number of stock orders processed.

Generally, automated test evaluation should be given at least the same priority as automated test execution because the effort required for test evaluation is at least as high as for test execution.

For evaluation of the test results mainly two types of experts are required: The application expert verifies whether the transactions and functions have operated correctly. The performance measurement expert validates the measured runtime data against expectations or – a more desirable situation – verifies exact performance requirements using the measurements taken.

The evaluation reports presented to management should not be overloaded with technical or business terms. This allows simple control of the test process, even by non-experts in performance testing, and new questions that arise during test execution can be easily recognised.

15.4 Risk management

An established risk assessment helps to identify and avoid potential pitfalls during test execution. Once a test environment (including tools) is available, four typical types of problems can still occur, namely functional, technical, organisational and methodological issues. Some important examples of each problem type are recommended as a standard risk assessment checklist. They are listed below.

Functional issues

- Missing or misinterpreted functional information leads to incorrect use of the application.

- Data, for example input data from external systems, is missing or dependencies between data are hidden.
- Error messages, warnings and software outputs are misinterpreted.
- Runtime errors and even data corruption occur due to mass data and functional defects.

Technical issues

- Installation of new software versions or technical components leads to significant downtimes.
- Capacity of (disk) storage is exceeded.
- Additional hardware is required or hardware that is ordered is not delivered on time.
- Load machines are not capable of generating the required load.

Organisational issues

- The work of different departments adversely influences the test environment. For example, server administration, client administration and network experts change system settings without co-ordination.
- Performance test resources, e.g. network bandwidth, are shared with external parties.
- Key persons are not available to clarify technical and functional questions.
- The time needed to execute certain tests exceeds the time planned and thus blocks the test environment so that for example a conversion step for production data is also delayed.

Methodological issues

- Use of an unrealistic load profile leads to false results.
- Use of an inappropriate testing environment makes reliable predictions almost impossible. Typical pitfalls for a testing environment are:
- significantly less powerful machines than in production,
- significantly smaller database than in production,
- configuration settings different from those in the production environment.
- Runtime data is misinterpreted.

Solutions to these problems involve the careful planning of activities and transparent test organisation. The validity of assumptions upon which the test is based should be checked regularly. Limit values for key parameters of the test environment should be defined. If these limits are not met a performance test should not be executed because this would mean that the test environment does not meet the expectations and is not a good simulation of the target production system – in other words performance test results cannot be transferred to reality. Examples of such limit values are:

- The CPU of the application server should run at more than 90% idle time. (This would mean that the CPU of the application server in the performance test environment is at least 90% available for the performance test.)
- The network transfer rate should be less than 800 KB. (This would mean that the bandwidth required for a reasonable load test is actually available.)

15.5 Experiences from real life

In a large Internet banking project the following striking phenomenon was observed in production: All servers still had enough resources but occasionally the application slowed down severely and even returned incomplete pages. A performance test was conducted in order to identify the source of the problem. The performance test environment matched the production environment very closely. The loads from production were taken and matched by performance test loads. Finally, the performance test reproduced the phenomenon in the test environment. The test revealed the following reasons for the problem:

The production environment was tuned by each administration team individually. The firewall team configured a load-balancing mechanism using a second backup firewall, while the web server team set up a fixed routing between the web servers and the application servers with no knowledge of the additional firewall. Therefore, under production load some network packets were routed through the backup firewall and got lost. This led to poor response times and even incomplete pages.

Database connection pooling was configured but not enabled.

It was shown that the response time highly depended on the type of customer using the application. Under certain rare circumstances, the application needed about 60 seconds longer for some customers than for a typical customer. This was due to a design problem (in order to avoid multiple database connections all account information for all accounts was picked at once – even if it was not yet needed)

After these problems had been fixed, the performance test showed that the application then ran stable and fast enough. The most important factors for the success of this performance test were:

- Do not overwhelm the testing focus. Placing too many demands on a performance test makes test design as well as test evaluation complicated and expensive.
- Concentrate the focus in an interative top-down manner. A very general performance test is often much cheaper to implement then a test designed to reveal very specific performance problems. Therefore, specific

performance tests should only be carried out when performance is identified as having problems on the general level.

• Facilitate communication between all involved parties. User and IT departments should be involved in performance-test design and execution. Often performance requirements are defined but not generally made known to all project members. Well-prepared performance test meetings with users and IT-staff often answer all questions pertaining to performance testing.

Acknowledgements

The author would like to thank Paul Keese, Michael Kuss and Frank Simon for their valuable suggestions and the performance testing team at SQS AG – headed by Heike Hefner – which provided many practical insights used to compile this chapter.

References

- Anderson, M. (1999), The top 13 mistakes in Load Testing Applications, in: *Software Testing and Quality Engineering*, Volume 1, Issue 5, September/Oktober 1999

- Basili, V., R Selby, and D. Hutchens (1986), Experimentation in Software Engineering, in: *IEEE Transactions on Software Engineering*, vol.SE-12, no.7, July 1986, pp.733-743.

- Beizer, B. (1990), *Software Testing Techniques,* 2nd edition, Van Nostrand Reinhold, ISBN 1-850-32880-3

- ISO/IEC 9126-1 (2001), *Software engineering - Software product quality - Part 1: Quality model,* International Organization of Standardization

- ISO/IEC DTR 9126-2 (2001), *Software engineering - Software product quality - Part 2: External metrics,* International Organization of Standardization

- Killelea, P. (1998), *Web Performance Tuning,* O´Reilly & Associates

- Loukides, M. (1990), *System Performance Tuning.* O´Reilly & Associates

- Meyerhoff, D., H. Berlejung (2000), Guidelines for Performance Testing in Commercial Client/Server Software Projects, in: *Conquest 2000*, ASQF – Arbeitskreis Software-Qualität Franken

- Meyerhoff, D., S. Caspers (1999), Performance and Robustness Test – Factors of Success for Development and Introduction of Commercial Software, in: *Conquest 1999*, ASQF – Arbeitskreis Software-Qualität Franken

- Performance SIGiST (2002), *Performance testing standard* (draft), BCS Special Interest Group in Software Testing

- Pol, M., R.A.P. Teunissen and E.P.W.M. van Veenendaal (2002), *Software Testing, A Guide to the TMap approach,* Addison-Wesley, ISBN 0-201-74571-2.

Part 5

Incident management

16 The Bug Reporting Processes[1]

Rex Black

There is an internal test process that produces results that are very visible: the bug reporting process. In a sense, bug reports are the only tangible product of the testing process itself, solid technical documentation that describes a behaviour or potential behaviour in the system under test that could negatively affect the customer's experience of quality. These negative behaviours are variously referred to as anomalies (the IEEE 1044 preferred term), bugs, incidents, flaws, problems, or defects, among other names. These bug reports also give management the information they need to decide the priority of the problems and provide developers with the information they need to fix them. Why is the bug reporting process is so critical? First and foremost, bug reporting is critical because bug reports are the vehicle by which we as testers influence increased product quality. Second, bug reporting is something that we do every day, and many times a day, usually during test execution periods. Third, bug reports are often highly visible, read by developers and senior managers alike. The successful test manager must master this process, and help their test team master it as well, in order for the test team to fully realize their potential contribution to the development effort.

16.1 Definitions

While the questions of "What constitutes a bug?" and "What is a bug report?" seem obvious from a high level, frequent semantic problems arise. A bug can be defined as a problem present in the system under test that causes it to fail to meet a reasonable user's expectations of behaviour and quality. Straightforward, right? Well, one person's reasonable expectations can be another person's wild-eyed pipe dreams. When standards of quality or expectation of behaviour are neither obvious nor documented in requirements, specifications, business rules, or use cases, experiences show

---

1   This chapter by Rex Black is based on chapter 11 from his book "Critical Testing Process" © 2002 Rex Black reprinted by permission of Pearson Education, Inc.

that the reasonableness of an expectation is usually decided by iterative consensus, e.g. discussion between the various concerned managers and staff, or by management decree.

Having mentioned quality, what can one say about that elusive trait? J.M. Juran, one of the fathers of the quality movement, defines quality as, "Features...decisive as to product performance and as to 'product satisfaction'...[and] freedom from deficiencies...[that] result in complaints, claims, returns, rework and other damage. Those collectively are forms of 'product *dis*satisfaction." (Juran, 1988). So, the definition can be rephrased to say that a bug exists when the product passively fails to satisfy the customer or actively causes customer dissatisfaction. More specifically, a bug is either a defect in the system under test that leads to quality-reducing behaviours or the absence of support in the system under test for quality-increasing features (that a reasonable user would expect). Here we need to be specific because one common objection to some bug reports is along the lines of, "that's not a bug, it's an enhancement request." The question of whether a quality issue should be resolved in the current release or some subsequent release is a matter of business priority for executive management, but it doesn't affect whether a quality issue exists.

A further source of confusion about bug reports arises because the word "bug" is not ubiquitous. Some people prefer "fault," "error," "glitch," or "defect." among other words. The symptom of a bug is sometimes called the "failure," "failure mode," "event," "issue," or "anomaly." As mentioned earlier, anomaly is the generic term used in the IEEE 1044 standard. These terms are generally recognized as synonymous, we use the word "bug" because of its quaint historical connotations. This brings us to the topic of this chapter, the bug report, which is defined as a technical document written to describe the symptoms of a bug for the purposes of
1) communicating the circumstances, effects, and classifications of a quality problem;
2) prioritizing the bug for repair;
3) helping the developer locate the underlying defect and fix it.

16.2 IEEE 1044 bug process

In IEEE Standards 1044 (IEEE, 1993) and 1044.1 (IEEE, 1995), a generic process for reporting, managing, and resolving bugs is laid out. This process includes four major steps:
1. Recognition
2. Investigation

3. Action
4. Disposition

Within each step, three activities take place, identifying, classifying, and recording. For the most part, steps 2, 3, and 4 of this process take place as part of the duties of the programmers, system engineers, and hardware engineers who repair the bugs, and the project management team that prioritizes and assigns bugs to specific participants for repair. Testers are primarily responsible for step 1, which is the subject of this chapter, along with final confirmation of repair for bugs which are fixed.

16.3 Bug reporting process

How can one write the best possible bug reports? The following outlines a number of generic rules for a thorough bug reporting process:

Structure
Good bug reporting begins with solid, organized testing. Testing may be manual or automated, scripted or exploratory, but it must be something other than just hacking on the product in an aimless attempt to break it. Sloppy testing yields sloppy bug reports.

Reproduce
Bugs almost always take us by surprise. If we could predict in advance when we would find a bug, we would hardly need to test the product. Reproducing the problem sharpens our understanding of the issue and allows us to document a crisp set of steps that will recreate the failure. Three tries is a good rule of thumb. Of course, some bugs have intermittent symptoms. For bugs that do not reliably reproduce their symptoms, the tester still writes the report, but notes the frequency of symptom occurrence. For example, "This failure occurred two out of three tries." This has the substantial political side-benefit of addressing the issue of irreproducibility head-on, which I'll revisit later.

Isolate
Many factors can affect the behaviour of software, and some of those factors will affect bugs. The way in which a change in the test environment manifests itself in terms of bug behaviour is often significant. By changing some key variables, one at a time, in an attempt to change the behaviour of the bug, the tester can write more insightful bug reports. Isolating a bug is not easy; one must understand to some extent how the system under test works and think through some experiments before running them. The tester also must take care not to voyage into the land of debugging (more about this later) or expend

inappropriate amounts of time on trivial issues. However, good bug isolation builds tester credibility and gives the developer a head start on debugging.

Generalize
Often the failure mode observed when first finding a bug is just one, possibly minor, case. For example, a problem was found where a program wouldn't import a specific worksheet from an Excel file. When the tester dug a bit deeper, though, he realized that it wouldn't import *any* worksheet from any Excel file if the name of the worksheet contained parentheses. It's important, though, when looking for the general case, not to generalize to the point of absurdity. Not all program crashes, for example, come from the same bug. Nevertheless, trying to find the general rule for how the bug occurs deepens understanding and helps convince developers and managers that the problem is not an isolated case.

Compare
Testing often covers the same ground, both when a tester runs the same tests against a later version of software and when a tester runs tests that cover similar conditions. These results can provide important clues to a developer when you connect the dots. Is the failure a regression? Does the same feature work in other parts of the product? While this kind of research is not always possible, e.g. when a test was blocked against a previous version, it can save the developers a lot of time if the tester can find this information.

Summarize
At this point in the process, the failure is probably understood well enough to answer the all-important question: "How will this problem affect the customers?" To translate that to manager-speak, that is, "Why should I waste my time listening to testing talk about this bug?" Manager-speak is mentioned because much of the reason we want to write a summary (or title) for our bug reports is to communicate to managers in a single sentence the essence and significance of the problem testing has found. This summary is invaluable when it comes time to prioritize the bugs. It also gives the bug report a "handle" or name for developers. "Hey, have you fixed that font-change bug yet?" is a question a tester might ask a developer which is far more meaningful than, "How's work on bug 1716 coming?" Writing a good summary is harder than it looks. The American President Thomas Jefferson once concluded a long letter with the sentence, "I would have written a shorter letter but I didn't have time." Spend the time to write good summaries, because it's the most important sentence in the bug report.

Condense

Speaking of writing a shorter letter, how about trimming some unnecessary words from our bug reports? The author once read a bug report that had nothing to do with computer video games that happened to mention that the tester had just set the high score in Tetris, an 80's video game. Do we care? No. Do we need to spend time reading about that? No. Did the tester who wrote that report make us want to pay close attention to his subsequent reports? No. The best bug reports are neither cryptic commentary nor droning, endless, pointless documents. Use just the words needed and describe only the steps and information that actually pertain to the bug being reported.

Disambiguate

To disambiguate is to remove confusing or misleading phrases that might make a reader wonder what is meant; e.g., this paragraph could be disambiguated by using the alternative phrase "be clear" instead of disambiguate. All kidding aside, the idea is for the bug report to lead the developer by the hand to the bug. Clarity is key.

Neutralize

As the bearers of bad news, testers needs to express themselves calmly and impartially in bug reports. Attacking the developer, criticizing the underlying error in the code, or using humour or sarcasm to make a point generally backfire. We should be temperate and fair-minded in our words and implications, and confine bug reports to statements of fact, not conjectures or hyperbole. As Cem Kaner has pointed out, you never know who's going to read the bug reports—plaintiff's counsel, perhaps?—so to avoid unnecessary appearances as a witness for the prosecution of your employer, you should write only exactly what you mean. (Kaner *et al.*, 1993)

Review

As I mentioned earlier, a bug report is a technical document. One thing we've learned about quality assurance is that peer reviews, inspections, walkthroughs, and the like are powerful tools for early detection of defects. The same applies to bug reports. Before dismissing this step as too time-consuming or a needless roadblock to getting bug reports filed as quickly as possible, consider the delays and frustration that can result when a developer wastes time trying to reproduce a bug that was actually a test problem or when a developer can't figure out what a bug report is about and so returns it as "irreproducible."

In following this process, testers should perform the three major types of activities specified in IEEE Std 1044 for the recognition step of the test management process: Identify, Classify, and Record.

Three points need to be mentioned about this process before going on. First, writing is creative: two good bug reports on one problem can differ in style and content (but not substance). The purpose of the bug reporting process is not to "standardize" bug reports, but rather to ensure quality. Think of this process as mixing paint or preparing a canvas for a portrait, rather than a "paint-by-numbers" diagram. Second, this process works best when thought of as a checklist rather than a strict sequential process. The first and last steps, structured testing and a peer review, are logical bookends, but proficient bug reporters practice all eight intervening steps in parallel. Finally, most test teams manage bugs in some sort of bug tracking tool, generally a set of screens, queries, and reports, together with business rules implementing a workflow, all built on top of a database. A good tool should adapt itself to the process, and the process should be optimized for the tool.

16.4 A hypothetical case study

To illustrate the bug reporting process, a Speedy Writer case study is provided. Suppose you are testing release 1.1 of a Web-based word processing program called Speedy Writer. Under a waterfall development model, the project entered the system test phase last week, and the system administration group just installed the second build on the test network. Your team has just started the second cycle of testing. Let's look a gradually refined failure (anomaly) description that L.T. Wong, a test engineer, writes during this cycle.

L.T. Wong is running an edit functionality test. She creates a new file, inserts some text, then tries to change the font of the text by selecting it, pulling down the font menu, and selecting the Symbol font. Based on the expected result documented in the test case, L.T. expects to see the sentences changed into Greek characters. (This is the behaviour for one popular PC-based word processing application.) However, the screen displays a bunch of flashing pixels, question marks, control characters, and other meaningless and seemingly random stuff where nice normal English sentences once were. L.T. starts her bug report and notes:

> *Nasty bug trashed contents of new file that I created by formatting some text in Symbol font, wasting my time.*

This might be the way one would describe this problem in a hallway conversation, but it's of limited use. With an eye towards helping some lucky developer understand what's going on, suppose that L.T. goes back and reproduces the problem a couple more times, refining her thinking about what went wrong and how to make it happen again. Subsequently, she might write the failure description as follows:

> ### Steps to Reproduce
> 1. *I started the SpeedyWriter editor, then I created a new file.*
> 2. *I then typed in four lines of text, repeating "The quick fox jumps over the lazy brown dog" each time, using different effects each time, bold, italic, strikethrough, and underline.*
> 3. *I highlighted the text, then pulled down the font menu, and selected Symbol.*
> 4. *This nasty bug trashed all the text into meaningless garbage, wasting the user's time.*
> 5. *I was able to reproduce this problem three out of three tries.*

This is much better. A developer can read this and get a head start on debugging the problem. However, remember that the SpeedyWriter product, as with any other application, supports a wide range of features and configurations that may affect the behaviour of this bug. What happens if an attempt is made to isolate the key variables that affect the bug? L.T. tries a few experiments and adds the following section to the bottom of her bug report:

> ### Isolation
> *On the vague suspicion that this was just a formatting problem, I saved the file, closed SpeedyWriter and reopened the file. The garbage remained.*
> *If you save the file before Symbolizing the contents, the bug does not occur.*
> *The bug does not occur with existing files.*
> *This only happens under Windows 98.*

This is a very specific failure mode, so L.T. decides to try a few other fonts, as well as checking to see if the font effects and styles have anything to do with the bug. She finds that both Wingdings and Arial fonts suffer from the same problem, while the bold, italics, and underlining have no effect on the bug's manifestation. (Note that the general condition here, with the popular Arial font suffering the same bug, gives this problem a much higher priority than before.) She deletes the potentially misleading reference to font styles from step two of the report and adds the following line to the Isolation section:

> *Also happens with Wingdings and Arial fonts.*

Next, L.T. reviews the test logs from the previous cycle of system test as well as looking at some test reports from the component test and integration test phases. She finds that this particular feature has been tested quite a bit, which tells her that this problem is a regression in product quality. She adds the following line to the Isolation section:

> *New to build 1.1.018; same test case passed against builds 1.1.007 through 1.1.017.*

Now that L.T. has a solid understanding of the bug, how it manifests itself, and how that affects the user, she writes the summary line (or title) for the bug report:

> **Summary**
> *Arial, Wingdings, and Symbol fonts corrupt new files.*

Here, L.T. has captured the impact to the user and the basic nature of the problem in eight words. No one reading this summary will fail to understand what the problem is and why it matters. At this point, the bug report is written. All that remains is to spend some time polishing it. First, L.T. condenses the report a bit by eliminating extra verbiage, for example rephrasing

> *If you save the file before Symbolizing the contents, the bug does not oc-cur.*
> as
> *Saving file before changing font prevents bug.*

and dropping the word "I" from the steps to reproduce. Next, L.T. reviews the report for ambiguous or confusing wording. She changes step three from

> *3. Highlighted the text, then pulled down the font menu, and selected Symbol.*
> to
> *3. Highlighted all four lines of text, then pulled down the font menu, and selected Arial.*

Step four goes from

> *4. This nasty bug trashed all text into meaningless garbage, wasting the user's time*
>
> to
>
> *4. This nasty bug trashed all text into meaningless garbage, <u>including control characters, numbers, and other binary junk</u>, wasting the user's time.*

In the Isolation section, she changes

> *Also happens with Wingdings and Symbol fonts*
>
> to
>
> *<u>Reproduced with same steps using</u> Wingdings and Symbol fonts.*

She adds the some detail to the Isolation line that reads

> *This only happens under Windows 98.*

expanding it to say that the bug

> *Only happens under Windows 98, not Solaris, Mac, or other Windows flavours.*

To wrap up, L.T. scours the report for any extreme or biased statements. She decides step four is a bit harsh, so she rephrases that as follows:

> *4. All text converted to control characters, numbers, and other apparently random binary data.*

Finally, L.T. asks you to review the report. You ask her if perhaps this bug is related to the file-creation problem she found in the first test cycle. You also ask her to remove the word "garbage" from the isolation section, being possibly inflammatory. The final bug report as submitted follows:

> **Summary**
> Arial, Wingdings, and Symbol fonts corrupt new files.
> <u>Steps to Reproduce</u>
> 1. Started SpeedyWriter editor, then created new file.
> 2. Typed four lines of text, repeating "The quick fox jumps over the lazy brown dog" each time.
> 3. Highlighted all four lines of text, then pulled down the font menu, and selected Arial.
> 4. All text converted to control characters, numbers, and other apparently random binary data.

> 5. Reproduced three out of three tries.
> <u>Isolation</u>
> New to build 1.1.018; same test case passed against builds 1.1.007
> through 1.1.017. *Possibly related to the file-creation bug fix in this rele-*
> *ase?*
> Reproduced with same steps using Wingdings and Symbol fonts.
> Saved file, closed SpeedyWriter and reopened file. *Still saw same cor-*
> *ruption of the text.*
> Saving file before changing font prevents bug.
> Bug does not occur with existing files.
> Only happens under Windows 98, not Solaris, Mac, or other Windows
> flavours.

This is a good, solid failure description for the bug that L. T. has observed.
(Again, the IEEE 1044 standard refers to this section of a bug report as the
anomaly description.) It communicates the problem, it will help management
decide whether to fix it based on impact to the customer, and it gives the
development team some solid leads for their debugging activities.

16.5 Classification: beyond the failure description

So far, the focus has been on the failure description, which is the heart of the
bug report. However, there are some other pieces of information commonly
captured by bug tracking systems that are important to making the overall bug
management process work.   These pieces of information are classifying
information and other supporting data. These pieces of information can take
the form of text, identifiers (codes with special significance), measurements
(numbers, dates, and other metrics), pointers or references to other
information sources, and administrative information.

In what IEEE 1044 refers to as the "recognition" step of the "generic anomaly
process," it provides for the following classification information to be gathered
during the bug reporting process:
* *Project Activity* (Mandatory): What was the person who reported the bug
  doing when the bug was recognized? The standard choices are: Analysis,
  Review, Audit, Inspection, Code/Compile/Assemble, Testing, Validation/
  Qualification Testing, Support/Operational, and Walk-through.
* *Project Phase* (Mandatory): At what stage in the system lifecycle was the
  project when the bug was recognized? The standard choices are:
  Requirements, Design, Implementation, Test, Operation and Maintenance,
  and Retirement. Some of these classifications include subclassifications as
  well.

- *Symptom* (Mandatory): What kind of problem does the person reporting the bug observe? The standard choices are: Operating System Crash, Program Hang-up, Program Crash, Input Problem, Output Problem, Perceived Total Product Failure, System Error Message, and Other. Some of these classifications include subclassifications as well.
- *Suspected Cause* (Optional): What does the person reporting the bug think might be failing or causing the failure? The standard choices are: Product, Test System, Platform, Outside Vendor/Third Party, User, and Unknown. Some of these classifications include subclassifications as well.
- *Repeatability* (Optional): As mentioned in section 16.3, how often can the person reporting the bug get the symptom of the bug to recur? The standard choices are: One Time Occurrence, Intermittent, Recurring, Reproducible, and Unknown.
- *Product Status* (Optional): What state is the system in due to and/or following the failure observed by the person reporting the bug? The standard choices are: Unusable, Degraded, Affected (Use Workaround), and Unaffected.

In addition, IEEE 1044.1 provides a number of additional classification data items that testers can use for bugs. Any of these classification schemes, according to IEEE 1044 and IEEE 1044.1, can be extended or customized as needed. For example, IEEE 1044.1 shows a way to expand the Project Phase classification to accommodate the DoD-STD-2167A and Spiral Life Cycle Models.

Two additional classification items that should be entered during the bug reporting process are severity and priority. While the IEEE 1044 and IEEE 1044.1 do not require the entry of the data items until investigation, a tester who has followed the process described in this chapter is sufficiently informed to estimate these.

Severity is defined as the technical impact on system under test. The following scale is the IEEE 1044.1 scale for severity:
1. Urgent: The failure causes a system crash or unrecoverable data loss or jeopardizes personnel.
2. High: The failure causes impairment of critical system functions and no workaround solution exists.
3. Medium: The failure causes impairment of crucial system functions, though a workaround solution does exist.
4. Low: The failure causes inconvenience or annoyance.
5. None: None of the above, or the anomaly concerns an enhancement rather than a failure.

Regarding priority, meaning the business importance, such as the impact on the project and the likely success of the product in the marketplace. The following scale is the IEEE 1044.1 scale for priority:
1. Urgent: Extremely urgent, resolve immediately.
2. High: Resolution requirement for the next external release.
3. Medium: Resolution required for first customer ship or deployment.
4. Low: Resolution desired for first customer ship or require for the subsequent release.
5. None. Resolution not required.

Priority and severity are distinct concepts and priority is the more important one. However, all too often project teams get into heated arguments over whether a particular bug was "severity one" or "severity two", the subtext being that only severity one bugs matter. Such discussions are beside the point. When deciding whether to fix a bug, one should focus on how the associated symptoms, behaviours, and failure modes affect the customers. Imagine a bug that involves display of an inappropriate message. That's a severity four or five bug on the scale described above. What if the inappropriate message includes a profane, lewd, or racist word? Less dramatically, suppose that the product name is displayed incorrectly in the splash screen? These kinds of problems are must-fix for release, severity notwithstanding. Conversely, a data loss bug that only occurs under certain obscure circumstances on unlikely and obsolete configurations may be severity one but priority five under the definition provided. What if our SpeedyWriter editor loses data when we save to a 360 kilobyte 5 ¼ inch floppy diskette? Perhaps, instead of fixing such a bug in the software, one should just document that our product doesn't support such drives. Boris Beizer provides a good discussion of bugs and what he calls "bug importance" (Beizer, 1990)

In IEEE 1044, the authors recommend a number of supporting data items during the bug reporting process (i.e., the IEEE 1044 "recognition" step). These are pieces of information that will help in the subsequent investigation, action, and disposition for the reported problem. One of these key pieces of information for a bug report is the tested version of the software. In the case study, L. T. reported a bug against "build 1.1.018" and reported that "builds 1.1.007 through 1.1.017" did not suffer the same failure mode.

In the case of integrated test management systems, where the bug and test repositories are in the same system, these two repositories can often be linked. Test case results can link to specific bug reports and bug reports can link to test cases. If the bug tracking system doesn't support this feature, the bug reporting process perhaps should include entering a test identifier in the failure description. Speaking of traceability, some bugs can be tied to specific requirements, business rules, use cases, or quality risks. Again, testing will use whatever built-in support your test management systems has for such tracing, or, if no such support exists, add a step in your process where the tester notes this information in the failure description.

Since bugs can be quite dependent on the specific configuration tested, testers should make a habit of noting this as well. Ideally, the bug tracking system will support a look-up table for test system configurations, but, if not, the tester needs a text description that captures the key items.

Another piece of information useful to capture is affected subsystem, component, or function. For example, in the case of word processor we might have the following categories:

- User interface
- Edit engine
- Installation and configuration options
- Documentation and packaging
- Other

- Tools and utilities
- File operations
- Unknown
- Not Applicable

Capturing this information is useful for various metrics, including tuning on-going and future testing to focus on those areas of the product that create the most problems.

In a typical bug tracking system, the developer who fixes the bug and possibly the release engineer who integrates the fixed code into the code repository will fill in some fields. (IEEE 1044 and IEEE 1044.1 define a number of mandatory and optional classification fields for the investigation, action, and disposition steps of the "generic anomaly process" defined in those two standards.) These fields don't typically have a lot of impact on the test team, except if they include a notation about which build contains the code fix associated with a given bug. Testers may find it useful to run reports on this information when preparing to confirmation test the bug fixes in a given test release. Going beyond the solitary bug report, bug tracking information also has an aggregate dimension. Metrics related to find and fix rates, defect injection phases, closure period, root cause, subsystem affected, and the like are critical project dashboard data. For more information on bug tracking systems, what they should capture, and what metrics one can obtain from them, please see "Managing the Testing Process, Second Edition" (Black, 2002), IEEE 1044, and IEEE 1044.1.

16.6 Process quality indicators

Based on the discussion so far, what quality indicators apply to the bug reporting process?

Clear, concise bug reports

Since writing a bug report *is* writing, albeit very technical, the usual quality indicators for good technical writing apply. Testers should write clearly and to the point. Testers should speak in a way that connects with the audience on their terms. Where bug reports do contain jargon and acronyms, testers should use well-understood project terms. They should produce clear, concise bug reports that everyone understands.

Bugs fix ratio

Bug reports are written to document problems, to help establish priority, and to provide information for fixing them. Kaner, Nguyen, and Falk put this slightly differently when they wrote that:
- the purpose of testing a program is to find problems in it;
- the purpose of finding problems is to get them fixed. (Kaner *et al.*, 1993)

This definition may minimize the broader risk-management function of the testing group, but it shows that the test team must have a positive return on the testing investment in terms of increased product quality. A must-fix bug found by the test team is a must-fix bug that won't reach the customer, with attendant order-of-magnitude savings in fix costs. Of course, it takes two to tango, as the saying goes, and even the best bug reports won't get fixed if a recalcitrant development team disregards them or an incompetent project management team ignores the ever-increasing bug backlog. However, disregarding such dysfunctional circumstances, when the bug reporting process provides managers with the information they need to prioritize bug fixing efforts and provides developers with the information they need to fix the bug reports assigned to them, that bug reporting process will have a better bug fix ratio than one which does not meet these criteria.

Duplication rate

Bug reports are about symptoms - observed anomalous behaviour - while bug fixes address defects in systems. It is certainly the case that some disparate bug reports lead to the same underlying bug. However, typically this number is fairly low. Testers can't do anything about such situations, but they can work to minimize having two testers reporting the identical misbehaviour in two separate bug reports. Such duplication of bug reports means duplication of effort by testers, developers, and managers. As with the entire process, balance is required, though. Most test and software professionals prefer have two bug reports on a must-fix bug than no bug report, e.g. a test escape. The author's rule of thumb is that a tester should not spend more than five minutes searching the bug tracking system for an existing bug report before filing a new one. A good practice is to have testers circulate their bug reports via e-mail to the entire team, either as part of the review process or just for general information. This level of effort normally keeps the duplication rate down to around five to ten percent, which is tolerable.

Bug report "ping-pong"

Bug report ping-pong is a game played between tester and developer where bug reports bounce unproductively back and forth. Typical reasons for these ping-pong games are that the developer says a reported bug is irreproducible or is inappropriately assigned to their component or piece of code. The former problem can be resolved through careful bug reporting as described earlier, particularly documenting the steps to reproduce and noting if the problem is intermittent. The latter problem requires dealing with the development manager to make sure that they, not testing, are ultimately responsible for assigning bug reports to developers.

Delineate a clear boundary between testing and debugging

As Boris Beizer has pointed out, in the earliest stages of test effort maturity, testing is seen as an adjunct to the debugging process. As the testing effort matures, though, testing is seen as a distinct set of tasks devoted to locating bugs and managing quality risk (Beizer, 1990). In companies with independent test teams, testers focus on testing and developers handle the debugging tasks.

Look at the process associated with finding a failure, fixing the underlying bug, and confirming resolution as shown in figure 16.1. The first three steps of this process are test activities, which belong to the test team, and occur as part of or in parallel with the bug reporting process. The next three steps are debugging activities, which belong to the development team, and happen as part of fixing the problem described in the bug report from the test team. The final step is confirmation and regression testing of the fix, which is again a testing activity. Therefore, this is a seven-step collabourative process that improves the quality of the system under test through closed-loop corrective action driven by bug reports. While the process is collabourative, each individual task belongs clearly to either the test team or the development team

In the IEEE 1044 and IEEE 1044.1, what this means is drawing a clear distinction between recognition, the first step of the bug management process in the IEEE model, and investigation and action. Disposition involves in part management guidance in terms of which bugs to defer, which bugs to fix, and who should do the fixing. It also involves the final step shown in figure 16.1, the confirmation and regression testing of the bug fix and, if appropriate, the test release containing the bug fix.

A good bug reporting process supports this separation of duties, because as pointed out earlier, a good bug report gives the developer all the information he needs to reproduce the problem and start tracking down the bug. The bug reporting and bug management processes are the only vehicles required for communication between the two teams. The hand off in the centre of the figure signifies this. The metaphor is a hand off, not a dialog, inquiry, or team activity, because a good bug reporting and management process protects the developer from having to ask the tester questions about what their bug report means and the protects the tester from having to spend time duplicating effort reproducing the problem for the developer.

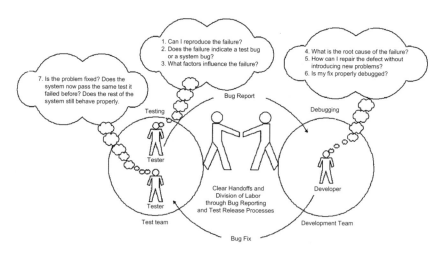

Figure 16.1: The find/debug/confirm process

Some test engineers consider it as something of a killjoy to discourage tester involvement in debugging, so let's explain the test manager's position:

1. The test manager has a lot of testing work for his testers to do. He's held accountable for that work getting done. When testers help developers fix problems, they're not testing.
2. Test managers can't manage their test operations when people loan themselves to the development organization at their discretion. Part of

managing is allocating human resources to meet corporate objectives. Test managers can't have re-allocation happening on the say-so of a tester who, frankly, may not have insight into the evolving priorities.

3. Debugging assistance by testers is seldom a wise use of resources. Even if the tester is a competent programmer, presumably the reason he is testing, not programming, is that he is more valuable to the company in a testing role.

4. Working side-by-side with developers on debugging may boost egos and feel like teamwork, but it doesn't build careers. An organisation will be happy to structure someone's job to support a programming career path, usually by adding test toolsmith and test automation tasks to their workload. Such activities are much more conducive to learning about programming than participation in debugging, which is more programming tourism than a resume highlight.

5. As hinted above, these activities often indicate a poor job of bug reporting being done by the tester. If the developer can't figure out what's going wrong based on the bug report and must ask the tester, then the solution is a crisper bug reporting process, not tester participation in debugging.

All that said, on some occasions testers should or even must participate in debugging, especially when unique test configurations or tools are required to reproduce the problem. It's really the exception to the rule, though, and a good bug reporting process minimizes the occurrence.

No bug reports for management problem escalation

Since bug reports are written to communicate about a problem in the system under test for the purposes of getting that problem prioritized and possibly fixed, testing needs to be sure that it uses the communication channel the bug reporting and bug management processes exclusively for that purpose. Submitting bug reports that report failures of the *process* rather than the *product* should be avoided. For example, if the release engineer didn't deliver the Monday morning build at 9:00 AM, testing shouldn't write a bug report with the summary, "Build not delivered on time." Talk to the release engineer, explain the importance of timely receipt of builds, and, if the issue were an on-going situation, escalate the problem to management. Of course, if the build was delivered on time but then wouldn't work, testing may write a bug report titled, "Build 781 fails to install."

Distinguish between test problems and SUT problems

As shown in Figure 16.2, an observed anomaly, rather than indicating a quality problem with the system under test (SUT), might actually be a testing problem. Such testing failures can arise with automated testing when the software driving the test fails, and it can arise for both automated and manual testing when the expected result is defined or predicted incorrectly. There is no magic bullet for eliminating tester mistakes, if there were, it would work for developers, too, most likely, and testers would be out of a job, but there are steps testing can take. In terms of the bug reporting process, reproducing the problem and isolating the causes of the failure helps, as does the peer review at the end.

Metrics support (project dashboard)

The test execution process needs to support gathering key metrics for managing testing and the project as a whole. Some of those metrics arise from the bug tracking system. So, the bug reports that the test team writes must gather all the important information needed for these metrics. The process must work crisply, so that metrics that are driven by dates have accurate date information. Testers must take care to categorize bugs appropriately, e.g., in terms of affected subsystem, so that metrics that analyze bugs by categories are meaningful. Above all, bug reports must be honest and complete. The tester will go to a great deal of trouble to report bugs, so one should make sure that the process supports gathering all the data as you do so. As mentioned earlier, *Managing the Testing Process, Second Edition*, IEEE 1044, and IEEE 1044.1 can provide you with further information on metrics to gather in your bug reporting process.

16.7 Handling challenges

Writing good bug reports and managing those reports to closure presents the test team, and especially the test manager, with a number of challenges, even when the perfect process *is* in place for writing these reports. These challenges are both technical (related to how hard it is intrinsically to report about the unknown) and political (related to the need to manage the interpersonal and team dynamics of criticizing the work of others).

Bug or feature?

As mentioned earlier, ambiguity in, or a complete lack of, requirements or specifications can complicate the bug reporting process. When developers respond to bug reports with comments like, "Well, that's the way XYZ is supposed to work," testers often have no clear way to refute that claim. Rather than becoming ego-involved in the issue, the course of action is to resolve the ambiguity through discussions with the various concerned parties. People like the technical support manager, the sales and marketing team, the development manager, and others on the management team will probably have opinions as well. As long as you don't escalate *every* bug report for arbitration, these people are probably ready, willing, and able to let testing know how they think the product ought to behave.

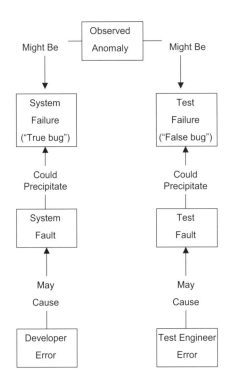

Figure 16.2: Test problem or system under test problem?

Bugs that get fixed by accident

The author once worked on a project where the development manager released new software daily. Testing chose not to accept builds into the test lab that often, as it disturbed our execution process to have to do confirmation testing that often. Every time there was a bug review meeting with this person, in response to any serious bug, whether his team had spent even a second trying to fix that bug or not, he would say, "Well, you need to retest that bug with release ABC because I bet we fixed that problem." Finally, we became so exasperated with this response that we told him, "You know, I'm sure you're convinced that you fixed all these bugs by accident, but in my experience a lot fewer bugs get fixed by accident than development managers would like. Until you actually expend some time trying to reproduce the problem and repair the bug, I am not going to ask my team to waste their time on retesting bugs."

The delivery was a bit raw, but these comments were needed in terms of course of action. Bugs don't typically get fixed by accident. By experience, requests to retest every bug against every release in the off chance that somehow many of them magically went away are a form of development manager squid ink designed either:
1. to obfuscate the fact that the product's quality is abysmally bad;
2. to slow down the onslaught of bugs reported by the test team.

Being a team player is good, but allowing yourself to be hoodwinked into squandering the test team's time retesting bugs that no one has tried to fix is not exactly the pinnacle of good management. Again, this brings us back to the IEEE 1044 model for bug management: Recognition, Investigation, Action, and Disposition. Until the proper entities have undertaken investigation and, if necessary, action on a recognized bug, then disposition work by the test team is seldom appropriate.

Irreproducible bugs

As difficult as this fact makes the lives of testers, and developers, some bugs just won't produce the same symptom again and again on command like a trained seal. For example, memory leaks depend on specific conditions arising repeatedly over an extended period of time before the system crashes or the application locks up. On one project, modem connections dropped sporadically, but testing couldn't make the problem occur deliberately. Ultimately, the developers had to put special probes in the software to track down the problem. Many times, intermittent bugs are also serious bugs. Crashes, losses of modem or LAN connections, or terminal mishandling of inputs (e.g., the Wintel PC "crazy mouse" bug) can disrupt a user's work and even destroy their data.

So, be skeptical of claims that a bug "just went away" (see above) when neither developers nor testers can reproduce the symptom. It is recommended to keep such bug reports open for a few test cycles (about two or three weeks) to make sure the symptom is not seen again. Testing may ask developers what they want us to do if they do observe the problem. (For example, rebooting a hung system usually destroys the state data that might help a developer track down the bug; perhaps the developer will want to try to probe the system through the network to capture this information.). Make sure to keep a record of every time the failure *does* rear its ugly head again. Some sense of the kind of system unreliability that the bug will cause is crucial to intelligent prioritization of the fix effort, and that means that testing need to be able to report on its frequency.

Deferring trivia or creating test escapes?

Sometimes bugs are reported that even testers consider nit-picky or insignificant. Perhaps testers should skip writing those reports? Or, when someone suggests that no one will care, the tester should defer or cancel the report? Doing so is arrogating the right to make decisions about what quality means for this product; that decision really lies with the customer whose needs and requirements the testers usually understand only imperfectly. Testing might decide to ignore a particular problem in the belief that no user would care, but then sales and marketing people can come back later and ask us how such an obvious bug escaped from the testing process. Once again, testing must strive for a bug prioritization process that sees the impact of the problem through the customer's eyes, and make decisions about which bugs to fix and which to ignore based on that.

Build trust with developers

Some testers enjoy testing because they have a chance to "catch" developers. This kind of "gotcha" attitude can create real problems with bug reporting. If developers see testing as a game of tag, then the "ping-pong" issue discussed early is sure to arise. In addition to keeping a team-oriented mindset during testing, four specific bug reporting actions support a cooperative relationship between testers and developers.

1. Keep your cool during discussions about bug reports with developers.
2. Discuss bug reports with an open mind, considering the possibility that you are mistaken about correct behaviour.
3. Submit only quality bug reports and be open to suggestions for improving the quality of your bug reports.
4. Be flexible on the delivery and reporting of bugs; e.g., if a developer wants a particular file or screen shot attached to a bug report, assuming the bug tracking system support such attachments, be cooperative.

There's really no overstating the kind of mischief that can occur when developers perceive the bug reporting process as a whip used by testers to beat them. In extreme cases, developers and development managers have demanded the right to review and approve bug reports before these reports were entered into the bug tracking system.

Let the development manager drive the bug fixing process

Sometimes test managers fall into the trap of haranguing individual developers about when a particular bug will be fixed. This is usually a bad idea, for a couple reasons. First, since developers don't usually report to test managers, test managers don't have a lot of insight into what other tasks the developers might have assigned to them. Interfering with their priorities won't endear the test manager to them or to their manager. Second, test managers have little if any authority over developers, so one likely outcome is that the test manager will irritate people without achieving any useful result. The test manager might be able to inveigle them to work on your favourite bug through bribery (lunch) or intellectual challenge (writing a particularly engrossing bug report), but taking the liberty of managing another's team generally won't work in the short- or long-term.

As a corollary to this observation, testing should avoid using the bug report data to create charts or circulate reports that make individuals look bad. For example, many bug tracking tools have an "estimated fix date" field that developers fill in for their own manager to report when they expect a bug will be fixed. Running a report that shows, for each developer, which bugs they haven't yet fixed that are past due would be humiliating to people. Likewise, running a report on components or affected subsystems by owner name, e.g. implying that the owner introduced the bug, would be both misleading and harmful to the targeted developers. As mentioned in the previous subsection, developers must trust you with the bug tracking system, otherwise dysfunctional events occur.

16.8 Implementing changes

This chapter has hopefully challenged some your existing approaches for handling bugs, confirmed others, and maybe left you thinking of how you can implement some the ideas you like but haven't started yet. How you get your bug reporting process under control depends a lot on where you are now, but here are some suggestions:
1.   Testers usually have strong opinions about bug reporting. However, be careful not to let your opinions blind you to the fact that other people are the customers for these bug reports. Talk to your customers, the technical support people, the developers, your fellow managers, and your test team, to find out what about the current process they like and dislike, as well as how they'd like to see the bug reports improved.
2.   As mentioned in the context of test execution, it's important to have a bug tracking system in place. There is a simple Microsoft Access database

provided with the book, *Managing the Testing Process, Second Edition,* (Black, 2002) which is available for free if you don't have the time or resources to buy or build you own. You can use a spreadsheet, if absolutely necessary, but text files, word processing documents or collection of e-mails won't work. Remember, we want to support gathering metrics, and you won't be able to do any good analysis from these kinds of files.

3. If you have an existing system in place, you should try to adapt it to support this process or some usable variant of it before deciding you must replace the system because you can't do everything you want. Changing your bug tracking system is a big decision, especially if you are in the middle of a project. The technical issues associated with moving data from one tool to another are not trivial and there are political issues, too. Bug tracking systems are often shared with other groups, such as release management, development, and technical support, and managers of these groups often develop personal dashboards that use bug tracking data. At the right time, changing bug tracking systems can make sense, but this process has been used with some of the worst bug tracking tools on the market.

4. In some cases rigidity and consistency of process are critical, but in the case of bug reporting, flexibility and sensitivity to priority are more important. The only iron-clad rule on this process is that every bug report undergoes a peer review. In some cases, reproducing the problem three times makes sense, but in some cases it doesn't. For example, if you have found a very trivial problem and it takes an hour to reproduce the failure, is that a wise use of two hours?

5. Some people have commented that they don't see how to make the peer review work. It is recommend that you give it a try before you dismiss it as a roadblock to efficient testing. Bad bug reports can waste a lot of time. Think of it this way: Testers are in the information business, we deliver an assessment of quality and risk, so the last thing we want is for our primary, highly-visible information products to be inferior. Do you think that an editor reviews every word on the front page of the "Wall Street Journal" before it gets published? You bet! Peer reviews are proven methods for improving the quality of technical documents, and those of us in the quality business should use the tools at our disposal to do a good job.

6. The bug reporting process suggested is a lot of work. It might help to come up with a metric that can show the improvement of the process. For example, what is the reopen rate on bug reports? In other words, how many come back to test marked as fixed or irreproducible when they are not fixed properly or are easy to reproduce? Another metric might be the closure period - how long, on average, do bug reports stay open? A good bug reporting process should help drive both these numbers down.

Whatever changes you implement, patience and perseverance are important. People develop habits of working, especially when it comes to tasks they do over and over again. You'll need to keep this in mind as you work with these folks to improve your bug reporting processes. However, the payoff is there. By applying the techniques discussed in this chapter, bug report fix rates have been achieved, e.g. closure of the bug report with an associated code change, of between 70 to 80%. If three out of four of your bug reports address a customer-facing, must-fix problem, then your bug reporting process will be a success.

References

- Beizer, B. (1990), *Software Testing Techniques*, 2nd edition, Van Nostrand Reinhold, ISBN 1-850-32880-3

- Black, R. (2002), *Managing the Testing Process*, Second Edition, John Wiley and Sons, New York.

- Black, R. (2000), Effective Test Status Reporting, in: *Software Testing and Quality Engineering*, Volume 2, Issue 2, March/April 2000

- IEEE 1044 (1993), *Standard Classification for Software Anomalies*, IEEE Standards Board

- IEEE 1044.1 (1995), *Guide to Classification for Software Anomalies*, IEEE Standards Board

- Juran, J.M. (1988), *Juran on Planning for Quality*, The Free Press, New York

- Kaner, C., J. Falk and H. Nguyen (1993), *Testing Computer Software*, Second Edition, John Wiley and Sons, New York.

Part 6

Test Process Improvement

17 Testing Maturity Model

Erik van Veenendaal and Ron Swinkels

For the past decade, the software industry has put substantial effort in improving the quality of its products. This has been a difficult job, since the size and complexity of software increases rapidly while customers and users are becoming more demanding. Despite encouraging results with various quality improvement approaches, the software industry is still far from zero defects. To improve product quality, the software industry has focused on improving their development processes. A guideline that has been widely used to improve the development processes is the Capability Maturity Model. The Capability Maturity Model (CMM) is often regarded as the industry standard for software process improvement. Despite the fact that testing often accounts for 30-40% of the total project costs, only limited attention is given to testing in the various SPI models such as the CMM. As an answer, the testing community has created its complementary improvement models. This chapter focuses on the Test Maturity Model (TMM). The TMM[1] is a model for test process improvement and is positioned as being complementary to the CMM. The ISEB practitioner syllabus (ISEB, 2001) identifies test process improvement as one of the key areas within the testing profession and identifies TMM as one of the major models.

17.1 History and background

The TMM framework has been developed by the Illinois Institute of Technology (Burnstein *et al.*, 1996) as a guideline for test process improvement and is positioned as a complementary model to the CMM (Paulk *et al.*, 1989) addressing those issues important to test managers, test specialists, and software quality professionals. Testing as defined in the TMM is applied in its broadest sense to encompass all software quality-related activities. Just like the CMM, the TMM also uses the concept of maturity levels for process evaluation and improvement. Furthermore process areas, goals

---

1   TMM is a registered servicemark of Illinois Institute of Technology

and key practices are identified. Applying the TMM maturity criteria will improve the testing process and have a positive impact on software quality, software engineering productivity, and cycle-time reduction effort.

For defining the maturity levels, the evolutionary testing model (Gelperin and Hetzel, 1988) has served as a foundation for historical-level differentiation in the TMM. The Gelperin and Hetzel model describes phases and test goals for the 1950s through the 1990s. The initial period is described as "debugging oriented", during which most software development organizations had not clearly differentiated between testing and debugging. Testing was an ad-hoc activity associated with debugging to remove bugs from programs. Testing has since progressed to a "prevention-oriented" period, which is associated with current best practices and reflects the highest maturity level of both the CMM and the TMM.

Furthermore, various industrial best-practices and testing surveys have contributed to the TMM development providing it with its necessary empirical foundation and the needed level of practicality (e.g. Durant, 1993). They illustrate the current best and worst testing environments in the software industry, and have allowed the developers of the TMM framework to extract realistic benchmarks by which to evaluate and improve testing practices.

Also the concepts associated with Beizers' evolutionary model on the individual testers' thinking process (Beizer, 1990) have been incorporated. Its influence on TMM development is based on the premises that a mature testing organisation is built on the skills, abilities, and attitudes of the individuals who work within it.

Whereas some models for test process improvement focus only on high-level testing or address only one aspect of structured testing e.g. test organisation, the TMM addresses both static and dynamic testing. With respect to dynamic testing, low-level and high-level testing are within the scope of the TMM. Studying the model more in detail one will learn that the model addresses all four cornerstones for structured testing (life cycle, techniques, infrastructure and organisation) (see chapter 2).

17.2 TMM maturity levels

The TMM consists of 5 maturity levels that reflect a degree of test process maturity. For each maturity level, a number of process areas are defined. A process area is a cluster of related activities within the test process, e.g. test planning or test training. When these activities are executed adequately, they will contribute to an improved test process. The five levels of the TMM will support an organisation to determine the maturity of its test process and to identify the improvements that are necessary to achieve a higher level of test maturity. Within the structure, a clear distinction is made between parts that are required (the maturity goals) and parts that are strongly recommended (key practices, subpractices). The TMM also contains examples and a list of recommended literature for each process area.

The five maturity levels and related process areas of the TMM are (figure 17.1):
- Level 1: Initial
  No process areas are identified at this level
- Level 2: Definition
  Process areas: Test Policy and Goals, Test Planning, Test Techniques and Methods and Test Environment
- Level 3: Integration
  Process areas: Test Organisation, Test Training Program, Test Life Cycle and Integration, and Control and Monitor
- Level 4: Management and Measurement
  Process areas: Peer Reviews, Test Measurement and Software Quality Evaluation
- Level 5: Optimisation
  Process areas: Defect Prevention, Test Process Optimisation and Quality Control.

Figure 17.1: TMM maturity levels and process areas

As can be seen in figure 17.1, the TMM consists of five maturity levels. The maturity levels are characterised hereafter.

The five maturity levels show an evolution from a chaotic, undefined test process to a controlled and optimised test process and largely reflect the five evolutionary periods that are described by Gelperin and Hetzel. TMM level 1 is related to the "debugging-oriented" period, level 2 to the "demonstration-oriented" and "destruction-oriented" periods, level 3 to the "evaluation-oriented" period and level 4 and 5 to the "evaluation-" and "prevention-oriented" periods. The five maturity levels are also strongly related to the CMM levels. In many cases a given TMM level needs specific support from key process areas at its corresponding CMM level or from lower CMM levels. An overview of supporting CMM key process areas required for TMM level achievement is shown in table 17.1 (Suwannasart, 1996).

TMM	CMM	Supporting CMM Key Process Areas
2	2	Requirements Management, Software Project Planning, Software Configuration Management
3	2	Software Project Tracking and Oversight, Software Quality Assurance
3	3	Organisation Process Focus, Organisation Process Definition, Training Program
4	3	Intergroup co-ordination, Peer Reviews
4	4	Quantitative Process Management, Software Quality Management
5	5	Defect Prevention, Technology Change Management, Process Change Management

Table 17.1: Support for TMM maturity levels from CMM key process areas

Level 1: Initial

At level 1, testing is a chaotic, undefined process and is considered as a part of debugging. The objective of testing at this level is to show that the software runs without major failures. Software products are released without adequate visibility regarding the quality and risks. In the field, the software does not often fulfil needs, is not stable, or is too slow to work with. Within the test project there is a lack of resources, tools and well-educated testers. There are no process areas at this level.

Level 2: Definition

At level 2, testing is a defined process and is clearly separated from debugging. In the context of structuring the test process, test plans are established containing a test strategy. For deriving and selecting test cases from requirement specifications, formal test design techniques are applied. However, testing still starts relatively late in the development life cycle, e.g. during the design or even during the coding phase. The main objective of testing in TMM level 2 organisations is to verify that the software satisfies the specified requirements.

Process areas at level 2 are:
- Test Policy and Goals
- Test Planning
- Test Techniques and Methods
- Test Environment

Level 3: Integration

At level 3, testing is fully integrated into the software life cycle. It is identified and defined at all levels of the V-model. Test planning is done at an early project stage by means of a master test plan. The test strategy is determined using risk management techniques and is based on documented requirements. A test organisation and a specific test training program exist, and testing is perceived as being a profession. Reviews are carried out, although not consistently and not according to a documented procedure. In addition to verifying that the software satisfies the requirements, testing is extended with invalid testing.

Process areas at level 3 are:
- Test Organisation
- Test Training Program
- Test Life Cycle and Integration
- Control and Monitor

Level 4: Management and Measurement

In TMM 4 organisations testing is a thoroughly defined, well-founded and measurable process. Reviews and inspections are taking place throughout the software life cycle and are considered to be part of testing. Software products are evaluated using quality criteria for quality characteristics such as reliability, usability and maintainability. Test cases are gathered, stored and managed in a central database for re-use and regression testing. A test measurement program provides information and visibility regarding the test process and product quality. Testing is perceived as evaluation; it consists of all life cycle activities concerned with checking software and software-related work products.

Process areas at level 4 are:
* Peer Reviews
* Test Measurement
* Software Quality Evaluation

Level 5: Optimisation

On the basis of all results that have been achieved by fulfilling all the improvement goals of the previous maturity levels, testing is now a completely defined process and one is capable of controlling the costs and the testing effectiveness. At level 5, the methods and techniques are optimised and there is a continuous focus on test process improvement. Amongst others "Defect Prevention" and "Quality Control" are introduced as process areas. The test process is characterised by sampling based quality measurements. A procedure exists for selecting and evaluating test tools. Tools support the test process as much as possible during test design, test execution, regression testing, test case management, etc. Testing is a process with the objective to prevent defects.

Process areas at level 5 are:
* Defect Prevention
* Test Process Optimisation
* Quality Control

17.3 TMM structure

The structure of the TMM is partly based on the CMM and the staged version of its successor: the Capability Maturity Model-Integrated (CMM-I). This is a major benefit, because many people/organisations are already familiar with the CMM(I) model structure. The CMM(I) structure makes a clear distinction between practices that are required (goals) or recommended (key practices, subpractices, etc.) to implement. This aspect is also included in the TMM. In this paragraph, the structure elements are described. The descriptions of the structure elements are adapted from the CMMI-SE/SW staged representation (Phillips and Shrum, 2000).

Maturity level

A maturity level is a degree of organisational test process improvement across a predefined set of process areas in which all goals within the set are attained. By identifying to what extent the goals are satisfied the maturity level of an organisation can be determined.

Process area

A process area is a cluster of related practices in an area that, when performed collectively, achieve a set of maturity goals considered important for establishing process capability in that area. A maturity goal is a required TMM structure element within a process area. A process area may contain several goals. Each goal within a process area must be achieved to consider the process area to be achieved.

Key practices

Key practices describe the activities that contribute to the effective implementation and institutionalisation of a maturity goal regarding a process area. They are the operational elaboration of the TMM. Key practices were selected based on their effectiveness in improving the capability in a certain process area. The key practices address the tasks, activities and responsibilities for management, development, testing and users/customers.

Subpractices

Subpractices are practices that describe activities that may be implemented in establishing the key practice. Subpractices are for informational purposes only and are intended to provide clarification of the key practices and to generate ideas for the user. Examples and a list of recommended literature are provided to clarify the (sub)practices and to support the TMM user.

17.4 TMM Level 2: Definition

To provide the reader with more insight and detailed understanding, guidelines for the TMM level 2 process areas are described in this paragraph, including the accompanying maturity goals. Since most companies are still at level 1, the level 2 guidelines probably reflect the test improvement areas for most companies and projects.

Test Policy and Goals

The purpose of Test Policy and Goals is to develop and establish a test policy and an overall test approach containing test goals, responsibilities and main tasks for each test level.

When an organisation wants to improve its test process, it should first clearly define a test policy. The test policy defines the organisation's overall test objectives, viewpoints regarding testing and the level of independence. It is important that the test policy is aligned with the overall business (quality) policy of the organisation. A test policy is necessary to attain a common view on testing between all relevant stakeholders within an organisation. This common view is indispensable to align further test process improvement activities.

Within the test policy the objectives of test process improvement should be stated. These objectives should be translated into a set of high-level key test performance indicators. The establishment of performance objectives and indicators provides clear direction and communication of expected and achieved levels of performance.

Within this process area an overall test approach is also defined. The overall test approach is a high-level test process description. The overall test approach can be based on existing generic overall test approaches for example: the V-model or the incremental model (IEEE 610.12, 1990). Within the overall test approach, test levels are identified, for example: unit, integration, system and acceptance test. In addition, goals, responsibilities and main tasks for each test level are defined. The overall test approach serves as a starting point for the test projects. Test projects are set up according to the overall test approach. When an overall test approach is defined and followed, less overlap between the test levels is likely to occur leading to a more efficient test process.

Maturity goals of the Test Policy and Goals process area are:
• A test policy, aligned with the business (quality) policy, is defined and agreed upon.
• An overall test approach is defined and deployed, identifying the test levels including goals, responsibilities and main tasks for each test level.
• A set of test process performance indicators is defined and deployed.

Test Planning

The purpose of Test Planning is defining a committed test strategy and approach, and establishing well-founded plans for performing and managing the test. Planning is essential for a process that is to be repeatable, defined and managed.

After confirmation of the test assignment, a general study is made of the system to be tested, the project, the functional and quality requirements, and the organisation of the development process. As part of test planning, the test strategy is defined by means of a risk assessment. Depending on the risks, it is decided which properties of the system will be tested, and in what depth. For it is impossible to test the entire system, as test techniques providing 100% coverage exists only in theory. Moreover, no single company would be willing to afford the resources required for this purpose. The objective is to provide the best possible degree of coverage in the right place. Such matters are, of course, agreed specifically with the stakeholders. Testers should not take these decisions themselves. Within test planning, the test organisation is also set up, the test deliverables that are to be provided are identified, and aspects relating to infrastructure and management are defined. Finally, the test plan is prepared and agreed upon.

Maturity goals of the Test Planning process area are:
* A project's test strategy is defined and agreed upon.
* Test project activities and commitments are planned and documented.
* Estimates are documented for use in planning and monitoring the test project.

Test Techniques and Methods

The purpose of Test Techniques and Methods is to improve test process capability during test design and execution by applying basic test techniques and methods.

Well-founded testing means that formal techniques and methods are applied, supported (if possible and useful) by tools. Test design techniques are used to derive and select test cases from requirements and development documentation. A test case consists of the description of the starting situation (including the test input), the change process, and the expected result. The test cases are documented in a so-called test design. At a later stage, as more information becomes available on the actual implementation, the test designs are translated into test scripts. In a test script, the specific test actions and checks are arranged in an executable sequence. The tests can subsequently be executed using these test scripts. The test design and execution follow the predefined test strategy in the test plan.

During the test execution test incident reports are documented and tracked until closure. Incidents are logged using an incident management system and a clear communication about the incidents with the stakeholders is realised.

Maturity goals of the Test Techniques and Methods process area are:
* Test design techniques are evaluated, recommended and consistently applied throughout test design.
* Test execution is performed using formal test scripts.

- Supporting tools are evaluated, recommended and consistently applied where possible for test design and test execution.
- Incidents found during testing are managed and reported.

Test Environment

The purpose of Test Environment is to establish and maintain an integrated software and hardware environment in which it is possible to execute tests in a manageable and repeatable way.

A test environment is needed to obtain test results under conditions which are as close as possible to the "real-life" situation, at least as far as high level testing is concerned. Furthermore, at any test level the reproducibility of test results should not be endangered by undesired or unknown changes in the test environment.

Specification of the test environment is carried out early in test projects. Specifications are reviewed to ensure their correctness, suitability, feasibility and its representativeness towards the "real-life" environment. Early specification has the advantage that there is more time to develop any special simulators, like stubs or drivers.

Availability of a test environment encompasses a number of issues, which need to be dealt with: Is it necessary for testing to have an environment per test level? A separate test environment can be very expensive. It must therefore be decided how to use them as efficiently as possible. Maybe it is possible to have the same environment shared between testers and developers. But then strict management and control is necessary as both testing and development activities are done in the same environment. When poorly managed, this situation can cause many problems ranging from conflicting reservations to people finding the environment in an unknown or undesired state when starting one's activities. Reconfiguring an environment to reach a known initial state can take days, depending on its size and complexity. Another approach for test environments is to let them 'grow' in parallel with the test levels. For example, one can decide to test a certain requirement at a higher test level to prevent the development of stubs that are needed to simulate specific subsystems that are available at higher levels.

Throughout the project the test environment is subject to changes due to for example hardware changes, incremental test environment development and changes in the test object. Thorough (configuration) management on the test environment is needed to cope with these changes.

Maturity goals of the Test Techniques and Methods process area are:
- Test environments are specified and their availability is ensured on time in projects.
- For higher test levels the test environment is as much as possible "real-life".
- Test environments are managed and controlled according to documented procedures.

17.5 From detection to prevention

Software systems play an increasingly important role in the society, making it necessary to link quality both to the process and the product. The TMM is focused on the test process as a complementary model to the CMM. It has been developed to support software organisations at evaluating and improving their test process. Within the TMM, testing evolves from a chaotic, ill-defined process with a lack of resources, tools and well-educated testers to a mature and controlled process that has defect prevention as its main objective.

Practical experiences are positive and show that TMM supports the process of establishing a more effective and efficient test process. Testing becomes a profession and a fully integrated part of the software development process. The focus of testing will change from defect detection to defect prevention.

References

- Beizer, B. (1990), *Software Testing Techniques*, 2nd edition, Van Nostrand Reinhold, ISBN 1-850-32880-3

- Burnstein, I, T. Suwannasart and C.R. Carlson (1996), *Developing a Testing Maturity Model: Part 1,* in: *CrossTalk*, August 1996

- Burnstein, I, T. Suwannasart and C.R. Carlson (1996), Developing a Testing Maturity Model: Part 2, in: CrossTalk, September 1996

- Burnstein, I, A. Homyen, T. Suwannassart, G. Saxena and R. Grom (2000), *A Testing Maturity Model for Software Test Process Assessment and Improvement,* in: T. Daughtrey (ed.), *Fundamental Concepts for the Software Quality Engineer,* American Society for Quality, Milwaukee, USA, ISBN 0-87389-521-5

- Durant, J. (1993), *Software testing practices survey report,* (TR-5-93), Software Practices Research Center

- Gelperin, D. and W.C. Hetzel (1988), *The growth in Software Testing.* In: *Communications of the ACM,* June 1988, Vol. 31, No. 6

- IEEE 610.12 (1990), *Standard Glossary of Software Engineering Terminology,* IEEE Standards Board

- ISEB (Information Systems Examination Board) (2000), Practitioner Syllabus V1.0, British Computer Society, UK

- Paulk, M.C., C.V. Weber, B. Curtis and M.B. Chrissis (1993), *The Capability Maturity Model; Guideline for Improving the Software Process,* Addison-Wesley Publishing Company

- Phillips, M. and S. Shrum, (2000), *Creating an Integrated CMM for Systems and Software Engineering,* in: *CrossTalk,* September 2000

- Software Engineering Institute (2000), *CMMI for Systems Engineering/Software Engineering,* Version 1.02, Staged Representation, TR-CMU/SEI-2000-TR-028, Pittsburgh, November 2000

- Suwannasart, T. (1996), *Towards the development of a Testing Maturity Model,* Diss. Illinois Institute of Technology.

18 Test Process Improvement

Tim Koomen and Martin Pol

This chapter presents the TPI-model. The model gives practical guidelines for assessing the maturity level of testing in an organisation and for step by step improvement of the process. The model consists of 20 key areas, each with different levels of maturity. The levels of all key areas are set out in a maturity matrix. Each level is described by several checkpoints. Improvement suggestions, which help to reach a desired level, are part of the model. The chapter includes a general description of the application of the model, which deals with how to implement and how to consolidate the improvements.

18.1 How good is your test process?

This seemingly easy question turns out to be very hard to answer in practice. Testing is often experienced as a troublesome and uncontrollable process. Testing takes too much time, costs a lot more than planned, and offers insufficient insight in the quality of the test process and, therefore the quality of the information system under test and the risks for the business process itself. But can we do something about this? Many organisations realise that improving the test process can solve these problems. However, in practice it turns out to be hard to define what steps to take for improving and controlling the process, and in what order. A comparison can be made with software process improvement where models like the Capability Maturity Model (CMM) offer support.

Based on the knowledge and experiences of a large number of professional testers the Test Process Improvement (TPI[®1]) model has been developed. The TPI model supports the improvement of test processes. The model offers insight in the "maturity" of the test processes within your organisation. Based on this understanding the model helps to define gradual and controllable improvement steps.

---

1   TPI is a registered trademark of Sogeti Nederland B.V.

18.2 The model

The model is visualised as follows:

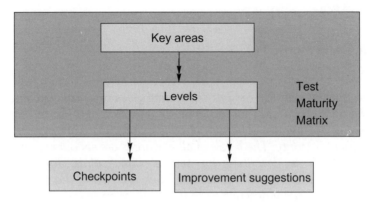

Figure 18.1 : TPI model overview

Key areas

In each test process certain areas need specific attention in order to achieve a well-defined process. These key areas are therefore the basis for improving and structuring the test process. The TPI model has 20 key areas. The scope of test process improvement usually comprises high-level tests like system and acceptance tests. Most key areas are adjusted to this. However, to improve more "mature" test processes, attention must also be given to verification activities and low-level tests like unit and integration tests. Separate key areas are included in order to give due attention to these processes as well. The key areas are organised by means of the four cornerstones of structured testing, life cycle, organisation, infrastructure and techniques.

The full list of key areas is given below, followed by an explanation.

Life cycle
Test strategy
Life-cycle model
Moment of involvement

Techniques
Estimating and planning
Test specification techniques
Static test techniques
Metrics

Infrastructure
Test automation
Test environment
Office environment

All cornerstones
Evaluation
Low-level testing

Organisation
Commitment and motivation
Testing functions and training
Scope of methodology
Communication
Reporting
Defect management
Testware management
Test process management

Key area	Description
Test strategy	The test strategy has to be focused on detecting the most important defects as early and as cheaply as possible. The test strategy defines which requirements and (quality) risks are covered by what tests. The better each test level defines its own strategy and the more the different test level strategies are adjusted to each other, the higher the quality of the overall test strategy.
Life-cycle model	Within the test process a number of phases can be defined, such as planning, preparation, specification, execution and completion. In each phase several activities are performed. For each activity the following aspects should be defined: purpose, input, process, output, dependencies, applicable techniques and tools, required facilities, documentation, etc. The importance of using a life-cycle model is an improved predictability and controllability of the test process, because the different activities can be planned and monitored in mutual cohesion.
Moment of involvement	Although the actual execution of the test normally begins after the realisation of the software, the test process must and can start much earlier. An earlier involvement of testing in the system development path helps to find defects as soon and easy as possible and perhaps even to prevent errors. A better adjustment between the different tests can be done and the time that testing is on the critical path of the project can be kept as short as possible.
Estimating and planning	Test planning and estimation indicate which activities have to be carried out when, and the necessary resources (people). Good estimating and planning are very important, because they are the basis of, for example, allocating resources for a certain time frame.
Test specification techniques	The definition of a test specification technique is "a standardised way of deriving test cases from source information". Applying these techniques gives insight into the quality and depth of the tests and increases the reusability of the test.
Static test techniques	Not everything can and should be tested dynamically, that is, by running programs. Inspection of products without running programs, or the evaluation of measures, which must lead to a certain quality level, is called static tests. Checklists are very useful for this.
Metrics	Metrics are quantified observations of the characteristics of a product or process. For the test process, metrics of the progress of the process and the quality of the tested system are very important. They are used to control the test process, to substantiate the test advice and also to make it possible to compare systems or processes. Why has one system far fewer failures in operation than another system, or why is one test process faster and more thorough than another? Specifically for improving the test process, metrics are important by evaluating consequences of certain improvement actions, by comparing data before and after performing the action.

Test automation	Automation within the test process can take place in many ways and has in general one or more of the following aims: - fewer hours needed, - shorter lead time, - more test depth, - increased test flexibility, - better visibility into the status of the test process, - better motivation of the testers.
Testing environment	The test execution takes place in a so-called test environment. This environment mainly comprises the following components: - hardware; - software; - means of communication; - facilities for building and using databases and files; - procedures. The environment should be composed and set up in such a way that by means of the test results it can be optimally determined to what extent the test object meets the requirements. The environment has a large influence on the quality, lead-time, and cost of the test process. Important aspects of the environment are responsibilities, management, on-time and sufficient availability, representativeness, and flexibility.
Office environment	The test staff needs rooms, desks, chairs, PCs, word-processing facilities, printers, telephones, and so on. A good and timely organisation of the office environment has a positive influence on the motivation of the test staff, on communication in- and outside the team, and on the efficiency of the work.
Commitment and motivation	The commitment and the motivation of the persons involved in testing are important prerequisites for a smoothly running test process. The persons involved are not only the testers, but also, for example, the project management and the line management personnel. The latter are mainly important in the sense of creating good conditions. The test process thus receives enough time, money, and resources (quantitatively and qualitatively) to perform a good test, in which co-operation and good communication with the rest of the project results in a total process with optimum efficiency.
Testing functions and training	In a test process the correct composition of a test team is very important. A mix of different disciplines, functions, knowledge, and skills is required. Besides specific test expertise, knowledge of the subject matter, knowledge of the organisation and general IT knowledge is required. Social skills are also important. For acquiring this mix, training etc. is required.
Scope of methodology	For each test process in the organisation a certain methodology or working method is used, comprising activities, procedures, regulations, techniques etc. When these methodologies are different each time or when the methodology is so generic that many parts have to be drawn up again each time, it has a negative effect on the test process efficiency. The aim is that the organisation uses a methodology which is sufficiently generic to be applicable in every situation, but which contains enough detail so that it is not necessary to rethink the same items again each time.

Communica-tion	In a test process, communication with the people involved must take place in several ways, within the test team as well as with parties such as the developer, the user, the customer, etc. These communication forms are important for a smoothly running test process, not only to create good conditions and to optimise the test strategy, but also to communicate about the progress and the quality.
Reporting	Testing is not so much "defect detection" as about giving insight in the quality level of the product. Reporting should be aimed at giving well-founded advice to the customer concerning the product and even the system development process.
Defect management	Although managing defects is in fact a project matter and not specifi-cally of the testers, the testers are mainly involved in it. Good manage-ment should be able to track the life cycle of a defect and also to sup-port the analysis of quality trends in the detected defects. Such analy-sis is used, for example, to give well-founded quality advice.
Testware management	The products of testing should be maintainable and reusable and so they must be managed. Besides the products of the testing themsel-ves, such as test plans, specifications, databases and files, it is impor-tant that the products of previous processes such as functional design and realisation are managed well, because the test process can be disrupted if the wrong program versions, etc. are delivered. If testers make demands upon version management of these products, a positi-ve influence is exerted and the testability of the product is increased.
Test process management	For managing each process and activity, the four steps from the De-ming circle are essential: plan, do, check and act. Process manage-ment is of vital importance for the realisation of an optimal test in an of-ten turbulent test process.
Evaluation	Evaluation means inspecting intermediate products such as the requi-rements and the functional design. The importance of evaluation is that the defects are found at a much earlier stage in the development pro-cess than with testing. This makes the rework costs much lower. Also, evaluation can be set up more easily because there is no need to run programs or to set up an environment etc.
Low-level testing	The low-level tests are almost exclusively carried out by the develo-pers. Well-known low-level tests are the unit test and the integration test. Just as evaluation, the tests find defects at an earlier stage of the system development path than the high-level tests. Low-level testing is efficient, because it requires little communication and because often the finder is both the error producer as well as the one who corrects the defect.

Table 18.1: Key areas

Levels

The way key areas are organised within a test process determines the "maturity" of the process. It is obvious that not each key area will be addressed equally thoroughly: each test process has its strengths and weaknesses. In order to enable insight in the state of the key areas, the model supplies them with levels (from A to B to C to D). On the average, there are three levels for each key area. Each higher level (C being higher than B, B being higher than A) is better than its prior level in terms of time (faster), money (cheaper) and/or quality (better). By using levels one can unambiguously assess the current situation of the test process. It also increases the ability to advice targets for stepwise improvement.

Each level consists of certain requirements for the key area. The requirements (checkpoints) of a certain level also comprise the requirements of lower levels: a test process at level B fulfils the requirements of both level A and B. If a test process does not satisfy the requirements for level A, it is considered to be at the lowest and, consequently, undefined level for that particular key area.
In the table hereafter a description is given of the different levels of the key areas.

Levels Key area	A	B	C	D
Test strategy	Strategy for single high-level test	Combined strategy for high-level tests	Combined strategy for high-level tests plus low-level tests or evaluation	Combined strategy for all test and evaluation levels
Life-cycle model	Planning, Specification, Execution	Planning, Preparation, Specification, Execution, Completion		
Moment of involvement	Completion of test basis	Start of test basis	Start of requirements definition	Project initiation
Estimating and planning	Substantiated estimating and planning	Statistically substantiated estimating and planning		
Test specification techniques	Informal techniques	Formal techniques		
Static test techniques	Inspection of test basis	Checklists		
Metrics	Project metrics (product)	Project metric (process)	System metrics	Organisation metrics (1 system)
Test automation	Use of tools	Managed test automation	Optimal test automation	

Levels Key area	A	B	C	D
Test environment	Managed and controlled environment	Testing in most suitable environment	Environment on demand	
Office environment	Adequate and timely office environment			
Commitment and motivation	Assignment of budget and time	Testing integrated in project organisation	Test engineering	
Test functions and training	Test manager and testers	(Formal) Methodical, technical and functional support, management	Formal internal Quality Assurance	
Scope of methodology	Project specific	Organisation generic	Organisation optimising (R&D)	
Communica-tion	Internal com-munication	Project com-munication (defects, change control)	Communica-tion within the organisa-tion about the quality of the test processes	
Reporting	Defects	Progress (status of tests and products), activities (costs and time, milestones), defects with priorities	Risks and re-commendati-ons, substan-tiated with metrics	Recommen-dations have a Software Process Improvement character
Defect management	Internal defect management	Extended defect management with flexible reporting facilities	Project defect management	

Levels Key area	A	B	C	D
Testware management	Internal testware management	External management of test basis and test object	Reusable testware	Traceability system requirements to test cases
Test process management	Planning and execution	Planning, execution, monitoring, and adjusting	Monitoring and adjusting within organisation	
Evaluation	Evaluation techniques	Evaluation strategy		
Low-level testing	Low-level test life-cycle: planning, specification and execution	White-box techniques	Low-level test strategy	

Table 18.2: Levels

Checkpoints

In order to determine levels, the TPI model is supported by an objective measurement instrument. The requirements for each level are defined in the form of checkpoints: questions that need to be answered positively in order to classify for that level. Based on the checkpoints a test process can be assessed, and for each key area the proper level can be established. As each next level of a key area is considered an improvement, this means that the checkpoints are cumulative: in order to classify for level B the test process needs to answer positively to the checkpoints both of level B and of level A.

Test Maturity Matrix

After determining the levels for each key area, attention should be directed as to which improvement steps to take. This is because not all key areas and levels are equally important. For example, a good test strategy (level A of key area Test Strategy) is more important than a description of the test methodology used (level A of key area Scope of Methodology). In addition to these priorities there are dependencies between the levels of different key areas. Before statistics can be gathered for defects found (level A of key area Metrics), the test process has to classify for level B of key area Defect management. Such dependencies can be found between many levels and key areas.

Therefore, all levels and key areas are related to each other in a Test Maturity Matrix. This has been done as a good way to express the internal priorities and dependencies between levels and key areas. The vertical axis of the matrix indicates key areas; the horizontal axis shows scales of maturity. In the matrix each level is related to a certain scale of test maturity. This results in 13 scales of test maturity. The open cells between different levels have no meaning in themselves, but indicate that achieving a higher maturity for a key area is related to the maturity of other key areas. There is no gradation between levels: as long as a test process is not entirely classified at level B, it remains at level A.

Scale / Key area	0	1	2	3	4	5	6	7	8	9	10	11	12	13
Test strategy		A					B				C		D	
Life-cycle model		A			B									
Moment of involvement			A				B				C		D	
Estimating and planning				A							B			
Test specification techniques		A		B										
Static test techniques					A		B							
Metrics						A			B			C		D
Test automation				A				B			C			
Test environment				A				B						C
Office environment				A										
Commitment and motivation		A				B						C		
Test functions and training				A			B			C				
Scope of methodology					A						B			C
Communication			A	B								C		
Reporting		A			B		C					D		
Defect management		A				B		C						
Testware management			A			B				C				D
Test process management		A		B								C		
Evaluation							A			B				
Low-level testing					A		B		C					

Figure 18.2: Test Maturity Matrix

The main purpose of the matrix is to show the strong and weak sides of the current test process and to support prioritising actions for improvement. A filled in matrix offers all participants a clear view of the current situation of the test process. Furthermore, the matrix helps in defining and selecting proposals for improvement. The matrix works from left to right, so low mature key areas are improved first. As a consequence of the dependencies between levels and key areas, practice has taught us that real 'outliners' (i.e., key areas with high scales of maturity, whereas surrounding key areas have medium or low scales) give little return on investment. For example, what is the use of a very advanced defect administration, if it is not used for analysis and reporting? Without violating the model, deviation is permitted, but sound reasons should exist for it.

In the example below, the test process does not classify for the lowest level of the key area test strategy (level A), the organisation is working conform a life-cycle model (level A) and the testers are involved at the moment when the specifications are completed (level A).

Scale / Key area	0	1	2	3	4	5	6	7	8	9	10	11	12	13
Test strategy		A					B				C		D	
Life-cycle model		A			B									
Moment of involvement			A				B				C		D	
etc.														

Based on this instance of the matrix, improvements can be discussed. In this example, a choice is made for a combined test strategy for high-level tests (=> level B) and for a full life-cycle model (=> level B). Earlier involvement is at this moment not considered to be of relevance. The required situation is represented in the following matrix.

Scale / Key area	0	1	2	3	4	5	6	7	8	9	10	11	12	13
Test strategy		A					B				C		D	
Life-cycle model		A			B									
Moment of involvement			A				B				C		D	
etc.														

Improvement Suggestions

Improvement actions can be defined in terms of desired higher levels. For reaching a higher level the checkpoints render much assistance. Beside these, the model has other means of support for test process improvement: the Improvement Suggestions, which are different kinds of hints and ideas that help to achieve a certain level of test maturity. Unlike the use of checkpoints, the use of improvement suggestions is not obligatory. Each level is supplied with several improvement suggestions.

18.3 The improvement process

The process of test improvement is similar to any other improvement process. The figure hereafter shows the various activities of an improvement process. These activities are discussed, with special attention for the places where the TPI model can be used.

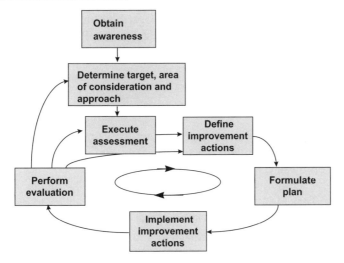

Figure 18.3 : The improvement process

Obtain awareness

The first activity of a test improvement process is to create awareness for the necessity to improve the process. Generally speaking, a number of problems concerning testing is the reason for improving the test process. There is a need to solve these problems and an improvement of the test process is regarded as the solution. This awareness also implies that the parties mutually agree on the outlines and give their commitment to the change process. Commitment should not only be acquired at the beginning of the change process, but be retained throughout the project. This requires a continuous effort.

Determine target, area of consideration, and approach

The improvement targets and the area of consideration are determined. Should testing be faster, cheaper or better? Which test processes are subjects for improvement, how much time is available for the improvement and how much effort is it allowed to cost?

Execute assessment

In the assessment activity, an evaluation is given of the current situation. The use of the TPI model is an important part of the assessment, because it offers a frame of reference to list the strong and weak points of the test process. Based on interviews and documentation, the levels per key area of the TPI model are examined by using checkpoints, and it is determined which checkpoints were met, which were not met, or only partially. The Test Maturity Matrix is used here to give the complete status overview of the test process. This will show the strengths and weaknesses of the test process in the form of levels assigned key areas and their relative position in the matrix.

Define improvement actions

The improvement actions are determined based on the improvement targets and the result of the assessment. These actions are determined in such a way that gradual and step by step improvement is possible.
The TPI model helps to set up these improvement actions. The levels of the key areas and the Test Maturity Matrix give several possibilities to define gradual improvement steps. Depending on the targets, the scope, the available time and the assessment results, it can be decided to carry out improvements for one or more key areas. For each selected key area it can be decided to go to the next level or, in special cases, even to a higher level. Besides this, the TPI model offers a large number of improvement suggestions, which help to achieve higher levels.

Formulate plan

A detailed plan is drawn up to implement (a part of) the short term improvement actions. In this plan the aims are recorded and it is indicated which improvements have to be implemented at what time to realise these aims. The plan deals with activities concerning the content of the test process improvement as well as general activities needed to steer the change process in the right direction.

Implement improvement actions

The plan is executed. Because during this activity the consequences of the change process have the largest impact, much attention should be spent on communication. Opposition, which no doubt is present, must be brought to the surface and be discussed openly. It has to be measured to what extent actions have been executed and have been successful. A means for this is the so-called "self assessment", in which the TPI model is applied in order to quickly determine the progress. Here, the persons involved inspect their own test processes using the TPI model. Another vital part of this phase is consolidation. It should be prevented that the implemented improvement actions have a once-only character.

Perform evaluation

To what extent did the implemented actions yield the intended result? In this phase the aim is to see to what extent the actions were implemented successfully as well as to evaluate to what extent the initial targets were met. A decision about the continuation of the change process is made based on these observations.

18.4 Conclusions and remarks

Current developments proceed at a very high speed. The productivity of developers is rising continuously and customers demand ever higher quality. Even if your current test process is fairly satisfactory, your process will need to improve in the future. The TPI model can help with this. The TPI model is an objective means to gain quick insight in the current situation of the test process. The model greatly offers help for improvement in the form of key areas, levels and improvement suggestions. It supports the definition of small and controlled improvement steps, based on priorities.

The reader might get the impression that use of the TPI model automatically leads to good analysis of the current and required situation. This is not true. The model should be seen as a tool for structuring the improvement of the test process and as a very good means of communication. Apart from the tool, improvement of test processes demands a high degree of knowledge and expertise of people involved, at least in the areas of testing, organisation and change management.

References

- Koomen, T. and M. Pol (1999), *Test Process Improvement, a practical step-by-step guide to structured testing*, Addison-Wesley, ISBN 0 201 59624 5.

Part 7

Test tools

19 Test tool overview

Erik van Veenendaal

The quality of test tools has matured during the past number of years. Their scope, diversity and application have increased enormously. By analogy with CASE (Computer Aided Software Engineering), there are also publications about CAST (Computer Aided Software Testing) available. CAST should be seen as a list of available test tools, classified according to application and platform. The use of such tools may often bring about a considerable improvement in the productivity of the test process. The description of test tools in this chapter is an indication of the current situation in a changing and evolving market. The reader should bear this in mind while reading this chapter.

19.1 A closer look

At a time when time-to-market is more critical than ever before, and applying the latest development methods and tools has shortened the time it takes to develop new systems, it is clearer than ever that testing is on the critical path of software development and that having an effective test process is necessary to ensure that deadlines are met. In this situation tools are needed to provide the necessary support. After all we're living in an IT-society. In past number of years tools have grown to maturity and can, if implemented correctly, provide support in raising the efficiency, quality and control of the test process.

The critical success factor for the use of test tools is the existence of a structured approach to testing and its organization. The implementation of one or more test tools should be based on the structured testing approach and the techniques that support it. Herein lies a major problem, as test tools do not always sufficiently fit in with an organisation's structured test approach. Within a well structured process tools will provide added value, however in an unstructured environment they can become counter productive. Automation requires a certain level of repeatability and standardisation regarding the activities carried out. An unstructured process does not comply with these conditions. Since automation imposes a certain level of standardisation, it can support the implementation of a structured approach. Structuring and automation should therefore go side by side, to put it briefly: "Structure and Tool".

Whereas, in the systems analysis and design phase, the introduction of methods and techniques preceded the arrival of supporting tools, the opposite appears to apply to testing. It is remarkable that the attention devoted to test tools is sometimes greater than that which is given to test methods and techniques.

There are areas in testing where activities need to be carried out accurately while they are relatively routine. This often applies, for instance, when two extensive reports are compared for the purpose of establishing whether they are identical, or during the repeated execution of the same test when discrepancies are not really expected. Such routine activities are often eminently suitable for automation and therefore require the support of a test tool.

A development of this kind occurred some time ago in the area of software development. Testers should learn from these developments. Programmers are no longer needed for writing object code. Compilers, 4GL tools or code generators are available instead. Nor are programmers required to key in their entire programmes again whenever they wish to make a change! At present it is often this latter eventuality which often occurs in testing software products: the test input is not preserved between test execution cycles, and the tester is therefore obliged to repeat the entire test each time. Similarly test designs may not be preserved between projects or shared across the organisation, and the test teams reinvent test designs for each project. Testers also produce test cases manually and assess the results manually. The application of test tools in support of a structured approach to testing is definitely a further step in the direction of high quality testing and software. In view of the present status of test tools, support during testing is mainly possible in test management and test execution and to a lesser extent in test design. Useful test tools to support test design techniques are still not available. Test tools therefore focus on the second half of the testing life cycle model, although there are some exceptions in practice already. A distinction should be made between tools for white-box testing and those for black-box testing: there are more, and, above all, more useful test tools available for white-box tests than there are for black-box tests.

Being able to use test tools can be assumed to be a basic skill for a tester these days. However, the wider concept of automation of the test process requires specialists and in-depth knowledge of (the possibilities) of automation and tools. This knowledge is certainly not present in all testers. This has created a new type of specialism: the test automation specialist.

19.2 Advantages

Applying tools throughout the test process may lead to less effort being spent on routine based tasks. As a result, employees with (often-scarce) test and domain expertise are able to concentrate on the more complex test activities and on providing higher test quality. Provided that test tools are used in conjunction with a structured test approach, there will be advantages in using them. These advantages may be quite considerable, as the application of most tools – the execution of the test – often claims about 40% of the total test effort for new development (even more in maintenance testing).

Automation of the test process offers amongst others the following advantages:
- A large number of tests can be carried out unattended and automatically, e.g. at night
- Automation of routine and often boring test activities leads to greater reliability of the activities than when carried out manually, and to a higher degree of work satisfaction in the test team. This results in higher productivity in testing.
- Regression testing can, to a large extent, be carried out automatically. Automating the process of regression testing makes it possible to perform a full regression test, so that it can be determined whether the unchanged areas still function according to the specification.
- Test tools ensure that the test data are the same for consecutive tests so that there is a certainty about the reliability of the initial situation with respect to the data.
- Some tools, e.g. static analysis, can detect faults that are difficult to detect manually. Using such tools, it is in principle possible to find all incidences of these types of faults.
- The automatic generation of large amounts of test data can be carried out automatically with the support of a test tool. Entering initial data sets need to be done only once instead of every time a test is run. But note that good test design is still needed to make a focused set of test data which addresses the risks - otherwise there is just a large volume of not very useful tests (Fewster and Graham, 1999).

In summary, it can be concluded that the use of test tools makes it possible to carry out more test activities in less time, and increases both the quality and the productivity of the test process.

19.3 Considerations

Test automation as the solution

Automation of the test process can contribute towards a higher level of quality regarding the product and the test process and towards a higher level of productivity, but is certainly not the answer to all problems. Within software engineering new technologies have often been received with overwhelming enthusiasm. Using 4GL and CASE-tools would result in defect free software. More recently code generators and object orientation were supposed to solve all the problems. Currently Component Based Development (CBD) and Rational Unified Process (RuP) are amongst the answers. The best solution is often a combination of more than one measure, by which the latest technology is not always the best choice. Automation of the testing process is no exception to this rule. At the start clear (business) objectives need to be defined. A tool should only become part of the testing process if it provides tangible improvements regarding the objectives.

Management commitment

Even if the testing discipline is mature enough to apply tools, the desired benefits are not always achieved. One of the most critical success factors of the automation of the test process is management commitment. Management needs to be aware that applying a test tool is an investment both in terms of cost and effort, that often only pays off after a period of time in terms of better and more efficient testing. If this awareness is not at an adequate level, there is a fair chance that the tool usage is stopped when the first problems occur. When a tool is applied for the first time in a time-critical project this phenomenon is strengthened. As soon as the project approaches its deadline, the chances are high that the tool usage is abandoned.

Another aspect of management commitment is the level of support it provides to structured testing. Some test tools contribute to more effective testing, others increase testing productivity. Both types of tools will not have the desired effect if testing takes place in an unstructured manner. Especially if test activities are carried out under time-pressure, the principles of structured testing need to be maintained. These moments will show to what extent management really supports structured testing and software quality.

Interpretation of tool results

Automation of the test process often results in a higher number of test cases being executed. Tools also offer measures regarding some quality attributes of the testing process. Since the measures are often quantitative and detailed, conclusions are drawn that are not always valid. If test coverage tools show that 100% statement coverage has been achieved, this does not mean that the system has been tested exhaustively! It is highly important to analyse the meaning of the results and measures produced by tools and to ensure that misinterpretations do not occur.

19.4 Test tool overview

Test tools may be classified according to the activities they support. The main support currently offered by test tools is intended for test management and test execution. In this paragraph the tools are categorised by the test life cycle phase they relate to. To provide a better understanding of the state-of-the-practice regarding test tools, some data is shown regarding the implementation of the various tools - the percentage of companies actually using a certain tool. The data is derived from a tool survey throughout 2000 and 2001 in over 200 European companies by Improve Quality Services BV. The data distinguishes between the areas of technical automation (e.g. embedded software and telecommunications) and information systems (e.g. banking, insurance and government).

Test management

For test management the same kind of tools may be used as in any other planning and control process, such as planning packages, spreadsheets, word processors and risk analysis packages. Special attention should be drawn to the automated version of test point analysis (TPA), the test estimation technique (see chapter 7).

- *Configuration management*
  During a project, a variety of deliverables are produced. It is very important for the deliverables to be controlled properly throughout their life cycle. After their creation and quality checks, the deliverables should be frozen. At this point, they become configuration items. A configuration management tool supports the management of configuration items and their changes. Such a tool supports version management of objects that have emerged in the course of time and the relationships between these objects. This includes configuration management for testware.
- *Incident management*
  To support the incident management activities, there are tools for registering defects and tracking and monitoring their life cycle. Some tools also provide the possibility of producing reports and statistics.

- *Test management*
  Test management tools offer an integrated set of features. Testware management is concerned with the creation, management and control of test documentation, e.g. test plans, specifications, and results. Some tools support the project management aspects of testing, for example the scheduling of tests, the logging of results and the management of incidents raised during testing. Incident management tools (also known as defect tracking tools) may also have workflow-oriented facilities to track and control the allocation, correction and re-testing of incidents. Traceability tools allow the link between test cases and their corresponding test coverage items to be recorded. Most test management tools provide extensive reporting and analysis facilities.

Test tool Implementation ratio	Technical Automation	Information Systems	Overall
Configuration management	50%	25%	37%
Incident management	59%	44%	51%
Test management	45%	30%	35%

Table 19.1: Implementation ratio test management tools

Test preparation

- *Requirements management*
  Requirements management or requirements testing tools provide automated support for the verification of requirements models, such as consistency checking and animation
- *Static analysis*
  Static analysis tools provide information about the quality of the software by examining the code, rather than running test cases through the code. Standard features of static analysis tools usually include checking against coding standards, structure analysis (e.g. call graphs and flow charts) and quality metrics (e.g. cyclomatic complexity)

Test specification

- *Test design*
  Test design tools generate test inputs from a specification that may be held in a CASE tool repository or from formally specified requirements held in the tool itself. Some tools generate test inputs from an analysis of the code.

- *Test data preparation*
  Test input data preparation tools enable data to be selected from an existing database or created, generated, manipulated and edited for use in tests. The most sophisticated tools can deal with a range of files and database formats. The tools are particularly useful for performance testing.

Test tool Implementation ratio	Technical Automation	Information Systems	Overall
Static analysis	22%	4%	12%
Test design	18%	13%	15%
Test data preparation	20%	9%	14%

Table 19.2: Implementation ratio test preparation and specification tools

Test execution

The following test tools are amongst those that may be used during the execution and checking of the tests:

- *Comparators*
  Comparison tools are used to detect differences between actual results and expected results. Stand-alone comparison tools normally deal with a range of file or database formats. Test running tools usually have built-in comparators that deal with character screens, GUI objects or bitmap images. These tools often have filtering or masking capabilities, whereby they can "ignore" rows or columns of data or areas on screens.
- *Coverage tool*
  Coverage measurement (or analysis) tools provide objective measures of structural (white box) test coverage when tests are executed. Programs to be tested are instrumented before compilation. Instrumentation code dynamically captures the coverage data in a log file and necessarily slows the program, which may affect the behaviour of the program under test. After execution, the log file is analysed and coverage statistics generated. Most tools provide statistics on the most common coverage measures such as statement or branch coverage.
- *Dynamic analysis*
  Dynamic analysis tools provide run-time information on the state of executing software. These tools are most commonly used to identify unassigned pointers, check pointer arithmetic, monitor the allocation, use and de-allocation of memory to flag memory leaks and highlight other errors that are difficult to find "statically".

- *Hyperlink testing tools*
  Hyperlink testing tools are used to check that no broken hyperlinks are present on a web site.
- *Monitoring tools*
  In order to gain insight into aspects such as memory usage, CPU usage, network load and performance, monitoring tools can be used during the test process. A variety of utilization of resources can be measured and stored. Monitoring tools are also used for testing e-commerce and e-business applications as well as web sites. The main function of this type of tool is to monitor web sites to ensure they are available to customers and to produce a warning if the service begins to degrade or has failed.
- *Performance tools (load and stress)*
  Performance test tools have two main facilities: load generation and test transaction measurement. Load generation can simulate either multiple users or high volumes of input data. Load generation is done either by driving the application using its user interface or by test drivers, which simulate the load generated by the application. Records of the numbers of transactions executed are logged. Driving the application using its user interface, response time measurements are taken for selected transactions and these are logged. Performance testing tools normally provide reports based on test logs, and graphs of load against response times.
- *Record (or capture) & playback (see also chapter 21)*
  Test running tools provide test capture and replay facilities. The tools capture user-entered terminal keystrokes and capture screen responses for later comparison. For Graphical User Interface (GUI) applications the tools can simulate mouse movement, and button clicks and can recognise GUI objects such as windows, fields, buttons and other controls. Object states and bitmap images can be captured for later comparison. Test procedures are normally captured in a programmable script language. When the script is executed this replays the user-entered keystrokes, etc. and can compare actual responses with those captured previously. Data, test cases and expected results may be held in separate test repositories. These tools are most often used to automate regression testing.
- *Security tools*
  Security testing tools are typically used for testing e-commerce and e-business applications as well as web sites. A security-testing tool will check for any aspects of a web-based system that are vulnerable to abuse by unauthorised access.
- *Simulators*
  Simulators are used to support tests where code or other systems are either unavailable or impracticable to use. A simulator imitates the operation of the environment of (part of) the system to be tested.

- *Stubs, test harnesses and drivers*
  Test harnesses and drivers are used to execute software under test which may not have a user interface or to run groups of existing automated test scripts which can be controlled by the tester. Some commercially available tools exist, but custom-written programs also fall into this category. Stubs are used to replace a program that is called upon. A stub is called from the program to be tested; a driver calls a program to be tested. Stubs and drivers are almost indispensable during component and integration testing.

Test tool Implementation ratio	Technical Automation	Information Systems	Overall
Comparators	39%	16%	27%
Coverage tools	17%	2%	9%
Dynamic analysis	19%	5%	11%
Monitoring tools	29%	14%	21%
Performance tools	35%	15%	25%
Record & Playback	29%	30%	29%
Simulators	51%	8%	29%

Table 19.3: Implementation ratio test execution and checking tools

References

- Fewster, M. and D. Graham (1999), *Automating Software Testing: Effective use of test execution tools,* Addison-Wesley, ISBN 0-201-33140-3

- Graham, D. (ed.) (1996), *Computer Aided Software Testing, The CAST report,* Cambridge Market Intelligence Ltd., London, ISBN 1-897977-74-3

- ISEB (Information Systems Examination Board) (2001), Practitioner Syllabus V1.1, British Computer Society, UK

- Pol, M., and E.P.W.M. van Veenendaal (1996), *Structured Testing of Information Systems,* Kluwer Bedrijfsinformatie, The Netherlands, ISBN 90-267-2910-3

- Pol, M., R.A.P. Teunissen and E.P.W.M. van Veenendaal (2002), *Software Testing, A Guide to the TMap approach,* Addison-Wesley, ISBN 0-201-74571-2.

20 Tool evaluation and selection

John Watkins

How many of you have infinite time, money and resource to test your software? How many of you are relaxing your requirement for software quality while increasing the timescales available for testing? Who believes you can develop defect free software? All those of you who put your hands up can stop reading this chapter now and can move on to the next one. As for the rest of us ...

The fact is that the majority of us are facing the paradox of ever-shorter development and testing timescales combined with the need for software of ever increasing quality. Improvements in the management of testing and testing process provide the means of making testing as effective and efficient as possible. Automated software test tools provide another possible strategy for saving time, effort and cost, and improving quality. However, if your organisation is already short of time, money and resource for testing, how can you be expected to spend more time, effort and money in identifying a suitable candidate test tool and determining if it is the right one for your organisation? Be reassured – you are not the first to face this dilemma.

This chapter describes an approach you can use to simplify the selection of an automated tool that matches your own particular testing requirements. The approach is based on a number of sources including work the author has conducted on behalf of numerous clients as well as a vast body of feedback from organisations engaged in the process of evaluating software test tools.

20.1 Do you really need a tool?

So, you have some issues with your current approach to testing - but do you really need a test tool? Before rushing out to buy a tool, you should first consider the following:
- Tools cost money – money that might have been spent more effectively. For example, could investing in training help address your testing problems?
- Are you managing your approach to testing efficiently – and could better management techniques be a solution?
- Could adopting an effective development and testing process be of benefit?

- If you have a short term or infrequent requirement for testing, would it be more cost effective to outsource the testing?

Finally, do not rush out and buy a test tool if your project is in the middle of a software-testing crisis in the hope that it will save the day. This is the very worst time to consider buying a tool – not only will you waste precious time and effort learning how to use the tool, but you are highly unlikely to make any productivity gains on the first or even second use of the tool (although some case studies do claim one organisation benefited after just two uses of a software test tool (Graham *et al.*, 1999)). There are genuine benefits to be gained through the use of tools – but only through their planned and managed introduction, and through continued use and re-use of the test suite that you will develop.

So when is it appropriate to use an automated test tool? Such products are particularly appropriate if you have:
- Frequent builds and releases of the software you are testing.
- A requirement for thorough regression testing, and particularly for business critical, safety critical, and secure or confidential software systems.
- Software involving complex graphical user interfaces.
- A requirement for rigorous, thorough and repeatable testing.
- The need to deliver the software across many different platforms.
- The need to reduce timescales, effort and cost.
- A requirement to perform more testing in shorter timescales.

If you have a requirement for one or more of the above, you should consider investigating what benefits you could gain from test tool use.

20.2 The need for a formal evaluation

The majority of suppliers will tell you that their tool is clearly the best, is incredibly easy to use, and will of course solve all your testing problems. The reality is that you have a unique set of requirements, and you must make sure that any tool you select satisfies those requirements. Furthermore, many suppliers will insist that you should buy their tool because it is the market-leading product and therefore, must be the best. Be careful not to place over-reliance on such claims – it is much more important that the tool matches your specific testing requirements. Recently commissioned studies showed that the top five issues for tool purchasers are: reliability of the tool, good match to requirements, adequate performance, ease of use and good documentation. Market leadership was ranked as the least important issue in fifteenth place!

The bottom line is that adopting a tool will mean a significant investment in time, effort and money, and before committing your organisation and its resources, you must assure yourself that the tool you choose will match your testing requirements. Because of this, you should adopt a formal means of identifying the right tool and be able to demonstrate the rigor of the process to your managers and colleagues.

20.3 Identify and document requirements

During the process of determining if you require a tool, you will have had to consider your specific testing requirements for such a tool. During this process, make sure that you document these requirements – they will be used later. Examples of such requirements could include: "the tool must support functional testing and regression testing", "process support must be available for the tool", and "the tool must seamlessly integrate with other development tools". As you compile your set of requirements, try to determine just how important each one is and assign a weighting to it to indicate its significance (in practice most organisations have found a simple three category "Essential", "Important" and "Desirable" approach to be effective).

Maintain the requirements information as a live document as you are almost certain to add additional requirements as the evaluation process continues, as well as relaxing or strengthening the weightings of specific requirements. Armed with your documented test tool requirements, you are now ready to do some market research. Annex E contains an extensive set of tool evaluation criteria.

20.4 Conduct market research

The next task in the evaluation process is to identify those test tools that most closely match your requirements. This is a two-phased activity:
*   First identify a collection of candidate tools which loosely match your high level or "Essential" requirements
*   Second, review the candidate tools more rigorously to reject those products that fail to match your "Essential" and "Important" requirements. This activity may involve contacting the supplier, obtaining product brochures and visiting the supplier Web site.

In performing the research to identify the candidate tools, there are many sources of information you can use, including:
*   Testing trade magazines

- Special interest group meetings (such as the BCS SIGiST group)
- Testing exhibitions, tools fairs and conferences
- Analyst publications ((Graham, 1996) and (Ovum, 2001))
- The internet.

The output from this task will be a short-list of tools and the contact details for their suppliers. Ultimately you should aim to identify just two tools, which you will then investigate in greater detail.

20.5 Organise supplier presentations

Once you have your short-list, it is time to do some further research in order to identify the tool that best matches your requirements as a prelude to formally evaluating that tool. A particularly effective strategy is to organise supplier presentations of the short-listed tools. Contact the supplier and outline your requirement (you might consider providing them with a copy of the requirements – trustworthy suppliers will quickly let you know if there is a good match to their tool or not to save wasting your time and theirs). Propose that the supplier organises a presentation of their tool based on your particular requirements and consider providing them with a copy or sample of your application so that they can demonstrate their tool using your software rather than some demonstration application. Prepare in advance for the presentation by reviewing your requirements and preparing questions for the supplier. It may be of benefit to produce an agenda describing what you expect to see and provide this to the supplier to review before the meeting.

During the presentation, make sure you take notes documenting the progress of the event, the answers to questions you ask, as well as any further questions raised. Do not be afraid to press the supplier if they appear to skip over some aspect of the tool or fail to answer any of your questions adequately. The reason may be quite innocent or it may reveal some weakness or limitation of the tool. Finally, remember that you are in charge, but be a good host too (you may end up working with these people if you purchase their tool).

If you have short-listed two suppliers, it can be very effective to see them both on the same day (one in the morning and one in the afternoon). If you plan to review the results of the presentations immediately after the events, both will be fresh in your mind. Also, it is likely that each presentation will raise further questions, and this will give you the opportunity to quickly contact the suppliers for any clarifications.

After each presentation, spend some time reviewing the results of the event. Review how well the tools met your requirements, and determine if there are any final questions or clarifications you need the supplier to answer. If you do have further questions, document them and provide them to the supplier. Finally, on the basis of the presentations and any supplier clarifications, select one of the short-listed tools for formal evaluation (although, if your organisation has sufficient time, resource and funds, you may consider conducting a formal evaluation of both tools).

20.6 Formally evaluating the test tool

After selecting the tool that you believe most closely matches your requirements, you will need to perform a formal evaluation of the product to demonstrate that it will be able to satisfy your requirements in practice (that is, in your test environment and with your software). This exercise is often termed a "Proof of Concept". Contact the supplier and ask for an evaluation copy of the tool. Most suppliers will provide you with a full working copy of the product, which is typically licensed for 30 days. Determine the level of support that is available to you during the evaluation period (for example, if needed will the supplier provide assistance with installation, who should you contact for technical support, and is there any documentation available to help support your evaluation?).

Run the evaluation as a formal project and ensure that adequate commitment is available from senior management in terms of timescales and resources. Within your evaluation plan, include a number of milestones at which you formally contact the supplier to review progress and address any issues raised by the evaluation. In evaluating the tool, you should use your formal requirements document, taking into account the weightings for each requirement and identifying how well the tool satisfies that requirement.

After evaluating the tool, you should document the results of the project in the form of an evaluation report. This report may be as simple as a record of the requirements, their weightings and the evaluation score held in a checklist or could be as formal as a written report. Consider providing the supplier with a copy of the report so that they can review your results – if you have misunderstood some aspect of the tool and given the associated requirement a poor score, the supplier will be able to advise you of the misconception and explain how the requirements can be satisfied. In addition to an evaluation report, you may also need to produce a business case document for senior management containing recommendations on the acquisition of the tool as well as return on investment calculations.

On completion of the evaluation, you should review the results of the evaluation and decide on your next actions. If the evaluation was satisfactory, then you will next need to consider acquiring the product.

20.7 Post evaluation activities

In purchasing the tool there are a number of issues to consider. The first thing to determine is the number of licenses that you will need to buy to allow your organisation to make best use of the tool. You will also need to consider the issue of fixed licenses (typically tied to a particular workstation) or floating licenses (typically installed on a server and issued on a first come first served basis). Floating licenses will give you more flexibility in making the tool available but will almost certainly cost more than the equivalent fixed license. In determining the number of licenses, you should also consider break points for discounts. Typically, suppliers provide discounts based on volume sales of licenses. Ask your supplier what these break points are so that you can take advantage of them if possible.

While in general terms, it makes good business sense to enquire about discounts, be careful not to let testosterone get in the way of obtaining a product which will be of benefit to your organisation. As incredible as it may seem, there have been many occasions where staff involved in the purchase of tools have walked away from a purchase just because the supplier is unable to reduce the purchase price by, in some cases, tens of pounds!

On the other hand, you should also be very wary of suppliers who will suddenly slash the price of their product as soon as they hear that one of their competitors is involved. You will have to work with the supplier following your purchase (perhaps for training and mentoring, as well as ongoing support), so it is worth considering the business ethics of any supplier who was perfectly happy to charge you £X one day and then suddenly charge you half that amount just a few days later for exactly the same product (while presumably still making a profit). This is not a good basis for a successful continuing business relationship, and suppliers who indulge in such activities are almost certain to find ways of recouping the discount at a later stage, otherwise their business would be unsustainable.

The organisations that gain the most benefits from tool use, plan and manage the introduction of the product into their organisation. For example, you should consider the need for training ahead of installation of the tool. Plan for some initial mentoring to ensure correct and effective use of the tool. Consider the benefits of planned consultancy visits at later points during the testing project as "health checks" to ensure continued effective and efficient use of the tool. Crown Management Systems provides an excellent case study of one such organisation that followed exactly this route and who claim to have made initial savings of some 35% on time and effort in testing as a result (Coles, 1999).

Finally, persevere. You will not realise benefits from the tool unless you continue to use it to support your testing activities. The more often you re-use the test scripts you have created, the more savings you will make in terms of time, effort and cost.

References

- Coles, C. (1999), *Crown Management Systems Limited Case Study*, Crown Management Systems and Rational Software

- Fewster, M. and D. Graham (1999), *Software test Automation*, Addison-Wesley

- Graham, D. (ed.) (1996), *Computer Aided Software Testing, The CAST report*, Cambridge Market Intelligence Ltd., London, ISBN 1-897977-74-3

- Krushten, P. (1998), *The Rational Unified Process*, Addison-Wesley

- OVUM (2001), Ovum Evaluates, CASE Products, Ovum Ltd.

21 Test excution automation

Chris Schotanus

Automated test execution is an area which is currently getting a lot of attention. In essence it is not a new area. Programmers have created solutions, ad hoc or structural, to test their products automatically for many years. The reason for the current attention is amongst others that modern applications with graphical user interfaces (e.g. client/server and browser based applications etc) are very complex and contain many characteristics that require extensive testing. Furthermore, new development techniques and methods like object orientation (OO) and component based development (CBD) demand for high quality regression testing since applications are built during iterative processes.

21.1 Advantages

PC's are becoming more and more powerful and have taken over the role of terminals, getting connected with mini and mainframe platforms using terminal emulators, client/server and/or web enabled applications, apart from the applications that run on the pc platforms itself. The pc therefore has become an ideal platform for Computer Aided Software Testing (CAST) Tools, even if the applications under test run elsewhere.

The general advantages of automated test execution are:
* *Better use of available time*
  Because of the easy repetition of the test (even during the night or week-end) the tester can spend time on other tasks (like interpretation of test results and test analysis)
* *Less boring activity*
  When test are to be repeated manually, activities become boring. This introduces the risk of the tester paying less attention.
* *Consistent test execution*
  By automating the tests the human factor is eliminated: the test tool will execute the tests in exactly the same way time after time.
* *More reliable results*
  Human tester can make mistakes during test execution or can overlook errors that occur.

- *Improved test planning*
  Since the test tool takes care of the test execution and the scripts contain the test knowledge, the test project becomes less dependent to the availability of testers.
- *Higher regression test coverage*
  In case of an application change testers tend to test only the changes (often due to lack of sufficient time to test it all). Automated test can be run out of working hours, so full regression tests can run without taking extra time.

In this chapter the focus is test execution tools and their possibilities. In essence four main techniques are available for using the test excution tools:
- Record and playback
- Test programming
- Data Driven Testing (a specific use of test programming)
- Testing with Action Words[1]

21.2 Record and playback

During Record and Playback (also known as Capture and Playback) the test tool acts as a tape recorder which records all keystrokes and mouse moves into a script file. Before starting the test actions the tool should be switched to "recording mode". The first time test actions are carried out manually and recorded by the tool. The recording is invisible to the tester and the application under test. The recording process can be interrupted to introduce checks, specifying that whatever is on the screen or part of the screen at a certain point during the test execution (recording) should also be there at the same point during the playback. Below a schematic overview of this process is drawn.

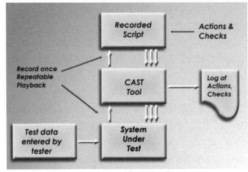

Figure 21.1 : Schematic Overview of Record and Playback

---

1   Testing with action words is a registerd trademark of CMG

The result of these actions is a script file containing all keystrokes and checks in one large sequence. An example of a such a script file recorded for an imaginary application is provided figure 21.2.

```
 1    attach_window("main_window");
 2    select_menu("client entry");
 3    attach_window("client entry");
 4    button_press("&new");
 5    enter_text("client_number","123545");
 6    enter_text("client_last_name","Newman");
 7    enter_text("client_first","Randy");
 8    enter_date("client_DOB","28-Now-43");
 9    button_press("&Ok");
10    attach_window("confirm");
11    button_press("&Ok");
12    attach-window("main_window");
13    select_menu("client entry");
14    attach_window("client entry");
15    button_press("&new");
16    enter_text("client_number","568910");
17    enter_text("client_last_name","Collins");
18    enter_text("client_first","Phil");
19    enter_date("client_DOB","31-Jan-51");
20    button_press("&Ok");
21    attach_window("confirm");
22    button_press("&Ok");
23    attach-window("main_window");
24    select_menu("client inquiry");
25    enter_text("client_number","12345");
26    button_press("Search");
27    check img1;
```

Figure 21.2 : A recorded script file

Each line in this file represents an action that will be performed on the application when the script is played back. Line 1 results in setting the focus to the system under test (similar to clicking with the mouse on the menu bar of the application). Then menu option client entry is selected (line 2), the mouse clicks on the button new (line 4) and the screen attributes are entered (lines 5 to 8). The action is finished by clicking on the Ok button (line 9). Then a confirmation dialog box pops up and the Ok button in that box is clicked (lines 10 and 11), from line 12 onwards these actions are repeated with different data. On line 27 a check is performed against a screen image stored in file img1.

As one can see from this example, the information in a script file is of a technical nature and therefore not very easy to understand by non-technical testers. Every keystroke is recorded (even the mistakes: see line 5 where a backspace corrects the mistyping of the 5). What is even more important, test data is mixed with the technical information in the file and the "flow" of the test is represented by the sequence of actions recorded in the script. This makes it difficult to show what has been tested. However, when the application has to be retested, a simple playback of this script will suffice, provided that the application does not change technically.

The reasons for using Record and Playback are mainly:
• It is *easy to create*, there is no need for technical knowledge of the test tools by the testers.
• Once a test script has been created it is *easy to repeat* : one keystroke is enough provided the application does not change;
• Tests can be executed *outside "office hours"*. A PC never gets tired and will work 24 hours a day if needed.

However, this method has a few disadvantages of which the most important is that test script file is difficult to maintain. All the actions are recorded in one file containing all information (both technical and test) in one large sequence. If a screen changes all the recorded actions will have to change too!. Another disadvantage is, that recording of test scripts can only start after delivery of a correctly working system and is therefore only applicable as regression test method.

21.3 Test programming

Test programming reduces the maintainability problem dramatically and increases the readability of the script. Most record and playback tools contain a script language, which can be used like any normal programming language, extended with special features for testing, e.g. functions for simulating mouse and keyboard events and capturing screen data. Using this script language it is possible to create routines that handle standard actions. By programming functions it becomes possible to group the technical issues and more or less separate them from the test data. Recording facilities of the test tool are used initially to create the script. After recording the script editor is used to change the script and create the programmed test. When the test from the previous example is programmed, it could look as shown in figure 21.3.

In the main script, on line 3 and 4 data is entered using the function *enter_client* (lines 100 to 112) and on line 5 data is retrieved using *select_client* (lines 113 onwards).

```
  1       ...
  2       ...
  3       call enter_client("12345","Newman","Randy","28-Nov-43");
  4       call enter_client("568910","Collins","Phil","31-Jan-51");
  5       call select_client("12345");
  6       check img1;
  7 end test
  ......
100 function enter_client(cl_nr,cl_last,cl_first,cl_dob)
101     attach_window("main_window");
102     select_menu("client entry");
103     attach_window("client entry");
104     button_press("&new");
105     enter_text("client_number", cl_nr);
106     enter_text("client_last_name", cl_last);
107     enter_text("client_first", cl_first);
108     enter_date("client_DOB", cl_dob);
109     button_press("&Ok");
110     attach_window("confirm");
111     button_press("&Ok");
112 end function;
113 function select_client(cl_nr)
114     ......
```

Figure 21.3 : A programmed test script

This example is already more readable and maintainable than a script created during record and playback. All technical items, that are sensitive to changes, are programmed in separate functions. In case of a change in the application only the functions may need to be adapted and the calls of these functions in the main script remain the same which reduces the maintenance effort. The test data and the test flow are still stored in the test script itself and therefore not easily accessible by non-experts like end-users, auditor etc.

21.4 Data driven tests

Data driven tests are a special implementation of test programming. In this case the scripts are programmed and contain all the functions for entry and checking of information. The data needed for the test is stored in separate files either in spreadsheet or ASCII format, in which case the data is separated by comma's or tab-characters. When we take a look at the script of the previous examples again, it could be programmed as shown in figure 21.4.

```
1    ...
2    ...
3    open_file("client");
4    until end_of_file("client");

5
read (nr,last,first,dob);
6    call enter_client(nr,last,first,dob);
7    loop;
8    close_file("client");
......
100 function enter_client(cl_nr,cl_last,cl_first,cl_dob)
101    attach_window("main_window");
102    select_menu("client entry");
103    attach_window("client entry");
104    button_press("&new");
105    enter_text("client_number", cl_nr);
106    enter_text("client_last_name", cl_last);
107    enter_text("client_first", cl_first);
108    enter_date("client_DOB", cl_dob);
109    button_press("&Ok");
110    attach_window("confirm");
111    button_press("&Ok");
112 end function;
```

Figure 21.4 : Programmed scipt for data driven testing

In the script a main loop is programmed that will read the file record by record and process the data. Like in the previous example a function is programmed that will take care of the data entry (lines 100 to 112). After reading a line from the input file (line 5) this input function is called (line 6).

The input file (speadsheet) used for this script could contain:

	Id	Last Name	First Name	Date of birth
1	12345	Newman	Randy	28-Nov-43
2	568910	Collins	Phil	31-Jan-51
3	....			

Figure 21.5 : Input file for data driven testing

As one can see, the function for data entry is similar to the one created during test programming. The main advantage of this way of working is the separation of the test input data from the script. This increases readability and reduces maintenance and data dependency. If the data has to be changed, or a test case has to be added, one only needs to change the data file. Various files can be used in the same script so reusability of the script is higher compared to the previously discussed way of working. However, only data in records of a pre-defined layout can be used, like in this example all columns will have the same type of contents throughout the file. If you want to process a file with a different record layout you will have to create another script. This makes data driven testing useful for large data entry but less usable for testing based on user scenarios. Since the input data varies it may be difficult to create and organise.

21.5 Testing with action words

The methods described so far, if used with care, can lead to improvements in the test execution process especially for regression testing. However, some important pitfalls exist. Record and playback is in fact automation of the existing manual test process. A good comparison is that of the first cars, which looked like carriages with a motor attached in place of the horses. It is a first step but not an optimal design. Test programming means higher programming effort, the system design has to be to be implemented in the test design. In both parts there is a lack of maintainabilty. If the menu structure or the location of a result on a screen changes, this will imply substantial effort to keep the tests running. In the worst case, for record and playback, the test will have to be recorded again.

A second potential problem with existing approaches to test automation is accessibility of both the tests and the test results. Because actions and data are mixed, in a very technical form, it is almost impossible to understand what exactly is tested, especially for a non-technical person. It is therefore hard to get a commitment for using automated tests. Of course data driven testing is a great improvement but the test flow (what has been tested, why and how) is still "hidden" in the test script.

In all of the described approaches, results checking is done by special functions of the test tool. In fact a "snap shot" is taken from the screen image during recording of the test. During playback the actual screen contents is compared with the file that contains the original one. Comparing pre-defined results with actual outcomes cannot be done!

There are a number of practical issues to consider in relation to starting the test preparations early. In case of record and playback methods, it is necessary to wait until the system is running. In "testing with action words", which is part of the TestFrame method for structured testing (Buwalda *et al.*, 2001), the tests are not registered in the test tool, neither as record playback scripts, nor as test programs. As with data driven testing the tests are stored in spreadsheets. These spreadsheets are called *test clusters*. To implement this approach a test language is introduced, specifying actions to be taken and the test data. The data can be either test input or (expected) test outcomes. The actions are specified as *action words* - short commands to the test tool.

Compared to the approaches described in previous paragraphs this "testing with action words" requires a different approach. In two more or less separated processes the tests are prepared. In test analysis, that can start as soon as the requirements documents are available, the actual tests are designed and the test clusters are created. In parallel the test navigation scripts are designed and created. In figure 21.6 the process is depicted with the most important products.

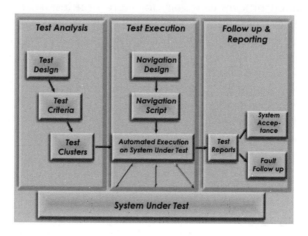

Figure 21.6: TestFrame process

Test Clusters

A test cluster contains the data that will be used during the test. This will cover both the input data and the expected results. So far it looks very much like data driven testing. The main difference is, that not only the test data but also the test instructions are specified in the cluster: column A contains the action word (the instruction), Columns B onwards contain the data that is used with the action word. Figure 21.7 shows an example in which an imaginary health insurance application is tested.

	A	B	C	D	E	F
1	**cluster**	Health Insurance Calculation				
2	**Date**	10-Aug				
3						
4	**begin**	Tc001 – Calculate yearly premium				
5		*Last*	*First*	*Date of Birth*	*Gender*	*Client ID*
6	**enter client**	Newman	Randy	28-Nov-43	M	&Keep[client-1]
7		*Client ID*	*Age*			
8	**check age**	&Client-1	58			
9		*Client No*	*Start date*	*Premium*		
10	**check premium**	&Client-1	&today()	5.000		
11						
12						
13						
14	**begin**	Tc002 – yearly premium must be greater than franchise				
15		*Last*	*First*	*Date of Birth*	*Gender*	*Client ID*
16	**enter client**	Collins	Phil	31-Jan-51	M	&Keep[client-2]
17		*Client ID*	*Age*			
18	**check age**	Client-2	50			

Figure 21.7: Example of a test cluster

This example starts with general information about the test that will be performed (rows 1 and 2). Rows 4 to 11 are the implementation of the test condition to calculate and check the annual premium for a health insurance. Reference to this condition is defined as a parameter to the action words "begin" and "enter client" and subsequently a client is entered. Since the system generates a unique Client ID the action word variable "&keep" is used to capture this value and store it in the variable "client-1". This variable is used in a special &-function in the next lines ("&client-1") as a key value to retrieve the correct client. After a check of the age of the client (action word "check age") a premium calculation is executed (action word "check premium") in order to check the annual premium calculated by the system. Here a value of 5.000 is expected. (Fewster and Graham, 1999)

The action words are usually specific for the application that is tested and the type of test that will be executed. This means there will be different action words for a stock trading system, a mortgage system etc.

Navigation

The test automation is regarded as a separate activity, completely seperate from the test design. To interpret and execute the commands in the test cluster a special script is written, so called navigation script. This navigation script is usually written in the script language of a record and playback tool. The navigation script consists of several components, some of which are general, others have to be specifically written for the application that is being tested. For example, there are general functions for reading the test lines from the tab separated ASCII text file (exported from the test cluster). The lines are interpreted one by one. The first field, the action word, is used to call a function for that action word. The action word functions are specific to the application. An example of a navigation script is provided in figure 21.8.

```
  1    ...
  2    get clustername from command_line;
  3    open_cluster(Clustername);
  4    while ReadTestLine = OK
  5    case action
  6      "enter client": EnterClient();
  7      "check age": CheckAge();
  8      "check premium": CheckPremium();
  9      "change client": ChangeClient();
 10    case else
 11      warning("unkown action")
 12    end case
 13 end while
100 function enter_client()
101    attach_window("main_window");
102    select_menu("client entry");
103    attach_window("client entry");
104    button_press("&new");
105    enter_text("client_number", arg2);
106    enter_text("client_last_name", arg3);
107    enter_text("client_first", arg4);
108    enter_date("client_DOB", arg5);
109    button_press("&Ok");
110    attach_window("confirm");
111    button_press("&Ok");
112 end function;
```

Figure 21.8: Example of a Navigation Script

In the example mentioned above there will be specific procedures for the action words used. The procedure for "enter client" will go to a client screen and fill all fields in the right order. This is not necessarily the same order used in the test cluster. Even the number of fields is not necessarily the same. The navigation procedure can replace unspecified fields with relevant default values. After entering the fields the navigation will close the entry screen by using "Enter" or any other means provided by the system under test.

The procedure for the other action words in the example, will follow a similar path. In case of "check age" it will select a screen were the value for the age can be found and capture this value from the screen. Next it will compare this value to the expected value which was specified, in this case 58. The result, "pass" or "fail", will be written into the test report. If it is not possible to capture a value from the screen other means can be used to obtain data like SQL queries or internal API calls.

Test Reports

The *report* consists of a header, a detail part and a summary. The content of the report is dependent on the project. In our example (see figure 21.9) the test has failed. The fail is marked, with the expected and recorded value, and in the summary the fail is marked again with a line number so that it can be easily used for analysis.

Test results reported as "Failed" are input for further analysis. They do not necessarily mean that the system is wrong. As with other test methods also the tests themselves can contain errors. The defects must be regarded as a starting point for further analysis.

The test report, produced under control of the navigation script, contains, along with the results, other data relevant to evaluate the test. It will usually contain a print of the test lines interpreted, version information in the header and a summary of the test results. It is also possible to report the test results in an alternative form, for example to store them in a database or a defect management system.

21.6 Consequences

Testing with action words has been applied in number of large and small projects, both for on-line and batch systems. This technique has a number of effects on the test automation process.

```
Licensed to   : Chris Schotanus
Company       : CMG
Serial number : 500-000123-0-01

Engine version       : 5.00
Cluster name         : Client Entry
Sheet                : 1
Cluster author       : Chris Schotanus
Cluster version      : 3,1
Cluster date         : 10-8
===============================================================
 4: ***** Begin Tc001 - Calculate yearly premium

 6: enter client    Newman Randy 28-Nov-43     M       &keep[client-1]
      value 12345 kept in client-1

 8: check age          &client-1      58
       check of:       age
       expected:       58
       recorded:       58
       result:         passed

10: check premium   &client-1     &today()      5.000
       check of:       premium
       expected:       5.000
       recorded:       5.000
       result:         passed

14: ***** Begin Tc002 - yearly premium must be greater than minimum premium

16: enter client    Collins Phil 31-Jan-51     M       &keep[client-2]
      value 768762 kept in client-2

18: check age          &client-2      50
       check of:       age
       expected:       50
       recorded:       51
       result:         failed
......

......

109: end      cluster
         * * * * end Cluster

===============================================================
Number of test lines : 109
Succeeded test lines : 91%
Number of errors : 0

Number of checks : 25
- Checks passed : 22        88%
- Checks failed : 3         12%
Failed on lines        : 18, 44, 45

Start time : Mon Aug 06 12:40:14
Stop time : Mon Aug 06 12:41:40
Time used : 00:07:26
===============================================================
```

Figure 21.9: Test Report

The first effect is on flexibility. The test set, test clusters and navigation script, are more maintainable than with the other described techniques. When a change is made to the system under test, this will usually lead to a change in the autamated tests but this change is often limited. In most cases a change only has consequences for the navigation. For example a change in the menu structure only means a change to the relevant action word procedures. When there is a change in the requirements implemented by the system, the change will only affect the test cluster. For example a change in the tax laws will have an effect on a payroll system and therefore on the clusters testing that payroll system.

A second effect is on the accessibility of the test clusters and the reports. Although they are direct input for an automated test process the test clusters can be designed in such a way that also non technical people can understand them. It is possible for end users to directly prepare the test cases by setting up the spreadsheets.

The third effect is concerned with planning. The preparation of the test clusters can start in an early stage in a project, without a knowledge of all functional details of the system. In particular the business oriented test cases can be produced as soon as the requirements are available. The navigation script can be developed when a system is in its detailed design or implementation phases.

There is a benefit in cost effectiveness. The implementation of the navigation script is an additional activity in a project. This activity must be compared with the manual testing effort for the first test. An important difference in this respect with the traditional record and playback approach is that also the initial test execution is automated; there is no recording phase. Payback on the cost of navigation scripting will start as the test execution is repeated. Of course the expected benefits will be higher if the tests have to be executed more often, either tests of new releases in the project or in the maintenance phase.

Last but not least in projects an increase in motivation has been observed. Reasons for that are that the less intersting parts of the testing work are carrried out by a computer and that the separation of test design and navigation make it possible for people to work on the job they like most and they can do best, either the more business oriented test design or the more technically oriented navigation.

With all techniques described in this document there is an effect on quality when test automation is applied. Because testing is carried out automatically it is very reliable. Also it is possible to always run all tests, catching the notorious unexpected faults resulting from unexpected changes to other parts of a system. Automated testing is appealing: instead of a person having to test an application manually an automated test tool does the work – if necessary over and over again. This saves valuable human resources and makes the best use of computing resources.

However, introducing test automation is not something that should be taken lightly. Investigations need to be carried out, users and testers need to be trained and a technical infrastructure needs to be implemented. Techniques that seem to be easy to implement are often difficult to maintain and produce products that are not reusable and not easily accessible by non-technical persons. Far too often tools are bought and implemented, without considering the processes those tools will have to support adn without proper planning and control. As a result these tool end up on a shelf and are never used again. Tool vendors have recognized this aspect and have added functionality to ease planning, programming and data driven testing. Testing with action words often provides the most flexible solution, but requires the largest investment. Which technique fits best for an organisation or project depends on the business objectives, risks of the system-under-test, system life cycle, skills available, etc. Remember, the main goal of test execution automation is to reduce the effort needed for test execution and increase the accessibility of the test by non-technical personnel.

References

- Buwalda, H., D. Janssen and I.Pinkster (2001), *Integrated Test Design and Automation*, Addison-Wesley

- CMG TestFrame research Centre (2001), *TestFrame, a practical guideline for testing information systems* (in Dutch), Ten Hagen & Stam Publishers

- Dustin, E., J. Rashka and J. Paul (1999), *Automated Software Testing*, Addison Wesley

- Fewster, M. and D. Graham (1999), *Software test Automation*, Addison-Wesley.

Part 8

People

22 Team Building

Chris Comey

This chapter has been produced to identify the technical, team, and management skills required to make a test team effective. It will draw upon information from various sources; books, magazines, and conference presentations as the basis for discussion. Testing has now reached the stage where it is recognised as a profession in its own right and as such, skilled, experienced, and motivated professional testers are required to carry it out successfully. In order to attract and retain the expert testers required, it is essential to bring the test role into line with other IT specialist areas. Testers need training and development, career paths, and parity to other IT roles regarding respect and remuneration. One needs to look at the individual skill set required in a test team, the individual characteristics and mindset that make a good tester, and the management and controls required to direct and motivate the team. Each individual should look at his or her own skill set and actions to ensure that they are all contributing to maximum effect.

22.1 Steaming along or just plodding?

> *Team'work - Co-operative work by a team acting as a single unit*
>
> *Collins English Dictionary*

As any sports fan will tell you there is no such thing as a 'dead cert' – the team that cannot be beaten. At some time or another you will have seen the so-called 'underdog' come out fighting and cause an upset by beating the red hot favourites. The favourites tend to be labelled a class above, and it is accepted that they have the far more skilful players. So, why does this happen? How can it happen? Is it a one-off? They just happened to play better on the day or something more fundamental, perhaps motivation, discipline, drive, or the will to succeed, maybe.

Taking the example of a simple game with clearly defined targets, i.e. score more goals than the opposition; what can be said about the workplace? In the existing IT workplace where the complexity of products is ever increasing and time to market is at a premium, it is essential that our delivery teams are as effective and efficient as possible. Having the right skill set amongst the teams, or being able to call on an expert when one is needed, is essential, but is it enough? The answer is no. What is also essential is to ensure that the skills are applied at the right time and place in the project and that team members understand their role and what is required of them. The team must all pull together and communicate effectively, sharing successes as well as any issues. To succeed you need to build a confident team that wants to achieve, understands the difference that they make to the project, and can be proud of what they do.

22.2 What makes a successful team?

- The correct combinations of skills and experience
- The correct combination of people
- The correct leadership and management
- The correct processes and controls

> *Skill – Practical ability, cleverness, dexterity*
>
> *Collins English Dictionary*

Skills in a test team

It is impossible to list the specific technical skills that are required for testing all IT projects. Every project is different, with a different customer base, project goals, technical architecture, technologies and hardware. What you must ensure is that the information detailing these variables is made available to the development and testing teams as soon as possible in the project lifecycle. The team managers will then be able to allocate the resource with the required skills to the project, identify any training needs that may be required, or recruit to fill any gaps in the existing skill set.

Specific Testing Skills

The "Professional Tester" Magazine in its March 2000 issue (Quentin, 2000) listed the following necessary skills for the approach to testing:
- The professional tester will need good general knowledge of testing and the influence of testing throughout the development and support of software systems.
- Knowledge of how testing fits into the different lifecycles.
- Knowledge of different test levels and approaches from component testing to acceptance testing and the related entry and exit criteria for each phase.

- The testing professional should be prepared for the iterative nature of regression testing.
- Knowledge about change control and configuration management and the risks associated with failure of any part of the development or deliverables from development.
- The tester will need knowledge of how to help management to create a suitable policy for quality in general and testing in particular
- Knowledge of how to establish strategies for traceability of test objectives to user required functionality, formal test specification and design techniques.
- The test professional should be familiar with both external and site-specific standards.

The following skills can be added to the list above. These specific skills will help an individual to be a good tester:
- Experience of development/coding is an advantage.
- Experience of static and dynamic test methods.
- Technical support experience is useful for the test environment support.
- Data analysis experience for production of test data.
- Business analyst experience.
- Automated testing tools experience (CAST Tools).
- Experience of metrics.
- Knowledge of improvement models such as CMM
- Knowledge of test process improvement (TMM and other models).

When building teams it is advisable to have a diversity of skills and also that there is strength in depth across the team. Having all these skills is impossible for one individual; nowadays one needs to specialise, e.g. test tools is almost a discipline within itself.

Remember testers all have skills but does the test team have the right combination of skills? It is no good putting eleven defenders or eleven attackers out on a football field. They may win the odd game purely by scoring more goals than the opposition, but at the end of the season the league table will show that they finish well below a balanced team of defenders, midfielders, attackers, and of course a good goal keeper.

Phase Specific Skills

Testing itself has been divided up into stages, levels, and functions; component testing, integration testing in the small, system testing, integration testing in the large, and acceptance testing, each of which will be executed by different people. This approach gives the required test focus at the required development phase, but is often prepared and executed by individuals in isolation from the other test areas. The Internet has changed the priorities of the test levels with security, usability, and performance now coming to the fore. Test tools are advancing very quickly which allows more testing to be executed quicker and easier. The changes will keep coming thick and fast, so be prepared for change and keep the communication chain open. It is reasonable to expect that as each test phase has a different focus, the skills required to execute the testing at each stage may be different.

A high level set of skills that would be valuable for each test level may look like:

Component Test
- Knowledge of coding languages
- Knowledge of the code under test
- Experience of white box testing techniques – path analysis, statements & branch testing, LCSAJ, etc as detailed in BS7925-2 (BS7925-2, 1998)
- Knowledge of static analysis techniques (complexity measures, paths, etc.)
- Experience with static test tools (complexity measures, syntax testing, pre-compilers, etc.)
- Experience of code inspections

Integration Testing in the small
- All the skills for component test will also apply for integration testing in the small. Other experience that may be useful would be:
- Experience of integration strategies
- Experience of testing component interfaces
- Experience of testing using variables and data exchange.

System Test
- Knowledge of white box and black box test techniques
- Knowledge of functional and non-functional testing
- Experience of dynamic test tools (capture playback tools)
- Experience of test management tools (test planning and tracking, incident management and configuration management tools)
- Experience of test automation

Integration Test in the large
- Experience of interfaces and files
- Knowledge of the business processes from end to end
- An understanding of operational profiles

Acceptance Test
- An understanding of the principles of testing

- Expert business knowledge from each business area such as operations, accounts, finance, compliance, live support etc
- An understanding of requirements test coverage
- Experience of test case design and execution methods

Useful skills for all stages

Knowledge of static analysis techniques (reviews and inspections etc)
Knowledge and experience of static and dynamic test tools
An understanding of project management, incident management, configuration management, delivery management, and implementation.
Knowledge of test environments and test data requirements this item should be at each level although it has a different meaning at each level, e.g. for component testers they need to understand stubs and drivers

22.3 People in a team

Anyone who has investigated this area will be familiar with the work of Dr. R. Meridith Belbin (Belbin, 1993), who carried out research over a number of years into the factors that most effect management teams. Results from this research showed that there are a finite number of behaviours, or team roles, which comprise patterns of behaviour adopted naturally by the various personality types found among people at work. By surveying individuals with a simple questionnaire, Belbin helps to identify the personal characteristics in each individual to identify their natural strengths and weaknesses. By carrying out this exercise it becomes clear that no one is perfect, that everyone has strengths, and everyone has allowable weaknesses. By identifying the team members' strengths and weaknesses, they will know what they are good at and, more importantly, where they need to develop.

> *There is no 'I' in Team – but maybe there should be!*

This expression would indicate that successful team members give everything up for the team, sacrificing their personal goals and needs to help achieve the team goals. This is admirable but not realistic; people are individuals and have different needs, the team ethos should recognise this and act appropriately. Once knowing people's natural roles, their strengths and weaknesses are known. People naturally feel more relaxed when they are doing work that they feel comfortable with, they will make a good job of it, and enjoy the process. If you thrust work onto individuals who are not capable of it because of a lack of the required skills, or they do not feel comfortable with it, then they will not do the best job possible. We need to play to existing strengths as well as strengthen weaknesses in order to develop our team members.

22.4 How to build a more effective team?

There is no magic wand that can be waved over a group of individuals to transform them into a fully functioning team. However, there are processes and practices that can be put in place. This chapter will discuss a few of the accepted principles that contribute towards good team working within an organisation and factors for motivation. One needs to bear in mind that everyone is different and each individual is motivated differently. Some people need reward, some accolades, some merely seek acceptance or to be heard, others just need to feel that they belong. The more each individual's needs are met by the team, the more each individual will feel part of that team. This will result in more individual input and, by default, a better overall team achievement. An example of a successful team can be found in "Practical quality assurance for embedded software" (Van Veenendaal, 1999).

> *If people have the right attitude then you can train them, develop them, and they can achieve anything given time. "Recruit for attitude, train for excellence"*

The IT industry can be compared to a white water raft ride: we're shooting down the rapids and if people are not prepared to paddle when you need them to, then we are all going to drown. If they won't paddle then don't let them on the boat; leave them behind. If they are paddling slowly then everyone else has to paddle that much harder.

22.5 Management

The management role in the formation and continued running of successful teams is key, regardless of job title e.g. team leader, test manager, test co-ordinator etc. You need to know what you are doing, believe in what you are doing, and you must take the initiative in all things that involve your team. You need sufficient knowledge of testing principles to evaluate the risk when a situation arises. You may or may not do something about it, but you must know why!

Some attributes of a good manager:
• Communicate and encourage communication
• Lead by example

- Hold progress meetings and share successes as well as problems
- Encourage people to take part in team meetings and canvas for opinions
- Involve people in the work allocation process
- Get individuals to take ownership of tasks and be accountable to you for their completion
- Encourage group problem solving
- Identify individuals strengths and weaknesses diplomatically but openly
- Identify individual career paths, training requirements, and personal development plans
- Introduce mentoring, shadowing, or buddies to promote cross fertilisation of skills and reduce single points of failure in individual team members
- Foster open and honest communication in both directions
- Maintain individual's self esteem
- Encourage team members to take responsibility and make them accountable where appropriate.
- Do something a bit different every now and then, a curry lunch maybe, a night out somewhere; try and make it mandatory.
- If they are working in accordance with your guidelines ensure they know that you will always back them up and fight their corner for or with them.

Remember, being a good leader is a skill too, and not everyone is a natural leader. People can learn to lead by being trained to do so, or through their experience of being led by others. Be careful though; if you have only ever experienced poor leadership, you may find that you have adopted bad practices and are a poor leader yourself. If you foster open constructive criticism within the team you can ask for feedback on your own performance, although this can sometimes bruise your ego, it is valuable. We never see ourselves quite as others see us, and this could be an opportunity to learn some new team leadership skills ourselves.

> *"What a wondrous gift to give us, to see ourselves as others see us"*
> *Robert Burns*

If a team member is obviously not contributing fully take him or her to one side and ask if there is a problem. There may be a domestic problem, or a medical condition, of which you are not aware. Always ask first before taking any form of action. If there is such a problem try and come to an understanding that is acceptable to both parties. If an individual is constantly late in the mornings ask why. It may be that as a single parent he or she has to drop the children at school every morning. You could ask if they would like to start and finish half an hour later. If you can be flexible then be so, after all you are the person with the power, so use it. Ensure that where extenuating circumstances do exist, the team are made aware before any bad feeling or rumours start.

If your team is made up of the different character types there will on occasion be confrontation between team members on any number of issues. The team leader role is required to make decisions at this point and to carry out a certain amount of peace brokering. Remember that a truly successful team once established should be able to function without any single individual being present. Some of the most successful managers make themselves obsolete and the team carries on functioning on a day- to-day basis without their presence, leaving the managers to concentrate on the more strategic concerns and of course their golf handicaps!

Delegation

You can delegate the responsibility but you cannot delegate the blame!

This means that you are responsible for the completion of the task regardless of the fact that you may have delegated it to another person. If the task is not completed satisfactorily then you delegated to the wrong person, unless of course the problem was unavoidable. Regardless of the excuses;
- too busy (check workload first and agree ownership)
- didn't understand (ensure the task is clear)
- something else came up (need them to inform you)
- didn't know how (you chose a person with insufficient skill set)
- thought you meant 'next' Monday (communication)

Choosing which tasks can be delegated and to whom is a fine art. You will probably recognise the 'micro manager' who cannot delegate anything to anyone. They have no confidence that the task will be done right if at all. It is difficult to work for a 'micro manager' as they often become a bottleneck for everything and often think it is everyone else's fault. There is only one way to do the task and that is their way, you are not so much a team as a machine and they are the operator, when they stop for tea, the machine stops too. Often, the only thing they are capable of delegating is the blame. If you find you cannot trust your staff enough to delegate to them, look first to yourself; you could be micro managing!

At the other extreme there is the absentee manager. He is always busy doing something else, never has time for meetings with his staff and pushes everything down the line onto his team. He is a notoriously poor communicator purely because he is too busy to do so, he is very hard to pin down and seldom returns his calls. he may delegate purely because he doesn't know what to do in the first place.

Fortunately, most managers are somewhere between the two extremes, which makes them bearable to work for. At this point let me say a few words about the perfectionist. The poor old perfectionist works so hard to try and get everything perfect and of course he can't, thus he is always frustrated and never happy with his achievements. Do not aim for perfection, as it is unlikely that you will be able to achieve it, aim for the agreed level of quality, which is appropriate and fit for purpose. Apply the 80/20 rule, which states that you can do 80% of the task in the first 20% of the time and the final 20% of the task takes the remaining 80%. You need to challenge yourself and ask is it good enough now? And, if the answer is yes then stop.

Individuals versus Teams

Do you believe that teams are better than individuals?

If you have any doubts that teams are more effective than individuals you can try a simple experiment. Take any twenty fairly tricky questions on general knowledge or a technical subject and ask half a dozen individuals to answer them individually without recourse to any literature or documentation. Then get the six people together and let them answer the same questions as a team, you will get discussion and disagreement on certain questions and consensus on others. The total correct score of the team will almost always be greater than the highest individual score, and certainly it will be higher than the average score achieved individually. This exercise proves that the whole is greater than the sum of the parts, two heads are better than one, and teams are more effective than individuals.

22.6 Retaining test expertise

The following is an excerpt from "Investors in test people" (Van Gool, 2000).

"Although the company was enjoying more and more success with TestFrame in the European market for testing, the retention of testers was becoming a problem. Once a test consultant had been recruited, it was important to keep them happy and motivated and to keep them interested in the testing profession, as many were being lured away by the closely related and attractive worlds of trends, new technologies and applications. Too often testing is seen as a stuffy and boring profession that is easy to learn and presents few challenges; in short. A profession which is merely an easy stepping stone into the world of IT."

"Testers said that the main reasons for them wanting to leave were that:
- Other IT disciplines had more to offer
- Testing wasn't challenging enough and didn't involve a broad enough range of disciplines
- The testing discipline was too isolated from other disciplines and was not a serious career move
- The test profession didn't offer sufficient career opportunities"

The company combated this trend by introducing career paths for testers, with training requirements identified for specific roles and also personal development plans for individuals. This resulted in a reversal of the trend and a successful application to the investors in people organisation. The key points of the process were as follows:
- Position testing as a multidisciplinary discipline (which in fact it is), which will stress the variety of the work and the opportunities for assignments and personal development
- Show clearly what the career opportunities are, as this will demonstrate what a position or career in testing has to offer
- Put supporting training courses in place, this will motivate employees and show them what the career opportunities are and facilitate the achievement of their goals and ambitions
- Ensure that the right man/woman is in the right job: in consultancy this means a greater focus on matching the right test consultant with the right assignment
- Implement internal marketing activities and PR, to improve the image that testing has
- However the most important task is still: talk to your employees, ask them what they want to achieve and help them to achieve it.

As can be seen the organization achieved some success in their approach. By talking to the people concerned and listening to what they had to say, taking action where possible to improve the situation, and monitoring the success of the process. Remember when dealing with people there are rarely one off solutions you need to follow through and make any changes part of your working culture.

Rewards – Motivators or De-motivators?

People are always looking to increase productivity for individuals and teams and rewards are one way of recognising an outstanding contribution. It is often the fact that the actual effort expended has been recognised that motivates people, not any bonus payments that may be made. It is the people you work for saying "Well done, you have done a good job and I am rewarding you for it", it's a pat on the back.

Beware! This subject can be a minefield. You must ensure that whilst recognising an individual you are not de-motivating other team members or damaging any individuals standing within the team by singling them out. A manager once informed me that I had been recommended for a bonus payment for my work on a certain project. I was not expecting this and as my chest started to swell with pride, the manager followed up with, "I am allowed to authorise one of these payments a month. You can have this one and Jim can have next month's." This left me totally deflated. What I thought was recognition of my efforts had turned into a bonus 'rota' irrespective of personal contribution or effort. This whole experience was counter-productive and even though I had the money from the bonus it actually managed to de-motivate me.

It is very difficult to establish who has made a significant contribution unless you are close enough to the day-to-day running of the project to be able to identify outstanding effort. You will have come across the 'self promoters' who makes sure that everyone, especially the management, is made aware how busy they are and how little time they have, whilst the rest of the team have their heads down doing the work. If you reward the self-promoters you will not only encourage them, you will de-motivate the hard workers and probably loose face with them.

Team bonuses are a much more productive approach. If the bonus criteria are set at the start of the project and the goals to achieve the bonus are clear then they can be a powerful motivator. If an individual within a team is seen to be slacking and endangering the team bonus then it is much more likely that peer pressure will be applied to that individual. Peer pressure is a very strong force as can be seen in the fashion world. It some times appears that the old adage "You are what you eat" has transformed into something more like "You are what you wear". Peer pressure can work on individuals that may well rebel against the approaches of management regarding their performance; remember everyone wants recognition, respect, and appreciation. The bonus itself need not be cash, it could be a special day off or a team event such as bowling or go karting.

22.7 Your career belongs to you!

An obvious statement, really that's why it's called 'your' career. What this means is that it is up to individuals to take responsibility for their own personal development and to keep their skills finely honed and up-to-date. If you know that you have a weakness in a particular area then try and strengthen that weakness rather than backing away from those particular tasks. Talk to your manager and discuss the ways in which you can develop not only technical skills, but also the so called 'soft skills'; ask what your weaknesses are. There are many techniques that allow learning opportunities varying from formal or in-house training through to mentoring and shadowing. If there are team members who are strong in a particular discipline, try shadowing them for a while and learn how they carry out that particular task, ask why they do things a certain way and not another way. You may not always find that the approach someone else adopts will work for you but you are still learning, developing, and becoming a more rounded individual.

It is not only training and experience that will help you further your testing career, you can increase your knowledge and awareness in the following ways:
- Read the books that have been written on the subject of testing
- Subscribe to the testing magazines and circulars
- Join the appropriate professional organisations for testers
- Attend the relevant testing focused conferences
- Achieve formal qualifications in testing
- Listen to others. Even if you don't agree with what they are saying, they may just point out another angle that you have not considered.

In order to succeed as a tester, one needs to become a rounded individual. As a tester we need a wider range of skills to allow us to handle the ever-increasing rate of change in our industry. Testers will also need to learn their strengths and weaknesses, learn to integrate with their colleagues, and learn to work together more closely.

22.8 How do we spot a good tester?

Testers need to have a combination of the technical skills and the soft skills that have already been talked about. Testers need to:

• Be skilled and experienced	• Be pedantic
• Be confident	• Be diplomatic
• Be good communicators	• Pay attention to detail
• Be conscientious	• Stay calm in a crisis
• Be self motivated	• Have a sense of humour
• Be reliable	• Be stress resistant
• Be tenacious	• Be accurate

There are ways that you can gain an insight into an individual's character, without using the Belbin questionnaire, by asking a few simple questions.

- When you interview potential employees take some time to try and assess their character, what their strengths are and how they will fit into the team.
- Look not only at the answers that they have given to any technical questions but also the way in which the questions were answered. Did they think about the answer or offer an answer straight away, did they ask for further information when the question was not clear, did they confirm their understanding before answering the question?
- You could ask them a few opinion questions to see if they have views or strong feelings on certain subjects. "How do you feel about testing without any CM in place?" should be enough to render a strong response if indeed it does not send them scurrying for the door.
- Offer the candidate the chance to ask you any questions that they may have, listen to what they want to know. It can give you information on their level of experience or what is important to them.

Once the technical interview is complete and the atmosphere has relaxed a little you could ask some of the following questions:

- Do you prefer to work closely as part of a team or have your own tasks?
- What was your greatest achievement at work?
- What are your hobbies?
- What are you really good at?
- What character trait do you find most annoying in other people?
- What do you think other people find annoying about you?
- Do you prefer to talk face to face or use email?
- Who was the worst boss you ever worked for and why?

You could prepare a multiple-choice test paper, or give them a section of specification and ask them to produce the test conditions. You could even produce a small Visual-Basic application and ask them to test it for you to see how many of the known faults they can find. Any or all of these will assist in determining an individual's testing ability and aptitude towards testing. Assess if they are easy going or highly strung, testing can be a stressful role. Look for a sense of humour. Sometimes you need to be able to laugh in the face of despair.

22.9 Communications

> *Communicate – impart, convey, reveal, to give or exchange information*
> *Collins English Dictionary*

One part of team working that can always be improved is communication both within the team and externally to other teams and project personnel. Various studies have shown that when two people are talking face to face, the information contained in the words spoken amounts to around 7% of the message. The other 93% of the communication is relayed from the context of the conversation, the emphasis placed on the words by the speaker, the tone of voice, body language, facial expressions etc. So beware the written word, as the human aspect of the communication is lost in emails and other non-verbal communiqués.

Communication is of course a two-way thing. The onus is on the person imparting the information to do so in a structured, logical, and if possible an easily understandable manner. The people receiving the information also need to be involved in the information exchange, active listening and employing the use of questioning, clarifying, and checking understanding should be the order of the day. As the listener if you come away with the wrong information or have misunderstood the message then you are partially responsible. Summary of the information is a very useful process to confirm your understanding of the information provided. Once you have listened to what you have been told, asked any questions that you may have, and checked your understanding, try putting the information into a summary in your own words and get confirmation that you have truly understood what is required.

When relating information to a third party where ever possible avoid the use of jargon and the dreaded three letter abbreviations that we all know and love! Sometimes it seems that the object of the exercise is less one of information sharing and more a political exercise to let everyone know how clever that particular "expert" is. Testers need to know what is happening with the product at all levels in order to be able to test at the most effect level possible. Testers really need to know everything in order for us to test to the best of our ability and add the maximum value to each level of development. Use plain

English in your plans and all test ware documentation, test reports, and progress reports, and encourage other teams to do the same.

Projects tend to run more smoothly if the design, development, and test teams can be located in a reasonable proximity to each other, and can go and talk any problems through with the concerned parties face to face. This allows personal relationships to form between the members of the teams and the very important individual and team communication to be fostered.

> *Communication breakdown, its always the same, you give me a nervous breakdown, you drive me insane*
>
> *(Led Zeppelin)*

The lyrics from Led Zeppelins Communication Breakdown were of course written for a personal relationship. Numerous personal relationships do fail with a communication breakdown being attributed as one of the main contributing factors. If communication between two individuals can break down then it is obvious that maintaining good communications between varied and diverse teams will be difficult. Good communications rarely just happen; they need to be worked at. This can be done by scheduling regular team meetings and one-to-ones. Have an area set aside where people can go and discuss an issue, maybe over a coffee, and actively encourage the test team members to meet all the people involved in their projects. At post-implementation reviews include a section on communication and look to improve any areas where problems arose.

Making decisions

Trained experienced professionals rarely make a wrong decision, however the decisions can only be made based on the information available to the person making that decision. If the information available to them is incorrect, out of date, or incomplete then the chances of an incorrect decision being made are multiplied. Sometimes, of course, decisions do need to be made without the full set of information in order for the project to continue making progress. This is a different scenario, and so long as the assumptions that were made are logged to support the decision it is a normal project activity.

The problems arise where information is available but not distributed, documents are updated but not circulated, requirements change and are not propagated, project drivers change and are not communicated. One way around this is to say, "send me everything and I will throw it away if I don't need it". A good manager can plan around anything except the unknown. Managers cannot of course perform miracles, they can only do the best thing under the constraints that apply to the specific problem in hand. In order for them to do this they need to know where the project is going, what the status is, what is going on, and what has changed. In the real IT development world a plan is current for a nano-second and is likely to already be out of date on production, because things are continually changing. Rapid change is a fact of life in IT. The test team is involved with every aspect of the project from the requirements capture stage, if not before, to support for the live operations team once the product is live. The test team will interface with all parties concerned in the project at some point during the lifecycle.

Customer – The test team will be involved in the requirements review process. Testers can often help with missing requirements analysis, testability analysis, and identification of environment and data requirements for testing. The test team often assists the customer with production of acceptance test case and sometimes test execution.

System users – The test team needs to learn from the users how the system is used in real life, what problems exist, and how to overcome them. The system test cases are derived from the functional specification but involving the users in the review of the test cases can be a very valuable exercise. It also makes the users feel involved and a part of the overall process rather than isolated and just given a system at the end of the project.

Business analysts – Business analysts often assist the customers with production of the requirements and often the acceptance test cases that will be used for product sign off. They tend to have an in depth knowledge of the business needs, why we are producing the system and how the system is intended to work, and are a very useful source of information to the test team

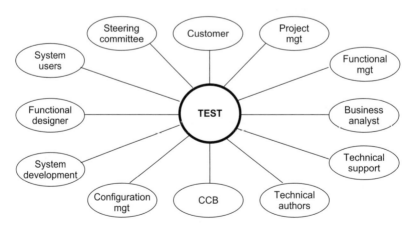

Figure 22.1: The great variety of communication links

Project managers – Good project managers are very important to the success of any project. They are ultimately responsible for all the project deliverables and products. They need to communicate any changes that impact the project teams as soon as possible and likewise the team mangers need to advise the project manager of any problems or slippage as soon as they occur.

Design team – The design team have a key role to play and therefore testing will have a large interaction with them. During test case design numerous queries will arise of a technical design nature, which will require confirmation. Including a designer in the review process for testing is useful as it can often highlight areas that have been missed or are considered to have insufficient coverage from a technical design viewpoint.

Development team – The test team will interact with development team, and other key stakeholders, when agreeing the release timings, content, and procedures. They will also interact regarding faults and change management, consult regarding technical queries, and discuss faults that have been raised. A good tester/developer relationship is vital if rapid progress is to be made. Development can assist the test team with the production of test harnesses and test data if a solid working relationship has been established.

Technical support team – Both live support and test team will benefit from a good working relationship. Technical support can consult with testing regarding live faults, quick fixes, and potential workarounds. A quick fix to a serious problem in live will need the test team to carry out regression testing as a priority. Testing can gain information on test effectiveness by looking at the faults that have been found in the live environment.

Technical authors – Technical authors can gain information on the system operation and performance by working with the test team. The test team can validate any products, such as user guides, that are produced, which will help to guide test case production and give an insight into how the business intend to use the system once it is live.

Configuration management team – The test team should fully support the configuration management processes as they are key to the production and execution of controlled and repeatable testing. The test team needs to be involved with the CM team at the early stages so that the test teams needs are incorporated into the CM strategy.

Change control board – The test team must have a representative on the Change Control Board to provide details of test effort, costs, and timescales for each change. Testing also needs to be aware of the changes that are approved and which release they are scheduled for in order to maintain the test cases, test data, and other test ware.

Fault management area – The majority of faults found during the development phase are raised by the test team. The fault management area will decide the action to be taken for each individual fault. The faults are prioritised and agreement is reached regarding which faults will be fixed in each release of code. The test team can answer any questions regarding these faults and provide further details where required. The test team needs to be kept informed regarding the release contents and when they are scheduled so that the test cases can be updated and prepared in advance.

Basically, all of the above individuals and teams are working together as a single project delivery team. Every team member has interdependencies on certain tasks that will impact other areas if there are problems encountered or delays happen along the way. This is IT, there will always be problems, people need to be confident that they can flag them early without fear of recrimination because we do not work in a blame culture. Planning around problems is what managers do so give them the information and let them do it! When it comes to project communications the test team needs to lead by example. Every communication sent needs to be clear, concise, easily understandable and to the point. Make sure that ALL the people who need to know are included on the circulation list. Make sure that the test team is included on all the correct distribution lists; it is down to you to check, take nothing for granted.

If problems arise, communication is often so complex that solutions are sometimes hard to find. Keeping that fact in mind, try the following basic and practical approach that have worked for other people (Perry and Rice, 1997).

Keep talking even if it means disagreeing

About the worst thing that can happen on a project is when the eventual users of the system and the sponsors of the system are in the dark as to what is going on with developing the system. Constant communication is what keeps surprises at a minimum. A common tendency is to avoid communications when people disagree. Although disagreements are sometimes difficult to work through, they should not cut off communication.

Don't confuse meetings, memos, and e-mail with effective communication

Meetings, memos and e-mail are vehicles of communication, but are not the message. You can write twenty e-mail messages to the same person in one day and perhaps convey the wrong message completely. In addition, communication is not only *what* you say, but *how* you say it. Some organisations actually encourage their employees to take frequent breaks together because it facilitates informal communication, which is vital to a project.

Whatever you do remember to communicate tactfully !!

> *Tact is the knack of making a point without making an enemy*
> *Howard W. Newton*

22.10 The end game

So the keys to a successful team are as follows:
• Have a clear, common understanding of the team goals.
• Have the technical skills to enable the team to carry out all composite tasks.
• Have the personal skills to allow the team to work together.
• Have the management, processes, and controls to allow the team to function efficiently without excessive constraints.
• Communicate effectively.

There must be a career path for professional testers, train them, increase their skills, motivate them, and reward them. All testers need to be ambassadors for the test discipline and make sure that the benefits that formal testing adds do not go unnoticed.

Should you find that you disagree with the content of this chapter, fine, but ask yourself this "Do I embrace a challenge? Do I go the extra mile? Am I ready to learn new skills? Am I prepared to change?" If the answer is no to any of these questions then you will need to look to your own attitudes and performance first or you may not last in the IT arena. The IT industry is changing at an ever increasing rate, new technology drives out new skills and new test tools and you will need to run just to keep up. Setting up balanced teams is a lengthy task, but it will pay dividends in the long run, for the individual, the team, and the company.

References

- BS7925-2 (1998), *Software Component Testing*, British Standards Institution

- Belbin, R.M. (1993), *Team Roles at Work*, Butterworth Heinemann, ISBN 0-7506-2675-5

- Brooks, F.P. (1995), *The Mythical Man Month*, Addison-Wesley, ISBN 0-201-835959

- Gool, B. van (2000), Investors in test people, in: *Proceedings EuroStar conference*, Kopenhagen 2000

- Ould and Unwin (1986), *Testing in Software Development*, Cambridge University Press, ISBN 0521-37860

- Patnode, B. (2001), A Recipe for Success, in: *Software Testing Quality Engineering,* Vol. 3, Issue 2 March 2001

- Perry, W.E. and R.W. Rice (1997), *Surviving the top ten challenges of Software Testing, A people oriented approach,* Dorset Publishing House, SBN 0-932633-38-2

- Quentin, G. (2000), Skills development, Section 1: The strategic approach, in: *Professional Tester*, Vol. 1, Issue 2, March 2000

- Sabourin, R. (2001), At Your Service, in: *Software Testing Quality Engineering*, Vol. 3, Issue 3 May 2001

- Straw, A. and M. Shapiro (1998), *Succeeding at Interviews in a week*, Hodder and Stoughton, ISBN 0 340 627379

- Veenendaal, E.P.W.M. van (1999), Practical Quality Assurance for Embedded Software, in: *Software Quality Professional*, Vol. 1, no. 3, American Society for Quality, June 1999.

23 Test career paths

Ruud Teunissen

This chapter will discuss a model for defining test career paths. The first step is to find out what special skills define a good tester – of course technical skills are important, but personal skills and an "attitude" are equally important! Once testers are recruited, the challenge is to keep them motivated, fascinated, enchanted, ... Good testers are ambitious and want to be "tested" themselves – time and time again. That is why the test career cube has been developed – a guideline for test career paths.

23.1 Three dimensions

To treat testing as a profession within an organisation, a career perspective must be offered to the test personnel. Essential components within a professional approach include (theoretical) training, personal preferences, personal skills, work experience, and coaching and support. The test career cube allows testers to grow from test engineer to test manager (first dimension). Not every tester has the same interests and strong points: the test career cube allows testers to differentiate: technical, methodical and managerial (second dimension). The final dimension is the backbone for each successful career: theoretical background, training, coaching, and (social) skills.

The cube is a tool for career guidance by the human resource manager in order to match the available knowledge and skills, and the ambition of the professional testers, to the requirements of the organisation.
The test career cube is part of the Test Management Approach (TMap), (Pol *et al.*, 2002)

The first dimension: Growth

Growth is the progress that an employee can make, for example from tester to test manager, from test engineer to test advisor. Growth is usually directly related to the responsibilities and the involvement an employee has within a project or the organisation. A test engineer can grow from execution to preparation to co-ordination to planning. Another possibility is to grow from execution to preparation to coaching, e.g. test design techniques, to test process improvement consultant.

A distinction should be made here between vertical growth and horizontal expansion. When further growth is no longer an option - remember Peter's Principle - there is the possibility of horizontal expansion: a higher performance level within the same level.

Improvement of the conditions of employment can be achieved in this structure by reaching either a higher function level or a higher performance level.

The second dimension: Differentiation

To treat testing as a profession is to treat your testers as individuals. Although not all testers are the same, they all have to start at the basis: the preparation and execution of test scenarios, test scripts and test cases. After gaining enough experience at the starting level, the logical step is to differentiate ,based on individual skills and preferences:

There are three different career paths described in TMap:
* *Team and project leadership*
  For test personnel that are capable of and interested in leading a test project.
* *Methodological advice*
  For test personnel that want to give test advice, for example when a test strategy is being established, in the selection and application of test specification techniques, etcetera.
* *Technical advice*
  Test personnel that feel attracted to the technical side of testing opt for technical (test) advice. This includes the organisation and utilisation of test tools or the set-up and management of a test environment.

The first step is specialisation in the chosen field to create a solid base for becoming an expert. The following table shows examples of function levels, the function name being indicated for each direction.

D	General test management		
C	Test project leadership	Methodological test advice	Technical test advice
B	Test team leadership	Methodological test specialisation	Technical test specification
A	Test execution		

Table 23.1: Test functions and levels

Function level A   for these functions there is as yet no clear
                         demarcation in "columns". At these levels, people
                         gain a wide knowledge of testing and test execution
                         in all its aspects.
Function level B, C   differentiation applies to these functions.
Function level D   differentiation does not apply to this function.
                         Employees at this level are expected to be capable
                         of successfully implementing each of the three
                         differentiations and/or managing them.

The third dimension: Knowledge and Skills

Building up knowledge and skills is the third dimension of the career cube. The
following components are distinguished:
- (test) training;
- social skills;
- experience;
- coaching and support.

Coaching and support are essential conditions for a sound career path, in
particular in the case of (a start in) one of the lower function levels. Each
employee receives support in various ways. This is implemented by the test
manager, the personnel official and/or by experienced employees. Testers
who have just started receive extra attention from a coach, who supervises all
aspects and developments. As the function level increases, the importance of
practical experience and social skills training also increases considerably in
relation to (test) training and coaching and support.

23.2 The test career cube

Finally, the full "career cube" is completed on the basis of the above. It shows
the required knowledge and skills for each function (differentiation).

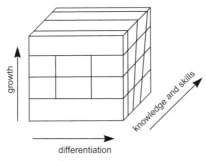

Figure 23.1: The test career cube

The main idea behind this chapter is the fact that testing is a profession and that you as a company should treat it as one. You can do so by offering your personnel career opportunities, based on individual choices and coaching. Appreciate individual skills and preferences, offer the possibility of differentiation - team leader, methodical or technical advice.

To keep your testers motivated you have to "test" your testers continuously and appreciate them by offering them a career and - naturally – by paying them the right salary.

References

- Pol, M., R. Teunissen and E. van Veenendaal (2002), *Software Testing: A guide to the TMap approach*, Addison-Wesley, ISBN 0-201-74571-2.

Annexes

Annex A. Testing standards assessment

In this annex brief subjective comments on each of the standards mentioned in chapter 3 "Testing standards" are provided. Each standard is also given a rating on its usefulness to a software tester.

* Ratings	
M	Mandatory - all testers should have this
HR	Highly Recommended
U	Useful, but not necessary
O	Other - only acquire if necessary

Standards	Comments	*Rating
Terminology	Good coverage of this area. Little scope for misunder-standings.	
IEEE 610	Useful reference text, but not necessary for a typical tester (over 200 pages of definitions!)	U
IEEE 610.12	The software engineering definitions. Necessary, only terms not defined here are included in BS7925-1.	HR
BS7925-1	Excellent component testing terminology source. Some general software testing terms, but needs expanding to become a true general software testing vocabulary. A draft copy of this document is available free from: Stuart.Reid@rmcs.cranfield.ac.uk.	M
Specific Software Testing	These standards are specifically written to support soft-ware testing and verification and validation (V&V).	
BS7925-2	Excellent coverage of the component (unit) test process and testing techniques and measures. The techniques and measures are also applicable to other test phases. A draft copy of this document is available free from: Stuart.Reid@rmcs.cranfield.ac.uk.	M

IEEE 829	Good test documentation standard, but the standards supporting the processes should include guidelines on the necessary documentation. For instance BS7925-2 for component test documentation, and IEEE 1044 for incident (anomaly) reporting.	HR
IEEE 1008	Good coverage of unit testing process, but now superseded by BS 7925-2.	U
IEEE 1012	Excellent V&V standard, using integrity levels. A must when writing a test strategy.	M
IEEE 1028	Excellent introduction to software reviews.	M
Supporting	Standards covering those processes that support the test process.	
IEEE 1044	Includes an anomaly (incident) classification process and standard lists of anomaly classification schemes. If you're setting up the incident reporting activity then there's no need to look any further, apart from.....	HR
IEEE 1044.1	Guidance on the above, if you feel you need it.	U
IEC 60300-3-9	A harmonising generic standard on risk analysis. Ideal if your industry does not have an application-specific version – and may be better anyway.	HR
ISO 15026	An excellent generic (non-safety-specific) process for determining integrity levels. The only minor problem is that it attempts to specify means of achieving levels of integrity – this is best left to the development and test process standards.	HR
High-level	Process and QA standards that contain requirements related to software testing	
ISO 9000(-3)	What can you say about the ISO 9000 series? More than a quarter of a million certified organisations can't be wrong. Testers need to be aware, but coverage of software testing is minimal.	U
ISO 9126	A useful source of quality characteristics definitions (see annex B) and metrics for non-functional testing. Contains both internal (white box) and external (black box) metrics.	HR

ISO 14598	Defines a product evaluation process. Often used in concert with ISO 9126.	U
IEEE 730	Very high level – states a requirement for the inclusion of·V&V and testing in QA plans, but not much else of use to the tester.	O
ISO 15288	Will contain (due for release in late 2000) systems level requirements and simply require compliance with ISO 12207, below for software components of systems.	O
ISO 12207	The integrating software life cycle processes standard. Those in software not using this standard in five years time will be negligible (and negligent?).	M
Application-specific	This is only a small sample of the available application-specific standards. As is typical of this genre, nearly all are safety-related and consider both software development and testing.	
IEC 880	An old (1986) standard that has a guidelines annex on software testing. Aimed at very high integrity systems, its surprising its not been superseded.	O
DO-178B	The best application-specific standard. Uses integrity levels. Its only failings are the expectation of 100% coverage and the inclusion of modified condition decision coverage.	HR
Def Stan 00-55	Appears biased towards the use of mathematical proof for verification. Defines required coverage in terms of code constructs rather than requiring techniques to be used.	U
MISRA	A reasonable set of guidelines, available free on the Web at: www.misra.org.uk/license.htm. No special automotive features discernible in the software testing.	U
NIST 500-234	Guidelines that specialise in V&V. Ostensibly for healthcare, but actually generic. Unusually contains special topics on testing reused software and knowledge-based systems. Available free on the Web at: 234/val-proc.html.	U
Generic Development	These consider both software development and testing.	
PSS-05-0	No integrity levels. Testing requirements are largely based on references to IEEE testing standards.	U

IEC 61508	Not completely generic (for safety-related software). Uses integrity levels, but allocation of software testing requirements to levels looks flawed.	U
Process Improvement	Apart from TMM, these process improvement standards cover both development and testing, but concentrate on development.	
ISO 15504	Allows existing process improvement models (e.g. CMM, CMMI, Bootstrap, etc.) to be cross-referenced to a common base for measurement and comparison.	U
CMM-SW	A framework for software development process improvement, it also gives guidance on what to add to increase the level of maturity of the process. Not a high software testing content. Will eventually be superseded by CMMI-SE/SW.	U
CMMI-SE/SW	A combined framework that used to be in two parts —one for systems engineering and one for software engineering. Not a high software testing content.	U
TMM	A tester's version of the CMM-SW (so based on maturity levels), which focuses primarily on testing (see chapter 17).	HR

Annex B. ISO 9126 Quality Characteristics

Functionality	*The capability of the software product to provide functions which meet stated and implied needs when the software is used under specified conditions.*
Suitability	The capability of the software product to provide an appropriate set of functions for specified tasks and user objectives.
Accuracy	The capability of the software product to provide the right or agreed results or effects with the needed degree of precision.
Interoperability	The capability of the software product to interact with one or more specified systems.
Security	The capability of the software product to protect information and data so that unauthorised persons or systems cannot read or modify them and authorised persons or systems are not denied access to them.
Compliance	The capability of the software product to adhere to standards, conventions or regulations in laws and similar prescriptions relating to functionality.
Reliability	*The capability of the software product to maintain a specified level of performance when used under specified conditions.*
Maturity	The capability of the software product to avoid failure as a result of faults in the software.
Fault-tolerance	The capability of the software product to maintain a specified level of performance in cases of software faults or of infringement of its specified interface.
Recoverability	The capability of the software product to re-establish a specified level of performance and recover the data directly affected in case of a failure.
Compliance	The capability of the software product to adhere to standards, conventions or regulations relating to reliability.

Usability   The capability of the software product to be
                             understood, learned, used and attractive to the user,
                             when used under specified conditions.

Understandability   The capability of the software product to enable the
                             user to understand whether the software is suitable,
                             and how it can be used for particular tasks and
                             conditions of use.

Learnability   The capability of the software product to enable the
                             user to learn its application.

Operability   The capability of the software product to enable the
                             user to operate and control it.

Attractiveness   The capability of the software product to be
                             attractive to the user.

Compliance   The capability of the software product to adhere to
                             standards, conventions, style guides or regulations
                             relating to usability.

Efficiency   The capability of the software product to provide
                             appropriate performance, relative to the amount of
                             resources used under stated conditions.

Time behaviour   The capability of the software product to provide
                             appropriate response and processing times and
                             throughput rates when performing its function,
                             under stated conditions.

Resource utilisation   The capability of the software product to use
                             appropriate amounts and types of resources when
                             the software performs its functions under stated
                             conditions.

Compliance   The capability of the software product to adhere to
                             standards or conventions relating to efficiency.

Maintainability   The capability of the software product to be
                             modified. Modifications may include corrections,
                             improvements or adaptations of the software
                             changes in environments, and in requirements and
                             functional specifications.

Analysability   The capability of the software product to be
                             diagnosed for deficiencies or causes of failures in the

	software, or for the parts to be modified to be identified.
Changeability	The capability of the software product to enable a specified modifications to be implemented.
Stability	The capability of the software product to avoid unexpected effects from modifications in the software.
Testability	The capability of the software product to enable modified software to be validated.
Compliance	The capability of the software product to adhere to standards or conventions relating to maintainability.
Portability	*The capability of the software product to be transferred from one environment to another.*
Adaptability	The capability of the software product to be adapted for different specified environments without applying actions or means other than those provided for this purpose for the software considered.
Installability	The capability of the software product to be installed in a specified environment.
Co-existence	The capability of the software product to co-exist with other independent software in a common environment sharing common resources.
Replaceability	The capability of the software product to be used in place of another specified software product for the same purpose in the same environment.
Compliance	The capability of the software product to adhere to standards or conventions relating to portability.

Reference

- ISO/IEC 9126-1 (2001), *Software engineering - Software product quality - Part 1: Quality model,* International Organization of Standardization.

Annex C. Review and inspection forms

This annex provides an example of the two review and inspection forms discussed in chapter 8. They can be used with any type of formal review. The responsible software quality engineer can generate the relevant metrics with the information on these forms.

The purpose of these forms is first of all to support the author in updating his/her document and the moderator in acting upon change requests and other improvement suggestions. Secondly the forms are used (by the software quality engineer) to monitor and improve the inspection process based on the metrics gathered, using feedback sessions.

Review Process Form

This form is used to log information with respect to the formal review. Information about the document (id, size, type), participants and effort (to be) spent is logged on this form. It is also used to invite participants to a formal review and control the process.

The formal review process form is divided in four main parts:
- When, where and what to review;
- Who is performing the formal review, with what role;
- Time used and defects found;
- Result of the review.

Review Logging Form

The logging form is used for logging the different reviewers' comments regarding the document during preparation and during the meeting. This form is used during rework as an action list by the author. Reasons why issues or defects are not solved are also noted on the logging form. The moderator can use the logging form during follow-up, to check whether all defects and issues have been addressed.

FORMAL REVIEW PROCESS FORM

❑ Walkthrough ❑ Technical Review ❑ Inspection

Doc-id(s):	Version:	Start date:	Project:
Kick-off meeting	**Date:**	**Time:**	**Location:**
Logging meeting	**Date:**	**Time:**	**Location:**

Document Name:

Review Size	Pages / lines of code
Document type	❑ Requirement ❑ Functional Spec. ❑ Architectural design ❑ Interface Spec. ❑ Design ❑ Code ❑ Test Spec. ❑ Project File ❑ Other:
Goals/Specific questions:	
Related documents / standards:	
Applied rules and checklists:	

	name		role	time (min)
Moderator:				
Author:				
Reviewer 1:				
Reviewer 2:				
Reviewer 3:				
Reviewer 4:				
Reviewer 5:				
Reviewer 6:				
Reviewer 7:				

Planning time:	x 1	min	New items logged:	
Kick-off meeting time:	x n	min		
Total preparation time:		min		
Logging time:	x n	min		
Discussion time:	x n	min	Critical items logged:	
Rework time:	x 1	min	Major items logged:	
Follow-up time:	x _	min	minor items logged:	
Total time:		min	Total items logged:	

Decision:	❑ Only Moderator ❑ New Formal Review ❑ Participants: ..
Completion date:	Moderator signature:
Remarks on formal review procedure:	

Improve Quality Services B.V.	**Formal Review Process Form**	**SEQ-Number:**

Notes to the Formal Review Process Form

Formal review type: the type of formal review: walkthrough, technical review or inspection.

Doc-id(s): the unique identification number(s) of the document under review including version or date.

Version: the version or the date of the document under review.

Start date: the date on which the author request for review.

Project: the name of the project.

Kick-off meeting: the date, time and place where the kick-off meeting will take place.

Logging meeting: the date, time and place where the logging meeting will take place.

Document name: the full name / title of the document under review. If the document is only partly reviewed also specify which pages / lines will be reviewed.

Review size: the number of pages that are under review. For code documents the number of lines of code to be reviewed must be given.

Document type: the type of the document under review.

Goals/Specific questions: specific questions / attention points that need to be answered / addressed during the review. These questions are formulated by the author in co-operation with the moderator.

Related standards/documents: standards and/or documents to be used or known by the participants of the review.

Applied rules/checklists: the rules and checklists to be used by the participants during the checking of the document.

Moderator: the name of the moderator and if applicable the description of the additional role and the preparation time of the moderator.

Author: the name of the author of the document.

Reviewer: the name and the description of the role assignment and the preparation time of the reviewers. The individual preparation time of the reviewer must be filled in at the start of the logging meeting. It can be used to calculate the overall preparation time.

Planning time: the number of minutes spent by the moderator (and author) for performing the planning, invitations and the entry-check.

Kick-off meeting time: the total number of minutes spent in the kick-off meeting by all participants of the kick-off meeting.

Preparation time: the total number of minutes spent in the individual checking of the document and associated documents, standards and checklists by all review participants including the moderator.

Logging time: the total number of minutes of the meeting spent in logging activities times all participants in the logging part of the meeting.

Discussion time: the total number of minutes of the meeting spent in discussion activities times the number of participants in the discussion part of the meeting.

Rework time: the number of minutes spent in addressing all items on the logging form by the author, this includes updating the document, the logging form and submitting change requests. This also includes the time spent by others than the author in solving open issues (only related to the documents used in the review. Not the time of solving change requests or Software Process Improvement proposals).

Follow-up time: the number of minutes spent by the moderator and participants in checking the rework.

Total time: the total of all the above mentioned times.

New items logged: new items discovered during the meeting, and which were not found in the individual checking by the participants.

Critical items logged: the number of critical items reported in the logging meeting. The same item found by more than one participant is only counted once.

Major items logged: the number of critical items reported in the logging meeting. The same item found by more than one participant is only counted once.

Minor items logged: the number of critical items reported in the logging meeting. The same item found by more than one participant is only counted once.

Total items logged: The total number of items reported.

Decision: decision whether the updated document should be checked by the moderator only, or that a new formal review is needed or that a review is needed with only some participants. In the last case the initials of the new reviewers must be noted in this field.

Completion date: the date the formal review of a document has been completed.

Moderator signature: the signature of the moderator after completion of the formal review.

Remarks on formal review procedure: remarks on the formal review procedure, these can be forwarded by the moderator to the central Software Quality Assurance group (if in place).

SEQ-Number: the (subsequent) number of the formal review held in the project, reference to the Master Review Plan.

FORMAL REVIEW LOGGING FORM

☐ Walkthrough ☐ Technical Review ☐ Inspection

Doc-id(s):

Project:

Document name:

N	Location		Defect / Issue description	C	M	m	N	Q	Rework / action performed / outcome discussion
	Who / Rule	Page Line							

| Improve Quality Services B.V. | Formal Review Logging Form | Page totals | SEQ-Number ... | Page ... of ... |

Notes to the Formal Review Logging Form

Formal review type: the type of formal review: walkthrough, technical review or inspection.

Doc-id(s): the unique identification number(s) of the document under review including version or date.

Project: the name of the project.

Meeting: the date, time and place where the logging meeting has taken place.

Document name: the full name / title of the document under review.

Nr: the (subsequent) number of defect logged.

Location: the exact location, page-number and line-number, of the item in the document under review.

Who: the initials of the participant who reported the defect.

Rule: The tag number of the rule that is violated with this defect (optional).

Defect / Issue description: the description of the defect so that the author can understand the item.

C: marked if the noted defect is a critical issue.

M: marked if the noted defect is a major issue.

m: marked if the noted defect is a minor issue.

Q: marked if the noted defect will be dealt with in the discussion part of the meeting.

N: Marked if it is a new item that is logged. This means that the defect was not found during preparation, but during the meeting.

Rework/action performed/ outcome discussion: remarks by the author during rework and/or additional remarks during the discussion meeting, e.g. proposed solutions.

Page totals: The totals of critical, major and minor defects on this page.

SEQ-Number: Sequence number of this review. The same number as with in the process form.

Page ... of ... : The page number of the total number of pages from this formal review.

Annex D. SUMI Case studies

SUMI is a rigorously tested and validated questionnaire based method to measure software quality from a user's perspective. Using SUMI the usability of a software product or prototype can be evaluated in a consistent and objective manner. The technique is supported by an extensive reference database and embedded in an effective analysis and reporting tool. SUMI has been applied to a great number of projects. This annex discusses three practical applications. Results, usability improvements, cost and benefits are described.

What is SUMI?

Within the European ESPRIT project MUSiC a method has been developed that serves to determine the quality of a software product from a user's perspective. Software Usability Measurement Inventory (SUMI) is a questionnaire-based method that has been designed for cost-effective usage. Software Usability Measurement Inventory (SUMI) is a solution to the recurring problem of measuring the user's perception of the usability of software. It provides a valid and reliable method for the comparison of (competing) products and differing versions of the same product, as well as providing diagnostic information for future developments

SUMI consists of a 50-item questionnaire devised in accordance with psychometric practice. Each of the statements is rated with "agree", "undecided" or "disagree". The following sample shows the kind of questions that are asked:
- This software responds too slowly to input.
- I would recommend this software to my colleagues.
- The instructions and prompts are helpful.
- I sometimes wonder if I am using the right command.
- Working with this software is satisfactory.
- The way that system information is presented is clear and understandable.
- I think this software is consistent.

The SUMI questionnaire is available in English (UK and US), French, German, Dutch, Spanish, Italian, Greek and Swedish.

SUMI is intended to be administered to a sample of users who have had some experience in using the software to be evaluated. In order to use SUMI reliably, a minimum of ten users is recommended based on statistical theory. Based on the answers given and statistical concepts, usability scores are calculated. Of course SUMI needs a working version of the software before SUMI can be performed. This working version can also be a prototype or a test release.

One of the most important aspects of SUMI has been the development of the standardisation database, which now consists of usability profiles of over 2000 different kinds of applications. Basically any kind of application can be evaluated using SUMI as long as it has user input through keyboard or pointing device, display on screen and some input and output between secondary memory and peripheral devices. When evaluating a product or series of products using SUMI, one may either do a product-against-product comparison or compare each product against the standardisation database, to see how the product that is being rated compares against an average state-of-the-market profile.

SUMI gives a global usability figure and additional readings on five sub-scales:
- *Efficiency:* degree to which the user can achieve the goals of his interaction with the product in a direct and timely manner
- *Affect:* how much the product captures the user's emotional responses
- *Helpfulness:* extent to which the product seems to assist the user
- *Control:* degree to which the user feels that he, and not the product, is setting the pace
- *Learnability:* ease with which a user can get started and learn new features of the product.

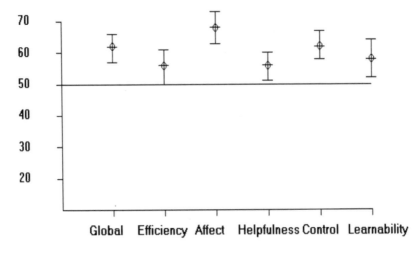

Figure C.1: a sample profile showing SUMI scales

Figure C.1 shows an example of SUMI output; it shows the scores of a test and the spreading of these scores (measured by the standard deviation) against the average score of the reference database, reflected by the value 50. Consequently the usability scores shown in the sample profile are positive, i.e. more than state-of-the-art, with a reasonable level of spreading.

SUMI is the only available questionnaire for the assessment of software usability, which has been developed, validated and standardised on a European-wide basis. The SUMI sub-scales are referenced in international ISO standards on usability (IS0-9241) and software product quality (ISO 9126-2). Product evaluation with SUMI provides a clear and objective measurement of the user's view of the suitability of software for his tasks.

Any SUMI test must be carried out by asking people to perform realistic, representative tasks. Employing a method such as usability context analysis helps identify and specify in a systematic way the characteristics of potential users, the tasks to be carried out and the circumstances of use (see paragraph 14.2). The results can be used to identify the various user groups and to define how these user groups are to be represented during testing.

Practical applications

Project 1: Project Management Package

Approach
A software package offering project administration and control functionality was subjected to the usability evaluation by means of SUMI. The software package is positioned as a multi-project system for controlling the project time, e.g. in terms of scheduling and tracking, and managing the productivity of projects. The package has been developed by a Dutch software house that specialises in the development of standard-software packages.

The SUMI test was part of an acceptance test carried out on behalf of a potential customer. Usability was an important characteristic due to the very high number of users, different user groups, their inexperience with project management software and the great variety of information needs. It was even looked upon as the critical success factor during implementation. Two main user groups were distinguished. One user group was mainly involved in the input of effort and time spent. Operability and efficiency are of especially great importance for this user group. Another user group was characterised as output users. Receiving the right management information is especially important for the output users. A SUMI test was carried out for each user group.

Specific acceptance criteria were applied regarding the usage of the SUMI technique for the usability evaluation. SUMI provides quantitative values relating to a number of characteristics that lead to a better understanding of usability. As part of the acceptance test, the SUMI scale was used that provides an overall judgement of usability, the so-called "global scale". Based on the data in the SUMI database, it can be stated that the global score has an average value of 50 in a normal distribution. This means that, by definition, for a value exceeding 50 the user satisfaction is higher than average. For the test of the project management package the acceptance criteria required that for each user group the global scale and the lower limit of the 95% confidence interval must both exceed the value of 50.

Results
The "global scale" regarding both user groups was below the desired the value of 50. For the input user group the score was even a mere 33. The output user group showed a slightly better score. Not only the "global scale" but also most other sub-scales were scoring below 50.

Because the results did not meet the acceptance criteria a number of usability improvement measures needed to be taken. Examples of measures that were taken based on the results of the SUMI test are:
• extension and adaptation of the user training;
• optimisation of efficiency for important input functions;
• implementation of specific report generation tools for the output user with a clear and understandable user-interface.

Project 2: PDM system

Approach
A Product Data Management System (PDMS) was implemented in the R&D department of a large copier manufacturer. During the trial phase usability appeared to be an issue and could have become a major risk factor during implementation. The time and effort needed to be spent on usability formed a point of discussion between development and the user organisation. It was decided to apply SUMI to acquire an insight into the current user perception of the PDMS.

A number of randomly selected users who were involved in the PDMS trail phase were requested to fill out the questionnaire. Twenty-six users were selected, of whom twenty-one returned the questionnaire. Six users stated that they didn't use the PDMS often enough. The feedback thus resulted in a 77% response rate.

Results

The table below shows the overall scores for the various SUMI sub-scales:

	Global	Efficiency	Affect	Helpfulness	Control	Learnability
Median	36	31	43	36	36	35

Table C.1: SUMI scores PDMS

The various scores were relatively low all round. There didn't seem to be too large of a divergence of opinion, except perhaps for learnability. An analysis of the individual user scores did not show any real outliner (see next table). Two users (one and five) had an outliner score for one scale (too high). Since it was only on one scale, they were not deleted from the respondent database.

	G	E	A	H	C	L
User 1	60	52	59	**69**	47	32
User 2	57	48	53	62	41	61
User 3	25	19	46	35	22	33
User 4	17	14	28	11	26	23
User 5	61	63	55	44	**60**	64
User 6	24	23	23	36	22	14
User 7	53	62	44	..	..	..
User ..	..	..	..	..	..	..

Table C.2: SUMI scores per user

As stated earlier the various scores were relatively low all round. In general one can say that the user satisfaction regarding the system is too low and corrective action is needed. Some more detailed conclusion were:

- *Efficiency*
  According to the users PDMS doesn't support the user tasks in an efficient manner. Too many and too difficult steps must be performed. Consequently, one cannot work efficiently and feels that the system is insufficiently customised to users' needs.
- *Helpfulness*
  An important conclusion is the fact that the messages are often not clear and understandable; as a consequence the system doesn't provide much help in solving a problem. The possibilities provided to the user in each situation are not clearly shown.
- *Control*
  Users often have the feeling of not being in control and find it difficult to let the system behave in the way they want it to. They feel safe when they only

use commands they know. However, they do find it easy to jump from one task to another.

On the basis of the SUMI evaluation it was decided to define a number of follow-up actions:
- a detailed analysis of the problems as perceived by the users. A number of users are interviewed and asked to explain, by means of practical examples, the answers given to the SUMI questions;
- a study on outstanding change requests and an increase in their priority;
- an improved information service to the users on changed functionality to provide them with more knowledge on how to operate the system; a re-evaluation of the training material with user representatives;
- a SUMI test was to be carried out on a regular basis (every two/three months) to track the user satisfaction during implementation of the PDMS.

Currently the follow-up is in progress and no new SUMI test has yet taken place. Consequently, nothing can be said regarding the improvement of the usability. However, by means of the SUMI test, usability has become a topic within the PDMS project that gets the attention (time and effort) it apparently needs.

Project 3: Intranet site

Approach
By means of MUMMS, a specialised multimedia version of SUMI, the usability of an Intranet site prototype of a large bank was evaluated. The Intranet site was set up by the test services department to become better known and to present themselves to potential customers. Since during the test only a prototype version of the Intranet site was available some pages were not yet accessible. A special sub-scale has been introduced for MUMMS, with the objective of measuring the users' multimedia "feeling":
- *Excitement:* extent to which end-users feel that they are "drawn into" the world of the multimedia application.

In total, ten users (testers) were involved in the MUMMS evaluation. The set of users can be characterised in the following ways:
- not involved during the development of the intranet site
- potential customers
- four users with Internet experience
- six users without Internet experience
- varying age and background (job title).

Results

The table below shows the overall scores for the various MUMMS sub-scales:

	Affect	Control	Efficiency	Helpfulness	Learnability	Excitement
Average score	69	74	62	67	67	68
Median	71	77	67	69	67	72
Standard deviation	9	12	11	8	6	12

Table C.3: Overall MUMMS score table

The various scores were moderately high. However, there seems to be a divergence of opinion on the control and excitement scales. Some low scores pull down the control and efficiency scales (see next table). Two users from the sample gave exceptionally low average scores. They were analysed in detail but no explanation was found.

	A	C	E	H	L	E	Average
User 1	71	81	67	71	74	77	73
User 2	74	74	74	71	67	71	72
User 3	81	84	67	67	74	74	74
User 4	54	51	54	57	64	44	**54**
User 5	71	74	43	58	55	76	63
User 6	64	84	67	81	67	69	72
User 7	51	81	74	54	74	64	66
User 8	71	81	64	74	71	81	73
User 9	77	81	76	84	77	74	78
User 10	64	47	51	57	57	44	**53**

Table C.4: MUMMS scores per user

As stated the usability of the Intranet site was rated moderately high from the users' perspective, although there seemed to be a lot of divergence in the various user opinions. Some more detailed conclusions were:

- *Attractiveness*

  The attractiveness score is high (almost 70%). However some users (4, 7 and 10) have a relatively low score. Especially the questions "this MM system is entertaining and fun to use" and "using this MM system is exiting" are answered in different ways. It seems some additional MM features should be added to further improve the attractiveness for all users.

- *Control*
  A very high score for control in general. Again two users can be identified as outliners (4 and 10) scoring only around 50%, the other scores are around 80%. Problems, if any, in this area could be traced back to the structure of the site.
- *Efficiency*
  The average score on efficiency is the lowest, although still above average. Users need more time than expected to carry out their task, e.g. to find the right information.

On the basis of the MUMMS evaluation it was decided to improve the structure of the Intranet site and to add a number of features before releasing the site to the users. Currently an update of the Intranet site is being carried out. A MUMMS re-evaluation has been planned to quantify the impact of the improvement regarding usability.

Applicability of SUMI

On the basis of tests carried out in practice, a number of conclusions can be drawn regarding the applicability of SUMI and MUMMS:
- It is easy to use and at low costs. This applies both to the evaluator and the customer. On average a SUMI test can be carried in approximately three days; this includes the time needed for a limited context analysis and reporting.
- During testing the emphasis is on finding defects, this often results in only negative quality indications, e.g. the number of defects found. SUMI however, provides an objective opinion that can also be a positive quality indicator, e.g. a SUMI score of 70 or more.
- The usability score is split into various aspects, making a thorough more detailed evaluation possible (using the various output data).
- SUMI provides, after detailed analysis and discussion, directions for improvement and directions for further investigation. SUMI can also be used as a risk analysis method to determine whether more detailed usability testing is necessary.

However, some disadvantages can also be mentioned:
- A running version of the system must be available; this implies SUMI can only be carried out at a relatively late stage of the project.
- A high number of users (minimum of ten) with the same background are needed to fill out the questionnaire. Quite often the implementation or test doesn't involve ten or more users belonging to the same user group.
- The accuracy and level of detail of the findings is limited (this can partly be solved by adding a small number of open questions to the SUMI

questionnaire). In practice a SUMI evaluation is often carried out in co-operation with a Heuristic Evaluation, the latter can in such a case provide a thorough interpretation of the SUMI score and concrete direction for improvement.

Conclusions

A system's end users are the experts in using the system to achieve their goals. Therefore, their voices should be listened to when the system is being evaluated. SUMI does precisely that: it allows quantification of the end users' experience with the software and it encourages the tester to focus on issues that the end users have difficulty with. A heuristics evaluation (preferably with user involvement) is also important, but it inevitably considers the system as a collection of software entities.

A questionnaire such as SUMI represents the end result of a lot of research effort. The tester gets the result of this effort instantly when SUMI is used: the high validity and reliability rates reported for SUMI are to a large measure due to the rigorous and systematic approach adopted in constructing the questionnaire and to the emphasis on industry-based testing during development. However, as with all tools, it is possible to use SUMI both well and badly. Care taken in establishing the context of use, characterising the end user population and understanding the tasks for which the system will be used supports sensitive testing and yields valid and useful results in the end.

SUMI is a testing techniques that can be applied to start usability testing or when limited resources for usability testing are available. Of course it is always a risk management decision, if usability is the most critical success factor, more thorough techniques such as full usability laboratory test should be applied. However, looking at current industrial usability practices, a large take-up of the discussed discount usability testing techniques would provide a great improvement for most projects and organisation ultimately leading to more usable and more user-friendly systems. User interfaces account for almost 50% of the code in modern software. In contrast, how much are you currently spending on usability testing?

References

- Kirakowski, J. and M. Corbett (1994), SUMI: the Software Usability Measurement Inventory, in: *British Journal of Educational Technology*, Vol. 24, No. 3, 1994

- Veenendaal, E. van (2000), Questionnaire-based usability testing, in: *Professional Tester* Vol. 1 Issue 4, September 2000.

Annex E. Tool Evaluation Criteria

This annex contains a list of criteria to be used in evaluating automated software testing tools and a suggested approach to conducting the evaluation. A simple scoring scheme with weightings is described, which can be used to score each of the evaluation criteria. The values for weightings and criteria scores may be modified through experience and use. An evaluation summary checklist is provided, which can be used in evaluating testing tools.

In conducting a review or evaluation of testing tools, the following approach should be employed:

Review the evaluation criteria and assign weighting to each of them:
- 1 for an essential criteria
- 0.75 for important criteria
- 0.5 for desirable criteria
- 0 for non-applicable criteria

When evaluating the tool, consider each criterion and score them as follows:
- 1 if the tool satisfies the criteria fully
- 0.75 if the tool largely satisfies the criteria
- 0.5 if the tool partially satisfies the criteria
- 0 if the tool does not satisfy the criteria

On completing the review, multiply the score for each criterion by its weighting and total the scores. The resulting value can be used to compare different automated testing tools. A supporting form is provided at the end of this annex.

Hereafter the evaluation criteria are listed; they are grouped under the following high-level headings:
- Support for Testing Types and Techniques
- Support for Test Management
- Tool Technical Issues
- Tool Defect Analysis Facilities
- Tool Documentation Issues
- Tool Integration Issues
- Tool Usability Issues
- Supplier Issues
- Training and Consultancy Issues

- Contractual and Financial Issues
- Miscellaneous Issues.

Support for Testing Types and Techniques

In selecting a testing tool, it is important that the tool is capable of supporting the key testing types your organisation in involved in.

Does the testing tool provide support for the following testing types:
- Functional Testing
- Regression Testing
- Installation Testing
- Configuration Testing
- Maintenance Testing
- Network Testing
- Performance Testing (including load, stress, volume and scalability testing)
- Multi-user Testing?

Support for Testing Management

Management of the testing process is key to successful, effective and efficient testing. It is important that any testing tool supports effective management of testing; providing good support for the typical testing management tasks.

Does the testing tool provide the following test management facilities:
- Support for multiple users with varying user privileges?
- The ability to record test plans or integrate with a project planning tool?
- The ability to integrate with a requirements management tool in order to represent and store and manage test requirements?
- The ability to design test scripts and verification points against requirements (and for this information to automatically be updated when requirements change)?
- The ability to integrate with a defect management and change request tool to allow the creation, monitoring, reporting, and resolution of defects?
- The ability to run pre-defined reports on all aspects of the testing process?
- The ability to customise existing / create new reports?

Tool Technical Issues

In selecting a testing tool, you will need to consider how well the tool facilities match your testing requirements (for example, does the tool support testing against the programming language you are developing in or does the tool perform on your operating system?).

Does the tool provide the following technical capabilities:
- The ability to record and playback test procedures?
- The ability to work with a particular development language or environment (e.g. C++, Powerbuilder, Visual Basic, Java, Delphi, Oracle, etc.)?
- Ability to test object container technologies (e.g. OCXs, VBXs, Data Windows)?
- Ability to test hidden objects (e.g. non-visual objects)?
- Ability to test the attributes of objects (e.g. Visible, Focus, Greyed, etc.)?
- Object-oriented recording / playback of scripts?
- The option of using low level or co-ordinate based recording / playback of scripts?
- Clarity / simplicity of the scripting language?
- Ability to manually edit scripts?
- Ability to playback scripts in W98/NT/W2000 without modification?
- Ability to trap unexpected windows and act on them?
- Ability to store all information in a single repository?
- Ability to integrate with other tools (e.g. CASE Tools)?
- Ability to update/maintain test cases and test procedures?
- Cross platform support (e.g. mainframe and PC testing)?
- The ability to automatically recover from crashes and continue to test?

Tool Defect Analysis Facilities
Does the testing tool provide the facilities for inspecting and analysing defects:
- The ability to view the test log following testing or at a later date?
- The ability to determine which test scripts and verifications passed or failed?
- The ability to examine the first failure and subsequent failures?
- Context sensitive facilities for viewing defects?
- The ability to enter a defect into the defect management system?
- Full traceability from the original requirement the test was based on through to the point of reporting the defect, and on through the defect tracking facilities?
- Ability to update/maintain test cases and test procedures (e.g. to update master data with observed data)?

Tool Documentation Issues
Irrespective of how technically good the testing tool is, the lack of clear and comprehensive documentation may compromise how successfully you use the tool. Some manufacturers now provide complete tool documentation on CD to save shipping bulky manual sets and to protect the environment. Such on-line documentation can provide a powerful means of accessing information, allowing the user to search for specified information. Also check manuals can be ordered as a free option.

Does the testing tool support the following documentation issues:
- An adequate installation documentation?
- A user manual?
- Tutorial information?
- Quick start information (such as "try it" sheets)?
- Trouble shooting information?
- A Scripting Language Manual?
- Is the documentation robust, durable and of good quality?
- Is the documentation clear, unambiguous and usable?
- Are additional copies of specified documentation available on request?
- Does the documentation provide further references to source material (e.g. definitive testing books, conference proceedings, testing technical reports)?
- Does the testing tool provide adequate contact information (e.g. help desk telephone number, web Site address and e-mail address)?

Tool Integration Issues

Integration is an increasingly important issue as senior software development managers appreciate the need to provide good communications between all the members of their projects, from analysts, through developers and onto the testers. IT professionals are increasingly looking for cross development lifecycle tool support rather than stand alone point solutions. Also, in considering the level of integration a given testing tool supports, beware of clumsy solutions where the user is expected to open the source tool (such as a requirements management tool), save the information held in that system into an intermediate file form, after which they have to run up the target tool (such as the testing tool) and then load the information into that tool. Such solutions are notoriously unreliable and in practice maintaining the currency of the information such integrations provide is at best difficult, and at worst, results in the tester working with out of date information, jeopardising the success of the testing project.

In evaluating a testing tool, the following tool integration issues should be considered:
- Does the tool have an integrated requirements management facility to ensure that each of the requirements for the System Under Test can be verified?
- Does the tool fully integrate with design and/or visual Modelling tools to allow automatic generation of test scripts based on design information (e.g. automatic generation of code stubs and test drivers for component test, automatic generation of integration tests from sequence diagrams, automatic generation of boundary and partition test data from design information)?

- For performance testing tools, is it possible to automatically generate test scripts from design information before any code has been written and execute them against the server logic to test the architecture and scalability of the proposed software?
- Does the tool have an integrated defect management facility to ensure that defects are automatically reported to the staff who need to know about them (e.g. as developer, project manager, QA manager, etc.)?
- Does the defect management facility provide traceability of the original requirement the defect is associated with?
- If the testing tool is a functional testing product, does it have a integration to other testing tools, such as:
  - reliability testing tools
  - code coverage tools
  - low level performance testing tools (to identify code bottlenecks)
  - high level performance testing tools (e.g. load, stress, volume and scalability testing tools)?
- Does the tool provide integration with a complete cross life cycle software development and testing process, where requests for help within the tool take the user directly to context sensitive process information, and where the process provides explicit advice on how to perform specified tasks within the testing tool?
- Does the tool provide integration with configuration management tools, allowing each artefact generated during testing (e.g. test scripts, reports, etc.) to be under rigorous configuration management?

Tool Usability Issues

Any testing tool should provide facilities that directly support the process by which testers typically test software in a natural and intuitive manner. The tool may be very powerful, but if the user interface to the tool is poor, the user may not be able to realise the full potential of the tool.

This section considers the usability issues associated with the testing tool (it is important to note that the criteria presented here represent only a sample of the usability issues that would need to be addressed in a full usability review):

- Does the tool adhere to user interface standards (e.g. Windows on PC platforms)? For example, does the tool use a standard "File, Edit, <tool specific menus>, Help" menu structure?
- Is the tool consistent in its use of menus and toolbar buttons? For example, is the "Open" toolbar button icon standard or is it some form of custom icon? Consistency is key in ensuring rapid familiarisation with the GUI.
- Where other tools integrate with the tool, do the other tools employ the same style of menu and toolbar buttons (or identical toolbar buttons where the function is the same) and is the look and feel the same? For example, try

comparing the "Open" toolbar button icons between "integrated" tools to see if they are the same.

- Are the Toolbar button icons standard and easily understood?
- Does the tool provide consistent short cut key access to its facilities?
- Is the tool simple, intuitive and easy to understand and use (e.g. can you easily guess what action to take next in most situations)? Beware tools, which have "modal" menus - i.e. menus where the menu items, which change with the state of the tool - such tools, will be difficult to learn how to use
- Does the tool provide good user help facilities?
  - Is there a help menu providing help topics?
  - Is there a help button on the toolbar?
  - Do the toolbar buttons have tooltips (the MS yellow pop up help labels)?
  - Are there help buttons providing context sensitive help in dialog boxes?
  - Does pressing the F1 key provide context sensitive help?
  - Is there a "point and click" help button? As a test of "attention to detail", find out what happens if you click on this button and then select the button again (i.e. Help on Point and Click Help).
- Where text is used in the tool, is it legible and free of technical terms or jargon?
- Does the tool allow the user to customise its look and feel?
- Does the tool allow the user to configure its facilities to match user preferences?
- Does the tool have good choice of colour for background and text (e.g. is there good contrast)?
- Is the tool attractive and enjoyable to use?

Supplier Issues

It is essential that you assure yourself about the size and financial stability of the tool vendor. The best tool in the world will be worthless if the supplier business fails. Similarly, small sized suppliers with few technical consultants may be unable to provide you with adequate technical support, mentoring, consultancy or training. Small sized vendors with poor finances may also have difficulties in performing adequate R&D, have problems keeping to promised release schedules, and suffer quality problems with releases. Another problem facing such organisations is the threat of take over, with no guarantees that the new owners will continue to support the old product range.

Think carefully before adopting tools from point solution vendors as you may experience integration issues if you need to use other tools in your software analysis, design and testing process. Consult with the other stakeholders in your organisation to find out what tools they use for analysis, design, change management and configuration management to determine if the suppliers of those tools also provide integrated testing tools before making a decision.

In evaluating a testing tool, the following supplier issues should be considered:
- Is the supplier financially and commercially sound?
- Is the supplier part of a larger IT company providing a range if IT services?
- Have you dealt successfully with the supplier in the past?
- Does the supplier have a web site which provides:
  - Company information
  - Product release news
  - Technical papers on the testing tool
  - Help and tips on the testing tool use
  - Sample/re-usable scripts?
- Help desk issues:
  - Is there a help desk available for user support calls?
  - Is the help desk UK based / European based / US based (this may affect availability of the service)?
  - Does the help desk provide 24 hour support?
  - Is there an e-mail address for support information?
  - When you need support, how quickly does the help desk respond?
  - When you need support, does the help desk understand your problem?
  - When you receive support, is the help correct and useful?

Training and Consultancy Issues
Despite what some vendors may tell you, no competent testing tool can be used without some level of user training. Even if you purchase a tool that has comprehensive on-line tutorial material, the users will still have to find the time and free resources to make use of the tutorial. In practice, training of staff is essential; otherwise lack of investment in training will cause a greater loss of investment when the staff struggle to use the tool effectively. Similarly, it can be very cost effective to put budget aside for mentoring and consultancy in order to show staff how to best use the tools, and to allow regular "health checks" to ensure continued effective use.

For these reasons, the following testing tool training and consultancy issues should be considered:
- Will the supplier install the testing tool at your site and provide introductory information (such as a half-day walk-through of the tool)?
- Does the supplier offer introductory training, and if so:
  - Can you obtain a copy of the prospectus?
  - What is the cost (per person / per day)?
  - Is there a minimum number of attendees?

- Can the training be performed at your site?
- Does the supplier offer advanced training? (This is often a good discriminator.)
- Does the supplier offer testing fundamentals training? (Another good discriminator of the depth and quality of the training that is available.)
- Does the supplier offer software development and testing process training? (A particularly important criteria for organisations with a mature approach to development and testing.)
- Does the supplier offer mentoring and skills transfer consultancy?
- Does the supplier offer tool consultancy?
- Are there third party organisations offering tool training / consultancy and are they certified and by the supplier before they are able to provide training? (This is a very good criterion to show widespread use and acceptance of a particular tool.)

Contractual and Financial Issues

This section addresses a number of financial and contractual issues that must be considered. Some of these issues may be difficult to resolve, but must be considered in evaluating a particular tool (such as estimating the value of the tool in terms of the benefits of using or not using the tool). While it makes good business sense to enquire about discounts, be careful not to let testosterone get in the way of obtaining a product, which will be of benefit to your organisation. As incredible as it may seem, there have been many occasions where staff involved in the purchase of tools have walked away from a purchase just because the supplier is unable to reduce the purchase price by, in some cases, tens of dollars!

On the other hand, you should also be very wary of suppliers who will suddenly slash the price of their product as soon as they hear that one of their competitors is involved. You will have to work with the supplier following your purchase (perhaps for training and mentoring, as well as ongoing support), so it is worth considering the business ethics of any supplier who was perfectly happy to charge you £X one day and then suddenly charge you half that amount just a few days later for exactly the same product (while presumably still making a profit). This is not a good basis for a successful continuing business relationship, and suppliers who indulge in such activities are almost certain to find ways of recouping the discount at a later stage, otherwise their business would be unsustainable.

The following contractual and financial issues should be considered:
- Does the price / pricing structure for the testing tool represent good value (this issue may require cost benefit analysis to be resolved)?
- Is the testing tool priced on a per licence basis?

- Are there any discounts for purchasing multiple licences?
- Are they fixed or floating licences?
- Does all of the tool functionality come in the "basic package", or do additional facilities cost extra (e.g. does the basic tool support network testing or is this a separate additional purchase)?
- How is multi-user testing priced (e.g. is it based on the number of "virtual users" that are required)?
- What is the cost of maintenance and does it include upgrades?
- What does maintenance provide?
- If priced separately, what is the cost of upgrades?
- How expensive is training (basic and advanced)?
- What is the cost benefit of purchasing and using the tool (this issue may require cost benefit analysis to be resolved)?

Miscellaneous Issues

The following issues are associated with obtaining further information on the testing tool and its use:

- Is there a user group for the tool?
- Is the user group independent of the supplier?
- How vigorous is the user group?
    - How often do they meet?
    - Do they publish proceedings?
    - Do they hold seminars, is there a mailing list?
    - Do they have a point of contact for testing tool issues / advice?
    - Do they have a web site?
- Is there any independent documentary support for the testing tool?
    - Are there textbooks available on the tool?
    - Technical reports/journal papers?
- Annual conference:
    - Is there an annual tool specific conference?
    - Where is it held?
    - Are the proceedings available?

Testing Tool	Version	Date of Evaluation	Evaluator Name

Criteria	Weighting (0-1)	Score (0-1)	Result
Support for Testing Types			
Functional Testing			
Regression Testing			
Installation Testing			
Configuration Testing			
Maintenance Testing			
Network Testing			
Performance Testing (Load, Volume, Scalability)			
Multi-User Testing			
Sub Total			
Support for Test Management			
Support for Multiple-Users			
Test Planning facilities			
Test Requirements facilities			
Design of Test Procedures/Test Cases			
Defect Management			
Pre-Defined Reports			
Customisation/Creation of new Reports			
Sub Total			
Tool Technical Issues			
Record and Playback facilities			
Required language/environment			
Object Container technology testing			
Testing of "hidden objects"			
Testing attributes of objects			
OO recording and playback			
Low level/co-ordinate recording & playback			
Clarity/Simplicity of Scripting Language			
Manual editing of Scripts			
Playback in W95, W98, NT, W2000			
Unexpected Windows			

Repository based			
Integration with other Tools			
Update/Maintenance of Tests			
Cross Platform Testing – mainframe/PC			
Automatic recovery from GPF / Crashes			
Sub Total			

Tool Defect Analysis Facilities			
Viewing the Test Log			
Determine Test Procedure/Test Case failure			
Examine failures			
Context sensitive defect analysis			
Entering defect reports			
Full traceability of original requirements			
Update/Maintenance of Tests			
Sub Total			
Tool Documentation Issues			
Installation documentation			
User Manual			
Tutorial information			
Quick Start information			
Trouble Shooting information			
Scripting Language Manual			
Robust, durable and good quality documentation			
Clear, unambiguous and usable documentation			
Additional copies of documentation			
References to source material			
Adequate contact information			
Sub Total			
Tool Integration Issues			
Fully Integrated Requirements Management			
Fully integrated with Visual Modelling tool			
Fully Integrated Defect Tracking			
Full Integration with other testing tools			

Integration with Development & Testing Process			
Integration with Configuration Management tool			
Sub Total			
Tool Usability Issues			
User interface standards			
Consistent Menus and Toolbar buttons			
Standard Toolbar Icons between Integrated Tools			
Standard Toolbar buttons used within the tool			
Consistent Short Cut key access			
Simple, Intuitive and easy to use			
Help facilities			
Legible and jargon free text			
Customise Look and Feel			
Configurable user preferences			
Good choice of colour and contrast			
Attractive and enjoyable to use			
Sub Total			
Supplier Issues			
Financially and Commercially sound			
Part of larger IT company			
Dealt successfully with Supplier in past			
Supplier Web site			
Help Desk			
Sub Total			
Training and Consultancy Issues			
Install and introduce tool			
Introductory training			
Advanced training			
Testing Fundamentals training			
Software Development & Testing Process training			
Mentoring and skills transfer			
Tool consultancy			

Third party training/consultancy			
Sub Total			
Contractual and Financial Issues			
Estimated value of Tool			
Pricing Scheme			
Multiple licence discount			
Fixed / Floating licences			
Packaged functionality			
Multi-user pricing			
Cost of Maintenance			
Maintenance Features			
Cost of Upgrades			
Cost of Training			
Cost Benefits			
Sub Total			
Miscellaneous Issues			
UK User Group			
User Group independence			
Vigorous User Group			
Documentary support			
Tool conference(s)			
Sub Total			
Total Score			

Literature

- Albrecht, A.J. (1984), *AD/M productivity measurement and estimate validation*, IBM Guideline

- Amland, S. (1997), Risk Based Testing of a Large Financial Application, in: *Proceedings of the 14th International Conference and Exposition on Testing Computer Software, June 16-19, 1997, Washington, D.C., USA*

- Anderson, M. (1999), The top 13 mistakes in Load Testing Applications, in: *Software Testing and Quality Engineering, Volume 1, Issue 5, September/Oktober 1999*

- Arksey, C. (1989), *Fagan method pilot, final report, Internal Technical Report*, Boeing, Seattle

- Bach, J. (1997), Good Enough Quality: Beyond the Buzzword, in: *IEEE Computer, August 1997, pp. 96-98*

- Bach, J. (1998), A framework for good enough testing, in: *IEEE Computer Magazine, October 1998*

- Bach, J. (1999), Heuristic Risk-Based Testing, in: *Software Testing Quality Engineering, Vol. 1, Issue 6, November/December 1999*

- Bach, J. (2001), Where does Exploratory Testing fit? in: *StickyMinds, Issue July 2001*

- Bach, J. (2001), What is Exploratory Testing? in: *StickyMinds, Issue January 2001*

- Basili, V., R Selby, and D. Hutchens (1986), Experimentation in Software Engineering, in: *IEEE Transactions on Software Engineering, vol.SE-12, no.7, July 1986, pp.733-743.*

- Basili, V., S. Green, S., O. Laitenberger, F. Lanubile, F. Shull, S. Sørumgård, and M. Zelkowitz (1996), The Empirical Investigation of Perspective-Based Reading, in: *Empirical Software Engineering, 1996, pp. 133-164.*

- Bawa, J., P. Dorazio and L. Trenner L (2001), *The Usability Business - making the web work*, Springer

- Beizer, B. (1990), *Software Testing Techniques, 2nd edition, Van Nostrand Reinhold, ISBN 1-850-32880-3*

- Belbin, R.M. (1993), *Team Roles at Work, Butterworth Heinemann, ISBN 0-7506-2675-5*

- Bevan, N., (1999), *Industry Standard Usability Test Reports, Industry USability Reporting project (IUSR) CIF IEEE*

- Bisant D.B. and J.R. Lyle (1989), A two-person inspection method to improve programming productivity, in: *IEEE Transactions on software engineering, October 1989*

- Black, R. (2002), *Managing the Testing Process, Second Edition, John Wiley and Sons, New York.*

- Black, R. (2000), Effective Test Status Reporting, in: *Software Testing and Quality Engineering, Volume 2, Issue 2, March/April 2000*

- Black, R. (2002), *Critical Testing Process,* Pearson Education, Inc.

- Boehm, B.W. (1979), *Software engineering economics, Prentice-Hall, Englewood Cliffs, NJ*

- Brooks, F.P. (1995), *The Mythical Man Month, Addison-Wesley, ISBN 0-201-835959*

- BS 7925-1 (1998), *Software Testing – Vocabulary, British Standards Institution*

- BS 7925-2 (1998), *Software Component Testing, British Standards Institution*

- Burnstein, I., T. Suwannasart and C.R. Carlson (1996), Developing a Testing Maturity Model: Part 1, in: *CrossTalk, August 1996*

- Burnstein, I., T. Suwannasart and C.R. Carlson (1996), Developing a Testing Maturity Model: Part 2, in: *CrossTalk, September 1996*

- Burnstein, I., A. Homyen, T. Suwannassart, G. Saxena and R. Grom (2000), A Testing Maturity Model for Software Test Process Assessment and Improvement, in: T. Daughtrey (ed.), *Fundamental Concepts for the Software Quality Engineer, American Society for Quality, Milwaukee, USA, ISBN 0-87389-521-5*

- Business Week (1994), Quality: How to Make It Pay, in: *Business Week, August 8, 1994*

- Buwalda, H., D. Janssen and I.Pinkster (2001), Integrated Test Design and Automation, Addison-Wesley

- Ciolkowski, C., C. Differding, O. Laitenberger, and J. Muench (1997*), Empirical Investigation of Perspective-based Reading: A Replicated Experiment, Technical Report ISERN-97-13, International Software Engineering Research Network.*

- CMG TestFrame research Centre (2001), TestFrame, a practical guideline for testing information systems (in Dutch), Ten Hagen & Stam Publishers

- Coles, C. (1999), *Crown Management Systems Limited Case Study, Crown Management Systems and Rational Software*

- Collard, R. (1999), Developing test cases from use cases, in: *Software Testing Quality Engineering, Vol. 1, Issue 4, July 1999*

- Graham, D. (ed.) (1996), *Computer Aided Software Testing, The CAST report, Cambridge Market Intelligence Ltd., London, ISBN 1-897977-74-3*

- DDA (1995), *Disability Discrimination Act 1995 (c. 50), Stationery Office Ltd, ISBN 0-10-545095-2*

- DO-178B (1992), *Software Considerations in Airborne Systems and Equipment Certification, RTCA*

- Def Stan 00-55 (1997), *Requirements for Safety-Related Software in Defence Equipment, Issue 2, UK Ministry of Defence*

- Durant, J. (1993), *Software testing practices survey report, (TR-5-93), Software Practices Research Center*

- Dustin, E., J. Rashka and J. Paul (1999), *Automated Software Testing, Addison Wesley*

- Evans, I, S. Mills and R. Warden (1996), Fit for Purpose? In: *SiGiST, February 1996*

- Fagan, M.. (1976), Design and code inspections to reduce errors in program development, in: *IBM Systems Journal, Vol. 15, no. 3: 182-211 (Reprinted in IBM Systems Journal 38, no. 2: 259-287)*.

- Fagan, M. (1986), Advances in software inspections, in: *IEEE Transactions on Software Engineering, Vol. 12, no 7, July 1986*

- Favaro, J. (1996), When the pursuit of quality destroys value, in: *Testing Techniques Newsletter, May-June 1996*

- Fewster, M. and D. Graham (1999), *Software test Automation, Addison-Wesley*

- Freedman, D.P. & G.M. Weinberg (1990) *Handbook of Walkthroughs, Inspections, and Technical Reviews, Dorset House Third edition, New York, ISBN 0-932633-19-6*

- Garvin, D. (1984), What does product quality really mean? In: *Sloan Management Review, Vol. 26, No. 1, 1984*

- Gelperin, D. and W.C. Hetzel (1988), The growth in Software Testing. In: *Communications of the ACM, June 1988, Vol. 31, No. 6*

- Gilb, T. and D. Graham (1993), *Software Inspection, Addison-Wesley, London, ISBN 0-201-63181-4*

- Gool, B. van (2000), Investors in test people, in: *Proceedings EuroStar conference, Kopenhagen 2000*

- Graham, D. (ed.) (1996), *Computer Aided Software Testing, The CAST report, Cambridge Market Intelligence Ltd., London, ISBN 1-897977-74-3*

- Haley, T., B. Ireland, E. Wojtaszek, D. Nash, and R. Dion. (1995), *Raytheon electronic systems experience in software process improvement, (CMU/SEI-95-TR-017), Software Engineering Institute, Carnegie Mellon University, Pittsburgh, USA*

- Hendriks, R., E. van Veenendaal and R. van Vonderen (2001), Measuring Software Product Quality during Testing, in: *Professional Tester, Volume Two, Issue No. 1, March 2001*

- Hetzel, W.C. (ed.) (1973), *Program Test Methods, Englewood Cliffs, N.J., Prentice-Hall*

- Hetzel, W.C. (1984), *The Complete Guide to Software Testing, QED Information Sciences Inc., ISBN 0-89435-242-3*

- Holland, D. (1999), Document inspection as an agent of change, in: *Software Quality Professional, pp. 22-33, December 1999*

- Humphrey, W.S. (1995), *A discipline for software engineering, Addison-Wesley, New York, ISBN 0-201-54610-8*

- IEC 880 (1986), *Software for computers in the safety systems of nuclear power stations, Industrial Electrical Committee*

- IEC 60300-3-9 (1995), *Dependability management - Part 3: Application guide - Section 9: Risk analysis of technological systems, Industrial Electrical Committee*

- IEC 61508 (1998), *Functional safety of electrical/electronic/programmable electronic safety-related systems, Industrial Electrical Committee*

- IEEE 610 (1990), *Standard Computer Dictionary, IEEE Standards Board*

- IEEE 610.12 (1990), *Standard Glossary of Software Engineering Terminology, IEEE Standards Board*

- IEEE 730 (1998), *Software Quality Assurance Plans, IEEE Standards Board*

- IEEE 829 (1998), *Standard for Software Test Documentation, IEEE Standards Board*

- IEEE 1008 (1987), *Standard for Software Unit Testing, IEEE Standards Board*

- IEEE 1028 (1998), *Standard for Software Reviews, IEEE Standards Board*

- IEEE 1044 (1993), *Standard Classification for Software Anomalies, IEEE Standards Board*

- IEEE 1044.1 (1995), *Guide to Classification for Software Anomalies, IEEE Standards Board*

- IFPUG (International Function Point User Group) (1999), *Function Point Counting Practices, release 4.1, IFPUG, January 1999*

- ISEB (Information Systems Examination Board) (1999), *Foundation Syllabus V2.0, British Computer Society, UK*

- ISEB (Information Systems Examination Board) (2001), *Practitioner Syllabus V1.1, British Computer Society, UK*

- ISO 9000-3 (1997), *Guidelines for the application of ISO 9001 to the development, supply, installation and maintenance of computer software, International Organization for Standardization.*

- ISO 9001 (1994), Quality systems – *Model for quality assurance in design, development, production, installation and servicing, International Organization for Standardization*

- ISO/IEC 9126-1 (2001), *Software engineering - Software product quality - Part 1: Quality model, International Organization of Standardization*

- ISO/IEC DTR 9126-2 (2001), *Software engineering - Software product quality - Part 2: External metrics, International Organization of Standardization*

- ISO/IEC DTR 9126-3 (2000), *Software engineering - Software product quality - Part 3: Internal metrics, International Organization of Standardization*

- ISO/IEC DTR 9126-4 (2001), *Software engineering - Software product quality - Part 4: Quality in use metrics, International Organization of Standardization*

- ISO/IEC CD 14598-5 (1996), *Information technology – Software product evaluation - Part 5: Process for evaluators*, International Organization for Standardization.

- ISO 9241-1 (1997), *Ergonomic requirements for office work with visual display terminals (VDT's), part 1: General introduction, International Organization of Standardization*

- ISO 9241-11 (1998), *Ergonomic requirements for office work with visual display terminals (VDT's), part 11: Guidance on usability, International Organization of Standardization*

- ISO/IEC 14598 (1998), *Information technology - Software Product Evaluation, International Organization for Standardization*

- ISO/IEC 12207 (1995), *Information Technology - Software life cycle processes,* International Organization for Standardization

- ISO/IEC 15026 (1998), *Information Technology – System and software integrity levels,* International Organization for Standardization

- ISO CD 15288 (1997), *Life-Cycle Management - System Life Cycle Processes,* International Organization for Standardization

- ISO/IEC 15504 (1998), *Information technology — Software process assessment,* International Organization for Standardization

- Jørgensen, M. (1994), *Empirical studies of software maintenance, Thesis for the Dr. Sceintific degree, Research Report 188, University of Oslo*

- Juran, J.M. (1988), *Juran on Planning for Quality, The Free Press, New York*

- Juran, J.M. and F.M. Gryna (1970), *Quality Planning and Analysis, McGraw-Hill, New York*

- Juran, J.M. (1995), *Managerial breakthrough: the classic book on improving management performance, McGraw-Hill, London, ISBN 0-07-034037-4*

- Kaner, C., J. Falk and H. Nguyen (1993), *Testing Computer Software, Second Edition, John Wiley and Sons, New York*

- Kaplan, C., R. Clark, and V. Tang (1994), *Secrets of software quality: 40 innovations from IBM, McGraw Hill, New York*

- Karlsson, J. and K. Ryan (1997), A Cost-Value Approach for Prioritizing Requirements, in: *IEEE Software, September 1997*

- Kelly, J. C. (1990), An analysis of Jet Propulsion Laboratory's two year experience with software inspections, in: *Proceedings of the Minnowbrook Workshop on Software Engineering, Blue Lake, NY, USA*

- Kelly, J. (1990), An analysis of defect density found during software inspection, in: *Proceedings of 15th Annual Software Engineering Workshop, (NASA SEL-90-006), Jet Propulsion Labs, Pasadena, California, USA*

- Kelly, M. (ed.), (1994), *MUSiC Final Report Part 1 and 2: the MuSiC project, BRAMEUR ltd, Hampshire, UK*

- Khoshgoftaar, T.M., E.B. Allan, R. Halstead, G.P. Trio and R. M. Flass (1998), Using Process History to Predict Software Quality, in: *IEEE Computer, April 1998*

- Killelea, P. (1998), *Web Performance Tuning, O´Reilly & Associates*

- Kirakowski, J. and M. Corbett (1994), SUMI: the Software Usability Measurement Inventory, in: *British Journal of Educational Technology, Vol. 24 No. 3 1994*

- Kit, E. (1995), *Software Testing in the Real World, Addison-Wesley, London*

- Kohli, O.R.., and R.A. Radice (1976), *Low-level design inspection specification, IBM Technical Report (TR 21.629), Armonk, IBM, NY, USA*

- Koomen, T. and M. Pol (1999), *Test Process Improvement, a practical step-by-step guide to structured testing, Addison-Wesley, ISBN 0 201 59624 5*

- Krushten, P. (1998), *The Rational Unified Process, Addison-Wesley*

- Levendel, Y. (1991), Improving Quality with a Manufacturing Process, in: *IEEE Software, March 1991*

- Loukides, M. (1990), *System Performance Tuning, O´Reilly & Associates*

- Nielsen J., (1993) *Usability Engineering, Academic Press, ISBN 0-12-518406-9*

- Nielsen, J. and R.L. Mack (eds.) (1994), *Usability Inspection Methods, John Wiley & Sons, Inc.*

- Macleod M, R. Bowden, N. Bevan and I. Curson (1997*), The MUSiC Performance Measurement method, in: Behaviour and Information Technology, Vol.16, pp. 279-293.*

- Mays, R.G., C.L. Jones, G.J. Holloway and D.P. Studinski, (1990), Experiences with Defect Prevention in: *IBM Systems Journal, 29 (1), 4-32, 1990.*

- McCall, J.A., P.K. Richards and G.F. Walters (1977), *Factors in software quality, RADC-TR-77-363 Rome Air Development Center, Griffis Air Force, Rome, New York*

- Meyerhoff, D., H. Berlejung (2000), Guidelines for Performance Testing in Commercial Client/Server Software Projects, in: *Conquest 2000, ASQF – Arbeitskreis Software-Qualität Franken*

- Meyerhoff, D., S. Caspers (1999), Performance and Robustness Test – Factors of Success for Development and Introduction of Commercial Software, in: *Conquest 1999, ASQF – Arbeitskreis Software-Qualität Franken*

- Mills, D., and Linger (1987), Cleanroom software engineering, in: *IEEE Software, pp. 19-25, September 1987*

- Mills, H.D. (1972), *Mathematical foundations for structured programming, (FSC 71-6012), IBM Corporation Federal Systems Division, Bethesda, Md*

- MISRA (1994*), Development Guidelines for Vehicle Based Software, Motor Industry Software Reliability Association*

- Myers, G.J. (1979), *The Art of Software Testing, Wiley-Interscience, New York, ISBN 0-471-04328-1*

- NIST 500-234 (1996), *Reference Information for the Software Verification and Validation Process (Health Care), US Department of Commerce*

- Ould and Unwin (1986), *Testing in Software Development, Cambridge University Press, ISBN 0521-37860*

- OVUM (2001), *Ovum Evaluates, CASE Products, Ovum Ltd.*

- Patnode, B. (2001), A Recipe for Success, in: *Software Testing Quality Engineering, Vol. 3, Issue 2 March 2001*

- Paulk, M.C., C.V. Weber, B. Curtis and M.B. Chrissis (1993), *The Capability Maturity Model; Guideline for Improving the Software Process, Addison-Wesley Publishing Company*

- Pence, J.L.P., and S.E. Hon III. (1993), Building software quality into telecommunications network systems, in: *Quality Progress, p. 95-97, October, 1993*

- Performance SIGiST (2002), *Performance testing standard (draft)*, BCS Special Interest Group in Software Testing

- Perlman, P., (1995), Practical Usability Evaluation, in: *Conference Proceedings of ACM CHI'95, v2, no.13, pp.369-370 Perry, W.E. and R.W. Rice (1997), Surviving the top ten challenges of Software Testing, A people oriented approach, Dorset Publishing House, SBN 0-932633-38-2*

- Pfleeger, Hatton and Howel (2001), *Solid Software,* Pearson Education, Inc.

- Phillips, M. and Shrum, S., (2000), Creating an Integrated CMM for Systems and Software Engineering, in: *CrossTalk, September 2000*

- PSS-05-0 (1991), *Software Engineering Standards, Issue 2, European Space Agency*

- Pol, M., E. van Veenendaal (1996), *Structured Testing of Information Systems, Kluwer Bedrijfsinformatie, The Netherlands, ISBN 90-267-2910-3*

- Pol, M., E. van Veenendaal (1997), A Test Management Approach for structured testing, in: E. van Veenendaal and J. McMullan (eds.), *Achieving Software Product Quality, UTN Publishing, The Netherlands, ISBN 90-72194-52-7*

- Pol, M., R.A.P. Teunissen, E.P.W.M. van Veenendaal (1999), *Testing acording to TMap, 2nd Edition (in Dutch), UTN Publishing, ISBN 90-72194-58-6*

- Pol, M., R.A.P. Teunissen and E.P.W.M. van Veenendaal (2002), *Software Testing, A Guide to the TMap approach, Addison-Wesley, ISBN 0-201-74571-2*

- Quentin, G. (2000), Skills development, Section 1: The strategic approach, in: *Professional Tester, Vol. 1, Issue 2, March 2000*

- Radice, R.A., J.T. Harding, P. E. Munnis, and R. W. Philips (1999), A programming process study, in: *IBM System Journals 2 and 3.*

- Radice, R.A. and R.W. Phillips (1988), *Software engineering, an industrial approach, vol. 1, Englewood Cliffs, Prentice Hall*

- Roper, M. (1994), *Software Testing, McGraw-Hill, New-York*

- Sabourin, R. (2001), At Your Service, in: *Software Testing Quality Engineering, Vol. 3, Issue 3 May 2001*

- Shull, F. (1998), *Developing Techniques for Using Software Documents: A Series of Empirical Studies, Diss. Computer Science Department, University of Maryland*

- Shull, F. (2002), Software Reading Techniques, in *Encyclopedia of Software Engineering, ed. John J. Marciniak, John Wiley & Sons.*

- Solingen R. Van, E. Berghout (1999), *The Goal Question Metric method, a practical method for quality improvement of software development, McGraw-Hill, UK, ISBN 007-709553-7.*

- Software Engineering Institute (2000), *CMMI for Systems Engineering/Software Engineering, Version 1.02, Staged Representation, TR-CMU/SEI-2000-TR-028, Pittsburgh, November 2000*

- Splaine, S and S.P. Jaskiel (2001) *The Web Testing Handbook, ISBN 0-9704363-0-0*

- Straw, A. and M. Shapiro (1998), *Succeeding at Interviews in a week, Hodder and Stoughton, ISBN 0 340 627379*

- Suwannasart, T. (1996), *Towards the development of a Testing Maturity Model, Diss. Illinois Institute of Technology*

- Trienekens J.J.M. and E.P.W.M. van Veenendaal (1997), *Software Quality from a business perspective, Kluwer Bedrijfsinformatie, Deventer, The Netherlands, ISBN 90-267-2631-7.*

- Usability SIGiST (2000), *Usability testing standard (draft), BCS Special Interest Group in Software Testing (SIGiST)*

- Veenendaal, E.P.W.M. van (1995), Test Point Analysis: a method for estimating the testing effort (in Dutch), in: *Computable, May 1995*

- Veenendaal, E.P.W.M. van and J. McMullan (eds.) (1997), Achieving *Software Product Quality, UTN Publishing, 's-Hertogenbosch, The Netherlands, ISBN 90-72194-52-7*

- Veenendaal, E. van (1998), Usability Testing, in: *Proceedings EuroStar conference, Barcelona 1999*

- Veenendaal, E. van (1999), Practical Quality Assurance for Embedded Software, in: *Software Quality Professional, Vol. 1, no. 3, American Society for Quality, June 1999*

- Veenendaal, E.P.W.M. van and J.E. Dekkers (1999), Test point analysis: a method for test estimation, in: R. Kusters, A. Cowderoy, F. Heemstra and E. van Veenendaal (eds.), *Project Control for Software Quality, Shaker Publishing BV, The Netherlands, ISBN 90-423-0075-2*

- Veenendaal, E. van (2000), Questionnaire-based usability testing, in: *Professional Tester Vol. 1 Issue 4, September 2000*

- Weinberg, G.M. (1971), *The psychology of Computer Programming, Van Nostrand Reinhold, New York.*

- Weller, E. F. (1993), Lessons from three years of inspection data, in: *IEEE Software, pp. 38-45, September, 1993*

- Whittaker, J.A. and A.A. Jorgensen (2000), How to Break Software, in: *Proceedings EuroStar conference, Kopenhagen 2000*

Authors

Erik van Veenendaal has been working as a practitioner and manager in the IT-industry since 1987. After a career in software development, he transfered to the area of software quality. As a test manager and test consultant he has been involved in a great number and variety of projects, has implemented structured testing and carried out test process improvements activities in a large number of organisations in different industries. He is the author of numerous papers and a number of books on software quality and testing, including the best-seller "Testing according to TMap". He is a regular speaker both at national and international testing conferences and a leading international (ISEB accredited) trainer in the field of software testing. At EuroStar'99 he received the best tutorial award for a tutorial on usability testing. Erik van Veenendaal is the founder and managing director of Improve Quality Services ltd., a company that provides international consultancy and training services in the area of quality management, usability, inspection and testing. Erik is also a senior lecturer at the Eindhoven University of Technology, Faculty of Technology Management. He is on the Dutch ISO standards committee for software quality and board member of ESCOM Conference ltd.

James Bach is founder and principal consultant of Satisfice, Inc., a software testing and quality assurance company. He is the author of Lessons Learned in Software Testing, and is a frequent expert witness in the area of testing. James cut his teeth as a programmer, tester, and SQA manager in Silicon Valley and the world of American market-driven software development. He has worked at Apple, Borland, a couple of start-ups, and a couple of consulting companies, including a stint as chief scientist at STLabs, an independent software testing laboratory. In 1999, James designed the General Functionality and Stability Test Procedure for the Microsoft Windows 2000 Application Certification program, which may be the first published example of a formalised intuitive testing process.

Victor Basili is a Professor of Computer Science at the University of Maryland, College Park, the Executive Director of the Fraunhofer Center - Maryland, and one of the founders and principals in the Software Engineering Laboratory (SEL). He works on measuring, evaluating, and improving the software development process and product and has consulted for many organizations, including AT&T, Boeing, Daimler-Chrysler, Ericsson, FAA, GE, GTE, IBM, Lucent, MCC, Motorola, NRL, NSWC, and NASA. He is a recipient of a 1989 NASA Group Achievement Award, a 1990 NASA/GSFC Productivity Improvement and Quality Enhancement Award, the 1997 Award for Outstanding Achievement in Mathematics and Computer Science by the Washington Academy of Sciences, and the 2000 Outstanding Research Award from ACM SIGSOFT. Dr. Basili has authored over 150 journal and refereed conference papers, has served as Editor-in-Chief of the IEEE Transactions on Software Engineering, and as Program Chair and General Chair of the 6th and 15th International Conference on Software Engineering, respectively. He is co-editor-in-chief of the International Journal of Empirical Software Engineering, published by Kluwer. He is an IEEE and ACM Fellow.

Rex Black is the president and principal consultant of Rex Black Consulting Services, Inc., international software and hardware testing and quality assurance consultancy. He and his consulting associates help clients such as Bank One, Compaq, Dell, Schlumberger, Williams Communications, and others with implementation, consulting, training, and staffing for testing, test automation, and quality assurance projects. His book, Managing the Testing Process, was published in June 1999, by Microsoft Press. His current book, tentatively titled Critical Testing Processes, has been published by Addison-Wesley in 2002.

Chris Comey is a senior test consultant with Testing Solutions Group Ltd. He has been involved in the testing arena for over 20 years. Initially from a telecommunications background, he has tested computer systems and developments for a number of industries including telecommunications, electricity, financial, banking, gaming, and a wide variety of Internet based WEB sites. Chris has first hand experience in the roles of test analyst, test co-ordinator, test manager and test consultant, and has tested the range of products from individual components up to the integration of large systems. He has worked solo, as part of a team, and as a team leader, using a number of different software development approaches ranging from RAD/DSDM through to the more traditional lifecycles such as the V-model. Having delivered training courses on UAT, testing basics, VV&T, and the ISEB foundation course, he has a balance of theoretical and practical skills and understands how to apply the theory in the real world.

Ton Dekkers has been working as a practitioner and manager within the area of software quality for a great number of years. Within this area he specialises in estimation, risk analysis, priority management and quality assurance in projects. He is a regular speaker both at conferences and a trainer in software estimation, risk management and "Quality Tailor Maid". Ton Dekkers is senior quality consultant for division Software Control of Sogeti Nederland B.V. He is member of the NESMA working groups "FPA in Maintenance" and "FPA New Technology".

Isabel Evans has nearly 20 years experience in the IT industry, mainly in quality management, testing, training and documentation. She has helped organisations in development of procedures, standards and methods to aid testing of software during development and maintenance projects. She has managed test groups, and performed testing design and development for acceptance and system testing of packages and bespoke systems. She has also provided Quality Assurance Support, Release
Management, and Customer Support for IT organisations. Isabel is the author and an accredited tutor for an ISEB accredited Foundation Certificate in Software Testing course. She has presented at various conferences including EuroSTAR, Quality Forum, the BCS SiGiST and the Euro Summit in Rome. She is an active member of the BCS SiGiST Standards working party and her company is a key member of the British Quality Foundation.

Paul Gerard is the Technical Director and a principal consultant for Systeme Evolutif. He has conducted consultancy and training assignments in all aspects of Software Testing and Quality Assurance. Previously, he has worked as a developer, designer, project manager and consultant for small and large developments using 3 and 4GLs. Paul has engineering degrees from the Universities of Oxford and London, is Joint Programme Chair for the BCS SiGiST, a member of the BCS Software Component Test Standard Committee and Former Chair of the ISEB Certification Board for a Tester Qualification whose aim is to establish a certification scheme for testing professionals and training organisations. He is a regular keynote speaker at seminars and conferences in Europe and the US, and won the 'Best Presentation' award at EuroSTAR '95.

Tom Gilb was born in Pasadena in 1940, emigrated to London 1956, and to Norway 1958, where he joined IBM for 5 years, and where he resides when not travelling. He has mainly worked within the software engineering community, but since 1983 with Corporate Top Management problems, and 1988 with large-scale systems engineering. He is an independent teacher, consultant and writer. He has published eight books, including the early coining of the term "Software Metrics" (1976) which is the basis for SEI CMM Level 4. He wrote "Principles of Software Engineering Management" (1988, now in 13th printing), and "Software Inspection" (1993). Both titles are really systems engineering books in software disguise. His pro-bono systems engineering activities include several weeks a year for US DoD and Norwegian DoD, and Environmental (EPA) and Third-World Aid charities and organizations.

Les Hatton is an independent consultant in software reliability. He is also Professor of Software Reliability at the Computing Laboratory, University of Kent, U.K. He holds a B.A. (1970) from King's College, Cambridge, an M.Sc. (1971) and Ph.D. (1973) from the University of Manchester, all in mathematics; an A.L.C.M. (1980) in guitar from the London College of Music, and an LL.M. in IT law from the University of Strathclyde (1999). He received a number of international prizes for geophysics in the 1970's and '80s culminating in the 1987 Conrad Schlumberger prize for his work in computational geophysics. Shortly afterwards, he became interested in software reliability, and changed careers to study the design of high-integrity and safety-critical systems on which he has been a keynote speaker at numerous software conferences. He has published many technical papers and his 1995 book "Safer C" pioneered the use of safer language subsets in embedded control systems and influenced many later standards including the automotive industry's influential MISRA-C standard. He is the author of the Safer C Toolset based on his widely-published research on direct and indirect defect detection and is nearing completion of another book entitled Software Failure: avoiding the avoidable and living with the rest. In October 1998, he was voted amongst the world's leading scholars of systems and software engineering for the period 1993-1997 by the US Journal of Systems and Software.

David Hayman is a principal consultant at Testing Solutions Group Ltd., a leading software testing services and training company. He has been working in the IT arena since 1984. The last 13 years have been in the software testing discipline. All of that time has been spent as a practitioner, the majority in senior roles defining and implementing test strategies and managing teams of IT and business testers. He has considerable technical and practical experience testing and implementing applications across a variety of infrastructure platforms, for both public and private sector clients. David now uses that experience in his role with Testing Solutions Group as a consultant and trainer. He is a regular and popular speaker at conferences in the UK and Europe. He is accredited "ISEB Foundation Certificate in Software Testing" trainer and a team leader within the BCS SiGiST sponsored working party defining standards for "Non-Functional Testing Techniques".

Rob Hendriks is working in the field of software quality for technical systems, with a specialisation on software testing, since 1996. Currently he works as a quality and test consultant for Improve Quality Services BV. The past years he has been working as a test co-ordinator and consultant within projects for consumer electronics and professional systems. He has been involved in the definition and deployment of the CMM key process areas Software Quality Assurance within a large organisation. On a regular basis Rob is a trainer on inspections and software testing and he is an accredited trainer for the "ISEB Foundation Certificate in Software Testing". Rob is a certified moderator and a member of the ISEB Software Testing Examiners Panel.

Tim Koomen graduated in 1986 in Computer Science at the University of Amsterdam. Since 1992 he has been a professional tester and has performed most testing functions since then. He participated in several testing projects for clients of Sogeti Nederland, a Dutch company with over 300 dedicated testers and owner of the structured testing approach TMap. Tim is a member of the Sogeti Nederland R&D-team, covering issues like testing Component Based Development, testing e-business and Test Process Improvement. He is a co-author of the TPI-book, translated in Dutch, English and German, and a frequent speaker at international conferences.

Dirk Meyerhoff is a senior executive at SQS AG. He has almost 20 years of experience in software development and more than 15 years in software testing. Dirk studied computer science before taking on a research position. As a researcher he focused on software quality and software metrics. In 1994 he started as a consultant for SQS, working for large clients mostly from the financial services and telecommunications industries. He built up and managed a department for performance testing before he became head of Product Development at SQS. This business unit develops methods and tools for software quality management, software quality assurance and testing. Dirk has developed several seminars for SQS and is an experienced trainer for various topics in the software quality domain. He published numerous scientific papers, gave presentations at international conferences, and edited two books on software quality and testing. He is co-chair of the ICSTEST - International Conference on Software Testing and is also active in special interest groups on software quality and testing in Germany.

Martin Pol is one of the founders of structured testing in The Netherlands. As a test manager he has been involved in a great number and large variety of testing projects and implemented structured testing in several organisations. He is the co-author of a number of books on structured testing and is a frequent speaker at both national and international conferences. He is currently the CEO and a senior consultant for Polteq International Testing Services B.V. Martin twice chaired the EuroSTAR conference and received the European Testing Excellence Award for his contribution to the field of testing.

Stuart Reid is a Senior Lecturer in Software Engineering for Cranfield University at the Royal Military College of Science. His research interests include software testing and process improvement. He is Chair of the BCS SiGiST Standards Working Party, which was responsible for the development of the software component testing standard (BS 7925-2) and a vocabulary of software testing terms (BS 7925-1). This working party is now developing a standard on non-functional testing techniques. In addition Stuart is also Chair of the ISEB Software Testing Certificate Board. He has a BSc (Hons.) in Aeronautics and Astronautics from Southampton University, a MSc in Computing from the University of Wales (Cardiff), and a PhD in Software Testing from the University of Glamorgan.

Hans Schaefer is an independent consultant in software testing methods. He has been in the testing field for over 15 years, consulting major software suppliers in Scandinavian countries, especially in the telecommunications industry, and is known as "Mr. Software Test" throughout Scandinavia. Hans has a civil engineers degree in computer science from technical university of Braunschweig, Germany. Hans runs public and in-house seminars in software review and testing throughout Europe and is a regular speaker at conferences.

Chris Schotanus is a principal consultant for CMG in The Netherlands. He has over 25 years of experience in Information Technology. Since 1995 he is a member of CMG's TestFrame Research Centre, and thus strongly involved in the development of TestFrame (CMG's method for structured testing). He provides management consultancy services and training on testing and TestFrame to many major clients in the financial world, industry, trading and government throughout Europe.

Forrest Shull is a scientist at the Fraunhofer Center for Experimental Software Engineering, Maryland. He received his doctorate degree from the University of Maryland, College Park, in 1998. His work includes developing, tailoring, and empirically validating reading techniques for inspections of software requirements and design documents. He also provides training and tutorials on the use of reading techniques, most recently at ICSE2000 and the 2000 NASA Software Engineering Laboratory Workshop. His current research interests include empirical software engineering, software reading techniques, software inspections, and process improvement.

Ron Swinkels is working as a senior test engineer at Improve Quality Services BV. For several multi-national organisations, he has been involved in testing (embedded) software systems and improving the organizations' testing process. In addition, he has participated in the development of implementation guidelines for the Testing Maturity Model. Ron received a masters degree in "Industrial Engineering and Management Science" at the Eindhoven University of Technology and recently passed the Certified Information Systems Auditor (CISA) examination.

Ruud Teunissen is working in the testing world since 1989. He has been involved in a large number of ICT projects and has performed several functions within the testing orgnisation. Based on his experience, Ruud participated in the development of the structured testing methodology TMap and is co-author of a number of books on structured testing. In recent years he has been involved in implementing structured testing within several organisations throughout Europe. Ruud is a frequent speaker at conferences such ICS Test and EuroSTAR and currently the Business Unit Manager of the testing department at Gitek nv, employing over 50 test professionals.

Robert van Vonderen, MsC, has worked for Océ Technologies B.V. since his graduation from the Eindhoven University of Technology. He conducted a range of applied research studies in the areas of embedded software, geographical information systems and printer controller software. In recent years he has worked as a project manager and project leader for the Océ Printing Systems division in the area of printer controllers and maintenance. He is currently responsible for the integration, testing and QA activities of the newest line of controller development.

John Watkins holds Masters Degrees in both Computer Science and Object-Orientation, has over 20 years experience in the field of software development, with some 15 years in the field of software testing, and is a Fellow of the British Computer Society. During his 15 years experience as a testing professional, John has been involved at all levels and phases of testing. He has provided high level testing consultancy, training and mentoring to numerous Blue Chip Companies. John currently works for Rational Software Limited, where he is the Product Manager in Testing for the Northern Europe region. He has been an invited speaker at various BCS Special Interest Groups on the subjects of Object-Orientation and Software Testing, and is an accomplished author having published a number of articles in conference proceedings, learned journals and technical reports. Most recently, John has published a book on Testing Process with Cambridge University Press.

Mark van der Zwan has been working in the field of software quality and the quality of IT services since 1994. As a researcher at the Eindhoven University of Technology he has been involved in a number of projects in the IT industry. He is co-author of a book on the service level management method. A method to continually monitor and improve IT service needs on one hand and possibilities on the other. Since 1998 Mark works as a quality consultant for Improve Quality Services BV and focuses on improving software product quality and especially on "the most cost effective manual defect detection technique" inspections. He is a certified moderator and has successfully implemented inspections and reviews within a number of Dutch industrial organisations. Other areas of interest are setting up and supporting measurement programs used to gain visibility in the process and product quality. Mark is a regular international trainer in the area of reviews and inspections.

Improve Quality Services

Improve Quality Services BV was founded in 1998 by Erik van Veenendaal as an independent organisation that focuses on advanced and high quality services in the area of software quality. It offers international consultancy and training services with respect to quality management, usability, testing and inspections. Services include software process improvement, IT-auditing, software quality assurance, inspection programs, test engineering and test process improvement.

Improve Quality Services is accredited to run "ISEB Foundation" and "ISEB Practitioner Certificate in Software Testing" courses. They were the first company outside the UK to be accredited for the practitioner level.

Quality is a key issue in all aspects of the company, whereby quality is translated into both customer and employee satisfaction. Customers vary from large multinational companies to SME type companies and government agencies. Most important curstomers are a number of major banks and a number of industrial engineering organisations.

Employees choose software quality and testing as their profession and career. They hold ISEB testing certificates and are also accredited as Certified Information System Auditors (CISA). On a regular basis papers from employees are published in various international magazines. To provide leading edge services, Improve Quality Services has a close working relationship with the Eindhoven University of Technology and participates in (inter)national Research & Development projects.

Improve Quality Services BV
Waalreseweg 17
5554 HA Valkenswaard
The Netherlands

www.improveqs.nl
email: info@improveqs.nl

Index